Princeton Theological Monograph Series

Dikran Y. Hadidian

General Editor

46

ORTHODOXY AND DIFFERENCE

Essays on the Geography of Russian Orthodox Church(es)
in the 20th Century

Orthodoxy and Difference

Essays on the Geography of Russian Orthodox Church(es) in the 20th Century

Dmitrii Sidorov

Pickwick Publications

San Jose, California

Copyright © 2001 Dmitrii A. Sidorov

First published by:

Pickwick Publications
215 Incline Way
San Jose, CA 95139-1526 USA

Printed on Acid Free Paper in the United States of America

Library of Congress Cataloging-in-Publication Data

Sidorov, D. (Dmitrii)
    Orthodoxy and difference: essays on the geography of Russian
Orthodox church(es) in the 20th century / Dmitrii Sidorov
        p.   cm. -- (Princeton theological monograph series : 46)
        ISBN 1-55635-038-4
        1. Church property--Russia--History. 2. Church and state--
    Russia--History. 3. Russia--Church history. 4. Church property--
Soviet Union--History. 5. Church and state--Soviet Union--History.
6. Soviet Union--Church history. I. Title. II. Series.

BX485.S555 2001
281.9'47--dc21

                                                    2001021040

To the memory of my granny
Ol′ga Pavlovna Azarova
(1908-1998)

CONTENTS

LIST OF FIGURES

Front Cover Illustration: A view of the main church of the architectural complex on Kizhi Island, Kizhi Museum of Wooden Architecture, Karelia, Russia, 1990.

Figure 1.1. The Russian realm.

Figure 2.1. Spread of Eastern Orthodoxy from Byzantium by 1000 AD. Russian monasticism (1200-1600).

Figure 2.2. The Church of the Assumption of the Holy Virgin (a.k.a. the Church of the Tithe, or Desiatinnaia Church), Kiev, 10th cen.

Figure 2.3. The Trinity-St.Sergii Lavra monastery (Sergiev Posad, former Zagorsk, Moscow oblast), 1993.

Figure 2.4. The Assumption (Uspenskii) Cathedral in the Kremlin.

Figure 2.5. St. Isaac Cathedral, Leningrad (St. Petersburg), ca.1960.

Figure 2.6. Kazanskii Cathedral (former History of Religion and Atheism Museum of the Academy of Sciences of the USSR), Leningrad (St. Petersburg), ca.1960.

Figure 2.7. Orthodox adherents in the Russian Empire, 1897.

Figure 2.8. Old Believers in the Russian Empire, 1897.

Figure 2.9. An Old Belief village church, Trans-Baikal area (Buryat Republic).

Figure 3.1. Patriarch Tikhon with clergymen (n.d., perhaps early 1920s).

Figure 4.1. Number of Orthodox church buildings, the Russian Empire and the USSR, 1834-1994.

Figure 4.2. "Famine-spider strangles the peasantry of Russia: the gold of churches must go for saving the hungry from death" (poster, Russia, the 1920s).

Figure 4.3. Removal of bell from the belfry of the Holy Week (Strastnoi) monastery in Moscow, the 1930s.

Figure 5.1. Archbishop of Constantinople, New Rome, and Ecumenical Patriarch Bartholomew I (left) and the Patriarch of Moscow and All Russia, Alexii II, in the Kremlin, Moscow, 1993.

Figure 6.1. Types of 17th century settlements on the territory of contemporary Moscow.

Figure 6.2. Historic areas of downtown Moscow.

Figure 6.3. Location in Moscow of the areas discussed in Chapters 6 and 7.

Figure 6.4. Okhotnyy Ryad, downtown Moscow, 1930s.

Figure 6.5. New temporary chapel in a typical Moscow residential neighborhood (Otradnoe).

LIST OF TABLES

Supplement

NOTE ON TRANSCRIPTION OF RUSSIAN ALPHABET

It is common among historians working on Russia to utilize the Library of Congress system of transcription of Russian words, where, for example, the letter "я" is translated as "ia". In geography and several other social sciences a different system is prevalent. Its major exponents are such journals as *Post-Soviet Geography, Post-Soviet Affairs,* etc. In this second system the same letter would be transcribed here as "ya".

Since both historical terms and geographical names are important in this study, it would be a loss to neglect either of these systems totally. Therefore, this book has adopted both systems: the Library of Congress system of transcription is the principal one; however, geographical names were transcribed according to the second system.

LIST OF ABBREVIATIONS

ARK	Antireligious Commission of the Central Committee, All-Russian Communist Party (Bolshevik), also called the Commission for Separation of Church and State
CROCA	Council for Russian Orthodox Church Affairs under the Sovnarkom/Council of Ministers of the USSR
EAOCh	Estonian Apostolic Orthodox Church
GAMO	State Archive for the Moscow Region (formerly TsGAMO)
GARF	State Archive of the Russian Federation (formerly TsGAOR SSSR)
MP	Moscow Patriarchate
NKYu	People's Commissariat of Justice
NKVD	People's Commissariat of Internal Affairs
Politburo	Political Bureau of the Central Committee, All-Russian Communist Party (Bolshevik)
ORSCh	Orthodox Russian-State Church
POP	Potentially Orthodox population
RGIA	Russian State Historical Archive (formerly TsGIA SSSR)
ROCh	Russian Orthodox Church
RSFSR	Russian Soviet Federated Socialist Republic
RTsKhIDNI	Russian Center for the Preservation and Study of Documents of Modern History (formerly the Central Party Archive, now RGASPI)

SCR	State-Church relations
Sovnarkom	Council of People's Commissars
SS	Saints
SSSR	USSR
TsGIAgM	Central State Historical Archive for the City of Moscow
VTsIK	All-Russian Central Executive Committee
VTsS	Supreme Church Soviet (Council)

ARCHIVAL ABBREVIATIONS USING THE RUSSIAN SYSTEM

f.	*fond* (collection)
op.	*opis'* (inventory)
d.	*delo* (file)
l., ll.	*list, listy* (leaf, leaves)
ob.	*oborot* (verso)

LIST OF SOME TOPONYMIC (PLACE NAME) CHANGES IN THE 20TH CENTURY

Modern name	Previous name(s)
Almaty	Alma Ata
Ashgabat	Ashkhabad
Bashkortostan	Bashkiria
Belarus'	Belorussia
Bishkek	Frunze
Chisinau	Kishinev
Kyiv	Kiev
Kyrgyzstan	Kirgizia
Moldova	Moldavia, Bessarabia
Nizhniy Novgorod	Gor'kiy
Orenburg	Chkalov
Samara	Kuybyshev
St. Petersburg	Leningrad, Petrograd
Tatarstan	Tataria, Tatar ASSR
Turkmenistan	Turkmenia
Tver'	Kalinin
Vladikavkaz	Ordzhonikidze
Volgograd	Stalingrad, Tsaritsyn
Ul'yanovsk	Simbirsk
Yekaterinburg	Sverdlovsk

PREFACE AND ACKNOWLEDGEMENTS

This book grew out of my fascination with the coincidence of two phenomena in the early 1990s. On the one hand, while at that period Anglo-Saxon cultural geography was embracing new modes of inquiry borrowed from adjacent academic fields — such as cultural studies and feminism, postmodernist philosophy and discourse analysis — only its least advanced branches, such as the geography of religion, continued to use maps as a principal means of analysis. On the other hand, at the same time there were fields in the social sciences, which seemed to have barely been exposed to the advantages of mapping and geographical analyses in general. For instance, the multidisciplinary studies of the Russian Church, despite the wealth of relevant data, apparently had not yet produced a single map. Therefore, it was highly tempting to undertake a two-fold project that would involve both a geographical "re-visioning" of the studies of the Russian Church and, at the same time, the advancement of the traditional geography of religion. The former meant at least the introduction of maps, the latter — going beyond mere cartography. The result of this project was my doctoral dissertation at the University of Minnesota. This book, however, is the culmination of my long and geographically broad graduate program and post-graduate teaching and research at several universities.

Being a native of the world's largest, yet most isolated and atheistic country, the Soviet Union, I always attempted to gain a truly global and universal education, and my graduate program(s) in the so-called first, second and third worlds helped me to achieve this goal. In the process I was fortunate enough to study in some of the world's most prominent centers of geographical research (Moscow State University, Oxford University, the universities of Minnesota and Wisconsin), giving me an exposure to many influential figures in the field. Afterwards my experience beyond graduation included teaching and research at the University of Wisconsin Colleges, the University of Minnesota, the University of South Carolina, as well as at a Catholic school (the University of St. Thomas) and a Lutheran college (Gustavus Adolphus College), which further widened my worldview and exposed me to new ideas.

The greatest asset of my experience as an "eternal graduate student" was exposure to many remarkable people. While at Moscow State University, I benefited from the guidance of such prominent Russian geographers as the liberal-minded Dr. S. E. Khanin, the energetic and entrepreneurial Dr. G. L. Vasil'yev, diverse and idealistic Dr. P. M. Polian, and precise and computer-versed Dr. V. A. Svetlosanov. At Oxford University, I was extremely fortunate to be engaged by the Old English-style tutorial discussions with Dr. Eric Swyngedouw, Professor David Harvey, and Clive Barnett. This tradition is alive at the University of Wisconsin-Madison as well; as a C.I.C. Traveling Scholar I was given an important opportunity to learn in both formal and informal ways from Professors Robert D. Sack, Yi-Fu Tuan, Mark Bassin, John Fiske, and Jack Kugelmass. I also cherish the memory of the small reading and discussion club we organized with Ken Hillis and Jonathan Perry.

Yet, only at Minnesota was I able to complete my study. I believe that the genuine generosity that I met at the University of Minnesota's Department of Geography is unparalleled. The geopolitical transformations that I describe in this book had tangible personal dimensions. In the course of my Ph.D. program at the University of Minnesota my country of citizenship ceased to exist, many cities were renamed, the ruble was devalued a thousand times, and the society I grew up in was dramatically altered. I am grateful for the support that I received during all those years in Minnesota. For instance, the research for my dissertation was funded by a University of Minnesota Graduate School Fellowship (1991-93), the Thomas F. Wallace Fellowship for 1994-95, and the Doctoral Dissertation Fellowship for 1995-96 (both from the University of Minnesota); two Summer Research Fellowships (the Department of Geography, the University of Minnesota) and Doctoral Dissertation Special Grant, Graduate School, University of Minnesota (1996).

My doctoral advisory committee gave me more than I can possibly acknowledge. I can only feebly attempt to express my gratitude for their help, guidance, and encouragement. Professor Eric S. Sheppard, my advisor, helped me to grow both professionally and personally. His patience, wit, and trust I miss most. Eric maintains a tireless commitment to his students and I can only hope that I have not overexploited it. Professor of History Theofanis Stavrou in many respects served as a co-advisor. On numerous occasions in his book-dominated office and on the streets of Moscow he challenged my geographical determinism. Professor John Rice was the most meticulous reader of my work. I cherish his critical and always friendly comments. I was fortunate to have on my committee Professor Helga Leitner. Her passionate approach to scholarship is a model I would like to follow. Both in and out of the classroom, John Archer shared with me his gift of imaginative thinking about theories of space. His way of thinking has some haunting quality that I often feel has a continuing presence well after our conversation is over. It is indeed true that this study would not have been possible without my doctoral committee. All these years Barbara VanDrasek was very helpful on different occasions, and to her I say my special spasibo. In the last year of my program, Earl and Cecilia Larson provided me with more than just free accommodation in the best neighborhood in town. They made me feel at home in Minneapolis.

I am also grateful for the support for research done outside of Minnesota. In Moscow, unpaid workers at the State Archive of the Russian Federation (GARF) had to carry up all of the numerous files I ordered on their own because elevators (as well as heating systems) were sometimes shut down due to funding shortages. I cannot recall all of their names, yet their faces are with me. For access to the rare internal summary of religious periodicals at the Department of External Church Relations of the Russian Orthodox Church, I am grateful to Galina Gulichkina. Discussions with such Orthodox priests as fathers Vladimir (Divakov), Ioann (Ekonomtsev), Vsevolod (Chaplin), Innokentii (Pavlov), Georgii (Chistiakov), Georgii (Kochetkov), Mikhail (Ardov), Metropolitan Volodymyr (Romaniuk) and his press-secretary Gennadii Druzenko were most stimulating. Alexander I. Kudriavtsev (Ministry of Justice of the Russian Federation) helped me to obtain important religious statistics. Mikhail I. Odintsov (the Academy of State Service) and Tat'iana Goricheva (independent philosopher) have changed my vision of Russian Orthodoxy. I cherish my friendly relations with fellow Russian geographers Valentin Bogorov, Mikhail Mozolin, Marianna Pavlovskaya, and Alexei Krindatch.

My acknowledgements and thanks also go to those colleagues who both helped me to find my place beyond graduation and mature professionally: Cary Komoto, Robert Werner, Robert Douglas, Mark Bjelland, Jullian Minghi to name a few. For critical comments on a draft of this book, I am grateful to Professor Nathaniel Davis. Earlier versions of several chapters were presented at several professional meetings and published in The Annals of the Association of American Geographers and Historical Geography, and I am grateful for their permission to reproduce the greater parts of them here. I would like to thank Ron Judy for proofreading of the manuscript, Eric Stevens for some help with graphics, and Dikran Y. Hadidian, General Editor of Pickwick Publications, for his patience.

My elderly and lonely mother Nadezhda Nikolaevna and granny Ol'ga Pavlovna deserve my deepest respect for their patience and daily prayers for me. If only my dedication of this book to my granny Ol'ga Pavlovna Azarova could exhaust the sense of guilt for overexploiting her patience – a few hours after submitting my thesis to the graduate school and thus formally completing my doctoral program, I was informed of her fatal stroke. And English words fail me at this point.

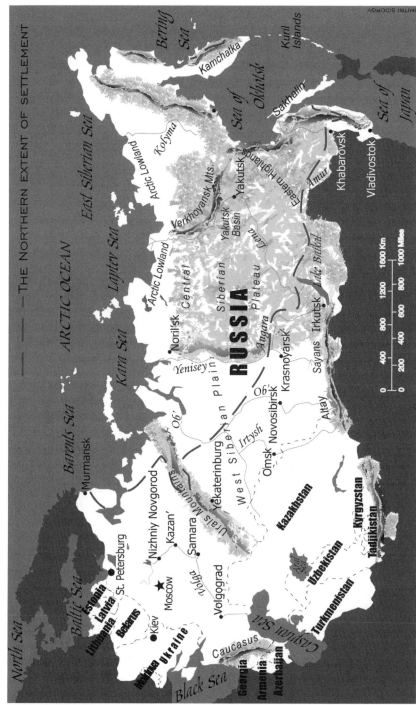

Figure 1.1. The Russian realm (drawn by the author and Eric Stevens).

Chapter 1. The Meaning of Space
in the Study of Russian Orthodoxy

> *It is customary to change the boundaries of the Churches as political entities and administrations change.*
> Photius I the Great, the Patriarch of Constantinople (ninth cen.)[1]

Introduction: The Diversity of Russian Orthodoxy

Since its acceptance as the official religion of Kievan Princedom by Prince Vladimir in 988, the Eastern version of Christianity, Orthodoxy, has remained the dominant religion of the Russian Realm. As a dominant ingredient in the social and cultural life of the people of Russia, this originally Byzantine form of religious organization has been a major ingredient of the realm's cultural and social life. As many political states of different structure and territory have succeeded each other in this realm, the Orthodox churches have continued to serve as the principal identifiers of the Russian landscape. Undoubtedly, the Russian Orthodox Church (henceforth the Church)[2] has been the main religious organization in the Kievan and Muscovite Rus' (Russia), the Russian Empire, the Soviet Union, the Russian Federation, and some other post-Soviet republics. In this light to talk about Orthodox diversity is a certain challenge. The existence of other Orthodox Churches remains overshadowed by its dominance.

In Tsarist Russia the Church occupied a dominant position, often merging with the state to form an oppressive political-economic system. The Church served to legitimize the tsarist regime, whereas the state protected the Church from external competition with other religions. The schismatic Orthodox Old Believers, for instance, were subject to various constraints. It was only in 1905-07, at the end of the empire, that some relaxation was permitted and other, non-Orthodox Churches received legal recognition.

This trend towards religious diversity in Russia was strengthened in the initial years of Bolshevik rule. The Church and the state were separated and all religious communities were granted equal rights.

The main Church not only lost its privileged position, but also faced various deprivations. Many of its church buildings were transferred to the Communist-inspired Renovationist Orthodox Church in a politics of religious diversification aimed at the fragmentation and suppression of the Church. Diversity as a political tool for subjugation of the Church was important for the new authorities. This situation had changed by the late-1920s as the majority of the Russian Orthodox Church took a more loyal stand towards the regime. The Renovationist Church had lost the authorities' support and gradually assumed a merely symbolic significance. In the 1930s, all Churches were subject to hursh state anti-religious policies, which included closures, nationalization, demolition, and juridical transfers of church buildings. In absolute terms, if judged by mere absolute numbers of church buildings these campaigns stopped the growth of religious diversity. Paradoxically, it preserved and balanced a higher-level diversity (diversity of Churches) in relative terms, since the campaignes were aimed at reducing the number of church buildings yet keeping some (of various Churches) opened for purpose of control.

This period of uncertainty for religious diversity ended in 1943. Following similar steps by the German occupational authorities, in order to gain popular support during the hard times of the war and post-war reconstruction, the Soviet state allowed the return of some church buildings to the main Church. However, strands of Russian Orthodoxy opposed to the regime, such as the Catacomb Church, were still not permitted to function. In addition, in an attempt to balance the geographical distribution of post-war churches and/or finally to eradicate religion, many churches were closed again in the early 1960s.

This situation changed dramatically in the late 1980s. The geo-political transformation of the former Soviet Union allowed various new communities to emerge. Throughout the Soviet period, the Communist authorities had paradoxically sheltered the Church at the national level due to the Iron Curtain and continuance of tsarist imperial policies. Thus a foreign branch of the Russian Orthodox Church, the Russian Orthodox Church Abroad, was separated and not allowed to enter Russian territory. The collapse of the Iron Curtain in the late 1980s opened Russia's biggest Church to various new influences from abroad, including the newly arrived foreign Russian Orthodox. Furthermore, the dissolution of the Soviet Union has fragmented the Church itself: new Orthodox churches have appeared, such as the Ukrainian Orthodox Church (Kievan Patriarchate), which is now attempting to open parishes in Russia.

The post-Soviet revival of the Church, after decades of harsh Communist persecution in which literally thousands of church buildings were closed, many priests killed or imprisoned and the Church was nearing total extinction (see, e.g., Pospielovsky 1984, 1988; Davis 1995), has been received by some analysts (see, e.g., Forest 1990, Hill 1989, 1991) as a sign of long-awaited religious freedom in the country. Indeed, many nationalized churches have been returned to the believers, the religious press is now free, and new religious communities have diversified the landscape. Yet this revival of the once-oppressed Church is raising not only hopes but also new anxieties about the democratization of the country. The success of these newly emerging alternative Orthodox communities, for instance, has been limited by some constraints on the allocation of religious property and space, both of which remain primarily in public hands. Facing opposition of a new coalition between the main Church and local authorities (e.g., in the case of Moscow), many such communities have already ceased to exist. This process is less visible at the level of the country as a whole, since some communities are often registered and, therefore, formally accepted by the federal authorities (even if their activities are blocked locally).

The new alliance between the state and the main Church has superficially resulted in a reversal of the previous Soviet anti-religious policies, most powerfully exemplified by the recent restoration of the Cathedral of Christ the Savior in Moscow. A more geographically nuanced analysis could show, however, that this "reversal" itself produces new injustices in a more sophisticated form. This privileging of the main Church in the broader process of religious revival in post-Soviet Russia, raises the danger that previous undemocratic practices in the religious field will be restored under a new guise.

In sum, the current revival of the Church exhibits divergent tendencies at the macro-level of geopolitical changes and at the local level of religious communities. At the large scale, the official Church often acknowledges the existence of other Churches, including some other Orthodox communities. Locally, however, the Church successfully resists this diversification by gaining a monopoly over the return of church property.

This study argues that scholars who traditionally study Russian society from different disciplines, should scrutinize the post-Soviet Orthodox religious revival more critically. While the revival is supposed to reverse the previous religious policies, it could itself be producing new injustices or justifying previous ones. To see, for instance, new manipulations of cult places in the revival, scholars must adopt a more active view of space and go beyond the treatment of space as a mere neutral container of social events.

More specifically, in this study I intend to critically re-examine basic spatial assumptions of both disciplines to understand why the two fields, the study of Orthodoxy and the geography of religion, did not encounter each other earlier. With regard to the essentials of the dominant vision of space in the studies of the Russian Church, I intend to reveal their origin in the official Soviet vision of space. For the geography of religion, it is the lack of the political dimension that is arguably the main disadvantage.

STUDIES OF THE RUSSIAN CHURCH IN THE 20TH CENTURY: A SOVIET ADMINISTRATIVE VISION OF SPACE?[3]

Studies of the Russian Church in the twentieth century stand as a distinctive and impressive body of multidisciplinary research by anthropologists, sociologists, historians, political scientists, architects, and others. To avoid unnecessary compartmentalization, this chapter profiles the field through its prevailing themes. This review is not comprehensive,[4] but it attempts to identify certain geographical "blind spots" which may not be obvious to insiders in this field. In addition, the review is limited only to themes directly related to this study.

In contrast to the drama of Soviet *history*, the *spatial* aspects of the social dynamics of the Soviet Union often seemed almost frozen, unchangeable. While, in general, history departments in western universities could not complain about the lack of students and researchers specializing in the Soviet area, this certainly was not the case in western geography departments. As a result, historians and historical thinking dominate studies of the Russian Church and culture in general. It is difficult to cite any major work on Orthodoxy in the Russian Realm written from a geographical position, although the list of historical studies is impressive. The dominance of historians and the discipline's associated mode of thinking certainly has contributed to the prevailing lack of geographical awareness in this field. This "historicism" is characteristic of the social sciences in general (Soja 1989) and is followed by a consequent under-representation of geography.

Documentation of the Church's Status and the Official Soviet Vision of Space

Given the closed nature of Communist society and the propagandistic bias of Soviet publications on religion (e.g., Moscow Patriarchate 1942, USSR Academy of Sciences 1986), it is understandable that the most important scholarly endeavor was to accurately document the state of religion in the country. One of the early works had the telling title *Communism and the Churches, a Documentation* (Barron and Waddams 1950). A number of studies were preoccupied with just this documentation (see, e.g., Alexeev 1954-55, Gsovski 1955, Spinka 1956, Szczesniak 1959, Kolarz 1961, Fletcher and Strover 1967, Marshall et al. 1971, Bociurkiw and Strong 1975, Boiter 1980, Konstantinov 1984, Petro 1990, Bourdeaux 1990). In addition, several works have addressed the status of believers *per se* (Marshal et al. 1971, Mol 1972, Lane 1978, Fletcher 1981).

The tradition of full-length comprehensive surveys of the Russian Church was started perhaps by John Curtiss' *The Russian Church and the Soviet State 1917-1950* (1953) and three volumes of Chrysostomus in German (1965-68), in which enormous quantities of data were collected at the expense of analytical depth (Ellis 1986). Nikita Struve's work (Struve 1967) was analytically deeper but focused primarily on the 1960s. Two decades later the first truly comprehensive study (Pospielovsky 1984) appeared. Its focus, however, was on the Soviet period of history.

Even if the more recent surveys attempt to go beyond mere documentation, this theme has remained important. For instance, Ellis (1986) was still concerned with "the problem of the true status of religious believers in the USSR," and even ten years later this topic is relevant as new archival data allow scholars to reconsider previous assumptions. For example, Davis (1995) has corrected widely accepted figures for registered Orthodox communities in the post-war period. In general, the field is very dynamic, and even updates (such as Pospielovsky 1995a) are important.

What these studies most obviously lack is a geographical awareness. Davis, for instance, has a wealth of data that are virtually incomprehensible since they are not presented cartographically (Davis 1995). Most often geographical diversity is conceptualized as variations between republics (see, e.g., Anderson 1994). Since enormous discrepancies exist within the Russian Federation itself, and since in most senses Russia is not equal to the smaller republics, this vision of space makes systematic comparative geographical analysis difficult (Sidorov 1994-95). Even when larger scale data are available, scholars seem unable to break with the official division of space and put Russia's provinces at the same level as the republics. In reality, as soon as governmental control weakened in the post-Soviet period, the official political-territorial hierarchy of the Soviet Union was challenged by the growing sovereignty of Russian constituitive regions. It would perhaps be correct to conclude that this strand in the studies of the Russian Church has tacitly assumed the Soviet administrative-territorial (di)vision of space.

The Soviet administrative-territorial division of space is often attributed to the so-called Administrative-Command System, an extremely bureaucratic kind of state, which existed from the late 1920s to *perestroika*. Space in this system was seen as totally ordered, rigid, and hierarchical, and oriented towards the center at expense of "horizontal" links between its constituent parts. Certain geographical concepts such as frontier, periphery, region, territorial discrepancies and interscalar processes do not fit easily with this rigid (di)vision of space, and thus are underutilized.[5]

As a result of implicit or explicit adoption of this vision of space, scholars can easily miss certain social and political characteristics of the country. For example, in a territorial sense scholars tend to delineate society and its cultural institutions by the state's internal and external divisions. Specialists on Russia and most social scholars often take this territorial match between the state, society, and its cultural institutions as axiomatic. Yet, as this study will show, territorial mismatches have not only been present, but also are politically significant. For instance, the emergence of the Renovationism, very much like the Old Believers' schism, could be interpreted as a result of the mismatch between expanded scope of the state and still national scale of consciousness of its society. Furthermore, territorial mismatches can help to understand the geography of Old Belief prevalence in Russia (Chapter 2). A similar mode of spatial reasoning will be utilized in Chapter 3 to explain the emergence and spread of the Renovationism in the Russian Orthodox Church.

State-Church Nexus and the Hierarchical Vision of Space

The theme of the relationship between the Church and the Soviet state remains a critically important one for it has implications for current Russian democratization and has long been a topic of special scholarly interest (Anderson 1944, Stroyen 1967, Bociurkiw 1969, Billington 1970, Simon 1970, P. Ramet 1987, 1989; S. Ramet 1993, Warhola 1993). Recent improvement in access to archival sources has allowed for some broad theorizations to emerge.

Having scrutinized virtually all facets of state religious policy in the post-Stalin years (1953-1993), John Anderson (1994) treats it mainly in terms of continuing but gradually easing anti-religious activity. Mikhail Odintsov (1994), in contrast, argues that the period of 1900-1965 is characterized not by a continuous policy, but rather by a prevailing, peculiar, and ever changing mix of elements of three consecutive patterns of religious policy developed, respectfully, under the tsarist monarchy (the pattern of Orthodoxy as the state religion), the bourgeois democracy (religious pluralism) and the Soviet state (atheism). For Odintsov, the very union of state and Church is the key unresolved problem. Mikhail Shkarovsky (1999) has already presented ten major periods of the Soviet religious policy.

In contrast, a *geographically* nuanced notion of the state and its religious policies is still required, especially given a time when various constituent parts of the former Soviet Union are growing in sovereignty. For instance, most studies along this lines used to lack research at the local level. At best, scholars have looked at the nexus of "central decision making bodies and on local implementers" (Anderson 1994: 215) or state organizations for religious affairs at the intermediate level (Odintsov 1994). This "top-down" assumption of how religious policy-making actually worked in the Soviet Union could be revised by assigning a much more interactive role to local and intermediate agencies. Anderson shows, for instance, that even under Khrushchev local authorities put theory into practice in different ways, evident in the differing rates of church closures in the republics. More detailed and geographically nuanced research is perhaps needed to answer the question *why* this was the case.

Similarly, this traditional "upside-down" vision must be corrected in the light of some post-Soviet developments when significantly more decisions on religious issues are being made at the local level. The restoration of the Cathedral of Christ the Savior in Moscow (Chapter 7) was managed by local decision-making bodies.

The Soviet imprint on this school of thinking's vision of space is visible in the lack of virtually any concept of periphery, i.e. the consideration of a multiplicity of "horizontal" processes at the local level, as opposed to thinking dominated by "vertical" linkages to processes in the ruling center. In this body of research, local-scale case studies are treated hierarchically, as cases reflecting (proving or accentuating) processes observed at the higher scale of republics. As this book will show, center-periphery discrepancies within the Russian Church are essential to understanding the geographical pattern of a schismatic movements like the Old Belief and Renovationism.

Anti-Religious Policy Studies as Mythology

The harsh anti-religious persecutions under the Soviet regime understandably provoked the emergence of a vast number of works with the prime goal of shedding light on these practices and possibly attracting public attention to them (see, for example, Bolshakov 1942, Fletcher 1965, Parsons 1972, Regel'son 1977, Babris 1978, Bourdeaux and Rowe 1980, Beeson 1982, Bourdeaux 1975, 1983; Buss 1987). Written with the best of intentions and by honest individuals, these works have recorded numerous cases and events, yet often at the expense of analytical depth and accuracy of conclusions.

This theme in studies of the Russian Church could benefit from a critical re-examination of its principal implication: that the interruption and reversal of Communist anti-religious practices is sufficient to restore and maintain religious justice. Current religious policies in Russia, with their self-proclaimed tolerance and spectacular returns of church property have been uncritically accepted as a sign of long-awaited justice in the religious sphere (see, e.g., House 1988, Boudeaux 1990, Forest 1990, Hill 1991). The unjust nature of Soviet religious policy was clearly visible to analysts for as long as it was clearly the obverse of religious policies in the developed western countries. The ability to foresee the emergence of religious injustices in a new, more sophisticated form poses the greatest challenge to this tradition in the post-Soviet period.

In addition, such modern developments in Russia as the return of church property could justify the previous manipulations of cult places if they ignore their geographical and interdenominational particulars. Few scholarly works (such as Pospielovsky 1988) still focus primarily on the main Orthodox Church and the state's ideology and practice. In short, despite the whole body of literature on the Soviet anti-religious persecutions, a fundamental comparative-analytical work is lacking, especially in terms of their religious and geographical characteristics. The current return of property to believers has come as a surprise to scholars.

There are three explanations for the underestimation of the property topic in the field. First, the traditional overconcern with the survival of religion resulted in the underestimation of the very possibility of its revival despite evidence from the WWII period (Alexeev and Stavrou 1976). Second, the very question of property has been left aside as a non-issue in a society with limited market relations. A study of the nationalization of monastic property by Zybkovets (1975) stands as a unique endeavor. To embrace the topic of church property in Russia, one must not only pay attention to the Soviet period of history, but also consider the problems of the pre-Soviet period. Yet, although the state of religion in Tsarist Russia has attracted scholarly attention (among others, Cunningham 1981, Smolitsch 1964-1991), it is difficult to cite a comprehensive work on church property that speaks to the post-Soviet concerns about the denationalization of property. Conventional historical frameworks for research (such as "Soviet period") prove to be constraining in the studies of post-Soviet developments. Finally, the concept of place is usually ignored in the field: until recently, few works have focused on such place-specific topics as a study of particular churches or parishes in the context of their history, geography, or politics.

In short, this strand of the studies of the Russian Church has contributed to the emergence of a certain myth of anti-religious Communist persecution. It is a myth in the sense that it overshadows the pre- and post-Communist religious manipulations; they become virtually negligible, and contradictory tendencies within the Soviet anti-religious policies are neglected themselves. The topic has become politically important and as such is reinforced constantly in a hegemonic way (meaning that only the point of view of the official Church is represented). In a geographical sense, this myth requires implicitly, and (in post-Soviet Russia) explicitly, the restoration of the pre-Soviet *status quo*. Scholars often see space not as a process but as a status which could be restored. Chapter 4 challenges this assumption by documenting the role of territorial mismatches in the anti-religious campaigns of the 1940-80s which were motivated by regional imbalances in church property distribution.

Nationalism and Religion

The topic of religion and nationalism in the former USSR should presumably assign a prominent role to space (Lang 1969, Markus 1985, Dunn 1987, Ramet 1987, 1989, Duncan 1991). However, close consideration shows that this is only partially the case. On the one hand, the religious dimension of nationalisms in the newly independent states is considered (e.g, Bourdeaux 1995) while on the other hand the role of spatial factors is largely ignored. In general, this strand of thinking is characterized by the same constraints as studies of the state-church relationship: the official Soviet political considerations and a corresponding vision of space dominate it. Confinement to official republic borders in these accounts is understandable yet limiting. As will be seen in the case of the post-Soviet development of the Ukrainian Orthodox Church-Kievan Patriarchate, borders of national identification and the Church's own geographical identification can be very divergent and certainly more complicated than official concepts would suggest.

Over-emphasis on the nationalist dimensions of Orthodoxy in the former Soviet republics neglects other trends at the international and sub-national scales. In particular, the recent surprising attempts by the newly independent Ukrainian Orthodox Church to open parishes in Russia and take under its jurisdiction some other alternative Russian religious communities (e.g. the underground Catacomb Church) warrant a new research agenda — one that can grasp the underestimated reformative aspirations of this Church as opposed to the traditionally expected nationalism.

What these studies fail to offer is a conceptualization of national identity in the Russian Federation since in this case, clearly, the methodology applied to other republics (for example, Batalden 1993) would be only partially successful. When it comes to the Russian Church and Russia specifically, it is worth applying a more diffuse vision of national identity. For instance, Pospielovsky, having described the national consciousness of the three Slavonic peoples in the tsarist Russian Empire, noted its vagueness and weakness: it was rather local (provincial) and international (religious, Orthodox) (Pospielovsky 1989). Unfortunately, the author fails to continue this consideration of the geographical components of post-Soviet Russian national identity, discussing only the growing significance of Orthodoxy in the national identity-formation process. The dramatic geopolitical transformations in post-Soviet space have presumably resulted in a mosaic of identities which scholars so far fail to grasp.

In short, studies of nationalism and the Russian Church have yet to surface. The related studies of nationalism in the republics suffer from a certain implicit identity of religion and region. Chapters 5 and 6 will challenge this "re(li)gion" concept, arguing that in these studies of nationalism scale must be taken more critically as a constructed and negotiated, rather than a "fixed," category. Consequently, national Orthodox religions do not necessarily coincide with the national "region."

The geopolitical transformation of the former Soviet Union has profoundly changed the Russian Church, both internally and externally. The protective Iron Curtain has been demolished, the empire has collapsed, and the Church's foreign alternative has appeared within the country. This appearance will be considered in the same chapter since scholars underestimate this phenomenon.

The Russian Church: The Local Dimension

The Soviet administrative-political view of space placed emphasis on the center, and most scholars of the Russian Orthodox Church, by implication, used to privilege "central" discourses. Descriptions of the top ruling body of the Church, the Moscow Patriarchate, often used to stand for the Church as a whole. Even if attempts were undertaken to add local "windows" to otherwise center-based accounts (e.g., Roslof 1994, Ellis 1996) the underlying understanding of space was still primarily hierarchical: local accounts are used to comment on the dominant central discourse. In other words, variations *between* as well as *within* the local were largely overlooked. It was the growing post-Soviet separatism which made scholars look "beyond Moscow" (*The Harriman Institute Newsletter* 1996).

Instead of going "beyond Moscow," Chapter 6 will look at the city as the unit of analysis. The argument is that the traditional lack of awareness of local as opposed to central problematics, and the new regional interests have paradoxically left Moscow as a blank spot in this research. It is difficult to cite any study devoted specifically to Moscow, not only on religious matters but in general. Only recently has the first comprehensive account of the city's modern governmental history been published (Colton 1995).

The local dimension provides useful perspectives on diversity issues. It would be an exaggeration to claim that religious diversity is a neglected area of study within the field. Yet this topic is most commonly present in studies as a mere concern for a balanced representation of different religions in Russia (see, e.g., Babris 1978, Hill 1989, 1991; Forest 1990). At best, scholars undertake studies into specific strands of Orthodoxy, such as the Old Believers, the Renovationists, the Catacomb, and the Foreign and Ukrainian Churches. What is lacking is an understanding of the role of religious differences in the democratization of the country. Chapter 6 looks at the politics of relations between the local state, the official state, and the new alternative communities. Finally, as shown in Chapter 7, on the reconstruction of the Cathedral of Christ the Savior, interscalar processes are important in themselves.

To conclude, the multidisciplinary studies of the Russian Church, dominated by historians, suffer from a long neglect of geographical approaches. Most importantly, they adopted a rigid, hierarchical, center-focused vision of space, which is characteristic of the official Soviet administrative-territorial division of the country. This "frozen" vision of space limits the scope of scholarly approaches. Each chapter of this book attempts to address different facets of this long neglect in a constructive way.

GEOGRAPHICAL STUDIES OF RELIGION: A-POLITICAL SPACE?

This section of of the chapter has a two-fold aim. First, it reviews the tradition of geographical studies of religion. Second, it explains why the geography of religion was not particularly useful for studies of the Russian Church. The argument is that the continuing neglect of the political dimension in religio-geographical studies makes this line of research obsolete for studies of the Russian Church.

Ecclesiastical Geography

Geography has elaborated a number of distinctive approaches in the tradition of studies of religion (see, for example, Sopher 1967, Kong 1990, Cooper 1992, Park 1994), which could possibly be fruitful for studying the Russian Church. It is appropriate, perhaps, to start by considering ecclesiastical geography since this approach is one of the oldest in the geography of religion.

The term "ecclesiastical geography" was coined by Isaak (1965: 10), for whom "[t]he spatial advance of the church in the world in terms of its own institutions and of political territories that assented to it, could be and were mapped by what we may call ecclesiastical geography." Ecclesiastical geography emerged in the sixteenth and seventeenth centuries and involved primarily the mapping of the spatial advance of Christianity in the world. In the nineteenth and twentieth centuries, ecclesiastical geography primarily emphasized the compilation of so-called missionary atlases. For example, King's (1964) missionary atlas not only provided information on previous accomplishments, but also served as a manual for further expansion. Christian positions were dominant, and atlases such as *The 20th Century Atlas of the Christian World* (Freitag 1963) were typical. Gradually, attempts were made to describe the spheres of influence of other religions. Although this was a seemingly liberating development, it had the effect of defining religions in terms of Christian missionaries' perceptions of what they encountered in different parts of the world and documenting how missions were progressing among them. The underlying impetus for geographical work, thus stemmed largely from Christian interests (Kong 1990: 357).

Ecclesiastical geography remains an essential part of contemporary study: "by and large, the bulk of work treating religion must be classified as ecclesiastical geography, even where geographers went beyond the more traditional range of things mapped and discussed by the older ecclesiastical geography" (Isaak 1965: 13). Recent research differs primarily in the use of progressively more sophisticated methods of mapping. Religious demography is another facet of ecclesiastical geography.

Gay (1971: 4-15) has documented some of the most definitive studies in this respect. In France, beginning in 1931, the work of Gabriel le Bras gave birth to a series of socio-geographic studies on religious distributions. Le Bras' concept of religious vitality went beyond a traditional mapping of institutions. He described vitality as the degree to which overt religious behavior is fundamentally religiously motivated and contrasted this with religious observance (i.e., practice), which is frequently devoid of religious meaning, reflecting instead the strength of social custom. In areas like Sweden, where folk (popular) religion reflects the area's religious personality far better than institutional practice, studies of the folk religious vitality would be important. Similarly, Fogarty (1957) has used all the available sociographic evidence in his attempt to analyze geographical variations in religious practice through-

out continental Europe by delimiting a belt of intensive religious practice of Protestant and Roman Catholic populations.[6]

In the USA, the geography of religion has a more complicated
picture. Two classic studies by Zelinsky and Hotchkiss are noteworthy
with regard to the development of ecclesiastical geography. Hotchkiss
(1950) identified denomination by a percentage of the total religious
community in each state and was able to show their relative distributions by plotting these variations. Zelinsky (1961) undertook a systematic account of the geography of religion within a given county. He
studied denominational allegiances, which varied greatly in strength
from place to place. It was on the basis of this that Zelinsky advanced
his vision of the religious regions of the US.

There were examples of ecclesiastical geography in Russia in
the pre-revolutionary period, yet new work followed only in the post-
Communist period (Krindach 1992). This book also contributes to the
ecclesiastico-geographical tradition, for each chapter analyzes, among
other issues, the spatial distribution of Orthodox communities and
churches, and provides a series of maps to assist with that.

Biblical Geography

Biblical geography is as old as ecclesiastical geography, also de-
veloping in the sixteenth and seventeenth centuries (Kong 1990: 357).
The Bible contains extensive historical materials and innumerable allu-
sions to the geographical background of that history. The intention of
biblical geography is to identify places in the Bible and to determine
their actual geographical locations. Although geographical references
range as far as India and Spain, at the center of the considerations is the
Holy Land under its various names. A number of atlases of the Bible
illustrate this body of scholarship. Although these studies vary in ways
of representing material and the degree of detail, most of them share
the same function of providing an illustration of biblical accounts (e.g.,
Grollenberg 1956, May et al. 1962, Al-Faruqi 1974, *Reader's Digest Atlas*
1981). On the other hand, the more recent *Atlas of the Bible* (Rogerson
1985) has a primarily geographic orientation. Ranging from urban geography to climatology and geomorphology, biblical geography is still
the "historical geography of biblical times" (Isaak 1965: 8).

The Influence of Religion on Landscape

Ecclesiastical and biblical geographies were not the only traditional links between geography and religion. Another avenue of communication between the two is the so-called physico-theological approach. This approach emerged in the late seventeenth century and
became particularly strong in the eighteenth and nineteenth centuries.
The line of reasoning in this tradition can be summarized as follows:
only a divine force for well-being could create the Earth in all its enormous complexity and fascinating order. The notion of a designed Earth
has been a commonplace idea since the Renaissance. The fundamental
questions for physico-theologians were proofs of God's existence, the
final causes of this world, and orderliness in nature (Glacken 1959: 504).

Theological explanations were seen as the only explanations able
to embrace the wholeness of nature and its purposefulness as evident
in any element or process. Fundamental to the physico-theological
stance was the idea that human beings attain control over nature. By
the nineteenth century, the decline of the older physico-theology had
already begun; with Lamarck and Darwin attention was turned to adaptation to environments (Glacken 1959: 549). Perhaps by the middle
of the nineteenth century, it became apparent that man's stewardship
over nature was no longer an accurate description "of his role, there
was disillusionment, and with it the realization that men could relent-
lessly destroy nature in ways that they did not even suspect themselves
capable of, that many of their efforts were not divinely guided, nor the
result of purposive control" (Glacken 1959: 427).

Though studies of how religion determines the environment
were replaced by environmental determinism the theory was revived
in the 1920s and 1930s by the spreading influence of Max Weber's book
The Protestant Ethic and the Spirit of Capitalism. This revival differed
from the previous physico-theological approach through its definition
of the subject matter of research. The call was to study religion's impact on the socio-economic sphere. This line of thought is still very
influential. Kong (1990) mentions recent writings (Curtis 1980, Laatsch
and Calkins 1986) on religion as a motivational force in environmental
and landscape change. However, the major influence and significance
of this "religious determinism" for geography was in the theoretical
domain, defining the questions geographers should be concerned with.
This line of thought has dominated much research over the last two
decades, and many attempts to delineate the field bear witness to this
approach (Kong 1990: 358). For example, Isaak (1959-60) was definitely

influenced by this line of reasoning. The emphasis on landscape, particularly in Sauer's school of cultural geography, is a result of the same religious determinism (Kong 1990: 359).

Similar modes of thought were also influential outside of geography. For example, Lynn White's "The historical roots of our ecological crisis" (1967) argued that increasing environmental degradation was the result of Christian thinking and, more specifically, of the Biblical belief that humans should dominate nature. White advocated either incorporating the more moderate position of St. Francis of Assisi into Christianity, or replacing it with a non-western religion.[7]

Environmentalist Influence on the Geography of Religion

The physico-theological approach to geographical studies of the interaction between the environment and religion was accompanied by another body of thought. In sharp contrast to the physico-theological ideas, this school explored the impact of the environment on religion. This body of thought developed in the eighteenth and nineteenth centuries under the influence of Montesquieu and Voltaire and flourished at the beginning of the twentieth century.

In geography, these ideas turned into a highly environmentally deterministic approach. The Russian anarchist and geographer Petr Kropotkin was one of the pioneers of this line of thought, supported by other leftist thinkers such as Plekhanov (Bassin 1992). Other proponents of an unrestricted environmentalism in geography were Semple and Huntington in the US and England, Le Play in France, and Ratzel in Germany. They aimed to explain the character of religions in terms of their geographical environments. Huntington (1926), for example, looked at the Bible and the history of the Israelite people from an environmental perspective, and Semple (1911) argued that the symbolism of a religion was affected by its place of birth.

Hultkrantz (1966) exemplified more recent variants of environmental deterministic thinking. He argued for a religio-ecological method of study. Hultkrantz (1966: 137) believed that "the old environmentalism is certainly dead, but a new trend, 'cultural ecology,' is appearing in its stead." The old environmental determinism can only give the hint, but no theology grows out of ecological, economic, or technical circumstances. According to Hultkrantz (1966: 142), "[i]t is only the religious form that may be determined by such impulses, at least partly... ." Hultkrantz's "determinism" is limited because this approach is intended primarily for tribal, simple religious groups, such as nomadic and arctic hunting cultures.

Thus, the legacy of environmental influence continues in different forms even after Huntington and Semple. In Sopher's (1967: 14) manifesto of the geography of religion we can find the following statement: "Geography can help to determine to what extent religious systems or their component elements are an expression of ecological circumstances." Although the context of the sentence is critical of the "etiological fallacy" in the geographical formulation of environmentalist generalizations, we read further on something similar to Hultkrantz: "In the simple ethnic systems, religion often seems to be almost entirely a ritualization of ecology. Religion is the medium whereby nature and natural processes are placated, cajoled, entreated, or manipulated in order to secure the best results for man" (Sopher 1967: 17).

Nonetheless, Kong (1990: 358) believes that Sopher's book (1967), as well as works of other authors (Fickeler 1962, Buttner 1974, 1980, Levine 1986), reflects the realization that relationships between religion and the environment are dialectical and that to study them as a unidirectional relationship would be unrealistic. A focus on reciprocity in the network of relations shows that religious geography, after utilizing the physico-theological and environmental deterministic precepts, now has entered a third stage of synthesis (Kong 1990: 359).

Studies of Sacred Places and Pilgrimages

Understanding what is "sacred" is a difficult, but necessary task in studies of religion, and geographers have attempted to elucidate what this may be. Sacred spaces and pilgrimages are characteristic of any society, whatever its religious practices. Still, issues of sacredness and pilgrimages have been explored primarily in the Christian domain. For example, Tuan (1977), approaching the idea of sacred space, implicitly explored Christian sacredness only. Nolan (1986) compiled a map of active shrines with sacred site features throughout western Europe, which amounts to a map of a Christianized continuation of pagan nature veneration. She tried to understand the relationship between natural features and the sanctity of religious pilgrimage sites such as dominant relief, hydrology, stones, caves, plants, and animals.[8]

Geographical studies of pilgrimages lack some systematic summarizing work. It is primarily anthropologists who attempt to grasp pilgrimages theoretically (e.g., Turner 1978). For example, Rutter (1929) has studied the Muslim Hajj pilgrimage and its impact on transportation and the economy of the region. Rinschede (1986) has profiled the pilgrimage town of Lourdes through the prism of its socio-economic character. Scott and Simpson-Housley (1991) provided a number of examples of sacred places and pilgrimages in Judaism, Christianity, and Islam.

Studies of Religious Symbolism in Cultural Geography

Although an increasing interest in the political symbolism of religious places has been labeled as part of the "new" cultural geography, these interests are, in fact, a focused expansion of past research (Kong 1990: 364). Deffontaines (1953), for example, examined the symbolic meanings of dwellings in religious terms. He looked at the manner in which the religious function of the house has modified its form, providing examples from different cultures where the symbolic function of a dwelling is of prime importance. The house can be a shrine and a tomb. Religion influences the orientation, shape, doors, and windows and other characteristics of houses.

Wheatley (1971) used a smaller scale in his studies of the symbolic religious meanings of cities. In particular, he examined the cosmological underpinnings of the Chinese city. No Chinese city was ever planned without the advice of a geomancer. Cardinal orientation and axiality were important characteristics of the cities. Wheatley argues that the major principle of the Chinese city is the parallel between the macrocosmos (the universe) and the microcosmos (the city).

The focus on symbolism can also furnish studies of pilgrimages with new insights. Tanaka (1981) studied the process of Buddhist pilgrimages. He explained how characteristics of pilgrimages, such as the number of sacred sites and the pattern of movement, are deeply symbolic. Nolan (1986) also put forward the argument that the roots of some Christian shrines' symbolism lie in pre-Christian belief-systems.

New Cultural Geography and Conflicts over Religious Places and Symbols

While studies of the symbolic meanings of religious places may be treated as traditional in geography, the recent growing interest of cultural geographers in the analysis of conflicts and power has indeed provided a new perspective on geography of religion. Interest in the political symbolism of religious landscapes is part of a broader trend in cultural geography. Focus on the interface between politics, symbolism, and religious landscapes reflects recognition in human geography of the symbolic as opposed to the purely functional meanings of places. There is rising interest in cultural politics among cultural geographers, with its associated concepts of ideology, hegemony,[9] and resistance. Landscapes are conceptualized as ideological in that they can be used to endorse, legitimize, and/or challenge socio-political control (see, for example, Jackson 1989).

Muir and Weissman's study (1989) of Renaissance Venice and Florence, Lewandowski's discussion (1984) of Madras, and Duncan's analysis (1990) of nineteenth century Kandy all show how religious landscapes can be used to endorse the political order and to contribute to the secular state's own political legitimation. Kong (1993) showed in the case of Singapore that the state plays a large role at a material level in deciding how space is to be used for religious purposes. The ascription of symbolic meanings is not lacking either. The state seeks to instill in people its particular set of values that will allow it to maintain political power. This power to define religious space is but one example of how the state has exercised its power. Not all individuals and groups respond amicably to the presumably all-embracing power of the state.

The symbolic meanings of religious buildings have not received sufficient attention in geography even though the material impacts of religion on the landscape have been researched. Religious buildings also are invested with a multitude of symbolic meanings — personal, sacred, social, and political. Cultural geographers have long ignored the association between the "religious" and the "political," concentrating instead on separating the "religious" from other sociopolitical and economic forces in society. As Kong (1993) has shown, contemporary meanings and values of religious buildings in Singapore are invested by the state and can be different from previous meanings and values. She showed this by highlighting the context of the religious buildings as influenced by the state. The state, thus, shapes the construction of the buildings' meanings. This line of religio-geographical research is relevant to Chapter 7, which looks at the pre-eminent Russian Orthodox monument, the Cathedral of Christ the Savior in Moscow, as an ever-changing inscription of the state's will.

Historical Materialist Perspectives on Religion

In contrast to major previous research approaches, Levine (1986: 428) suggests

"a research paradigm which geographers of religion have not generally adopted but which should prove directly useful to some and challenging to others. The adoption of phenomenological and historical materialist approaches have become commonplace in geography yet historical materialist approach is suggested as a research perspective for geographers who want to appreciate more fully the socio-environmental impacts of religious institutions. More specifically, [this] paper addresses the question of the nature of the relationship between religion and society and its operation as an institution in class society."

In Levine's words, phenomenologists tend to see religion as an attempt to comprehend reality. Functionalists in both sociology and anthropology have tended to see religion as a factor in creating social cohesion. Ecologists see religion as a system of symbols, which establish motives in people through a formulation of the general order of existence. Historical materialists have conveyed the idea that religion is of "the world and that it is illusion and mystification. Religion is an expression of real misery, of life's trials. Religion is produced by people" (Levine 1986: 432).

Levine (1986: 433) argues that, too often, Marxists and others have seen religion as false or illusory, and hence ideological. Religion is neither necessarily false nor illusory, yet it is ideological as a mental construct and physical practice that influences society and is influenced by it. The consequent function of religion is to legitimize social institutions. It is inevitably a social phenomenon as well as an institution. People are essentially social, and institutionalization is a constant, dialectical process. Institutions should be understood within the particular class structure of the society.

Levine claims that the geography of religion is primarily concerned with the institutionalization of a particular ideology and that geographers should be concerned with religion's role as a world-founding institution (Levine 1986: 437). Understanding the particulars of the institutionalization of a religious ideology will help the geographer attain a fuller understanding of the socio-environmental impact of reli-

gion on society and environment and their impact on religion. In order
to understand the role of religious institutions as socio-cultural agents,
it is necessary to appreciate the nature of society in terms of its institutional and class dimensions.

The exclusive focus on class suggested by Levine may be too
rigid a framework for applied studies. In addition, modern societies,
such as the US, are pluralist in their religious landscapes, and it is unclear whether Levine's focus on dominant ideologies and power fits
within the reality of diverse modern societies. Yet Levine's is a refresh-
ing project. The article is unique in geography, and the reason for that
may be the generality of the author's claims: not only geographers, but
also sociologists, anthropologists and others can benefit from adopting
the author's perspective. There have been few if any attempts to do
specifically geographical research along similar lines.

Two of Levine's emphases are very relevant to this study. First,
this book studies the institutional dimension of religion. Second, the
political, legitimative role of religion in society is often the focus of the
analysis. The latter emphasis stands in contrast to the new cultural
geography's seemingly exclusive interest in landscapes and cityscapes
as "texts." Cultural geographers are able to go beyond mere local studies of the religion-politics nexus as the whole book attempts to show.

Summary

Despite, or because of, its long history the geography of religion currently looks obsolete in light of new research challenges. Its
main deficiencies can be summarized as the lack of political interest, a
focus on object-descriptive themes, and theoretical indifference. In the
words of Kong (1990, quoted in Johnston et al. 1994: 523),

"[a] review of the geography of religion remains at present
largely an inventory of eclectic, and mainly descriptive, empirical studies, intersected with a smaller number of theoretically more ambitious works, and culminating in a handful of powerful research monographs, many of them addressing topics from the past. The global revitalization of
religious belief and its consequences in the past decade provide the contemporary research problems around which a
more theoretical and programmatic body of research in the
geography of religion might yet develop. In the light of the

salience of its subject matter and an incomplete intellectual development to date, there is certainly 'more room for geographical exploration (of religion) than has thus far been attempted'."

It is this void that has motivated this study. The remaining part of this chapter will explain how this book intends to overcome the deficiencies of both the studies of the Russian Church and the geography of religion, by conceptualizing the role of scale in the evolving geopolitics of Russian Orthodoxy in the twentieth century.

THE CHURCH, THE STATE, AND SOCIETY:
THE DIFFERENCE THAT SCALE MAKES

As the preceding reviews of literature from studies of the Russian Church and the geography of religion have shown, in both scholarly fields the Russian Orthodox Church (ROCh) remains an understudied geographical phenomenon. Therefore, it is only natural to expect a possible "marriage" of the two fields, meaning the expansion of religio-geographical methods into studies of the Russian Church. Although some initial examples are available (see, for example, Krindatch 1996), this possible "marriage" would arguably not be successful in insofar as it would not fully satisfy the demands of studies of the Russian Church. Two arguments are noteworthy in this regard.

First, there is a mismatch of interests between studies of the Russian Church and the geography of religion. While the former is predominantly concerned with *socio-political* issues, the latter has restricted itself to exclusively *cultural* matters. Second, there is a mismatch of research foci: the interdisciplinary studies of the Russian Church tend to analyze Church-society *relations*, while the geography of religion rather privileges more exclusive *object-based* studies with its predominantly anthropological descriptive concerns.

The two preceding arguments have geographical manifestations. Students of Orthodoxy would be most interested in a geography reflecting the broad *spatiality* of mutual relationships between the state, the Church, and society, while the arguable exclusivity and object-fixation of religio-geographical studies has resulted in its relative "relational ignorance" and a *fixation on territory*.

In the light of these arguments, this book attempts to reposition religio-geographical research from its current focus on cultural, mate-

rial, and territorial concerns to engage more broad socio-politico-cultural and spatial interests. I intend to focus on one important facet of
state-church-society relationships, namely their spatial non-coincidence:
the mismatch of the *territorial extents* of the Church, the state, and society. At different periods of the Russian Orthodox Church's modern
history, these mismatches have had not only territorial but also exceptional scalar dimensions.

Focus on spatial mismatch between the state, Church, and society has several research advantages. First, it allows some continuity
with the traditional "territorial" interests of human geographers and
specifically religio-geographers. Second, it allows the incorporation of
relational perspectives (discussed below) from the most recent alternative theoretical approaches, which can be seen primarily as a challenge
to traditional geography's preoccupation with (bounded) territory and
fixed scales as opposed to "ruptured territory" and "extensional scale."
Third, a concern for territorial non-coincidence can provide fresh geographical insights into two key concepts in contemporary social sciences — *power* and *difference*. The remaining body of this chapter elabo-
rates these claims, thereby attempting to provide a conceptual foundation for the book as a whole.

Meanings of Space and Meanings of Scale

John Agnew and Stuart Corbridge have identified two modes
of understanding space in the social sciences.

> "The first sees space as territorial. In other words, space is
> viewed as a series of blocks defined by state territorial bound-
> aries. Other geographical scales (local, global, etc.) are largely
> disregarded. This usually taken-for-granted representation
> of space appears dominant in such fields as political sociol-
> ogy, macroeconomics and international relations. A second
> understanding views space as structural. From this point of
> view, geographical entities of one sort or another, nodes, dis-
> tricts, regions, etc. have spatial effects that result from their
> interaction or relationship with one another. For example,
> an industrial core area is paired with a resource periphery in
> a structural relationship of superiority/subordination. This
> more self-conscious understanding is characteristic of much
> human geography, economic history, and dependency theo-
> ries in sociology" (Agnew and Corbridge 1995: 79-80).

In brief, Agnew and Corbridge identify two main problems with the territorial vision of space: its "boundedness" ("territorialization") and the privileging of the national scale ("nationalization"). Since for Agnew and Corbridge such structuralist schools as Marxism, Weberianism, and Durkheimian sociology share this "territorial" view of space. A less confusing term for "structural" space might be "relational" space. Although not all territories are "territorial" in the above sense, I would prefer not to use a different term (such as "divisional space") to avoid confusion.

Contrary to Agnew and Corbridge's classification, the dichotomy of territorial/relational space does exist within human geography. To see this, consider the way the two key concepts of territory and scale are treated in human geography. First, territory is usually associated with bounded space (Cox 1991), e.g., treated "territorially" (in the sense described above). Indeed, the problem of territorial non-correspondence has attracted limited attention by geographers (Cox 1996). Second, scale often is treated "territorially" as a space of certain size, bounded within some levels.

When it comes to scalar as opposed to territorial differences, traditional human geographers pay little attention to interactions or relationships. Scalar differences are viewed as "territorial": scalar space is conceived as divided into blocks, or levels, defined in part by state hierarchical divisions (federalisms of various kinds), which is a scalar equivalent of "territorialization" in the sense discussed by Agnew and Corbridge (1995). And of all scales, the national one is privileged (the scalar equivalent of territorial "nationalization").

This situation in human geography has recently been challenged from a number of perspectives. Localities studies in the late 1980s attempted to challenge the privileged position of the national scale in scholars' and practitioners' thinking, studying the relation between global, national and local phenomena (Smith and Dennis 1987, Duncan and Savage 1989). Another group of scholars addressed somewhat similar problems from primarily a supranational (global) viewpoint (Wallerstein 1991, Taylor 1989, Dalby 1990, 1993).

The situation of "territorialization" (fixity) of scale has become a target of a so-called constructionist approach.

> "Scale is, arguably, geography's core concept, for only through its resolution can we negotiate the boundaries between difference and similarity. It is scale which enables us to differentiate geographical landscapes, to delimit inclusion or ex-

clusion in such social constructions as home, class, nation, rural, urban, core and periphery. Despite its importance for the production and differentiation of landscapes, scale remains a theoretically and empirically problematic concept. This is particularly so with regard to mapping the translations between processes operating at different geographical scales... geographic scale is produced as the resolution of processes of cooperation and competition between and among social groups in building landscapes. Since scale is socially produced, there is a politics to its production" (Herod 1991: 82).

The concept of construction of scales has been advanced recently by some geographers (Smith 1992a, 1992b, 1993, Swyngedouw 1992, Meyer 1992, Leitner 1997, Delaney and Leitner 1997, Marston 2000). These studies of interscalar interactions — global-local connections, *glocalization* — are perhaps the first true attempts at a "relational" view of scales. Yet the discourse on the interscalar ties is reminiscent of the discipline of international relations (reviewed in Agnew and Corbridge 1995) in that it is built on the assumption that there are scales (analogous to states). Thus, the discourse on interscalar dependencies can indirectly reinforce the "territorialization" of scales (their fixity). In an implicit critique of this tendency, other scholars have focused on examples of "jumping scales," breaking imposed scales as part of social movements' resistance to "scalar territoriality" (Staeheli 1994, Miller 1995, Adams 1996).

What is lacking in this approach is any discourse on intra-scalar relations as opposed to external ones. In other words, although the fixity of scales has been shaken, this happened primarily with their external characteristics. Internally, scales are still perceived as arguably fixed, homogeneous, "territorial." Like territories, scales are not homogeneous. This study will focus on these omitted themes.

To make my point clear, an important distinction should be made between scale as extent and scale as level. Cartographically, scale is "the proportion between a length on a map and the corresponding length on the ground; it may be expressed in words, shown as a divided line or given as a representative fraction" (Small and Witherick 1989: 201). In human geography, scale is conventionally taken to mean "relative spatial extent (i.e., *spatial scale*), ranging from the *macro-scale* (e.g., the continent), through the *meso-scale* (e.g., the country), to the *micro-scale* (e.g., the region)" (Small and Witherick 1989: 201).[10]

This latter definition is somewhat problematic because it

conflates two different features of scale: (1) scale as extent and (2) scale as level in hierarchy of spatial units of different size. The difference is that "scale as extent" connotes existence of an original nucleus (extent of what?) and directed, therefore flexible, edge; "scale as level" refers only to its position relative to other scale-levels of the hierarchy. For instance, "local scale" in the first meaning refers to spatial extent of a locality; in the second sense, local scale means certain level in the hierarchy of levels (e.g., local level vs. national level). While the first feature connotes possible interpenetration of scales, the latter does not allow that.

It is important to distinguish between these two meanings for two reasons. First, this study focuses on mismatches in the extent of scales at different scale-levels. For instance, statistically considered as occupying at the same local scalar level, in reality the Moscow government, the city of Moscow, and Moscow diocese of the Church have different spatial extents. Second, this difference in meanings of scale can signify a profound watershed between two scholarly paradigms that I intend to discuss. In the earlier, "territorial" paradigm, exemplified here by traditional human geography, scale is understood primarily as level, as something static and delineated. In the latter, "relational," paradigm, exemplified here by social studies of power/difference, scale is treated rather as extent, and attempts are made to challenge the fixity of the extent at a particular scale-level. Both paradigms have something to offer, however. At the same time, as Agnew and Corbridge argue, "[o]ne feature both understandings commonly share is a lack of historical consciousness about the appropriateness of particular spatialities" (Agnew and Corbridge 1995: 80).

Power and Difference in "Territorial" Human Geography

The aim of this and the following section of this chapter is to elaborate on the dichotomy suggested by Agnew and Corbridge by discussing its scalar implications for understanding of power/difference problematics.

For purposes of identification, that tradition in human geography which is dominated by "territorial" views of scale, is called here "divisional" human geography. This term is highly conditional: it is meant only to mark a distinction between scale-bounded approaches and scale-relational ones. It includes a number of quite different theoretical traditions also outside of geography, e.g., Marxism and

Durkheimian sociology.

Its features can be illustrated by reference to Robert Sack's classic work (1986) *Human Territoriality*. Many other works could be used for our purpose, but this book is chosen for several reasons. First, it can be called a geographical manifesto on power and space because of its attempted abstract and unifying theoretical nature. Second, it contains a discussion of church power problematics. Third, some of its themes (discussion of the Panopticon) overlap with Foucault's (1977) *Discipline and Punish*, which will be used subsequently as an illustration of the "relational" vision of space. Finally, Sack's book popularized arguably the most explicit metaphor of the "territorial" spatiality of power, namely territoriality.

According to Sack (1986: 2), territoriality is "a human strategy to affect, influence, and control a territory." As Sack shows in a special chapter, the Roman Catholic Church contains complex examples of territorial effects in different historical periods, many of which are shared with the Eastern Orthodox Churches by nature of their common origin in the initially undivided Christian Church.

Similarly, many elements of Sack's approach to territoriality are essential for this study. He makes an important distinction between the invisible Church (the abstract system of belief and values) and the physical or visible Church. It is the latter, the physical Church, that constitutes the subject of this study. Of the three facets of the physical Church identified by Sack, its members, rules, and properties, the focus here is on its property, or church buildings. Characteristically, the book's subject index does not include the items "power" and "difference" (although it does include "Panopticon"). Perhaps, at that time, mid-1980s, the nuances of these words were not fully perceived.

In his analysis, Sack pays attention to scalar differences between types of territoriality. He focuses primarily on two types of territories: holy places and church buildings' interior spaces, and those that are representing administrative structures of the Church such as parishes, dioceses, and archdioceses. His focus is on boundaries, more specifically, on the fixed, stable lines of delimitation. As has been pointed out, this interest is characteristic of traditional theories of power. In general, Sack's vision of territoriality is relatively passive. Only in the conclusion of the book does he mention that "we must be aware that [territoriality] possesses its own potentialities to affect and control, and that some of these may be contrary to the goals of the society" (Sack 1986: 219). This underexplored dimension of territoriality's *own potentialities* will be explored in this study.

With the many socio-geographical ruptures and disjunctures in Russia's development during the period under investigation, it is only natural to expect from a system of territoriality a certain inertial force, or mismatch of territory, and the effects of a spillover of process. These are, according to Sack (1986: 38), among the primary characteristics ("combinations of tendencies") of territoriality, yet he has not explored these effects in length.

The Russian Church's physical infrastructural embodiment, like the strategy of territoriality under condition of spatial mismatch or temporal lag, can acquire potentialities of its own. In other words, at times of dynamic social change, the specific socio-spatial relations preserved by the Church infrastructure's inertia become not only visible, but also significant. One aim of this research is to explore these social potentialities of church infrastructure along the lines of power and difference.

In short, Sack's *Human Territoriality* has a number of underexplored dimensions, such as territorial mismatches and their importance for the exercise of power. Perhaps, there was no demand for these avenues at the time. However, it is of interest to note that, simultaneously with the appearance of Sack's work another book on territoriality was published (Dodgshon 1987). It also stressed the importance of geographical studies of territorial ruptures but did not pursue them. The reason for this continuing neglect of focus on spatial discontinuities may be in the unproblematic state view of power.

In subsequent years, however, no major study on the topic of territoriality have been produced, although a number of articles have utilized the concept (see, e.g., Adams 1996). Three factors can explain this relative neglect of territoriality. First, in a way, Sack's and Dodgshon's books may have exhausted the theme for a while. Second, with the general turn of geographers' interest to ward processes, the topic of territoriality was deemed static and exhausted. Finally, and this is the theme running through the following discussion section, new competing theories emerged which had the advantage of providing a more sophisticated treatment of power and its geography. Before they are considered, though, the essential characteristics of the "territorial" scalar view of power/difference must be summarized.

As has been mentioned, a number of influential social theories in geography have shared a "territorial" view of space. With regard to scale problematics this meant that "[r]eference to local or regional settings, except as 'case studies' of ostensibly state-wide processes, or to 'global' processes, was largely closed off by the 'nationalizing' of social science and its subservience to the territorial state" (Agnew 1987). Only outside the modern world, in the "traditional" societies where nation states did not exist, did other geographical scales of analysis seem appropriate. This sense of the territorial state as the container of (modern) society has been reproduced in the main currents of international relations. According Agnew and Corbridge (1995: 93), "[o]nly inside the state territory is there social order; outside is anarchy and danger." In short, the adoption of a "divisional" view of space resulted in the equation of society with the state.

The state has two main defining aspects in political theory: one involves the exercise of power, and the other entails the spatial demarcation of territory for this exercise. One of the implications of a "divisional" view of space is understanding power as power of the state, state authority, or state authorities at different levels: national, sub-national, local. As the state is considered "natural," so is power and its scalar "boundaries." The alternative to power, then, is chaotic diversity, meaning that the power/difference relationship becomes treated as (state) authority/diversity concept ("diversity" will be defined subsequently).

In short, with the divisional view of scale, power is unproblematic, because the very divisions used are preconditioned by some authority (e.g., first we have federal scalar units, and then scholars study processes within them). Even if scholars dealt with power systems different from the state, such as church and family, they still borrowed the essential ingredients of the authority/diversity concept of power: a divisional, bounding, view of both space and scale; that is, a taken-for-granted understanding of power as authority, and treatment of disorganized diversity as opposite to ordered power-authority.

In conclusion, one might say that human geographical studies of the relationship between power and difference suffer from the "territorial trap" (Agnew and Corbridge 1995). In particular, power is arguably limited to the authority of a dominant agent (usually, the state), diversity stands for difference, and (bounded) territory is privileged over scale-extent. As will be shown in the next section, power can be seen in an alternative fashion as a process in making. To see that, however, one must adopt a more relational approach.

Recent Social Theorists on Power, Difference, and Space

The purpose of this section is to show how the limitations of the traditional political geography described above have been challenged by recent social science's discussions of space/power/difference problematics. As has been mentioned, the weakest points in both Sack's and Dodgshon's visions of territoriality are their treatments of power and its geography. Indeed, in neither book was "power" even included in their subject indexes. Perhaps, at the time of writing these books, in the early 1980s, the concept of power was not seen as particularly problematic. With Sack, power was authority, and with Dodgshon, power was the advantage in the means of production and the degree of a society's complexity. In other words, Sack's ideas of power came primarily from anthropology and sociology (Weberianism), whereas Dodgshon's drew on Marxism (historical materialism) and systems theory, which, perhaps, best suited his grand scale of analysis.

Contemporaneously with these traditional sources of theorization on sociality and power, however, in the late 1980s human geography discovered mutual affinities with a number of new theoretical fields in social sciences, particularly post-structuralism. It would not be an exaggeration to suggest that the spatiality of power-difference was a main concern of post-structuralist thought. In many ways, it was a reaction to geographers' obsession with boundaries and their inability to occupy a more relational position.

Foucault's writings (1972, 1977, 1980, 1984) were particularly influential for this new relational paradigm (for interpretation in geography, see Driver 1985, Matless 1992, Philo 1992), his *Discipline and Punish* serving as a manifesto for the trend. Although widely cited in human geography, this classic study by Foucault is arguably misinterpreted by those who narrow it to the issue of "local sites of power" and surveillance mechanisms (e.g., Herbert 1996). In my opinion, the true innovation of the work was its insistence on the relational nature of power, in terms of both its social and spatial embodiments. Arguably, the first part of the book, which discusses the pre-modern period is historically dubious, but this section is only an introduction to what was the ultimate target of Foucault's project: to explain the mechanisms of normalization in modern societies and the role of space in this process.

Foucault's concept of power was a challenge to two major previous intellectual trends, which could be identified with Marxism and liberalism. While the former locates power in the dominant groups of class-divided societies, the latter stresses individual dimensions of power. Foucault's radical innovation is in placing power between these social and individual domains. Power is a medium, like knowledge or language. Language, for example, simultaneously belongs both to every individual and to society as a whole. It makes sense only as part of one Self and simultaneously of the Others. Foucauldian power, like language, belongs to no one, and to talk about power in terms of its quantity or location is to miss the whole point.

In this view, Bentham's Panopticon is not the example of Foucauldian power system because power there is precisely located (in the central tower) and it has some purpose (for some power groups). The Foucauldian Panopticon is different: the central tower is empty (or occupied by occasional visitors including the imprisoned people themselves) but through particular behavior relations, spatial practices, knowledge, and language people constantly re-create power. The Panopticon system is based not only on voyeuristic tricks, but also on relative rupture in spaces of certain social entities, such as the state and society. Everyone in modern society is simultaneously in the tower and in the cell, exercising and suffering from power. It, thus, would be wrong to claim that the much acclaimed Davis' (1990) portrayal of surveillance in modern Los Angeles in *City of Quartz* provides an example of the Foucauldian control mechanism because we can still localize power in his account in some classes whose interests it secures. Davis' approach to control is still a Marxian one, not Foucauldian.

It is noteworthy that, while discussing space continuously, Foucault is, in fact, a-territorial. There is no discussion of the variety of societies or of internal diversity within France itself (provinces, region, countryside vs. the city). Again, like language, power is "always-already there," everywhere, at every scale. There is no outside for Foucault's almost totalitarian account of power. By implication, there is also no viable alternative to power. Similarly, can there be any alternative to knowledge or language if the very discussion of that requires their use? Foucault is silent about how changes of power forms occur. His is an account of paradigms, highlighting differences between distinctive grids of relations from one epoch to another.

Foucault's project has been misinterpreted in human geography by overemphasizing its "micro-level" dimension. Foucauldian power embraces all scales. Power is always-everywhere. Power is relational: it is re-created by a certain positionality of social agents, not by clear boundaries between the powerful and the powerless. Within this paradigm, two alternatives to power are visible, however: social and spatial differences. Foucault was more explicit about the latter. In his

(1972) *Archaeology of Knowledge and the Discourse on Language*, he argued that attention should be paid to both the microscopic and macroscopic scales of social events, focusing on discontinuities and ruptures in social sciences because they are critical for both the exercise of power and the emergence of difference.

Yet, if one outcome of spatial disruptures is difference, Foucault seemingly ignored this theme. It was Lefebvre who elaborated on difference as opposition to power (Lefebvre 1991).[11] However, it is important to stress that Lefebvre's understanding of difference does not coincide with the concept of *différance* of the French post-modern thinker Derrida, for whom *différance* acts to "deconstruct" claims of consistency and truth in texts (e.g., Doel 1992, Lagopoulos 1993, Olsson 1993, Barnes 1994). Nor does his use of difference coincide with the concern with the Other prevalent in post-colonialist thought. For Lefebvre, difference is resistance to the totalitarian power space described by Foucault, and is resistance through the production of space in everyday life.

Unfortunately, despite the wide usage of the term, only vague definitions of difference exist.[12] Broadly understood, difference could be interpreted in terms of the appreciated multiplicity of meanings *as a part of* a commitment to equal rights in modern societies (such as cultural pluralism). In contradistinction, the more traditional term "diversity" is usually reserved for the multiplicity of meanings working *against* equal rights (such as ethnic multiculturalism with its celebration of group heritage) (Johnston 1994: 339). In the case of the Russian Church in the Soviet and post-Soviet periods, "difference" is arguably related to the alternative schisms within it.

Space is essential to theorizing both "difference" and "diversity." Although studies of areal differentiation and corresponding sociocultural "diversity" are traditional in geography, the growing interest in social "difference" is a relatively recent phenomenon. This has required, first, a profound change in the way space is analyzed in postwar human geography, namely by a reassertion of the social dimension of space (Soja 1989, Harvey 1989, Gregory 1993).[13]

It may be argued that traditional socio-politico-cultural geography is primarily concerned with boundaries, while more recent, post-traditional geography, with relations and their extent. These two groups of ideas are not mutually exclusive, but rather complementary. As early as 1987, Agnew claimed that

> "In two respects, then, conventional views of power
> are deficient. The first is the focus on either power *or*

structure with power referring to overt behavior rather than contingent outcomes. The second is the arrogation of power to the state or political system. An alternative view sees power as productive and enabling as well as repressive, and a feature of all social interactions rather than just those characteristic of the state or political system" (Agrew 1987: 24).

As Agnew and Corbridge's 1995 book showed, this problematic is still highly relevant.

Territorial Ruptures, Scalar Mismatches, and the History of the Church

The previous discussions provide conceptual grounds for a mismatch-focused approach to studying the Russian Orthodox Church. The empirical experience of the historical geographies of the Church, the state, and society also justifies the need for attention to these problems. It was a common belief in the pre-revolutionary Russian Empire that the key elements of the country's identity were its main Orthodox religion, its autocratic state system, and its generally compliant society. In fact, a popular formula was put forward: Russia is "Orthodoxy, Autocracy, Nationality." The lack of "and" between the last two words was not accidental: this formula reflected not so much a set of "ingredients," but their extreme interconnectedness. This societal match between the state, the Church, and society in pre-revolutionary Russia was presumably supported by their relatively close spatial correspondence.

The 1917 revolution dramatically altered the formula: autocracy was in theory demolished, the Church was officially separated from society and the state, and society pushed headlong into modernization. The Soviet period of Russian history can be treated, therefore, in terms of the divergent destinies of the Church, the state, and society. Metaphorically speaking, the state, as the most flexible of the three agents, looked into the future, the Church was most tied to the past, while society reflected the present. At the same time, this temporal divergence had clear, albeit understudied, geographical manifestations. The state created a series of new politico-territorial divisions of the country. Society was largely resettled through urbanization, modernization of the periphery, relocations of populations, and different conflicts/

wars. The Church became subject to changing political fortunes with resulting territorial rearrangements. In other words, contrary to scholars' implicit preconceptions, at different periods of Soviet history the Russian state, the Church, and society did not match one another geographically. More specifically, their territorial extents did not coincide. This disjunction has reached its most visible, manifestation in post-Soviet Russia: at both the large-scale level as well as the local one these three agents clearly occupy different territories.

Although the question of whether scale matters could be approached differently, this study will focus on the implications of these spatial ruptures for power/difference relationship. An overriding hypothesis is that territorial mismatches provide grounds for both progressive and conservative outcomes: they may facilitate the exercise of hegemonic power,[14] yet they may also support resulting difference.

Review of the Book

Four principles underlie the architecture of this study.

First, every attempt has been made to maintain chronological continuity with the Russian past; at the same time, historical frames of chapters slightly overlap because each chapter has a somewhat different theme. Second, every chapter has a particular scalar focus (or, to be accurate, inter-scalar focus), determined primarily by the state's shift from one scalar extent to another (e.g., shift from national level to imperial one). Third, every chapter considers a new facet of Orthodox difference, introducing a different schismatic off-spring of the pre-revolutionary Church. The order of considered schisms is based not on the date of their origins (most of this century's schisms have roots in the Church unrest of the 1920s), but on the time of their activity *in the Russian Federation*. For instance, the Foreign Church only recently arrived in Russia and is not considered in early chapters. Finally, the Russian Church is constituted by its believers, priesthood, physical embodiment (property), juridical name, and high authorities (Patriarch and the Moscow Patriarchate). Accordingly, each chapter attempts to show how the changing geography of *each* component influenced a specific schism. For instance, the Old Belief schism (Chapter 2) was led by believers while the Renovationist movement was initiated by priests (Chapter 3). Ukrainian Orthodox separatism can be interpreted not only in conventional nationalist terms, but also as a factor influenced by geographic unevenness of the Communists' church elimination campaigns (Chapter 4). Thus, every chapter focuses on a specific constitutive facet of the Church.

Chapter 2 considers the historical-geographical background to the close interrelationships of the Church, the state and society exemplified by the "Orthodoxy, Autocracy, Nationality" formula. It includes an historical introduction which considers the Byzantine origin of Russian Orthodoxy, its close links with the state, the first nationalization of church property under Peter the Great, the state Church, the messianic mission of Orthodoxy, and the emergence of religious diversity in response to Russia's shift from nation-state to empire (the Orthodox Old Believers and ethnic-religious difference).

The main body of the chapter considers late Imperial Russia (1897-1917), when the Russian Church was not only an institution of civil society, but also a pivotal element of the state's oppressive political-economic system. The Church legitimized the tsarist regime and the state protected the Church from external competition. The schismatic Orthodox Old Believers, for instance, were pushed to the geographical periphery. It was only after the 1905-07 revolution that some relaxation was permitted, and Churches, other than the main one, received legal recognition cracking the "Orthodoxy, Autocracy, Nationality" monolith.

Chapter 3 considers how the trend toward growing political, social, and cultural divergency in pre-revolutionary Russia was strengthened in the initial years of Communist rule (1917-27). The Church was separated from the state and society, society was polarized along modernization lines, and the state acquired new global ambitions through the creation of the Soviet Union. It is not a surprise that the Church was also internally fractured. To fragment and oppress the main Church, the state transferred many of its buildings to the Communist-inspired Renovationist Orthodox Church (1922-46). The Renovationist schism not only reflected society's modernization split, but also had an often overlooked connection with the state's new geographical mismatch with its society. Renovationism can be viewed as an attempt to create a church for the global ambitions of the Soviet Union. In fact, for many believers the watershed in the clash between the old and new branches within the Church came with the question of the old (Russian) versus the new (world, universal) calendar. In short, the Renovationist schism, like the Old Belief schism, can be interpreted as a result of the mismatch between the scales of state and society.

Chapter 4 covers two different scalar shifts of the state and two schisms within the Church. The first part describes the state's return to the previous imperial level and its implications for the Church (1927-48). When in the late 1920s the state had to minimize its global aspirations, the new Renovationist Church had few advantages over the old branch and even shared its fate: in the 1930s thousands of different churches were simply closed. Yet, even in this process, the state was politically selective in its construction of the new Soviet space. The 1941 German invasion, paradoxically, saved the Russian Orthodox Church from total extinction. In 1943, to regain popular support in German-occupied lands, Stalin allowed the main Church to revive itself. A new organization, the Russian Orthodox Church-Moscow Patriarchate, was finally born. This Church played a significant role in reconstruction of the imperial scale for the state. Other styless of Russian Orthodoxy (not only the Renovationists but also the Catacomb Church opposed to the regime) were not permitted to reorganize because they would undermine the main Church's credibility.

In contrast, the second part (1949-90) of Chapter 4 looks at the implications of the new post-war persecutions of the Church for the state's retreat from the imperial scale to the level of the nation-state. In 1949 church closures began again. This time the major assault, in 1959-63, was an attempt to balance an emerging post-war mismatch between the geographical extent of society and the Church. Through the 1939 territorial acquisition along the western margin of the USSR, and the Orthodox revival under the Germans, the Church had become primarily a Ukrainian phenomenon. The argument is that this late and incomplete assault on churches resulted in growing nationalism in Ukraine and other republics. The final dissolution of the Soviet Union fragmented the Church, and new Orthodox Churches have since appeared. For example, one such Church in Ukraine attempted to open its parishes outside of Ukraine, notably in Russia itself. Internal Orthodox differences, thus, have become an international political affair.

The remainder of the book focuses on the geopolitical transformations of the USSR and the corresponding Orthodox revival (1988-97). The retreat of the Russian state from the imperial level of the former Soviet Union left Russian society and the newly revived Russian Church in a scalar mismatch with one another. The remaining chapters of this study elaborate on these mismatches at three scalar levels: national, local-urban, and local-site.

At the national level (Chapter 5), these mismatches dramatically affected the Church. State authorities were paradoxically sheltering the Church at the imperial scale through self-isolationist policies and the continuation of the tsarist imperialist legacy. Thus, a branch of the Church abroad (the foreign Russian Orthodox Church) was not allowed to enter Russia. The collapse of the Iron Curtain opened Russia's biggest Church to various new influences, including that of the Church abroad.

Chapter 6 considers some outcomes of these processes at the local (Moscow) level. The current revival of the Church exhibits divergent tendencies at the large scale of geopolitical changes and, at the local scale, of religious communities. On the large scale, the federal state acknowledges the existence of many Churches, including different Orthodox communities. Locally, iregional authorities have often successfully resisted any diversification through their control of denationalization of church property. The success of newly emerging alternative Orthodox communities has, thus, been limited by local constraints on the access to religious property and space, which remain primarily in state possession. Facing the opposition of a new coalition between local authorities (e.g., those of Moscow) and the main Church (which is geographically limited to historical centers of cities), many alternative communities already have ceased to exist, while others have managed to survive by exploiting some territorial mismatches between the local state and metropolitan society.

Because it brings together the themes running through the entire study by focusing on a single site, Chapter 7 could be considered as an extended conclusion. The history of the (re)created, preeminent Orthodox landscape at this site not only reflects the major scalar periods of the country's socio-politico-cultural history, but also provides another example of the difference that scale makes. Initially a monument to the whole empire, the Cathedral of Christ the Savior now reemerges as a hegemonic endeavor of the powerful local Moscow state. This new alliance of the state and the Church, exemplified by the restoration of the Cathedral, only superficially results in a reversal of previous Soviet manipulations of cult places.

Chapter 1: Notes

1. This is the very first line of the act of the Patriarchate of Constantinople (1996) regarding the Estonian Church (Chapter 5).

2. In this study "the Church" refers to the main, official Church in the country (in the post-war period, the Russian Orthodox Church). In general, the term "Churches" (with capital "C") is reserved for (religious) institutions, while "churches" mean religious (Orthodox) buildings.

3. A version of this section of the chapter was previously been published in Russian (Sidorov 1997a). In English, see also Sidorov (1994-5, 1996, 1997b).

4. For other bibliographies see works of Pospielovsky (1984), Ellis (1986), and Davis (1995).

5. For a more detailed discussion of the specifics of the Soviet space see Kaganskii (1995).

6. Interestingly, the birthplaces of both Roman Catholicism and Protestantism lie in the "religious wilderness," according to Fogarty's mapping.

7. For an update on this debate, see Doughty (1994).

8. Another example of geographical research on sacred places is Fischer's (1990) study of Protestant monasticism.

9. Hegemony is the capacity of a dominant group to exercise control, not through visible rule or the deployment of force, but rather through the willing acquiescence of citizens to accept subordinate status by their affirmation of cultural, social and political practices and institutions which are fundamentally unequal (Johnston et al. 1994: 243).

10. For a general introduction to the concept of scale see Johnston et al. (1994), Meyer et al. (1992).

11. For an illuminating discussion, see Stewart (1995).

12. In my usage, the meaning of difference is consistent with such authors as Young (1990), Harvey (1992), The Minnesota Reading Group (1992). See also Sidorov (2000c).

13. For numerous articles on these issues see geographical journals such as *Antipode, Area, Environment and Planning D: Society and Space, Transactions of the Institute of British Geographers*.

14. The term "hegemony" used here is consistent with Antonio Gramsci's (1992) concept. In a nutshell, hegemony refers to implicit, legitimated exercise of power by some privileged political groups.

CHAPTER 2. "ORTHODOXY, AUTOCRACY, NATIONALITY": THE MATCH IN MAKING

> *... in the Russia of the Old Believers the Leninist Revolution would have been impossible.*
>
> Alexandr Solzhenitsyn[1]

Nation-building usually involves some aggregation: nations, "imagined communities," as Anderson (1983) has called them, are as much processes as they are outcomes. Although this dynamic understanding of nation-building has become widely accepted in the social sciences, discontinuities among participants of this process and associated territorial ruptures have not attracted sufficient scholarly attention. It perhaps would not be an exaggeration to claim that social scientists privilege too greatly the role of the state in nation-building, often at the expense of considering the contribution of other participants (such as the Church) to the process. In addition, the territorial, as opposed to temporal, discontinuities of nation-building have not attracted sufficient scholarly attention. Accepting a more "relational" approach (promoted in writings of Foucault and similar scholars, for example), this book treats nation-building as a process of bridging gaps between the territorial extents of the state, society and their cultural institutions such as religious ones. Although the pre-revolutionary Russian state insisted on the success of its imperial policy and popularized as its expression the formula "Orthodoxy, Autocracy, Nationality,"[2] in reality the territorial match between state, Church, and society was never completed. This chapter summarizes the historical background of this territory-matching process. More specifically, it focuses on the role of the territorial mismatch between the state and society in the emergence of the first major split in Russian Orthodoxy (between the mainstream and the Old Belief), and its implications for the survival of the schismatic movement of Old Believers.

The first part of this chapter discusses the role of Orthodoxy in three important historico-geographical developments which led

Figure 2.1. Spread of Eastern Christianity from Byzantium by 1000 AD. Russian monasticism 1200-1600. Source: based on Gilbert (1972: 15-16), drawn by Eric Stevens and the author.

to the creation of the pre-Soviet Russian Empire. First, the Orthodox baptism of the Prince of Kiev in 988 not only allowed the creation of the first Russian state (Kievan Rus'), but also later assured its survival when the country was again decentralized by a foreign invasion. Second, the post-invasion re-creation of the Russian nation-state around Moscow (Muscovite Russia) required a kind of second baptism: some of the Moscow Church's rituals were changed to facilitate the reincorporation of all Slavic lands (primarily the Ukrainian part of society). Third, the Orthodox Church was essential in securing the state's control over the new space of the eventually emergent Russian Empire. This first section also provides a necessary historical context for the remainder of the text, as well as a sketchy physico-geographical and socio-cultural review of the realm: the major subregions of the former Soviet Union (the Russian Empire) are identified. The first part also begins to address this chapter's main goal: an analysis of scalar factors in the emergence of the first main Orthodox schism, the Old Belief. The argument is that the emergence of the Old Belief schism was a result of a mismatch between the imperial scale of the state and the national scale of Russian (Muscovite) society.

The second part of this chapter builds on this foundation to further develop its main goal, and analyzes the scalar factors in the survival of the Old Belief. The argument is that the schism's geography reflects important internal thresholds in the country. The prosecuted Old Believers found escape in niches created within the mismatch between the state's extent and society's settlement frontiers.

In addition, this chapter speculates on some of the methodological particulars of doing a geographical analysis of religion in Russia: several religious sources for the pre-revolutionary Russian Empire allow a comprehensive and comparative examination of religious statistics which is not available for later periods.

THE CHURCH, THE STATE AND SOCIETY IN PRE-MODERN RUSSIA: SPATIAL HISTORY[3]

Christian Schisms and the Introduction of Christianity to Russia

The history of Christianity could be written as a history of its schisms, and this is arguably even truer with regard to its geography. Russian Orthodoxy is no exception to this generalization. Two fundamental Christian schisms provided a guiding context for the baptism of the ancient Slavic people by Byzantine missionaries.

First, in the fifth and sixth centuries, the "Lesser" or "Separated" eastern Churches became divided from the main body of Christianity. These Churches fall into two groups, the Nestorian Church of Persia, and the five Monophysite Churches of Armenia, Syria (the so-called "Jacobite" Church), Egypt (the Coptic Church), Ethiopia, and India.[4] As a result of this first division (and, later, Islamic rule, Figure 2.1), the eastern extent of Orthodoxy became restricted mainly to the Greek-speaking world (Ware 1963: 12).

Then came the second separation, conventionally dated to the year 1054, although its beginning could certainly be found much earlier. The main body of Christians divided into two communions: in western Europe, the Roman Catholic Church under the Pope of Rome; in the Byzantine Empire, the Orthodox Church of the East. Orthodoxy was now limited on its westward side as well (ibid.) (Figure 2.1).

The formal causes of the two splits now could look insignificant, but it is interesting to note how cultural and ecclesiastical divisions coincide. The three groups correspond to three major culture traditions: the Semitic, the Greek, and the Latin. So it has come about that in Orthodoxy the primary cultural influence has been that of Greece, and Byzantium was primarily a Greek civilization. In its initial centuries, the Russian Orthodox Church was known as the Eastern Church or the Greek-Russian Church.

As the Orthodox Church became bounded first on the southeastern and then on the western side, it expanded in the only available direction remaining to the north. In 863 Saints Cyril and Methodius, the Apostles of the Slavs, traveled northward to undertake missionary work beyond the frontiers of the Byzantine Empire. Their efforts led eventually to the conversion of the Bulgarians and Serbs, making Orthodoxy common in the Balkans and Eastern Europe (Figure 2.1). Russia was also converted. As Byzantine power dwindled, these newer Churches of the north increased in importance and, with the fall of Constantinople to the Turks in 1453, the Principality of Moscow was ready to take Byzantium's place as the protector of the Orthodox world (ibid., 13). Before we discuss these themes, however, it may be worth summarizing the essential features of Orthodoxy.

The Doctrine and Practice of Orthodoxy

Eastern Orthodoxy is a branch of Christianity; yet it interprets Christian theology slightly differently. The specifically Orthodox emphases in Christ's teaching could be summarized as follows.

First, the Russian word *Pravoslavie* ("Orthodoxy") has the double meaning of "right belief" and "right glory" (or "right worship"). Therefore, the Orthodox regard their Church as the Church which teaches the true belief about God and, equally important, which glorifies Him with the right worship, that is, as nothing less than the Church of Christ on earth.

Second, as a consequence, Orthodoxy places enormous emphasis on the church service. A better word would be "liturgy," because the Protestant word "service" does not reflect the beauty and sophistication of the Orthodox liturgy. Liturgy, ritual, and "right" practice are of equal importance to the teaching itself.

Third, one of the distinctive features of Orthodoxy is the place it assigns to icons. Icons are sacred images, two-dimensional symbolic representations of God. An Orthodox church today is still filled with them. Dividing the sanctuary from the body of the building there is a solid screen, the iconostasis, entirely covered with icons, while other icons are placed in special shrines around the church; and, perhaps too the walls are covered with icons in fresco or mosaic. Icons are only symbols and not idols: the Orthodox do not worship them, but rather venerate them. Respect for icons is part of the Church's teaching.

Fourth, worship in special buildings (churches) is very important, liturgy is not conceivable without a special, physically extant building. Orthodox churches have a distinctive architectural style, and are considered sacred structures. In pre-revolutionary Russia, churches, more than anything else, defined settlement type: a large settlement without a cathedral would not be considered a city (Chapter 4).

Fifth, in terms of the narrative of Christ's life, two Orthodox emphases are especially important for our understanding of Russia. First, the idea of martyrdom is emphasized. Russians have always laid great emphasis on the place of suffering in the Christian life. Martyrs were considered to be "other Christs." Later, the monastic life became an equivalent to martyrdom. Monasticism played a decisive role in the religious life of Byzantium, as it has in all Orthodox

countries. Second, the idea of Resurrection is emphasized in Orthodoxy. Whereas in the West many Christians tend to see Christmas as
the major holiday, in Eastern Orthodox countries it is undoubtedly Eas-
ter, the celebration of the Resurrection. Resurrection is one of the themes
that fascinates Russians' thinking, as will be shown in this book.

Sixth, Orthodoxy has always attached great importance to community and the place of councils in the life of the Church. It is believed
that the council is the chief organ whereby God has chosen to guide
His people. (In Russian the noun *sobor* means both "main church" and
"council".) In the Church neither dictatorship nor individualism was
expected, but harmony and unanimity; men remain free but not isolated, for they are united in love, in faith, and in sacramental communion. There were several Great Councils engaging all of Orthodoxy, and
the Orthodox Church takes these Councils as its standard and guide
alongside the Bible.

Finally, the communal life of Byzantium (where Orthodoxy
originated) formed a unified whole, and there was no rigid line of separation between the religious and the secular, between Church and state,
although each had its own proper autonomous sphere. Bishops were
appointed by God to teach the faith, whereas the Emperor, though not
its exponent, was the protector of Orthodoxy. Between the two was a
"symphony" or "harmony," but neither element exercised absolute control over the other. As a result of this form of belief, in Byzantium the
Emperor was considered to be God's representative on the earth; God's
living icon. This "symphony" was quite fragile, however, and it was
seen as dangerous if the "symphony" were disrupted by the Church's
subordination to the state as happened at one point in Russian history
(Chapter 4).

Structural Organization of the Orthodox Church as a Whole

Unlike Roman Catholicism, the Orthodox Church is a family of
independent self-governing national Churches, only one of which is
the Russian Orthodox Church. The Orthodox Church as a whole is a
federation of national Churches. The system of independent national
Churches made the link between Church and national people firm.
Christianity among the Slavs became in very truth the religion of the
whole people, a popular religion in the best sense. Like Islam, Orthodoxy emphasizes the cardinal importance of the local community in
the structure of the Church.

The organization of every national Church is characterized as a hierarchy, but Orthodoxy as a whole is not. In Orthodoxy as a whole, no one figure holds a position equivalent to the Pope in the Roman Catholic Church. The Patriarch of Constantinople is known as the "Ecumenical Patriarch," "the first among equals," but he does not have the right to interfere in the internal affairs of the various Orthodox Churches. This decentralized system of independent local Churches has the advantage of being highly flexible, and is easily adapted to changing conditions.

Orthodox Baptizing and Nation Building (988 — Mid-Late 15th Century)[5]

From its very first steps on Russian soil, the Orthodox religion played a socio-political role. In fact, it was this role which made a prerequisite the Orthodox baptism of the Kievan Rus' in 988: not only was the Kievan Prince open to testing different religious alternatives, he also attempted a reform to strengthen the dominant pagan religion a few years before the baptism (it largely failed). The state's conversion to Orthodoxy was an attempt to cement the integration of Slavic tribes (Odintsov et al. 1995: 27).

At the end of the tenth century, several competing Slavic peoples existed in the territory of the present-day Ukraine, Belarus, and western Russia on the eve of the Orthodox conversion (Figure 2.1). At that time, the southern part of the territory was a vast steppe that was a source of constant invasions by nomads. Though the northern portion of the region was forested and provided protection against the nomads, in general it was not so hospitable, so the Slavs there settled along rivers.

Given these environmental circumstances, it is not surprising that Kiev was of such importance. The city was, first, located on the cross-roads of the major water way (the Dniepr River) connecting the Vikings of Scandinavia to the Greeks of Constantinople, and, second, on the boundary between the forest and the steppe. So, the Kievan Princedom, one of the group of competing Slav peoples, was in a geographically privileged position to assume power.

In 988 Grand Prince Vladimir of Kiev replaced paganism with Eastern Orthodox Christianity as the official religion of his princedom and married the sister of the Byzantine Emperor. This was one of the defining dates in world history and, certainly one of the major turning points in Russian history (Figure 2.2). All scholarly accounts of the event agree that the Rus' did have some choice in religious orientation. The Rus' selected Christianity over Islam and Judaism and, within Christianity, the Byzantine rather than the Roman variant. As legend has it, it was the enormous beauty of the service in the St. Sofia cathedral in Constantinople that triggered the Prince's final decision in favor of Orthodoxy. Another explanation for the success of the conversion mission was that from the start the Slavs heard the Gospel and the service of the Church in a tongue which they could understand, a Slavic one. So the Slav Christians would enjoy a precious privilege which none of the people of western Europe would share until the Reformation – the right to conduct services in their mother tongue.[6] Old Slavonic is still the language of service in Russian Orthodoxy even though modern Russians have difficulty understanding it.

Of prime importance, however, was the fact that Prince Vladimir succeeded in accomplishing three geopolitical goals in this baptism. First, domestically, the replacement of the diverse pagan pantheon with the well-developed monotheist system of Christianity allowed him to solidify the process of Russian state formation. Second, within the new state, Kiev (Kyiv) became the undisputed leader of the union. Third, internationally, Prince Vladimir chose to have his country become the eastern flank of Christendom rather than an extension into Europe of

Figure 2.2. The Church of the Assumption of the Holy Virgin (a.k.a. the Church of the Tithe, or Desiatinnaia Church), Kiev, 10th cen.

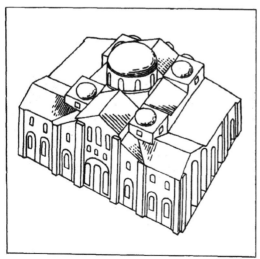

Reconstruction by Kenneth Conant. Source: Mezentseva and Mezentsev 1981. Designed and constructed by Greek artisans imported for the purpose, the church reflects precisely the features of Byzantine style. Built in 989-96, this church laid ground for monumental stone constructions in Russia. It collapsed under the weight of a crowd of fleeing refugees when the Mongol Tatars took Kiev in 1240 (Cross 1949: 6).

non-Christian civilizations. Alliance with the powerful Byzantine Emperor elevated Russia's position in the world.

Byzantium thus conferred two gifts upon the Slavs: a fully articulated system of Christian doctrine and a fully developed Christian civilization. The Russian Church during the Kievan period was subject to Constantinople and the Metropolitans of Russia were usually Greek. The capital city of Kiev became one of the most beautiful and powerful centers of the Russian realm (Figure 1.1), and its major spiritual center was the Monastery of Caves. Still, much of the countryside remained pagan until the 14-15th centuries because the Church was at first restricted mainly to the cities.

During the following 600 years of initial Christian influence, three major political developments had great significance for the fate of religion in Russia: the conquest of Rus' by the Mongols, the shift of Rus's cultural-political center from Kiev to Moscow, and the steady decline of Constantinople (Pankhurst 1996: 131).

The choice of Eastern Christianity as a model for ancient Russian culture had three major effects on the formation of a Russian Church. First, doctrinal rigidity and inflexibility in ritual practice became part of Russian religious culture. Second, virtually no internal diversity in religious perspective or practice could be accommodated, and intolerance toward dissent became a characteristic feature of the institution. Third, Eastern Christianity accords central importance to the principle that the church must be unequivocally subordinated to the state. Finally, as reflected in the split of the Christian church into Eastern and Western churches, there was sharp opposition to western ideas (ibid., 132).

It was Russia's greatest misfortune that she was allowed too little time to assimilate the full spiritual inheritance of Byzantium. In the mid-13th century Kievan Rus', the Golden Age of Russia, was brought to a sudden and violent end by the nomadic Mongol invasions from the east. Kiev was sacked and the whole of the Russian land was overrun by the invaders.[7] For two hundred years Russia ceased to exist politically, being subordinated to the Mongol Khans. However, this was only a relative disaster since the Mongols paradoxically helped to save the Russians from yet another possible conquest, from the West and North. The threat was quite serious. One of Russia's greatest Saints, Alexandr Nevskii from Novrogod, is revered for having defeated the Swedes and the Germans. It is noteworthy, however, that he submitted to the Mongols.

The period of Mongol invasion interrupted the country's de-

Figure 2.3. The Trinity-St.Sergii Lavra monastery (Sergiev Posad, former Zagorsk, Moscow oblast), 1993, photo by the author.

velopment, yet it did not affect church life: unlike other institutions in the country, the Church was not severely damaged by the invaders. On the contrary, its relative position was heightened since only the Church was left intact of the triad "state, society, Church." The Mongols did not touch churches. More than anything else, it was the Church that kept alive Russian national consciousness during this period.

Nation-Building II: from Kievan to Muscovite Rus' (Late 15th - Late 17th Century)

Finally, the Russians managed to drive out the Mongols and, gradually, another Russia was resurrected — Muscovite Russia, which existed for over two hundred years (the late 15th-the late 17th century). After the Mongol invasion, the Russian center re-emerged not in Kiev, but thousands of miles northeast, in Vladimir and Suzdal', and eventually in the lands of Moscow. The leading position of Moscow was secured by several factors. First, Kiev never really recovered after the Mongol sack and was later taken over by the Lithuanians. Second, other principalities competing for national leadership such as Vladimir and Suzdal' lacked the fortuitous central location on a river system that gave Moscow access to other trading sites and major surrounding seas. Finally, the rise of Moscow was closely bound up with the Church. When the town was still small and comparatively unimportant, the

Metropolitan[8] of Russia, Peter, decided to settle there; henceforth it remained the city of the chief Orthodox leader of Russia.

Sergii of Radonezh, the greatest national Saint of Russia, is closely connected with the recovery of the land around Moscow at this time. He founded a monastery which within his own lifetime became the greatest religious center in the land. What the Monastery of the Caves was to Kievan Russia, the Monastery of the Holy Trinity[9] (Figure 2.3) was to Muscovy. The difference was that this monastery was founded in the forest wilderness and not in the city as in Kiev. Thus, he greatly promoted a tradition of monastic colonization of the forests. Monks in search of the solitary life would make their way into distant forests, clearing fresh land for agriculture. From Radonezh and other centers a vast network of religious houses spread swiftly across the whole of north European Russia as far as the White Sea and the Arctic Circle (Figure 1.1). Sergii has been called a "Builder of Russia" in three senses: spiritually; geographically, for it was he more than any other who inspired the great advance of monks into the forest; and politically, for he encouraged the rise of Moscow and resistance to the Mongols.

In 1453, sixty-one years after the death of Sergii, the Byzantine Empire fell to the Turks. Only twenty seven years later, in 1480 the Golden Horde was defeated by Ivan III and Mongol domination of Russia came to an end. Because it was the only Orthodox country that remained independent at this time, the new Russia, which took shape after Sergii, was now called to take Byzantium's place as protector of the Orthodox world. To the Russians it seemed no coincidence that, at the very moment when the Byzantine Empire came to an end, they themselves were at last throwing off the few remaining vestiges of Mongol control in their own land. God, it seemed, was granting them their freedom because He had chosen them to be the successors of Byzantium. The idea of Moscow as the successor of Byzantium was promoted by the marriage of a Russian ruler to a niece of the last Byzantine Emperor. The Grand Duke of Moscow began to assume the Byzantine titles of tsar (a version of the Roman "Caesar") and the double-headed eagle of Byzantium (symbolizing the East-West duality of the culture) as his state emblem. People came to think of Moscow as "the Third Rome," arguing that Rome had fallen to the barbarians and then lapsed into heresy; and the second Rome, Constantinople, had been taken by the Turks. Moscow therefore had succeeded Constantinople as the Third and last Rome, the center of Orthodox Christendom. Russian bishops started to elect their Metropolitan without consulting

Constantinople, and eventually the head of the Church was raised from the rank of Metropolitan to that of Patriarch.

Unlike most other peoples in the world, the Russians called their country "Holy Russia." Guided by the religious metaphor of Moscow as the Third Rome, Muscovite Russia assumed imperial ambitions. Many princes and tsars were canonized as saints, and especially important were those who served as warriors preserving the integrity of the Russian nation.

Another implication of Byzantium's collapse was reflected in the relative resistance of Russian Orthodoxy to reforms of any sort — the Russians, receiving Orthodoxy as a well-developed system and, in the absence of the (Byzantine) Motherland of the Church did not see themselves as the ultimate arbiters of change. They preferred to keep preserving the gift intact. It is a common belief that most changes in Russian Orthodoxy were essentially conservative movements for the restoration of the original canons. As a result, schisms rather then reforms characterize its history.

Shift From Nation-State to Empire, and the Old Belief Schism

At the time of the 1917 revolution, the Church was called the Orthodox Russian-State Church (hereafter the ORSCh)[10] rather than the earlier common names of Greek-Orthodox or Eastern Church. This shift points to the general direction of the historical evolution of the Russian state: it had gradually been transformed from a nation-state into an empire. Religion played a significant role in this process.

The concept of Moscow as the Third Rome encouraged a kind of Russian messianism and led Russians sometimes to think of themselves as a chosen people called upon to save Orthodoxy. If this were taken in a political as well as a religious sense, it could be used to further the ends of Russian secular imperialism. Imperialism is understood here as the policy of extending a nation's authority by territorial acquisition or by the establishment of economic and political control over other nations.

The building of the Russian Empire began in the middle of the sixteenth century when Russians conquered the region of Povolzh'e to the east of the central Moscow core. A territory along the Volga River populated by several different ethnic groups, primarily Tatars, Povolzh'e became the first major cultural region of the Russian realm east of the Moscow core (Figures 1.1 and 2.1). However, reunification of the former lands of the Kievan Rus' was of prime importance. Western and south-western expansion would, among other things, also allow the Musco-vite Rus'to be closer to the original Greek core of Orthodoxy and, per-haps, one day take back Constantinople. In the 1650s, recovering from the period of unrest known as the Time of Troubles, Muscovy renewed its political interests in Poland, Ukraine, and Turkey. The state then decided to initiate the reunification of those Russian territories which had been annexed to Lithuania and Poland during the centuries of the so-called "Mongol yoke" (Zenkovsky 1957: 45-6).

Unlike Povolzh'e, the territories to the west (modern Belarus and Ukraine) were populated by ethnically similar Slavic people with the same dominant Orthodox religion. However, a period of long sepa-ration (under Lithuanian and Polish control) had, over time, caused some dogmatic differences to emerge between the way Orthodoxy was practiced in Muscovite Rus' and in these western Orthodox lands. Ac-cording to Serge Zenkovsky, the reunion of Ukraine and Belarus (Belorussia) with Muscovy and the plans for the eventual unification of all Orthodox peoples under the aegis of the Russian tsar required the unification of Orthodox practices and the adaptation by the Rus-sian Church of the ritual and the customs common to Greek-Orthodox tradition, which had been introduced in Ukraine in the mid-seventeenth century (ibid., 46). Therefore, the state of Muscovy had to undertake a massive religious reform. Correction of books and rituals began in 1653 and in 1654 Ukraine accepted "the Eastern Orthodox tsar." The schism of 1666-7 in which the Old Belief broke away from the Church was a reaction against this reform (Zenkovsky 1955: 118). "In 1653-1667, Rus-sia shifts from the policy of national cultural isolation, from great-Rus-sian state, to involvement into supranational (supra-great-Russian) cul-tural development, to creation of supranational empire" (ibid.). "The Great Duke and Sovereign of Muscovy became Tsar of Great, Little and White Russia,[11] a title which clearly indicates a transition toward impe-rial goals. Half a century later Peter I was officially crowned as Em-peror" (Zenkovsky 1957: 46).

The change from the old Muscovite to the new "All-Russian" cultural pattern occurred with astonishing rapidity — a sign, perhaps, that the old traditions no longer corresponded to the needs of new, expanding powerful state. Almost overnight monks from Kiev and Polotsk replaced Muscovite cultural leaders. The old Muscovite missal was re-edited by Kievan monks, and the Polish-educated White Rus-sian monk, Simon Polotsky, became the recognized state ideologist and educator of the tsar's children. From the beginning of the eighteenth

Figure 2.4. The Assumption (Uspenskii) Cathedral in the Kremlin. Source: *Moskva: Fotoetiudy* (1957).

Figure 2.5. St. Isaac Cathedral, Leningrad (St. Petersburg), ca.1960. Source: *Leningrad* (1960).

century, the hierarchy of the young Empire's Church leadership consisted primarily of Ukrainians. Little Russia, today's Ukraine, found a field of endeavor for its intelligentsia, and for two hundred years Ukraine remained the most tranquil part of the empire (ibid., 46-9).

It was not the fear of novelty but, rather, offense at the defamation of ancient traditions and repudiation of the Old Russian ideology which brought about the Old Belief opposition to cultural reform and the Empire's new policies. Among the opponents to the state's new policies were not only obscurantists and enemies of enlightenment, but also the majority of traditional Muscovites, the main part of its "intelligentsia," and its recent spiritual elite. While the court, officers, and some of the landed gentry supported the reforms, a part of the aristocracy also opposed the new order. The intellectual opposition of the Great Russians to Westernization and the refusal to bow to the new "general line" were so strong that for three-quarters of a century, from 1660 to 1735, almost no Great Russian names appear on a list of the writers, educators, and theologians of the official "governmental" cultural school. Thus, while the Empire was expanding and integrating its new citizens, a part of the Great Russian, former Muscovite, society remained in opposition to the cultural and political activities of the state and became increasingly isolated from it (ibid., 48-50). The Church reforms of 1666-67 can be seen as a "second baptism" of Russia: while in Kievan Rus' it helped to unite the Slavic lands, in Muscovite Rus' it helped to reunite them.[12]

The ideal of perfect unity of the religious and secular authorities ("symphony") was gradually eroded in this period. Politically, the Church re-emerged after the Mongol yoke as the supreme institution in society. Patriarchs in fact ruled the country, and the first Romanov tsar was a son of Patriarch Filaret. This imbalance eventually was overturned. In theory, the Church and the state remained two equal powers, and in Moscow, in the Assumption (Uspenskii) Cathedral of the Kremlin (Figure 2.4), there were placed two equal thrones, one for the Patriarch and one for the tsar. In practice, secular power came to control the Church more and more, as evident in the Church reforms of the 1660's. And with Peter the Great at the turn of the 18th century Imperial Russia took its final form.

Imperial Russia (Late 17th Century — 1917)

With Peter I (also known as Peter the Great), the ruler of Russia took the title of Emperor (*Imperator*) instead of Tsar, and the country came to be called the Russian Empire. The Russians had, by that time, conquered Povolzh'e, entered Siberia, and reunited the western lands, but it was Peter who dramatically changed some aspects of the country, and also created a basis for its further phenomenal territorial expansion. Significantly, he also launched an exploration into the enor-

Figure 2.6. Kazanskii Cathedral (former History of Religion and Atheism Museum of the Academy of Sciences of the USSR), Leningrad (St. Petersburg), ca.1960. Source: *Leningrad* (1960).

mous mineral resources of the Ural Mountains, another region of the Russian realm. Before that, Russia's major resources were honey, fur, leather, and bee's wax. The iron ore, gold, and other mineral treasures of the Urals gave Russian imperialism decisive economic and material support.

In contradistinction to Muscovite Russia, imperial Russia can be also called the Russia of St. Petersburg (Figures 2.5 and 2.6). This shift (until 1918) from conservative Moscow towards the northwest symbolized the beginnings of a policy of Westernization and marked the beginning of a conquest of another cultural region: the Baltics. In addition, the new capital city signified final submission of the Church to the state: Peter the Great not only left Patriarchal Moscow but also abolished the very Patriarchate itself and set up in its place a commission, or Holy Synod, headed by a secular appointee. This system continued until the end of monarchy, when, in 1917, the Council of the Church reestablished the Patriarchal system and elected a new Patriarch (Tikhon) (Figure 3.1).

For later discussion in this book (Chapter 4) it is important to note that, contrary to popular belief, exploitation of the Church's property was not a Communist innovation, but was rather already a common practice in imperial Russia. Peter the Great, for instance, by resolution of the Synod of March 28, 1722, ordered the dismantling of most old chapels in the country, and the reutilization of the buildings' construction materials for "other needs" (during the construction of St. Petersburg, he prohibited the use of stone anywhere else). In 1727, Peter II reopened the surviving chapels. Of 62 known monasteries on the territory of contemporary Moscow, 19 (30 percent) were closed in the 17-18th centuries (Burakov 1991: 16).

In the two hundred years after Peter the Great the Russians settled Siberia (between the Urals and Lake Baikal) and the Trans-Baikal region (although only their southern belt with its relatively bearable climate), and added Finland, Poland, the western portions of Ukraine, Belarus, and the Baltics, the Far East, the Caucasus, Kazakhstan and Central Asia. The late Russian Empire was an enormously large state. Since it is a constant reference point for any post-Soviet debates (and practices) on religious revival, it is worth considering some essential features of the religious situation in late imperial Russia. More specifically, it is important to stress the limitations of geographical correspondence between the state, society, and the Church.

The "Orthodoxy, Autocracy, Nationality" Match
in Late Imperial Russia

Imperial enlargement of the Russian state inevitably led to the incorporation of many cultural, ethnic, religious and social differences, and required some adaptation to them. The purposes of the second part of this chapter are two-fold: to continue the discussion of the geography of difference which emerged when the state shifted to the imperial level, and to examine the state's response to this new scale. The arguments are that the new imperial scale of the state brought about ethno-religious diversity, which was a challenge to the dominant Orthodox Russian-State Church. The ideal of perfect unity between the state, the Church and society ("Orthodoxy, Autocracy, Nationality" formula) had more ideological justification than real historical and geographical validity. This mismatch was beneficial for the schismatic Old Believers providing certain territorial niches for them to survive.

Note on Sources and Methodology

In contrast to both Soviet and post-Soviet eras, the state in its late-imperial period (defined for this study as 1897-1917) conducted extensive statistical religious surveys. Three main sources containing statistics on believers were utilized for this chapter: first, the 1897 population census; second, the 1913-14 reports of the Holy Synod, and, third, a report on the state of Old Believers in 1912. Statistics on Orthodox priesthood and property from these sources will be analyzed in Chapters 3 and 4 respectively.

In 1897 the Russian Empire conducted its first state-wide population census. It turned out that, of all population censuses in the following 100 years, this was almost the only one which would include religious questions. The only exception was the 1937 census, however, its results were not released by the state and, until their recent publication (*Vsesoiuznaia Perepis'* 1991), were shelved in secret archives. The regional breakdown of these data is still missing. In short, the 1897 census remains the only fully comprehensive, though outdated, source of statistics on the geography of religious believers in Russia (Tsentral'nyi Statisticheskii 1901a). The 1897 population census provides statistics on the numbers of adherents of different religions in statistical units of the Empire. For this chapter, they will be considered at the level of the Empire as a whole (52 provinces in the European part of the country and 42 in the rest of the Empire). Table A2.1 summarizes these statistics along interconfessional lines.[13]

The second major source of religious statistics for late Imperial Russia is the annual Report of the Holy Synod's overprocurator. The latest two published volumes cover 1913 and 1914 (*Vsepoddanneishii Otchet* 1914 and 1916). These reports are especially valuable for their provision of clergy and property statistics (analyzed in Chapters 3 and 4). In addition, they cover virtually all other facets of the Orthodox Russian-State Church life including affiliational mobility, personnel matters, finance, and organizational changes.

The third data source utilized in this chapter specifically covers the Old Belief movement's status in 1912 (Departament Dukhovnykh Del 1913).[14] Adaptation of the 1897 map for the system of 1912 provinces was done by the author (Figure A2.2). Areas north of the permafrost line were mostly unsettled (exept Yakutsk area and Kamchatka) and are ignored on all maps (Figure 1.1).

The Geography of Non-Orthodox Difference in Late Imperial Russia

This section provides a sketchy backround overview of non-Orthodox religious diversity on the eve of the Soviet period. The presentation follows the 1897 population census' order of statistical classification of religions. Table A2.1 shows the percentage of adherents to major non-Orthodox religions in Russian provinces in 1897.

Roman Catholics

Roman Catholicism and Protestantism are not the oldest non-Orthodox confessions in Russia. It was only in the two centuries between Peter the Great's reign (early 18th century) and 1917 that a small population of Protestant and some Catholic believers were introduced onto Russian soil. Their adherents included German and other foreign peasant farmers imported by Catherine II to foster efficiency in agriculture (Pankhurst 1996: 138). Not being the oldest, these confessions offered a noteworthy glimpse of alternative religious cultures.

Figure A2.3 (Supplement) shows the geographical distribution of Roman-Catholics in 1897. The western provinces constituted the principal core of this confession in late Imperial Russia, especially in the Polish provinces and Lithuania. Adjacent areas of Finland,[15] western Russia and Belarus, and the western half of Ukraine together constituted a wider Roman-Catholic belt along the western margin of the country. In the internal parts of the Empire, other clusters emerged either as a result of ethnic German settlement (the Middle Volga provinces), or Ukrainian migration (Yenisey region, the Far East). The Caucasus was a special case: it had the Armenian Catholic Church.

Protestants

The geography of Protestantism in Russia shares a certain similarity with the pattern described for Roman Catholics (Figure A2.4). In the Baltics, the highest proportion of Protestant population could be found in Estonia (90 percent) and part of Latvia. The belt of Protestantism was formed also by adjacent provinces of Lithuania, Russia (e.g., St. Petersburg), Belarus, and Ukraine).[16] Its extension into southern European Russian provinces was most noticeable (southern Povolzh'e areas were settled by German colonists).

Other Christians

This miscellany section of the 1897 census included primarily the Armenian Apostolic Church (Figure A2.5). As one of the best examples of ethnic confession, this Church in late Imperial Russia had most of its adherents residing in Armenia and adjacent provinces of Trans-Caucasia. A significant Armenian diaspora in Rostov province and Turkmenistan (Central Asia) provided the basis for the prevalence of this confession in these areas.

This category of the census data most likely also included figures for Christian sectarianism. Sectarians were prevalent on the country's margins (eastern Siberia, southern Ukraine and Russia) already in the end of the last century. Their continuing prevalence in these areas in Soviet time thus has some historical tradition (see discussions in Chapter 3 on Renovationism and 5 on the Catacomb Church).

Islam

Numerically, Muslims formed the second (after the Orthodox believers) largest confession in late Imperial Russia. Though Islam is also one of the oldest religions in the Russian realm, its presence was limited to Central Asia, Kazakhstan, parts of the eastern Caucasus, and Povolzh'e (Figure A2.6). The only other enclave outside this subregion was Crimea, with its Crimean Tatar population.

Judaism

Religious policies in the late Russian Empire had no greater restrictive effect on any other religion than on Judaism.

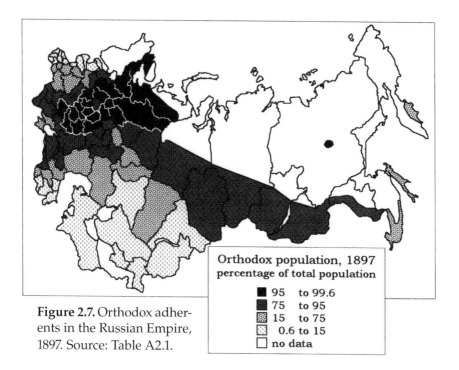

Figure 2.7. Orthodox adherents in the Russian Empire, 1897. Source: Table A2.1.

Orthodox population, 1897
percentage of total population

■ 95   to 99.6
▨ 75   to 95
▨ 15   to 75
▨ 0.6 to 15
☐ no data

"After the three partitions of the Polish-Lithuanian State in 1772-95 and the annexation of the Grand Duchy of Warsaw in 1815, a great many Jews found themselves within the borders of the Russian Empire. They did not receive the right of free settlement within the whole territory of the Empire, but had to remain in the 10 provinces of Poland and the 15 western provinces of the Russian Empire. An exception was made for merchants of the first guild, for persons with higher education, for dentists, pharmacists, *fel'dshery* (physician's assistants), midwives, mechanics, and craftsmen. According to the so-called temporary rules of May 3, 1882, the Jews, even inside the Pale, were forbidden to settle anew outside of cities, towns, and *mestechki* (settlements predominantly inhabited by traders and craftsmen) and to buy or to have mortgages on real estate outside of cities and towns. The legal limitations were directed against 'persons of Jewish faith,' and became invalid when a Jew adopted Christianity of the Eastern Orthodox, Roman Catholic, or Protestant denomination" (Pushkarev 1970: 7).

Figure A2.7 shows the geographical distribution of Judaism in 1897. The so-called Pale, the line of restricted Jewish settlement, is clearly visible on this map: Jews were prohibited from residing anywhere in the Empire outside the westernmost part of the country. Thus, the highest proportion of adherents to Judaism (up to 22 percent) was in Polish and Belarusian provinces, and the Baltics. Local ethnic Jews (the so-called "mountainous Jews," or Tats formed the clusters in the eastern Caucasus (Dagestan and Azerbaijan). The same goes for the enclave in Central Asia (Khiva). The prevalence of Judaists in parts of Central Siberia is somewhat puzzling. Noteworthy is the lack of any significant presence in the Far East, where the Soviet state later established a formal region of Jewish autonomy (so-called Jewish Autonomous oblast', or Birobijan).

Due to this extremely constrained settlement pattern in late imperial Russia, in the Soviet period, of all non-Orthodox confessions, Judaists experienced the greatest territorial change.

Other non-Christians

The "other non-Christians" section of the 1897 census included primarily Buddhists (Astrakhan', Irkutsk and Trans-Baikal provinces), as well as local pagan shamanist beliefs (the Far East and Povolzh'e) (Figure A2.8). These were the most exotic confessions in late Imperial Russia.

Summary

The Russian Empire prior to the 1917 revolution was a multi-religious country. This religious diversity was not characteristic of all regions, however. The territory of the country can be divided into the following three subregions in terms of religious diversification. First, the monolithic Orthodox provinces dominated by an ethnic Russian population (Figure 2.7). Second, the monolithic Muslim Central Asian subregion (Figure A2.6). Third, the subregions of religious diversification: the West of the country (Finland, the Baltics, Poland, Ukraine), the Caucasus, and parts of Eastern Siberia and the Far East.

Of these regions, three should be highlighted specifically as the areas of contact and coexistence of the dominant Orthodox religion and non-Orthodox belief systems: Ukraine, southern Russia (north Caucasus and the steppe belt), and eastern Siberia. As will be seen in the following chapters on Renovationism and Catacomb Orthodoxy, the legacy of this exposure to religions different from the dominant one is noticeable. Alternative movements within the Church found most fertile soil in the areas with some experience of religious tolerance and co-existence.

ORTHODOX DIFFERENTIATION IN LATE IMPERIAL RUSSIA: THE OLD BELIEF

Previous Accounts and Their Deficiencies

Ethno-religious diversity was not the only regional consequence of the shift from Kievan to Moscow Rus', from the nation-state to empire. Of equal, if not greater importance, to the main Church was the alternative of the Old Belief, which is the main subject of interest for this chapter. Unlike the non-Orthodox religions in Russia, the Old Belief is more difficult to map for four reasons.

First, the Old Belief is not a homogeneous and well-institutionalized phenomenon. Since no bishop consecrated new hierarchs according to the old ritual, Old Believers quickly found themselves bereft of canonical clergy. The decision on how to deal with that absence increasingly defined the stripe of any particular Old Believer. Differences within the Old Believer communities solidified into a number of branches (concords).[17] A number of them were priestless.

Second, statistics on Old Believers were never complete and reliable for political reasons: the state and adherents of the schism themselves had reasons to either downplay or hide the true scale of the movement. According to the 1897 census, only 1.72 percent of total population of the Russian Empire were Old Believers (Table A2.1). However, this figure is most likely not accurate because for centuries the state persecuted, in varying degrees, the schism's followers right up until the Act of Toleration of 1905. Thus, many Old Believers hid their religious identity. This secrecy had an economic rationale; under Peter the Great, for instance, the Old Believers were required to pay double tax. Therefore, they preferred to bribe the local priest (who served as informant for the state) and to be "uncounted". Moreover, the state itself had political motivations to downplay the importance of the schism.[18] It is speculated that as much as ten percent of the Russian population at the beginning of this century were Old Believers (Kirillov 1913: 12).[19] These figures are particularly impressive if one takes into account the constant repression of these people in imperial Russia.

The third factor that makes mapping of the Old Belief a relatively difficult endeavor is that it has not been mapped much. Whereas the geography of non-Orthodox religious diversity in the Russian Empire in general could be described in qualitative terms, a similar description of the Old Belief would be only a first approximation because the movement was relatively more dispersed territorially. Yet the best summary of Old Belief geography (Robson 1995: 21-2) has been purely descriptive. Robson concludes that

> "[a]lthough they debated the exact number of Old Believers and their perceived influence in Russian society, scholars agreed that the geographic centers of the Old Belief gravitated to the outskirts of the empire. These centers seemed to grow as far away as possible from state and ecclesiastical authority – except in Moscow, where Old Believers retained large and prosperous communities. The Vyg monastic complex exemplified this geographical phenomenon, providing spiritual leadership from the most remote part of European Russia, far in the north country. [...] While lacking numerical data, impressionistic evidence concurs with von Bushen's assessment of Old Believer strength in the borderlands. One missionary priest, D. Alexandrov, claimed that "all of Siberia is in the hands of the [priestly Old Believers] and the Baptists." An article in the Orthodox religious journal *The Wanderer (Strannik)* described three areas of particular Old Believer strength. These formed a band of provinces along the eastern border of European Russia, spreading from Nizhnii Novgorod and Viatka in the north, then circling south and through the Urals and west into the Don oblast'. [...] [T]he article noted areas of Siberia with a particularly high Old Believer population, especially Tomsk, Tobolsk, and Irkutsk. [...] The question remained whether a specific geographic area had created an environment wherein the Old Belief could thrive or whether the faithful had sought such far-flung locales in order to live better life of the Old Belief" (ibid.).

Robson cites sources indicating that both explanations are viable. Not only state persecutions, but also the moral climate in urbanized Russia pushed the Old Believers to the outside. "The schism of the old ritual, which caught fire in the center of Rus', reached to its borders."[20] In addition to the wilderness, the Old Believers emigrated to populous areas where the main Church held little influence, such as Poland, and even Turkey, Austria, the US and Canada (ibid.).

In short, Robson's account stresses two features of the movement: its centrifugal movement away from the historical core of the country, and its main concentration along the borders of European Russia. This summary of the geography of the Old Belief needs to be modified in three respects. First, it lacks specificity. Second, although Robson is aware of varying population densities over the space of the Russian Empire, his description has not taken population distribution into account. Finally, as this chapter attempts to demonstrate, Robson's general conceptualization of the Old Belief geography can be interpreted somewhat differently. More specifically, building upon statistical analysis, I intend to show that the geography of this schism shows correspondence with physico-geographical frontiers between major cultural subregions of the Russian Empire (Figure 1.1). The argument is that the scalar mismatch of the state and society not only caused the emergence of the Old Belief, it also provided several protective barriers for the schism's survival.

Fourth, the main shortcoming of previous geographical estimations of the movement was their lack of comparative analysis in covering all available statistical indicators. As has been noted, statistics on the number of Old Belief adherents were often unreliable or else distorted for political purposes. Therefore, it is important to utilize different indicators of the Old Belief's geographical prevalence.

Mapping the Old Belief: Indicators

There are three principal ways to assess the territorial distribution of a religion: the first is to look at the statistics of believers; the second, property distribution; and third, data on clergy and priests. The latter data is either not available or applicable for the Old Belief. Therefore, the geography of Old Believers in the Russian Empire in this study is estimated on the basis of the first two principal kinds of indicators.

First, two parameters characterize geographical prevalence of adherents of the Old Belief: their percentage in the total population (Figure 2.8), and the ratio of Old Belief relative to total Orthodox population prevalence (A3.9). The latter shows the relative strength of the alternative schismatic Old Believers against the main Church.

Second, property distribution can be assessed through analysis of the distribution of Old Belief churches (Figure A2.11) and worship houses (A3.12). In addition, prevalence of Edinoverie churches can serve as an indicator (Figure A2.13). (Edinoverie was a state attempt to regain control over the Old Belief after previous persecutions had failed. Edinoverie allowed communities to keep Old Belief specificity in practice and dogma, yet formally be part of the main Church.) Statistics on Old Belief property are summarized in Table A2.2.

As has been noted, the number of adherents of the Old Belief was likely downplayed for the political purposes. On the other hand, property data have their own limitations: they may better reflect the state's vision of where Old Believers should be than where they actually were (this is especially true with regard to Edinoverie churches).

Indices of Mismatch among Population, Ethnicity, and Religion

An additional index has been calculated for this study, the so-called index of "actual/potential Orthodox population deficit" indicating the intensity of deviance from the presumed strict correspondence between religious and ethnic identities of Slavs (Figure A2.10). Presumably, Orthodoxy is a religion primarily of Slavic peoples of Russia. Thus, Russians, Ukrainians, Belarusians, and Moldovans (who are Orthodox Romanians, not Slavs) constitute potential Orthodox populations. The index is calculated as follows:

$$\frac{\text{total actual Orthodox population - total potential Orthodox population}}{\text{the total actual Orthodox population}} \times 100\ (\%)$$

This index shows deviance from hypothetical full correspondence between actual and potential Orthodox population figures serving as a summary figure for non-Orthodox diversity. It shows the degree of under- or over-representation of the Orthodox population in a unit, relative to the ethnic (Slavic and Moldovan) composition of population, measured as a percentage of the Orthodox population. A negative value indicates that a certain percentage of Slavs in the district were non-Orthodox and chose other religions. A positive sign indicates that the number of Orthodox in the unit exceeds that of potential Orthodox peoples and, therefore, non-Slavic peoples constitute the difference. In general, this index shows the deviation from the presumed rigid link between religion and ethnicity, i.e. between Slavic/Moldovan and Orthodox identities.

The 1897 population census was the only one taken in the 19th century and had comparable data on total Slavic and Orthodox populations for units of the country. Given the absence of religious data in later censuses, a correlation analysis for 1897 will help determine whether total population or total Slavic population represents a better surrogate indicator of Orthodoxy for later chapters. For the territory of the whole Empire, the simple correlation between Orthodox and total population figures is 0.89, and between Orthodox and Slavic population figures — 0.97 (Table A2.3). Thus, the data on Slavic populations serves as a better substitute for missing (Soviet) statistics of Orthodox believers than figures of total population. However, a similar correlation analysis for provinces which later formed the Russian Federation reveals that total and Slavic population figures can serve as equally effective substitutes for the missing Orthodox population data in Russia alone: both correlation indexes are 0.96 (Table A2.3). This difference between the Imperial and Russian federal states is obviously attributable to greater diversity in the former.

Findings

My findings do not disprove Robson's estimation of the geography of the Old Belief; rather they confirm and detail it. The first point I would like to make is that Robson's assumptions correspond somewhat differently with the two kinds of indicators utilized for this study (the statistics of believers and the property statistics). Robson's assumptions closely correspond with the property statistics. Of them, the Edinoverie church data suits his description of the geography of the Old Belief by far the best. Indeed, on the map of Edinoverie churches (Figure A2.13) the main concentration of Old Believers is on the border of European Russia – Urals, northwestern Central Asia, southern European Russia (Don area), and the west (Baltics and St. Petersburg). The two other areas identified by Robson (Moscow and Siberia) are also clearly identifiable. Speaking about Siberia, Robson, however, mentiones Irkutsk, not Trans-Baikal province. The map of Old Belief property (Figure A2.12) shows that Irkutsk was indeed a prominent Old Belief province.

That being said, I must raise concern with the fact that it is the map of Edinoverie which reflects Robson's estimation the best. Of all available data, it is the most official which reflects his account the best.

It is likely that Robson's vision of where Old Believers were prevalent is essentially the official, state vision. Though this does not necessarily mean that his findings are incorrect, it does indicate that they are most likely biased in two respects. First, it reflects the absolute (e.g., numerical), not relative (against the main Church) strength of Old Believers in a particular area. Second, it is influenced by the state's interests. For instance, prevalence of Edinoverie churches in provinces close to the capital city of St. Petersburg reflects more the state's fear of the Old Belief there than it does their actual strength.

The second point I would like to make is that Robson's pattern reflects only one territorial mismatch, namely between the state and society. Arguably, the state's real influence was limited by the territory of European Russia, therefore its margins provided niches for Old Believers. The statistics of the Old Belief/Orthodoxy ratio (Figure A2.9) show the relative strength of the Old Belief against the main Church. Its spatial pattern is markedly different from Robson's description: Old Believers were in a relative sense strongest not on the margins of European Russia, but rather further away, on the extreme margins of the Russian Empire. Perhaps Figure A2.9 reflects a different kind of mismatch, namely the territorial mismatch between the official Church and society. In the case of this mismatch, protective niches for the Old Believers were available in the Baltics, Trans-Caucasia, and Central Asia (e.g. regions of predominantly non-Russian population). The map of the Old Believers' percentage of the total population (Figure 2.8) serves as a summary of the two identified mismatch-based patterns of Old Belief geography. There is no contradiction between them, rather they complement one another.

The third point I would like to make refers to both patterns. All these measures show relatively high concentrations of Old Believers along major *internal* frontiers of the Empire. These areas usually coincide with physical-geographical barriers or zones of contact of Russians with non-Russian cultural subregions. The barriers meant greater autonomy and protection from possible persecutions; the contact zones kept Russian nationalism alive. The Old Belief, again, was formed by the most nationalistic part of Russian society. In short, Robson's stress on the centrifugal movement of Old Believers and their marginalization in the Russian Empire is important, but also could be more specific if the mismatches between the state and society, and between the Church and society, are taken into account. They help us understand the Old Belief's survival in certain regions of the country.

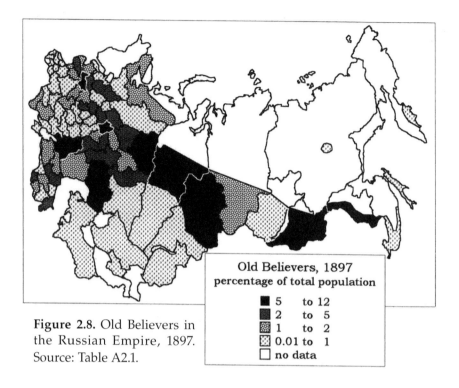

Figure 2.8. Old Believers in the Russian Empire, 1897. Source: Table A2.1.

Old Believers, 1897
percentage of total population

- 5 to 12
- 2 to 5
- 1 to 2
- 0.01 to 1
- no data

The Geography of Orthodox Dissidence in Late Imperial Russia

With the shift to Empire, the Church expanded across such a vast territory that internal differences became unavoidable. More than that, the newly incorporated cultures and religions provided not only new adherents for the Orthodox Russian-State Church, but also alternatives to its monopoly. Previous sections of this chapter have already described the geography of alternatives to the main Church. This section, in contrast, looks at the actual influence of the alternatives on the main Church, analyzing its affiliational dynamics. Data on the dynamics of affiliational membership in the Orthodox Russian-State Church in 1913 are summarized in Table A2.4, and are based on the Annual Report of the Holy Synod's overprocurator (*Vsepoddanneishii Otchet* 1914). This table allows several indicies common in the study of human migrations to be used. For our present purposes, however, it is important to stress that usage of these terms here is conditional: changes in affiliational membership do not mean any geographical move. Such common terms in the study of migration as in-, out-, net-, and gross-migration are utilized here to facilitate the reader's understanding of

Figure 2.9. An Old Belief village church, Trans-Baikal area (Buryat Republic). Source: Angapov (1979: 282).

congregational affiliational mobility (these indicies are calculated as the number of cases per 1 million Orthodox population).

Figure A2.14 shows the total gross-balance of both in- and out-transfers. Clearly, the European center of the country (with the notable exceptions of Moscow and St. Petersburg) was the most stable. Very surprisingly, such borderlands as Trans-Caucasia, Moldova, and Yakutia also appear as areas with low affiliational transfers. Areas of high intensity of transfers include the Baltics, northern Caucasus, southern and western Central Asia, the Far East and parts of Siberia.

In contrast, Figure A2.15 shows the total net-balance. The Church was gaining adherents almost everywhere in Central Asia and Siberia (with the highest rate in the closest Perm and farthest Vladivostok dioceses, with a negative rate in the central Siberian Yenisey diocese). The European part of Russia was relatively stable, yet, at its western and southern Ukrainian margins, the Church was losing believers. Figures A3.16 and A3.17 show total in- and out-transfers separately. The rest of the maps show out-transfers by category.

The most intensive out-transfers to the Old Belief were in three areas. First, to the east of Moscow province, second, on the northern and eastern margins of the European part, and third, in Tomsk province (Figure A2.18). The most surprising characteristic of this figure is the lack or insignificance of out-transfers in provinces on the southern and south-western margins of the country. At the same time, the northern European province of Archangel'sk, not an Old Belief stronghold on the previous maps, appears as one of the leaders of the out-transfers. The general eastward directionality of out-transfers to the Old Belief does not contradict Robson's and my own conclusions, but rather narrows them geographically. Judging by this indicator, the Old Belief had a potential for further growth primarily to the north and east of the historical European core of the country. Destinations for out-transfers in the western borderlands were, not surprisingly, other Christian Churches (Figure A2.19), while non-Christian alternatives were significant only in a few dioceses (Figure A2.20). The primary destination of out-transfers from the main Church in the southern and Siberian (including the Far East) provinces of the country was toward sects (Figure A2.21).[21] This map is remarkable in that it provides quite rare insights into the geographical prevalence of sects in the empire. Statistics on them were always less available than on the more organized confessions. Out-migration to sects indicates their prevalence in southern Ukraine, the north Caucasus, Central Asia and southern Siberia.[22]

These maps are important for further discussion of the Renovationist prevalence in Chapter 3. More specifically, it is important to highlight the two different patterns evident from these maps. Whereas the main Church was most challenged by Old Believers in the European part of the country, especially on its eastern and northern margins, sectarians were a greater alternative on the more distant margins (of the Empire as a whole), especially in the south, in Siberia, Far East, and in the west (Finland and the Baltics). Although both the Old Belief and sects were alternatives to the main Church (and might even co-exist on the same territory), their relative strongholds did not match one another geographically.

Conclusion

This chapter provides a necessary background for subsequent chapters and analyzes the role of territorial mismatches between the state, society, and the Church in the emergence and survival of the Old Belief.

The Church played an important role in the spatial history of the country, as it grew from the Kievan Princedom to the Russian Empire. The Church also changed from a branch of the Eastern (Greek)

Church to the Orthodox Russian-State Church. This chapter summarizes important periods of this spatial history and provides a necessary background for the rest of this study. Utilization of the relational-Foucauldian perspective, with its reliance on the role of discontinuities and ruptures in social processes, allows one to see clearly the importance of the fact that expansions of the state, society and the Church did not always correspond with one another. The scalar mismatch between the state and society, for example, resulted in the Old Belief schism. Similar mismatches in later periods allowed the Old Believers to survive. At the same time, this chapter profiles non-Orthodox diversity. The Empire incorporated many non-Orthodox peoples, who also challenged the dominant position of the main Church. In any case, the popular expression for the Russian Empire's essentials, "Orthodoxy, Autocracy, Nationality," had limited validity in a geographical sense.

Second, this chapter provides necessary specifics into the geography of the Old Belief in pre-revolutionary Russia. Previous geographical accounts of the movement were based on qualitative descriptions. Therefore, statistical and cartographic means were utilized to clarify what is already known about the geography of the Old Belief. My findings mostly concur with previous observations summarized above and detail areas along the margins of the country with Old Believer strongholds. Contrary to common belief, the Old Believers attracted the greatest out-transfers from the ORSCh in areas different from those of sectarian movements. At the same time, my findings hopefully contribute to a further understanding of the geography of the schism. My major finding is that, unlike the non-Orthodox diversity, the geography of Old Belief is not characterized by a concentration of adherents in distinctive subregions of the country; rather, it highlights the boundaries between them. In other words, this stress on boundaries is another manifestation of the importance of territorial mismatches between society, the state, and the Church.

Chapter 2: Notes

1. Solzhenitsyn made this statement while addressing a group of Russian Orthodox clerics in 1974. Quoted in Robson (1995: 3).

2. The "Orthodoxy, Autocracy, Nationality" formula was coined in the early 1830s by the Education Minister of the Russian state, Count S. Uvarov. It presented an attempt to popularize the state after the setbacks of the 1825 Decembrist Revolt in St. Petersburg and liberal movements in Europe. This ideology was propagated by historian M. Pogodin, literary critic S. Shevyrev, and philosopher F. Sidonskii. Pogodin's journal *Moskvitianin* in the period between 1841 and 1856 published a number of articles to prove the special (non-liberal) form of Russia's development, based on the idea of Russian society's uniquely strong attachment to the autocratic state and the official Orthodox Church (Godienko 1988: 181-2).

3. This historical account is drawn from Ware (1963).

4. The Armenian Church, present on the territory of the former USSR, is the oldest Christian Church there.

5. For further popular and scholarly readings regarding the baptizing see *Kak Byla Kreschena Rus'* (1988), *Russkoe Zarubezh'e* (1991), *Tysiacheletie Kresheniia Rusi* (1988), Tsarevskii (1991, 1898).

6. Old Slavonic is still the language of service in Russian Orthodoxy even though modern Russians have difficulty understanding it. Attempts of the Renovationists to introduce modern Russian as the language of service have failed together with the movement itself (Chapter 3).

7. The only exception was Novgorod in the North.

8. Metropolitan was the highest rank in the Church at that time since it was not formally independent.

9. The monastery is now known as Trinity-St.Sergii Lavra in Sergiev Posad (former Zagorsk).

10. The pre-revolutionary Church had a name (*Pravoslavnaia Rossiiskaia Tserkov'*) which is usually translated as Russian Orthodox Church. This name was different from the current name of the Russian Orthodox Church (*Russkaia Pravoslavnaia Tserkov'*) not only by the order of words, however, but also by the meaning of the word "Russian."

In the Russian language, there are two different words which are translated into English as "Russian:" *usskaia* refers to something ethnically Russian; *rossiiskaia* refers to something of the Russian state. The current official name of the Russian Orthodox Church refers to the ethnical Russianness; in contrast, the pre-revolutionary name of the Church referred to the Russian state. It is important for purposes of this study to keep this nuance of the Russian language and distinguish Churches, therefore a different word is utilized. "Russian-State" is a hybrid English equivalent of the word "rossiiskaia" meaning Russian by its citizenship, not ethnicity.

11. Little Russia (Malorossiia) is historical, although somewhat pejorative name for Ukraine (the same goes for "the Ukraine"). Belarus (Belorussia) literally means "White Russia."

12. Zenkovsky's works (summarized in his 1970 book) have been quoted here extensively because his concept of the influence of geopolitical change on a religious schism is very important for this study, providing a model for analysis of other schisms in Russian Orthodoxy.

13. Base maps of the country's division into civil units (provinces) in 1897 exist in Leasure and Lewis (1966), and are utilized for this study (Figure A2.1 of the Supplement).

14. Detailed statistics on the geographical distribution of Old Belief subgroups is published in Tsentral'nyi Statisticheskii Komitet (1901b).

15. The 1897 census provides data only for the Russian population in Finland. Finns are mostly Lutheran.

16. Although the 1897 census did not provide data on Finns, this belt clearly also included Finland.

17. For description of different strands of the Old Belief, see Robson (1995: 29-40).

18. For discussion of Old Belief statistics, see Kirillov (1913: 13-26). Also, Tikhomirov (1900), Robson (1995: 19-24).

19. Robson (1995: 21) cites von Bushen, who in 1863 noted that Old Believers constituted 10 percent of the population in the empire's border provinces (emphasis mine - D.S.).

20. A missionary priest, cited in Robson (1995: 23).

21. These data do not specify sects.

22. This map is supported by Klibanov (1982: 36) (see Figure A2.22).

Chapter 3.
"Liberation of Christ from the National Embrace": Renovationism as a Movement

> *The liberation of Christ from the national embrace, from confessional altars and from capitalist gold chains is the greatest gift of love, which Renovationism has laid at the foot of the global throne of the All-Mighty.*
>
> Alexander Vvedenskii, leader of Renovationism[1]

This chapter further continues our consideration of the social and political implications of the territorial non-correspondence between the state, society, and the Church. More specifically, it considers the first post-revolutionary decade (1917-27), when the mismatch between the global aspirations of the state and the parochial, traditional identity of society provided a fertile soil for a split within the Orthodox Russian-State Church. This split (the Renovationist movement) formally emerged in 1924 and continued until the death of its main leader, Alexander Vvedenskii, in 1944. The 1930s will be only briefly considered here because of the scarcity of available information and the general decline of Renovationism in that decade.

The period 1917-27 can be seen as an aftermath of two important, although abortive, events. First, the state and society had been dramatically shaken by the October 1917 revolution led by Vladimir Lenin. This transformation culminated in 1922 in the formation of the USSR as a union with global aspirations. However, by the late 1920s the country arguably had lost its revolutionary potential, and with the final emergence of Joseph Stalin as the undisputed ruler of the country in the late 1920s, the USSR had imperialist, rather than global aspirations. Second, the Holy Council of 1917-18 adopted a far-reaching program of church reforms, which were not implemented because of the state's continuing intervention. The formation in 1922 of the Renovationist movement within the Church can be seen as a culmination (although not canonical) of the 1917-18 "Church Revolution." Yet its eventual result was the appearance, in 1927, of the declaration of the Church's loyalty to the state which, among other things, marked the abortion of any further reform movements within the Church.

The history of the Renovationist movement can be summarized as follows. The Renovationists first seized control of the central church administration in May 1922 and soon thereafter held more than half of all parishes of the Church. In the later 1920s, however, following the state's release of imprisoned Patriarch Tikhon (Figure 3.1) in exchange for his adopting a more loyal position toward the new Communist authorities, the state stopped privileging the Renovationists. This led the various Church factions to begin competing for property and parish communities. However, by 1925 most parishes had abandoned Renovationism, and it finally became subsumed as a minor branch of the Church. During the 1930s, Renovationism was subject to the general anti-religious campaigns, and, unlike the Tikhonite Church, was not permitted by the state to revitalize itself in the post-war period.[2]

Renovationism was a broad program for the political, social, and religious modernization of the Russian Orthodox Church in the 1920s and 1930s. Although prototypes appeared prior to 1917 (see Cunningham 1981), the movement became a real force only with the clandestine support of Bolshevik authorities whose immediate goal was to fracture and eventually suppress the main Orthodox Church. The view commonly taken by historians is that the state during this period was the leading agent and society mainly a passive recipient of the state's decisions. To this explanation of the movement's emergence, this chapter adds a geopolitical argument, namely the role of the mismatch between the state and society. In addition, it challenges certain geographic characteristics of the movement which are often misinterpreted by historians in their dominant, state-centered discourse. Instead, I intend to show the continuing legacy of the pre-revolutionary geography of the Church in the territorial pattern of Renovationism.

Three major forces shaped Renovationism as a movement: first, the schism was promoted by several internal reformist drives within the Church; second, it was constrained by the resistance of the old Tikhonite part of the Church;[3] and third, when these two forces were approximately balanced and stable, the state changed its position from hidden support, to neutrality, and then to hidden antagonism. This chapter attempts to show that the movement was also shaped by a geographical factor ignored by historians, namely, the specific spatial extent of each of these agents relative to one another.

Figure 3.1. Patriarch Tikhon with clergymen (n.d., perhaps early 1920s). Source: Kirichenko (1992: 205), reproduced by permission.

The Renovationist schism was not only a historical phenomenon, but also a geographically differentiated movement, experiencing spatial expansion and decline, and possessing local characteristics and regional variations. Scholars of Soviet history tend to consider the regional and local dimensions separately. Regional accounts have been very general while specifically local investigations are not placed in the context of a broader regional contextualization. More precisely, two main theoretical constructs of the regional patterns of the Renovationist movement can be identified. Anatolii Levitin and Vadim Shavrov (1977: 255) explained the geography of Renovationism in terms of the class make-up of the population, and the resulting pro- and anti-Soviet regional attitudes. Dimitry Pospielovsky (1984: 68-9), in contrast, argued for the coincidence of Renovationist and the prevalence of regional sects. Both accounts are based on rough statistics which must be clarified before they can be precisely mapped.

Two important local accounts of the movement, provided by Edward E. Roslof (1994: 237-261) and Gregory L. Freeze (1995: 305-339), did not consider regional variations, yet their conceptions by implication lead to certain regional generalizations. Freeze's model is particularly suggestive in this regard and worth distinction as a third conceptualization by historians of the geography of Renovationism. Freeze (1995: 327, 338) explains the Renovationists' inability to prevail

primarily in terms of dispersion of power in the Church, i.e., the transfer of authority from central or diocesan church authorities to parish
councils. He cites such factors as the rising "parish power," the collapse of the Church administration, lack of communication, and the
revolution's weakening of the parish clergy. Since all these factors were
more significant in the country's periphery than in its historical, European core, this conceptualization, by implication, assumes that
Renovationism's failure was most marked in marginal regions. It remains to be seen whether or not this reasoning is supported by the
regional pattern of the Renovationists' prevalence.

       This chapter has three aims. First, it analyzes another mismatch
in recent Russian history, namely that between the global aspirations
of the early Soviet state and its more parochial society. Second, it uses
this to summarize and analyze what is already known about the regional geography of an important, if geographically obscure, socio-politico-cultural phenomenon in recent Soviet history, namely the
Renovationist movement in the Russian Orthodox Church. Finally, this
chapter attempts to prove the importance of geographical considerations
by utilizing them to challenge some of the historian's assumptions about
the Renovationist movement. To existing explanations of Renovationist
geographical patterns, it adds its own perspective based on center-periphery discrepancies in the Renovationist movement.

DOCUMENTING AND MAPPING RENOVATIONISM:
A NOTE ON SOURCES AND METHODOLOGY

Sources

       There are three principal bodies of geographical statistics on
Renovationism: 1) internal reports of the secret service (1922, 1924); 2)
data compiled by the Renovationists themselves for the 1925-27 period;
and 3) the archives of the state organizations in charge of religious affairs, which contain statistics for the 1930s. Statistics for the late 1930s
are sketchy.

Secret Service Reports
       For political reasons, data on the earliest stages of Renovationism
(1922-24) were of special interest to the secret services and the secret
Anti-Religious Commission of the Communist Party's Central Committee (1922-29) (see Roslof 1994). Two noteworthy regional reports of

the secret service to this Commission are located in RTsKhIDNI (formerly known as the Central Party Archive of the Institute of Marxism-Leninism). A survey of the 6th department of SOGPU (the Secret Service's Department for Religious Affairs) provides data on the state of the Renovationist movement in the provinces between July 15th and August 20th, 1922.[4] Unfortunately, these data are qualitative and cannot be mapped. A survey of early 1924 compiled by Evgenii Tuchkov[5] provides some statistics on the number of Renovationist parishes. It is not comprehensive (Table A3.1),[6] but it covers the important period immediately preceding the one for which the Renovationists' own statistical accounts are available.

Publications of the Renovationists

The major Renovationist journal *Vestnik Sviaschennogo Sinoda Pravoslavnoi Rossiiskoi Tserkvi* [Messenger of the Holy Synod of the Orthodox Russian-State Church] published several statistical reports that were compiled by the Renovationists themselves for the period 1925-27 (Table A3.2).[7] Although most analysts of the movement rely on these data for their estimates of its regional strength (see, for example, Stratonov 1932, Pospielovsky 1984, Roslof 1994), these data and the analyses they yield have two limitations. First, the original figures could be inaccurate or distorted for political purposes. Nevertheless, no comparable alternative figures from the Tikhonite part of the Church or the state for the same period of 1925-27 are available for verification. Second, although these figures are familiar to scholars, their geographical dimensions have not yet been studied. The data presented are simply the number of parishes in each region. This precludes comparative analysis, since the country's territory is so unevenly populated. One way to solve this problem is to adjust the data for population distribution, i.e., to compare the number of parishes to the total Slavic population.

State Data

Soviet archives with statistics on Renovationism have only recently been opened to scholars. Although some figures have already been published (Odintsov 1993, 1994), most still remain under-studied by historians. In addition, some archival *fondy* are still classified and thus accessible only to a limited number of scholars. Data for the state organizations which controlled religious affairs at the time of the Renovationist movement are primarily stored in the State Archive of the Russian Federation (GARF), formerly the Central State Archive of the October Revolution (TsGAOR).[8] Within are several collections containing materials of the state religious departments, primarily for the early 1930s and the post-war period.[9] Unfortunately, the 1920s and late 1930s, key periods for the movement, are under-represented in these materials.

The most important source of regional statistics on Renovationism in the 1930s are the materials of the March 1, 1931 All-Union survey organized by the VTsIK Presidium's Permanent Commission for Cult Issues. A uniform questionnaire was filled out by local authorities and summarized by the Commission. Although the accompanying correspondence contains much evidence of various misunderstandings, it is also certain that the Commission did its best to clarify the received data. For instance, doubtful questionnaires were repeatedly returned for correction. Table A3.3 shows the latest available version of these data.[10] Since some authorities at the lowest local level of *rayony* did not answer the questionnaire, these statistics are not comprehensive. However, the data are utilized in this chapter not in the form of absolute figures, as the percent data (e.g., percentage of Renovationist parishes in the total Russian Orthodox Church, which hopefully minimizes the effect of local underrepresentation).

Other Sources

Presumably, the Russian Orthodox Church should contain a wealth of data regarding Renovationism. Outside researchers, however, are repeatedly denied access to that material, because it is "uncataloged" and, therefore, "not available to outside researchers."[11] The author's inquiries about the Renovationist materials at the Moscow Patriarchate, its archive, and the Synodal Library also yielded no positive results. The standard answer was that the Church itself would like to know their current location. Some of these materials reportedly were destroyed, either by those former Renovationists who rejoined the Church and had reasons to hide information on the movement, or by the state authorities themselves.[12] Some social organizations which worked in the religious field (e.g., the Society of Militant Godless) can possibly provide additional data. Unfortunately, however, the author had only the chance to browse though a few such files in the GARF.

Published memoirs of contemporaries of the movement tend to focus on accounts of the top hierarchical level (Stratonov 1932, Levitin and Shavrov 1977, Krasnov-Levitin 1977). Some new papers and memoirs have recently surfaced, but their focus is on the local, Moscow scale (Kozarzhevskii 1989, Sventsytskii 1994). The many local Renovationist publications and periodicals (1922-28) may contain some statistics, although it is unlikely they would cover the movement as a whole. Previous analyses of Renovationism relying on local archival sources tend to focus on case studies, with no general comprehensive summary yet available (Shishkin 1970, Krasnov-Levitin 1977, Levitin and Shavrov 1977, Roslof 1994, Freeze 1995).

Methodology

Administrative Boundaries' Adjustment

In order to map the regional Renovationist statistics from the three major sources, appropriate territorial divisions of the country should first be reconstructed. The lack of maps showing the USSR's administrative-territorial division for appropriate historical periods is a major stumbling block for mapping the historical geography of the Russian Orthodox Church.

Until the mid-1920s, the USSR continued in principle to use the pre-revolutionary system of territorial-administrative division (*gubernii*). Tuchkov's survey of Renovationists for early 1924, for instance, gives figures for *gubernii* (Figure A3.1). However, the Renovationist figures for 1925 and 1927 utilize diocesan units based on a new system of territorial-political division of the country.[13] Therefore, in this study these data were used with a modified version of the territorial division, which was employed for the 1926 population Census (Figure A3.3).[14] This map of the Renovationist diocesan division in 1927 should not be taken as a completed and verified project, but rather seen as a necessary compromise for this particular chapter. Gubonin (1994) lists in his supplement all Renovationist dioceses and their bishops at different times; Lemeshevskii (1979-89) provides a listing of the Church's bishops and their dioceses. These listings do not coincide fully with the listings provided by the Renovationist publications, which, in turn, also differ from each other. Clearly, the Renovationist diocesan division was not stable, with many tiny and short-lived units.

In this chapter the discernment of the geographical affiliation of a particular diocese within the civil division in unclear cases relies on two additional sources of information: the political-administrative division of the country in the 1920s and bishop's titles given in the extensive listing of Lemeshevskii (ibid.). Russian Orthodox bishops traditionally use double geographical names in their titles. For example, the title "bishop of Kuznetsk, vicar of Tomsk diocese" could be taken

as an indicator that Kuznetsk oblast' together with Tomsk oblast' constituted the Tomsk diocese.

A new territorial division in the 1930s required a new base map
(Figure A3.4). The principal difference between the 1930s divisions
and those of the 1920s is the aggregation of many of the latter into large
statistical Oblasts (e.g., Moscow Oblast', the statistical aggregated unit,
is different from Moscow oblast', the administrative unit).[15] This change
in administrative-territorial division provides an obstacle in compar-
ing data for the 1920s with those for the 1930s; the problem is multi-
plied by the associated, yet not always corresponding, changes in diocesan division.[16]

Population Measures

The major sources of USSR population statistics for the 1920s
and 1930s are the December 17, 1926, January 6, 1937 and January 17,
1939 censuses (*Vsesoiuznaia Perepis' Naseleniia 17 Dekabria 1926* 1928,
Vsesoiuznaia Perepis' Naseleniia 1937 g. 1991, *Vsesoiuznaia Perepis' Naseleniia
1939 Goda* 1991). They provide not only absolute population figures,
but also the ethnic composition of the population for civil territorial
divisions. Orthodoxy in Russia is predominantly a Slavic religion.
Utilization of total population figures in this study would result in distorted representation in Central Asia, the Caucasus and Siberia, where
a significant part of the total population is non-Orthodox. Therefore,
data for the Slavic population, defined as Russians, Ukrainians,
Belarusians, and Moldovans (who are predominantly Orthodox although not Slavic), have been distinguished and form the basis for calculation. Since significant part of the Orthodox population of the
Povolzh'e and Ural areas were non-Slavic, this could result in general
over-representation of these areas on the final maps. However, the author believes that these distortions are minor. Two simplifications have
been permitted here. First, this unity of ethnic and religious characteristics of the population has only a limited validity. Second, although
these data are not accurate for calculating ratios except in the year of
the census, this study assumes that in the span of two-to-three years
the ethnic composition of the civil units either did not change significantly. In any case, no other comparable statistics on ethnic composition by region are available to the author.

RENOVATIONISM AS A SPATIAL MOVEMENT

Origins of Renovationism

Certain geographical factors must be taken seriously when scholars debate the origins of Renovationism. To date, discussions of this topic have been limited to considerations of historical, social, political, and personal issues. What is often missing in these accounts is the influence of a geographical factor, namely the mismatch between the state, society, and the Church.

It will be argued here that the Renovationist schism was facilitated by the territorial non-correspondence between the country's state and its society. More specifically, the state acquired global aspirations, while society obviously remained more parochial and national in its make-up. In this light, the emergence of Renovationism can be seen as an attempt on the side of both the state and some clergy to bridge the gap and to provide a global set of religious values for the traditional society. At the same time, Renovationism was to facilitate activities of the state at the global scale. Several arguments can be put forward to support this underexplored line of geographical (rather than exclusively historical) reasoning.

To start with, it arguably was not mere coincidence that the Renovationist movement emerged in the same year that the Soviet Union was formed (1922). It was expected that this union would become global, so construction of a gigantic Palace of the Soviets (discussed in Chapter 7) was proposed to accommodate the presumably ever-growing number of delegates joining the Union, and to serve as a symbol of the coming Communist global hegemony (Palamarchuk 1994: 174). Reflecting this tension between the state and society was the question of the calendar (Freeze 1995). The Renovationists suggested that the Church adopt the universally-accepted date system instead of the traditional Church calendar. In short, the emergence of the schism was in part a result of the state-society mismatch. The Renovationist schism in the Russian Church clearly reflected the general schism in society along modernization lines, yet its geographical dimension deserves greater attention by scholars.

Dogmatic differences between the traditional (Tikhonite, later known as Sergian) Church and the Renovationists can also be conceptualized along global/national lines. Detailed analysis of Renovationist ideology is beyond the frame of this study. Alexander Vvedenskii, the leader of the Renovationist schism, provides a good summary (cited at the beginning of this chapter): "the liberation of Christ from the national embrace" was the main goal of the movement. Similar supranational, interdenominational and macro-economic (meaning global-economic) rhetoric can be found in many publications in *Vestnik Sviaschennogo Sinoda*, the main Renovationist periodical. Although much of this rhetoric was motivated by attempts of the Renovationists to enlarge their importance and to capture allegencies and support of foreign Orthodox Churches, a surway of Renovationist publications and archival materials shows the gradual emergence of a different, although politically no less important, idea.

The Renovationist leaders were, for a very long time, if not always, aware that the movement had a good chance of surviving after the late 1920s when the state gradually lost interest in privileging the Renovationist Church and after the traditional Church was supressed domestically. And this chance had a spatial dimension: the Renovationist Church could become helpful in the foreign affairs of the state, in the domain beyond the formal territorial extent of the new union. With the gradual decline of the rhetoric of "proletariat world revolution" and "global Soviet union," the movement's leaders became increasingly involved in the attempt to be seen as indispensible in the state's effort to regain control over the enormous Church property abroad that remained largely autonomous after 1917.

The state in turn realized that these church properties abroad not only had enormous material value, but could also be very important politically, serving as possible nuclei for international Soviet influence. Full utilization of this potential was, perhaps, postponed due to the domestic political priorities of the 1920-30s, the lack of experience in international affairs, and the ineptness of the bureaucracy. Archival documents show that the Soviet Foreign Affairs Ministry and the Cult Commission were often acting in disaccord in the 1920s, for some time not even being able to organize a joint meeting.[17] One tragic and anecdotal case is particular telling about the spirit of the time. Father Vladimir Znosko, a WWI POW in Germany after 1915, served as a priest of the Soviet Embassy's church in Berlin. He bombarded the Renovationist Synod in the 1920s with appeals to regain the Church's property in Germany, but his forwarded appeals kept merely rebouncing between different state organizations. The Foreign Affairs Ministry, for instance, had doubts about the legitimacy of both the Renovationist Synod and father Znosko personally, so the sole supporter of all Russian churches in Germany was unable to get any support for himself and was in a desperate situation.[18]

Tragically for the Renovationists, need for a large-scale geopolitical intervention in international Orthodox affairs came only later, in the late 1940s, when the state had already wholly disregarded the movement. It is an irony of history and geography that the Renovationist geopolitical ideas were to be implemented after 1943 by the traditional (Sergian) Church (Shkarovsky 1999: 284-305)! In this sense, Renovationism survived the death of the movement itself.

Furthermore, in addition to Orthodox Renovationism, the state supported similar trends in some other religions in the USSR, another argument in support of the "global" underpinnings of Renovationism and criticism of consideration of it in mere national political terms. If the prime motivation for such schisms was a mere attempt to weaken an influential Church (this is the main conceptualization of historians with regard to the Orthodox Renovationism), then it is not clear why the Buddhists and the Armenian Church were selected. In all senses (including the geographical one) they occupied a marginal position in society, and this marginality, in accordance with the dominant theories of Renovationism, should have made them the last target of the state's purposeful fracturing. Yet this marginality becomes of prime importance if Renovationism is to be understood geographically. For instance, Buddhist Renovationism was associated with the foreign policy goal of bringing Tibet into the sphere of Soviet influence.[19] Similar motivations perhaps guided Renovationist schism in the Armenian Church, Russia's Muslims, and later among the Ukrainian Uniates and East German Protestants.

In short, the mismatch between the state, society and the Church was one of the factors behind Orthodox religious unrest in the 1920s. Geographical analysis is important in understanding the origin of Renovationism because it also helps to explain its consequences, meaning the particular regional forms it took. The rest of this section first clarifies the regional patterns of Renovationism during growth, stagnation and decline. It is important to do just this because the historians' accounts so far have been based on very rough estimations of regional patterns of Renovationism. Second, it compares the conceptualization developed here with prevalent theoretical constructs provided by historians.

Period of Growth (1922-23)

This section describes areas in the USSR where, in the period 1922-23, Renovationists were relatively strong and weak initially. A survey of the 6th department of SOGPU (the Secret Service's Department on Religious Affairs) provides data on the state of the Renovationist movement in provinces from July 15th to August 20, 1922.[20] Unfortunately, these data are qualitative. In addition, the survey focuses on the fight between priests of the two Orthodox groups for dominance in the top diocesan organizations. Apparently, Renovationism was not an immediate success. The central provinces of the country were seemingly most resistant to the movement. For example, the following characteristics were used to describe the Renovationism movement in Vladimir –"weak development", in Ivanovo-Voznesensk — "no movement" and in Tver' — "the Renovationist movement goes astray." The Renovationists also apparently faced troubles in other areas (for example, "In the city of Arkhangel'sk there are only two Renovationists").

However, "[a]t the end of 1922, the Soviet government handed over to Renovationists of all kinds[21] nearly two-thirds of all functioning churches in the RSFSR and Central Asia — close to twenty thousand churches. Churches in the Ukraine and Belorussia ... are not included in that figure" (Pospielovsky 1984: 62).

In April 1924, the head of the secret service's special department on religious affairs, Tuchkov, compiled data on the reported prevalence of Renovationists in the provinces at that time (Table A3.1; Figure A3.2). Central Asia was not included in Tuchkov's survey, and many numbers are only estimated. However, noteworthy for later discussion is the fact that North Caucasus, with the exception of Kuban', does not appear as a stronghold. Also, some growth of Renovationist prevalence to the north of the historical European center is visible.

The general pattern described by Tuchkov's statistics coincides with Levitin and Shavrov's picture of the movement (Levitin and Shavrov 1977: 255). They provide the first conceptualization of the geography of Renovationism. In their regional account of the movement they reach the conclusion that the movement was most successful in southern Russia and Siberia. Against all expectations, the pro-Soviet Renovationist movement was supported in these areas, which, since the end of the civil war, had been largely anti-Soviet and home to the White-guard Cossacks. Even more striking is the relative failure of Renovationism in the industrial urban regions of the country. The proletariat was more willing to support the Tikhonite strain in the Church. Levitin and Shavrov explain this seemingly contradictory geographical pattern in terms of the religious indifference of Cossacks and the religious and political awareness of the proletariat. This explanation seems questionable: it is not clear why proletarians would be willing to support the seemingly counter-revolutionary Tikhonite strain in the Church over the "progressive" Renovationists. In the same way, the link between the presumed indifference of Cossacks and prevalence of the Renovationists is not clear.

Period of Stagnation and Decline (1924-29)

What was the geography of Renovationism in the period of 1924-29, when the state withdrew its active support but had not yet started its active anti-religious assault? By November 1924, the Renovationist parishes "had been reduced to 10,016 in Russia, Siberia and Central Asia, plus some 3,000 in the Ukraine, 500 in Belorussia and 400 in the Far Eastern District... ."[22] The regional breakdown of these data is given in Table A3.2. These are absolute numbers which for a country like Russia with significant ethnic and territorial discrepancies, give a distorted perception of the movement's geographical dimensions. Figure A3.5 represents these data, expressed as the number of Renovationist parishes in a diocese relative to the size of its Slavic population.

As seen on this map, in the early period of its decline (ca. January 1925) the movement was already weak in the central areas of the country, that is, the historical European Russian core. The areas with a higher density of Renovationist parishes were the agrarian belts in southern and northern European Russia, parts of Central Asia and Eastern Siberia. The pattern on this map appears more concentric than regional, with an increase in the Renovationist presence with increased distance from the center in *all* directions.

The underestimated prevalence of the Renovationists in northern European Russia is especially remarkable in this regard. With varying clarity, this spatial pattern can be seen on the subsequent maps of the Renovationist prevalence in October 1, 1927 (Figure A3.6) and on January 31, 1927 (Figure A3.7). Unlike other Renovationist statistics, the figures used in Figure A3.7 are comparative, showing the percentage of Renovationist parishes in the Russian Orthodox Church's dioceses.

Given the relatively sparse presence of Renovationist parishes in the center of the country, the margins could be expected to show the greatest decline in the Renovationist presence after the state withdrew its active support in the late 1920s.

However, Figure A3.8 shows that, from January 1925 to October 1927, although nation-wide the movement was in decline, a significant number of dioceses saw a continuing growth in Renovationism. Notably, this growth tended to occur in the historical central and northern areas of the country. Thus, while the total number of Renovationist parishes in the country was declining, several dioceses of European Russia saw growth in the Renovationist presence. This might be attributed to a temporary revival of state support for the movement, or, conversely, a continuation of the fighting between the Tikhonites and the Renovationists. In any case, it is clear that the decline was not a geographically uniform process.

Period of Survival (the 1930s)

Table A3.3 and Figure A3.9 show the proportion of Renovationist places of worship in the Russian Orthodox Church on December 1, 1933, at a time when the state had started its anti-religious assault against both Renovationists and Tikhonites. Clearly the same regional uniformity is visible in this distribution: despite growth during 1925-27, the European core still lagged behind the nation-wide average by 15.5 percent. This while the southern European, Siberian and Central Asian regions of the country were uniformly above even the higher average figure for the 1927 estimation (21.7 percent). In these areas the movement still held between one-quarter and one-half of all parishes in the Church. The center-periphery pattern is even more sharply visible here than on the previous maps: with the exception of the Far East, the country is divided into a historical European core with a minimal proportion of Renovationist parishes, and the rest of the country.

Renovationist parishes were subject to the general anti-religious persecution in the late 1920s and especially in the early 1930s. For example, in 1928 the Renovationist Synod was seen repeatedly seeking opportunities to gain an audience with Soviet Prime Minister Rykov to present evidence that excessive taxation had brought a desperate ("catastrophic") condition for many Renovationist priests and bishops. As a result, in regions such as the Caucasus, Volga, Ryazan', some clergy were leaving the movement.[23] As a dramatic example, the famous Cathedral of Christ the Savior in Moscow belonged to the Renovationists at the time of its destruction in 1931. Yet, with a distinct geographical pattern similar processes were under way in virtually every area of the country.

Figure A3.10 depicts the percentage of all Russian Orthodox churches closed between 1918 and 1931 that were Renovationist places of worship.[24] The general trend appears to be that with growing distance from the center, there was an increasing proportion of Renovationist churches among all closed Russian Orthodox churches. This could be interpreted as a reflection of the growing indifference of local authorities to religious matters. On the other hand, this pattern in general coincides with the pattern of the Renovationist parishes' geographical distribution (Figure A3.9). This might be an indication that the anti-religious actions were planned to be paradoxically "just": their destructive effect was proportional to a religious organization's relative strength in a territorial unit. Indeed, in 1932 the chair of the Cult Commission under the VTsIK Krasikov explicitly demanded that, in places with both Tikhonite and Renovationist churches, closures should follow "the proportionality principle."[25]

End of the Renovationism

Given the relative lack of popular support, the future of Renovationist movement was always problematic. Nonetheless, it was the state which finally terminated the movement. Following the Germans' unwillingness to permit the revival of the "Communist" Renovationist churches on occupied territories, the Soviet authorities, too, in 1943 permitted only the revival of the conservative, Patriarchal (Tikhonite, Sergian) wing of the Church. Vladimir Karpov, the chair of the Council for Russian Orthodox Church Affairs (CROCA), wrote to Stalin in 1943 that the Renovationist movement had played a positive role in the past, but that lately it lacked "the same importance and following." It was their rival strain of the Church that occupied a "patriotic position" [during WWII]. Karpov proposed "not blocking the decline of the Renovationist strain and transfer of its clergy and parishes to the Sergian Church." On October 12, 1943, Stalin approved Karpov's proposal with just two words "That's right!", thereby crossing out any future for the schism.[26]

By December 12, 1943, five out of six remaining Renovationist parishes in Moscow had joined the Patriarchal Church. Out of the 147 remaining parishes in the USSR as a whole, 86 churches were in the

Krasnodar region, and 42 in the Stavropol region (both in the North Caucasus). Desperate attempts by the movement's leader, Alexander Vvedenskii, to help it survive by merging with the Old Believers, Roman Catholics or forming a separate sect, were rejected by the CROCA.[27]

There is evidence that the state's unwillingness to permit a Renovationist revival parallel to that of the main Church after 1943 was facilitated by a lack of communication between the parishes of the peripheral strongholds and the movement's leaders in distant core areas. For example, as Pospielovsky points out:

> "In the Central Asian area the Soviet government ... took care of the question: it simply blocked (confiscated or destroyed) all letters from those communities to Alexander Vvedenskii, by that time head of the Renovationist schism. Hearing nothing from him, they returned to the fold of the Patriarchal Church" (Pospielovsky 1984: 68).

In a country as large as Russia, space is never a neutral factor.

CLERGY AND WEALTH:
THE GEOGRAPHY OF PARISH INCOME BEFORE AND AFTER 1917

Regional Differences and Historical Explanations

Three existing theorizations of the regional geography of Renovationism have already been mentioned: one linking the Renovationist strongholds to the areas of widespread anti-Bolshevik public sentiments (Levitin and Shavrov 1977), the other arguing for a correlation with the geographical pattern of Russian religious sectarianism (Pospielovsky 1984), and the third suggesting the least success of Renovationism in peripheral areas (Freeze 1995). These views, while not fully defensible, are not always incompatible with my findings.

The first two conceptualizations (by Levitin and Shavrov, and Pospielovsky) do not contradict my findings. Levitin and Shavrov's concept needs a more detailed, quantitative and cartographic analysis unavailable to me at this point. Pospielovsky identifies the Renovationist areas as Central Asia, the northern Caucasus, the Don region and parts of southern Siberia; these were the only territories where the Renovationists had a major lay following and attempted some renewal after the war (Pospielovsky 1984: 68-9). Indeed, in Figure A3.7 Renovationist parishes in the European dioceses are almost uniformly below the average proportion of 21.7 percent, while more than half of the parishes in the more marginal dioceses were Renovationist in 1927.

Pospielovsky believes that "... these areas have historically had the highest concentrations of followers of the Old Believer schism and of popular sects, most of which were an extreme development of the priestless wing of the Old Believers" (Pospielovsky 1984: 68-9). Despite some macro-geographical correlation, micro-geographies of the Renovationist movement, the Old Belief, and popular sects do not always coincide. First, as Chapter 2 has shown, the Old Belief and sectarianism were most successful in challenging the main Church in different, non-coinciding areas. Second, Renovationism was not equally successful in all Old Belief strongholds, e.g., the western part of the former Russian Empire, the Baltics, was one of the prime centers of the Old Belief with no equivalent Renovationist prevalence. Similarly, while the Old Belief was most popular in the westernmost section of Central Asia, Renovationism was predominant in its extreme eastern and southern parts. Third, although both the Old Belief and the Renovationism were opposed to the official Church, their positions with regard to Orthodoxy were opposite, the former being ultra-conservative, the latter extremely liberal. In the same vein, Renovationists were harsh critics of any sectarianism, as is seen from their numerous publications. It is not clear why these competing movements should be equally prevalent in the same areas.

My findings (and the two first conceptualizations, despite their differences) strongly oppose Freeze's theorization: contrary to his theory, Renovationism was successful in the peripheral parts of the country. For instance, the regional variation in the overall pattern of Renovationism challenges Freeze's explanation of the movement's failure in terms of growing parochialization of power. Contrary to the author's conceptualization, the movement was relatively more successful in areas where the "breakdown of ecclesiastical administration," "lack of communications," "Renovationists' lack of preparation" and "inability to re-educate" were the worst.[28]

Leaving aside the factual dimension of these conceptualizations, one can point out some of their theoretical weaknesses. The stress on anti-Bolshevik public sentiments implicitly assumes that Renovationist believers (parishioners) were the guiding force of such a movement. Moreover, the "sectarian" argument implicitly excludes the clergy, since sects are often priestless. Yet, in sharp contrast to the Old Belief,

Renovationism was undoubtedly led by priests: they were the prime subjects of the Bolshevik pressure, and they (some of them) were receptive to new opportunities.

More specifically, it is well known that the movement was inspired by married ("white") priests who were dissatisfied with the privileged position of unmarried ("black") priests (according to the Orthodox canon, only unmarried priests had access to ruling positions in the Church [Pospielovsky 1984: 43-7]). Consequently, Renovationism was very much a grass-roots phenomenon. Paradoxically (or logically), the global rhetoric of the Renovationists was supported by primarily peripheral, local, activists. Although this observation can help us understand why the center-periphery pattern emerged, it does not explain intra-peripheral differences in Renovationist prevalence. In short, it is obvious that, before speculating on the role of parishioners in the movement, the geographical pattern of Renovationism should be linked with some clergy-based variations in the Church.

More specifically, the remainder of this chapter attempts to prove another suggestion: despite the movement's socialist rhetorics, its peripheral geography was determined by economic considerations of local clergy: Renovationism's principal promise to the priests, that of greater autonomy, had greater appeal among more prosperous parishes of the country.

In light of this discussion of the factual and theoretical weaknesses of previous conceptualizations, this study provides a third conceptualization. This is a center-periphery model in two senses. First, at the level of factual summarization, it highlights the geographical prevalence of Renovationists on the margins of the country as opposed to its historical European core. Figure A3.4, for instance, shows the lowest proportion of the Renovationist parishes in the central and Middle Volga dioceses surrounded by areas of growing Renovationist presence in all directions, including the European North. Second, at the level of theorization, the center-periphery model stresses the hierarchical opposition between the ruling center and the peripheral parishes. The Renovationist movement provided greater autonomy to regional units and ground-level parishes of the Church. The Renovationist attack on the top Church hierarchy and the promise of greater parish freedom was perhaps more appealing to the periphery of the country than to its central areas. To test my hypothesis, I analyzed the correlation between intra-peripheral differences in Renovationist prevalence and potential parish "separatism."

Having said this, I must again stress that, perhaps, my findings cannot be explained by one single factor, and that first the two theorizations must be included as well. First, the peripheral administrative authorities might have been more indifferent in religious and political matters, and the movement was not overly associated in public opinion with the Soviet regime. It is known that many Renovationist priests were honest people guided by the idea of the Church's renewal. Second, the central areas of the USSR did indeed have less experience with sectarian and schismatic movements than did the margins of the country (especially in the south). Finally, the settlement pattern in the less populated areas of the country did not provide much choice for believers in terms of parish affiliation (this idea is only partially explored in the rest of this chapter, and certainly deserves further inquiry).

State Subsidies

This section attempts to elaborate further on the principal finding of this chapter, namely the Renovationist movement's center-periphery pattern of geographical prevalence. The idea is to examine the correspondence between intra-peripheral differences in parish wealth and Renovationist prevalence. Overall, the Renovationists were more successful in the southern periphery of the country. Theoretically, this difference could be rooted in the specifics of parish income in the south, which were combined with differing effects of the 1917 revolution (it might have had a relatively less harmful effect on the southern flank of the country); however, I believe that the 1913 data are representative of other years for two reasons. First, the revealed patterns are strikingly uniform and unlikely to be subject to significant change. Second, statistics for 1912 reveal similar patterns.

The 1914 report of the Holy Synod's overprocurator (*Vsepoddanneishii Otchet* 1916: 149-60) provides an historical account of changes in parish (priests') income, particularly with regard to state subsidies. Since Peter the Great's failed attempt to issue a tax to replace the dominant payments for church services (*treby*), the state largely ignored the question of clergy income; payment for services was still the main, and often insufficient, source of income. Nicholas I in 1828 ordered the Holy Synod to find sources to finance the poorest priests. By the end of the 1830s all local priests were divided into 7 classes (*shtaty*) and, until 1860, were receiving growing subsidies from the state. However, after 1861 this growth was discontinued, and the state started to search for alternative, local sources of financing. The Rules of Local

Means, approved on March 24, 1873, identified the following items of local priest income: a) voluntary payment for services, b) church land profit, or its substitute in a different form, c) interests on bank accounts donated to churches and d) income from quit-rent items. Nevertheless, priests considered this insufficient and the Special Council (*Osoboe Prisutstvie*) failed to find new local sources of income. Instead, it recommended decreasing the number of parishes in the Empire; indeed, in the 23 years of its work 3,000 parishes were closed (pre-Soviet developments of this kind are usually ignored in popular post-Soviet discourses; see chapters that follow). Remarkably, at the same time state salaries were increased for priests in the borderlands of the Empire (for example, the west and the Baltics). By 1913, of the total number of parishes (41,270), only 76 percent (31,413) received state subsidies for priests. It is noteworthy that the highest state salaries were held by priests of the borderland provinces: Riga, Warsaw, Kholm (800-1500 rubles), followed by Turkestan (600 rubles), Finland and Yakutia (600 rubles), Far East (500-600 rubles), Belorussia and Lithuania (400-700 rubles), south-western Ukraine (300-500 rubles). The average for the remaining dioceses was above 300 rubles, while in some the state salary was only 100-180 rubles (e.g. almost one-tenth that in the 'strategically' important westernmost dioceses).[29]

After 1917 state subsidies to parish clergy ceased. Yet their legacy might have exercised continuing impact on the geography of Renovationism in the post-revolutionary period. As has been shown, before 1917 the Church was state institution. The borderland parishes were most privileged by the tsarist state, and this might have made them more loyal to the state in general. Therefore, if Renovationism was perceived as a state-sponsored development, then it follows that its largest support should come from the historically state-loyal borderland parishes.

Local Income

State subsidies were important, although not universal and certainly not the parish clergy's only source of income. This section considers so-called local income items. Since no geographical summary of pre-revolutionary local parish income differences in the Church is known to me, I must first analyze the available data.

Reports of the Holy Synod's overprocurator (*Vsepoddanneishii Otchet* 1914, 1916) provide statistics on income, expenditure, and fiscal balance of the Russian-State Church's dioceses (Table A3.4). When standardized by the number of parishes (churches) in each diocese, these data provide a basis for making geographical comparisons with the prosperity of parishes in different areas of the late Russian Empire.

Figure A3.11 shows the level of total income per church in dioceses of the Russian-State Church in 1913. By far the most prosperous parishes (judged by income) were in the dioceses with the two major cities, Moscow and St. Petersburg. The rest of the country can be divided into the following three categories: 1) prosperous parishes in dioceses of the historical center of Russia, between Moscow and St. Petersburg; 2) a prosperous southern belt of borderlands (southern Ukraine, northern Caucasus, Turkestan (southern Central Asia), Trans-Baikal; and 3) relatively poor dioceses between the central core and borderland crescent with two major clusters of low-income dioceses in Belorussia/Lithuania and the internal parts of western Siberia and south-eastern European Russia. It is worth mentioning that there is a correspondence between this income pattern and the pattern of religious dissidence discussed in Chapter 2. Chapter 4 will show its correlation with the geographical pattern of church property distribution.

Figure A3.12 shows the balance of an average parish in dioceses in 1912. Although the European core around the two capital cities had dioceses with the highest average remaining balance, the rest of the high-balance dioceses formed a northern-eastern belt which is in stark contrast to the parish income prevalence discussed above. Thus, the central European core, southern Ukraine, parts of the north Caucasus and eastern Siberia had both high income and high balance. In contrast, Belarus/Lithuania, south-eastern European Russia, and parts of southern Siberia had both low income and low balance. Presumably, the two parameters should correspond more closely, since balance is dependent on income (and expenditure). This non-correspondence of income and balance may mean a reversed relationship between them: income may be dependent on the remaining balance. It is important to look at the geographical particulars of income's categories (Table A3.5).

The Church as a whole in 1913 had the following income structure: salver dues (regular donations during service in church) — 14.4 percent; candle sales profit — 38.3 percent; quit-rent (*obrok*) items — 10.2 percent; donations to local churches — 19.1 percent; interest on capital of churches — 5.1 percent; miscellaneous income items — 12.8 percent. Patterns of each category's geographical prevalence exhibit remarkable regional patterns. Salver dues (Figure A3.13) provided a relatively high percentage of income in a latitudinal belt of dioceses stretching from Warsaw through Belarus to historical core of Russia (with notable exception of Moscow and St. Petersburg). The importance of salver dues declined, gradually and uniformly, southward and eastward, and had the lowest importance for the southern crescent of high income dioceses. In contrast, the pattern of candle sales income (Figure A3.14) seems almost reversed: more than half of the income of the southern crescent parishes came from candle sales. The importance of this income category declined, gradually and uniformly, towards the historical center of the country. Salver dues and candle sales together accounted for more than half of the total Church income. Unlike other categories of income, salver dues and candle sales are based on personal routine contributions of parishioners.

Unlike the southern, high-income parishes with their casual items, the northern high-balance parishes relied more on exceptional, periodical, items such as quit-rent (*obrok*)[30] (Figure A3.15), donations (Figure A3.16), and capital interest (Figure A3.17). They are exceptional in two senses. First, they were likely to be one-time and large payments, and second, they were exceptional in the sense that they were immediately and effectively eliminated by the Bolsheviks. However, the casual income items (such as candle sales) were relatively small continuing payments, which the Bolsheviks failed to eradicate.

It is unlikely that parishioners in the southern parishes were more prosperous than parishioners in the northern belt. Rather, two other factors should be cited. First, unlike the northern belt, the southern crescent is the area of contact with non-Slavic and non-Orthodox population: southern parishioners might not necessarily be more prosperous, but for nationalist reasons may be prone to be more generous than their northern counterparts. Second, for similar reasons the state used to privileged the borderlands; priests in these areas had greater governmental subsidies than in the rest of the country (*Vsepoddanneishii Otchet* 1916). Third, as Chapter 4 will show, the distribution of churches and Orthodox believers did not match up: the north had a relatively high number of churches and a relatively low density of believers per one church. Thus, an average parish income basis in the south was greater than one in the north. The settlement pattern should not be overlooked in this regard; while typical north European rural settlements were small, their counterparts in the south were the largest in the country.[31]

The difference between the southern and northern belt in amount and kind of income, perhaps, led the latter to the necessity of maintaining a high remaining balance, because its income base was narrower and less stable.

For a further discussion of links between high income and support of Renovationism, it is important to speculate on the divergent economies of the northern and southern belts. The general hardships brought by the 1917 revolution's aftermath and anti-religious laws of the Communists affected all parishes. Yet their harmful effect was arguably more severe for the northern parishes, since the main categories of their income, quit-rent, donations and capital interest, were all severed at once. In contrast, the southern (and central European) parishes relied on routine personal contributions which, though they certainly declined, could not be totally cut off.

In short, in late Imperial Russia the southern parishes were relatively more prosperous (judging by the level of income) than those in the north. While the Communist transformations most likely evened out this discrepancy, in relative terms the south continued to have a better income base.

In this light, the dominance of Renovationism in the southern, more prosperous, parts of the country's periphery seems reasonable since these parishes' desired greater autonomy and the Renovationist promised just that. This appeal to parishioners' desire for license would not work in the historical center because of geography. And the northern parishes could not wish greater freedom for their financial limitations.

Conclusion

Three points should be highlighted in this conclusion.

First, the Renovationist schism can be seen as a response to the mismatch between global aspirations of the ruling state and the national consciousness of Russian society. As can be seen in the failure to modernize the Church calendar, the Renovationists' preaching of supranational Christianity did not find a lay following. On the other hand, the movement was relatively more successful among local priests. Thus, the "liberation of Christ from the national embrace" can, paradoxically, be seen as a two-fold process: on the one hand, it uses a supra-national rhetoric while, on the other hand, its following is sub-national. In the similar fashion, as seen in the geographical pattern of the movement's prevalence, the rhetoric was focused on socialism, while local support was arguably based on economic considerations.

Second, it is clear that space deserves a greater appreciation among historians working in the field of Russian studies. This chapter shows that geographical factors are important to our understanding of some particulars of the Renovationist movement. Without attention to the spatial factor, the movement's initial failure to totally dominate the Church, its survival in the 1930s, and its final decline cannot be fully understood.

To previous conceptions of the geography of Renovationism, this chapter adds another, more nuanced notion of the movement based on center-periphery discrepancies. This pattern is important because it challenges some widespread assumptions of historians (such as Freeze 1995). Moreover it suggests a need for further investigation into the relationship between the Renovationist movement and such factors as regional separatist ideologies of different sorts, the legacy of sectarian and schismatic movements, the settlement pattern variations, and the parochialization of power of the peripheral executive authorities. Most important, as my analysis shows, the level of income in the parishes could be a factor affecting the regional patterns of Renovationism. The promise of greater autonomy for local parishes and opportunities for married priests was arguably more appealing for relatively stronger parishes. This chapter has analyzed pre-revolutionary geographical patterns of parish income and speculated on their possible influence on the regional geography of Renovationism.

Finally, there are avenues of possible further geographical inquiry in studies of Renovationism. A set of geographical questions has not been considered here, yet deserves mention. First, differences in the movement's trends at the national and local levels requires further investigation. Second, the specifics of the Renovationists' views of the diocesan division of the country, and their introduction of aggregated "metropolitan" divisions could be a topic of further analysis. Third, the foreign dimension of the movement, both outside the Russian Federation and the USSR, has been only briefly touched on by scholars (Roslof 1994: 234), even as new archival documents still surface.[32] Fourth, the Renovationist movement itself was not a monolithic whole, but rather fractured into three or four smaller unions whose comparative regional geography in the country remains unclear. All of these geographical dimensions of Renovationism will hopefully attract scholarly interest.

Chapter 3: Notes

1. Vvedenskii (1925, 21).
2. For historical accounts of the movement, see Kuznetsov (1956-9), Sergii (Larin) (1953-9), Levitin and Shavrov (1977), Roslof (1994).
3. The Tikhonite part of the Church included supporters of Patriarch Tikhon (elected in 1917, he ruled the Church until his death in 1924).
4. RTsKhIDNI (Rossiiskii Tsentr Khraneniia i Izucheniia Dokumentov Noveishei Istorii, now RGASPI) f. 17, op. 84, d. 309, ll. 124-140.
5. Evgenii Tuchkov was the head of the Secret Service's Department on Religious Affairs in the 1920s.
6. RTsKhIDNI f. 17, op. 60, d. 509, ll. 100-26; ibid., op. 87, d. 186 ll., 150-176. These data have been published in Roslof 1994, 211-2.
7. The journal had different titles. *Vestnik Sviaschennogo Sinoda Pravoslavnoi Rossiiskoi Tserkvi*, 1925 no.1: 15-16; 1926 no. 7; 1927 no. 2 (15). *Vestnik Sviaschennogo Sinoda Pravoslavnykh Tserkvei v SSSR*, 1928 no. 2: 8. Roslof (1994: 211-12) presents a summary table of most of these data. A modified and expanded version of this table is compiled for this chapter (Table A3.2).
8. The following state organizations controlled affairs of the Russian Orthodox Church at the time of the Renovationist movement (1922-46): the People's Justice Department's Section on Separation of the Church from the State and School (1918-24); the Central Executive Committee's Secretariat on Cult Issues (1924-29); the VTsIK Presidium's Permanent Commission for Cult Issues (1929-34); the USSR TsIK's Permanent Commission for Cult Issues (1934-38); no state body, only the special church section of the state security services, existed (1938-43); the Council for the Affairs of the Russian Orthodox Church (1943-65).
9. GARF (Gosudarstvennyi Arkhiv Rossiiskoi Federatsii) f. 5263, op.1; f. 6991, *opisi* 1-7.
10. GARF f. 5263, op. 1, d. 32, ll. 66-73.
11. Professor Edward E. Roslof, personal communication.
12. The GARF has a file listing Renovationist materials which were taken by the Council for the Affairs of the Russian Orthodox Church from the apartment of the movement's leader, A. Vvedenskii, in 1946 and destroyed on December 29, 1950 in accordance with the order of the Council's Chairman Karpov (GARF, f. 6991, op. 2, d. 82). Altogether, 103 folders (*dela*) were destroyed (of these, 15 contained diocesan materials with some possible statistics).

13. Traditionally, the diocesan division of territory in the Russian Orthodox Church coincides with the civil division; as a rule, parish boundaries are coincident with those of the civil division. At the same time, a diocese could contain more than one civil unit and vice versa.

14. Base maps can be found in Leasure and Lewis (1966), Central Statistical Board of the USSR (1927), Lorimer (1946).

15. A map of the statistical-administrative division of the country's territory for 1931 could be found in *Administrativno-Territorial'noe Delenie* (1931). A map for 1930 could be found in Santalov and Segal (1930).

16. Map digitizing work is laborious but unavoidable in the absence of a centralized database of historic-cartographic materials. It is worthwhile for specialists in Russian historical studies to share their cartographic resources, such as digitized maps, to avoid duplication of work.

17. GARF f. 5263 op. 2, d. 2, ll. 60-60ob., 77-77ob.

18. GARF f. 5263 op. 2, d. 2, ll. 63-65.

19. RTsKhIDNI f. 89, op. 4, d. 162, ll. 66-67, 141-142; *ibid.*, d. 171, ll. 1-4.

20. RTsKhIDNI f. 17, op. 84, d. 309, ll. 124-140.

21. There were several divisions in Renovationism. I was, unfortunately, unable to find any statistics that would compare them numerically or shed light on their regional specifics. It is possible that these divisions were limited primarily to the top leaders of the movement.

22. "By the end of 1926 the total figure for all 84 dioceses of the Renovationist Church, including the Ukraine and some 30 Renovationist parishes in North America, was 6,245 parishes... . This may be compared with some 30,000 parishes across the whole Soviet Union in the Patriarchal Church claimed by Metropolitan Sergii in 1930" (Pospielovsky 1984, 62), also Curtiss (1953).

23. GARF f. 5263 op. 1, d. 6, ll. 22, 25-26ob.

24. Strictly speaking, no Renovationist churches existed and could be closed prior to 1922.

25. GARF f. 5263 op. 1, d. 6, ll. 28-29.

26. GARF f. 6991 op. 1, d. 3, ll. 7-8 (also published by Mikhail Odintsov in *Istoricheskii Arkhiv*, 1994 (3)).

27. GARF f. 6991 op. 1, d. 3, ll. 7-8, ll. 137-9.

28. In Freeze's own words, "[p]redictably, conditions were particularly bad in Siberia" (Freeze 1995: 337), yet, as maps in this chapter show, the Renovationists were relatively successful there.

29. For additional accounts of Orthodox priests' status in the 18-19th centuries, see unique works of Freeze (1977, 1983) and his 1985 translation of Belliustin's *Description of the Clergy in Rural Russia: the Memoir of a Nineteenth-Century Parish Priest*.

30. Quit-rent (*obrok*) was common at the time of serfdom (before 1861). In addition to natural rent, in the end of 19th century it also included the rent for land.

31. The author is grateful to Professor Ihor Stebelsky (Canada) for this insight.

32. Such as *Russkaia Pravoslavnaia Tserkov'* (1996).

CHAPTER 4. PLAYING CHESS WITH CHURCHES: RUSSIAN ORTHODOXY AS RE(LI)GION[1]

The fight against religion must not be limited nor reduced to abstract, ideological preaching... .

Vladimir I. Lenin[2]

Historically and geographically, the Orthodox religion has been of the utmost importance to the Russian state and society (Chapter 2). In pre-1917 Russia the numerical growth of churches was steady (Figure 4.1), with Orthodoxy being the only religion represented locally in all regions of the late Russian Empire and its successor state the USSR (hereafter the Russian realm).[3] Thus, buildings of the Orthodox Russian-State Church (hereafter the Church) used to serve as the most visible landscape identifier of the realm. In dramatic contrast, the Bolsheviks, in their unprecedented crusade for the complete eradication of religion after 1917 closed, reused for secular purposes, or simply ruined thousands of Orthodox churches.

Although harsh Soviet anti-religious persecutions provoked the emergence of a vast number of works with the prime goal of shedding light on these practices and possibly attracting public attention to them, lack of data prevented the emergence of specific works dealing with the property dimension of the campaigns. Though generally written with the best of intentions, these early works have recorded numerous cases and events, often at the expense of analytical quality and accuracy of conclusions. They also contributed to the emergence of a myth of Communist anti-religious persecution. It is a myth in the sense that it overshadows the pre- and post-Communist religious manipulations. For many post-Soviet politicians in Russia, this myth explicitly requires the restoration of the pre-Soviet *status quo*. Here space is seen not as a process but as a status that could be restored (Chapter 1).

In addition, the contradictory tendencies within the Soviet anti-religious policies has also been neglected. A serious challenge to the early, "monolithic" view of Soviet history is the fact that within this period there were episodes when the state did allow new churches to be reopened.[4] The most recent scholarship is well aware of the inconsistensies of general Soviet religious policies. For example, for

Mikhail Odintsov (1994) the period of 1900-65 was not characterized by a continuous policy, but rather by a prevailing, peculiar, and ever changing mix of elements of different patterns of religious policy. In contrast, according to Anderson (1994), in the post-Stalin years (1953-93) state religious policy was characterized by continuing but gradually easing anti-religious activity. For Mikhail Shkarovsky (1999), there have already been ten major periods of the Soviet religious policy (Chapter 1).

Even if scholars disagree with one another over periodizations, these differences are important to the advancement of studies of state-church relations (hereafter the SCR). The first goal of this chapter is to contribute to this body of literature in two respects. First, so far no periodization of any kind has been provided for the specifical dimension of property in the SCR. This chapter attempts to fill this gap by relying on data from previously inaccessible archives in Russia. Second, it is important to put the Soviet campaigns in a larger historical context, revealing their predecessors in the tsarist state and successors in the newly independent republics. To do that, this chapter utilizes some under-studied tsarist reports on the status of the Church as well as some current but rare sources from Russia.

There are several explanations for the underestimation of the property topic in the studies of SCR. First, as a non-issue in a society with limited market relations, the very question of property has been left aside by Soviet scholars themselves. A study of the nationalization of monastic property by Zybkovets (1975) stands as a unique endeavor. Second, to embrace the topic of church property in Russia, one must not only pay attention to the Soviet period of history, but also consider the problems of the pre-Soviet period. Although the state of religion in Tsarist Russia has attracted scholarly attention,[5] it is difficult to cite a comprehensive work on church property which speaks to the Soviet and post-Soviet concerns with the (de)nationalization of property. Thus, conventional historical frameworks for research (such as "Soviet period") prove to be constraining in the studies of Church property and post-Soviet developments. In addition, such modern developments in Russia as the return of church property could justify the previous manipulations of cult places if their geographical particulars are ignored. Finally, the concept of region is usually ignored in the field: until recently, few works have focused on such place-specific topics as the study of particular churches or parishes in the context of their history, geography, or politics.

The second goal of this chapter is to apply the concept of geographical region to the study of SCR. Whereas historians have scrutinized periods of the state manipulation of the Church, regional variations in the state anti-religious policies have not attracted attention. The concept of region, perhaps a geographical equavalent of the historian's concept of period, remains an underutilized tool in studies of SCR. This chapter will show the importance of geographical (regional) reasoning in analysing SCR in the Russian realm. Presumably, in such an enormous and diverse country as the former Russian Empire/USSR, regional discrepancies within the Church did exist and were (and still are) significant, both statistically and politically. Different hypotheses explaining these discrepancies shall be tested.

The third goal of this chapter is to reveal the prognostic potential of church property statistics. My hypothesis is that the regional imbalance of church distribution excersizes a continuing legacy on other facets of the Church such as its believers, priests, dogmas, and, even schismatic nationalist aspirations. Whereas most scholars conceptualize the emergence of the Orthodox Churches in the newly independent republics of the former USSR in terms of state and/or popular nationalisms, this chapter suggests the spatiality of Russian Orthodoxy, as embodied in church buildings, is a factor for understanding Orthodox schisms and conflicts in the newly independent republics.

Hence, this chapter considers primarily the physical manifestation of the Church, its churches. First, I will summarize and analyze statistics on the state of church property in late Imperial Russia, then I will trace the changing geographical and political patterns of church property transfers in the USSR, and I will finally look at the continuing legacy of church property distribution for post-Soviet Orthodox internal and external politics.

CHURCH PROPERTY BEFORE 1917 AND RUSSIAN IMPERIALISM

Importance and Scope of Church Property

Ritual, or proper service, is of prime importance for Orthodox religious life, and is not conceivable without a special, physically extant building. Historically, Orthodoxy played a central role in Russian society, and the significance of its churches went well beyond the mere religious domain.

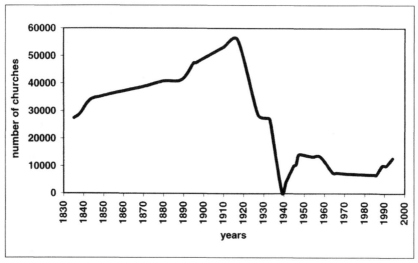

Figure 4.1. Number of Orthodox church buildings, the Russian Empire and the USSR, 1834-1994. Source: Sidorov (2000a: 209). Note: Figures for 1926-28 refer to RSFSR and for 1945-94 – to the ROCh's societies registered in the USSR and its successor states.

For example, whereas in modern countries the status of a settlement is usually defined by its population size and functional characteristics, in pre-revolutionary Russia, churches, more than anything else, defined the settlement type. There were differences among urban settlements: Moscow was often called the "first-altar city" (*pervoprestol'nyi grad*) because it had the main altar of the Church (the Assumption Cathedral in the Kremlin, Figure 2.4). The capital cities of provinces, as opposed to ordinary towns, were expected to have a major church or cathedral. Similarly, until the police reform of 1882 (and even after that), the addresses of people were linked to parish churches (e.g., "Moscow, specific parish, personal name") (Palamarchuk 1992: 11). In the same way, all rural settlements were traditionally divided into *derevnia* (churchless village) (*Slovar' Russkago Iazyka* 1895) and *selo* (rural settlement with church) with the intermediate *sel'tso* (small *selo* with estate, perhaps with its home church) and *sloboda* (big industrial settlement near a city) (Volin and Ushakov 1940: 270; Institut Russkogo Iazyka 1984: 73, 138).

Traditional Orthodox dogma requires "one bishop for one city" to avoid internal competition and disobedience. While the rural settlements tended to have just one church, this tradition resulted in the distinction of the so-called "sobor", or cathedral — the primary church of the local bishop in the cities. In the countryside, a priest's control over his parish often varied depending on the size of the settlement. It can be argued that in areas with a high ratio of Orthodox population per church there arose a greater opportunity for religious disobedience because a lower density of church buildings distances parish adherents from their priests. It is perhaps not a coincidence then that sectarian movements were stronger in the southern provinces (Safronov 1998), which also had the lowest density of churches relative to the Orthodox population. Thus, although it is not immediately visible, property distribution affected the Church, specifically with regard to its internal diversification and possibilities for control of parishioners.

In pre-revolutionary Russia, the Church[6] occupied the dominant position, often merging with the state to form an oppressive political-economic system. The Church legitimized the tsarist regime and the state protected the Church from external competition. This state support came primarily through the allocation of wealth. Along with land allocation, property provisions played a crucial role in state policies privileging the main Church.

Annual reports of the Russian Orthodox Church's Holy Synod's overprocurator provide a detailed picture of this dominance. According to the last pre-revolutionary report of 1914, the Church had the following property within the Empire (Table A4.1) (*Vsepoddanneishii Otchet* 1916, Sidorov 1998: 282-83). There were about 55,000 Orthodox churches in all. It is noteworthy that only one fifth of this number (11,000) were located in Ukraine. Provinces of the Empire in 1914 could be divided into the following groups according to the density of Orthodox churches (Figure A4.1). The highest density was in the historical European Russian core, especially in its northern part.[7] While a high density of churches in the western half of Ukraine can be attributed primarily to historical reasons (this area was among the first settled in the Russian realm), in the Baltics, Central Asia, Trans-Caucasia[8] and parts of Siberia, it is necessary to cite the colonialist aspirations of the Empire as an explanation for the high density of churches in these borderlands. The lowest level of church density characterizes three regions: first, the interior provinces in the area of the Urals; second, the provinces of Omsk and Tomsk in Western Siberia and the province of Semipalatinsk in Kazakhstan; third, and notably, the eastern Ukraine and southern European Russia.

The Geography of Orthodox Property by Its Type

In addition to over 23,000 chapels, the Church had about 55,000 thousand church buildings of various kinds with parish churches (41,000) constituting the largest component. Their geographical pattern, therefore, largely corresponds to that for all churches (Figure A4.2). The highest density was in the areas of northern European Russia (especially, Arkhangel'sk province), and the lowest in the southern rural areas (Kuban', eastern Ukraine).

A number of small churches in distant, declining, or priestless settlements were affiliated with a major parish church. Altogether, these "branch" churches accounted for about 5,800 buildings (Figure A4.3). The geographical prevalence of these "branch" churches also calls to mind the pattern on Figure A4.1, however, accentuating a north-south gradient formed by these churches. Most of them were located in the sparsely populated areas of the European North, with a gradual decline in prevalence southward. The southernmost (as well as westernmost and easternmost) borderlands show an increased prevalence of these affiliated churches. Perhaps this shows some similarities among these areas; while the European north was sparsely populated for physical-geographical reasons, the borderlands were the sociocultural equivalent of the physical desert. Since the Orthodox were minorities in these border areas, their sparse settlement pattern may have required more affiliated churches than in predominantly Slavic provinces. These areas were also zones of intense congregational transfers; the Church and the state presumably had an interest in keeping all buildings functional, despite declines in membership, and affiliations were a possible solution to such problems.

Monasteries and cemeteries accounted for about 2,000 structures each. Churches of these types differ from the others because of their longer history (Table 4.1). While average total construction time to build churches of all types was eighty-seven years, an average cemetery church would require 207 years, and a monastery church 180. Certainly, this table also reflects the changing demand for churches of these types.

The geography of monastic churches reflects the fact that many of them were built in different epochs, and in fact, in a state of a different scale (the original fifteenth-century Muscovite Russia had a relatively small territory, not reaching the margins of the Eastern European Plain, e.g. the Volga River, steppe belt, Caucasus). Three concentric circles could be identified: first, the Moscow core; then, an eastern crescent separating the Tatar-dominated Volga area; and finally, Trans-

Caucasia, a later frontier (Figure A4.4). In addition to defense considerations, monasteries were built in remote areas to provide seclusion
for the monks and to combat the wilderness — facts that should not be
dismissed in discussions of the geographical pattern of monastery
churches.

Table 4.1. Time of church property construction by type, 1913/1912.

Type	Number in 1913	Built in 1912	Of them, stone (%)	Years
Cathedrals	759	1	100	759
Cemetery	2067	10	30	207
Monastery	1985	11	72.7	180
Branch	5842	45	28.9	130
Edinoverie	541	5	40	108
Parish	40263	521	48.9	77
Home/state	2480	33	66	75
Movable	48	—	—	—
Missionary	49	—	—	—
Chapels	23288	203	21.2	115

Source: *Vsepoddanneishii Otchet* (1914: 6-7, 16-19), the author's calculations. Note: The last column shows the average number of years required for different types of church property to reach their 1913 size at
the rate of construction in 1912.

Unlike other types of churches, which are used by different generations, cemetery churches must be built as new cemeteries are developed. Therefore, the geography of cemetery churches reflects not only
the current status quo, but also the situation in all previous periods.
Figure A4.5 shows the pattern of cemetery churches in 1914, clearly
highlighting areas with a long history of settlement (Belarus, western
Ukraine, the central European part of Russia, and Trans-Caucasia).[9] A
similar pattern characterized the distribution of cathedrals (about 700
in 1914). Their high density in the borderlands in part can be attributed
to imperial colonization, but the population settlement pattern should
not be dismissed (Figure A4.6).

The remaining types of churches can be singled out as promoting the Church's territorial expansion. Missionary churches, of course,
did this explicitly. Most of them, however, were in central, not eastern,
Siberia, as well as some in southern Central Asia (Turkestan) (Figure

A4.7). Movable, field churches were also utilized in Turkestan, as well as in Finland (Figure A4.8). They were most likely army churches or temporary houses of worship.

Only one fifth of 23,000 chapels were built of stone (Table 4.1). Generally, chapels served as expected forerunners of churches in the sparsely populated peripheral areas of the realm. Chapels were most prevalent in the European north, stretching all the way to the Far East. In contrast to the pattern of missionary churches, chapels were not widespread on the non-Russian margins of the Empire (Figure A4.9).

With regard to the role of church buildings in the expansion of the Church and the state, it is important to look at the geographical pattern of home/state churches (Figure A4.10). Unlike other types of churches, these were not formally part of the Church, but were built and owned by private people or the state. State and private churches accounted for about 2,000 buildings in 1914. In late Imperial Russia, they had a relatively short construction time, and a higher proportion were built of stone (Table 4.1), which might reflect not only their better financing, but also their political importance. Figure A4.10 shows that most of the home/state churches were located in the borderlands with high religious mobility.

Finally, 541 churches were of Edinoverie affiliation (schismatic Old Belief communities that formally accepted the jurisdiction of the main Church, yet made no changes in their service).

Although many buildings of the Church were erected by money collected in parishes, the state provided significant selective support for church construction. The relatively high density of churches of some kind along the southern flank of the country most likely indicates the imperialist functions of these buildings and certainly the nationalism of ethnic Russian residents there. In contrast, the interior, protected areas of the country had the lowest densities.

The close link between the Church and the state was forged during the very foundation of Russian Orthodoxy based on the Byzantine model. Historically, this connection with the state was generally beneficial for the Church. Yet at times of change, the church's close association with the state could become its Achilles heel, as in posttsarist Russia. For the remainder of this chapter, it is important to note that, contrary to popular belief, manipulation of the Church's property was not a Communist innovation, but already a common practice in imperial Russia (Chapter 2).

THE SOVIET POLITICS OF CHURCH PROPERTY TRANSFERS[10]

The First Wave of Church Closures:
Political Motivation and Prime Rural Targeting

After the Revolution, the new Bolshevik authorities immediately issued a series of decrees targeting the Church. Lenin's decree of November 8, 1917, nationalizing all land, made it illegal for the Church or parish priests to own land. The decree of December 11, 1917 confiscated all of the Church's educational institutions; those of December 17 and 18, 1917 denied legality to Church marriages; that of January 16, 1918 expelled the clergy from the armed forces;[11] and that of January 20, 1918 canceled state subsidies to the Church. Finally, a decree published on January 23, 1918 separated the Church and the state and nationalized all Church property (Mitrofanov 1995: 5).[12]

Although these legal provisions formally separated religious and civic matters, the state continued its assault on church property. The first major attack on churches started in 1922, formally to find resources to fight the famine (Figure 4.2). However, analysts argue that the first wave of the Church property closures was actually an attack

Figure 4.2. "Famine-spider strangles the peasantry of Russia: the gold of churches must go for saving the hungry from death" (poster, Russia, the 1920s). Source: Kirichenko (1992: 207), used by permission. This propaganda poster shows a map of the European part of Russia with the region of Volga shaded in black. The sign in the center reads "Famine."

on the Church and that the famine was only a convenient excuse (Nezhnyy 1993d). The rural churches perhaps were the prime targets, and the eastern and Central Asian, less-urbanized part of the country suffered most (Table A4.2; Figure A4.11).[13]

The Second Wave (1931-34):
Socio-Economic Reasons and Urban Focus

A second wave of church closures was carried out in the early 1930s. In contrast to the political objectives of the first wave of the Church property closures, the second attack had arguably both direct and indirect socio-economic motivations. After the final 1927 declaration of the Church's loyalty to the Soviet state, control over the main Church was no longer a prime political issue. The Church, therefore, came to be seen primarily as a potential resource of material goods for building the new world within the country. During the late 1920s, and especially in the early 1930s, the previous rhetoric about a global Soviet union was replaced by the ideology of the superiority of the USSR in international economic and technological competition. Its domestic implications were industrial modernization, urbanization, collectiviza-

Figure 4.3. Removal of bell from the belfry of the Holy Week (Strastnoi) monastery in Moscow, the 1930s. Photo by A. Sheykhet. Source: Kirichenko (1992: 207), used by permission.

tion of agriculture, and the accompanying politico-architectural reconstruction of the landscape.

The property transfers that followed (demolitions, closures, recycling, and juridical re-allocations) were an important part of these processes. Their effect on churches was devastating. Rare metals from church bells, precious stones and the debris of demolished churches were recycled in new constructions; gold and precious stones were exported to finance modernization; and empty buildings were used to house new rural-urban migrants or new enterprises and offices (Figure 4.3).

Table A4.2 and Figure A4.12 show the percentage of churches closed between 1931 and 1933 in the Russian Federation.[14] In this period, in contrast to the first wave of church closures, urban areas were most affected. These areas — the Moscow-Leningrad core, central Volga, the Urals — were the main urban regions of the USSR. Was this a sign that there were too few churches left in the countryside to continue the closures there?

My hypothesis is that Ukraine initially lagged behind the USSR as a whole in the number of churches closed. In 1926, explaining the relative lack of success in Ukraine, the main Soviet anti-religious theoretical journal *Antireligioznik* cited several factors (Livanov 1926: 39-47). According to the journal, Ukraine was one of the central stages of the civil war, and this delayed, until 1920, beginning of implementation of the laws on separation of state and church. Furthemore, the relative complexity of social, religious and ethnic composition of Ukraine resulted in tensions that further delayed until 1924 anti-religious work. Some other arguments could be added.

First, the Ukrainian dioceses were a potential challenge to the main Church, and the state could be interested in using the autocephalous (independent) Ukrainian Church in attempts to weaken the overall power of the Church. There is some archival evidence that in 1922 the commission on separation of state and Church had, at least, serious doubts about whether to support autocephalists.[15] However, by the 1930s the main Church had already been suppressed and this hypothesis might be wrong about the second wave of church closures. Hewryk also indicates that in the case of Kiev the assault on church property was conceived in the early 1930s (Hewryk 1982: 7). Second, Ukraine was the breadbasket of the USSR. In 1929 the secret Anti-Religious Commission of the Central Committee of the All-Union Communist Party of Bolsheviks specifically recommended that churches in rural areas not be closed during harvest season lest the combined resistance of peasants distract them from their work.[16] Third, the same commission also recommended that church closures be conducted very carefully in the borderland areas of the USSR.[17]

Unfortunately, I failed to find in the archives figures similar to those for the RSFSR to prove my hypothesis for other republics. These regional statistics have yet to surface.

The Third Wave (1936-38):
Totalitarian Motivations and Regional Victims

In any event, in Ukraine the third wave of church closures started earlier and was most harmful. Hryhor Luzhnyts'kyi provides indirect support for my hypothesis. Drawing on data of Mytrophan Yavdas, he states that

> "[i]n the years 1934-36, the Soviet government intensified its drive against Ukrainian churches, chapels and monasteries, and other priceless monuments of Ukrainian culture... . Altogether, the Soviet government destroyed in 1934-36 about 75 to 80 percent of all churches in Ukraine... . According to official statistics compiled by the 'Union of Fighting Atheists', the number of closed churches in Ukraine was given by years: in 1924-25 – 46 churches closed; 1926 — 28 ; 1927 — 58; 1928 – 97; 1929 – 136; 1930 – 234; 1931 – 350" (Luzhnyts'kyi 1960: 41, 43, 44).[18]

A state archival source provides the following percentages of all religious buildings existing in 1917 that had been closed by April 1, 1936: the USSR as a whole — 57 percent, the RSFSR – 51 percent, Belarus – 78 percent, Ukraine – 59 percent, Armenia – 86 percent, Azerbaijan – 87 percent, Georgia – 79 percent, Uzbekistan – 62 percent, Kyrgyzstan – 62 percent.[19] Thus, quite rapidly, Ukraine had a larger proportion of closed religious buildings than the Russian Federation. This may mean that many of them were not demolished, but closed or just not functioning.[20] By Sept. 1, 1936, 28 percent of all pre-revolutionary churches were still functioning in the USSR as a whole, 36 percent in the RSFSR, and only 9 percent in Ukraine. This data should not be misinterpreted: non-functioning churches were not necessarily officially closed, and, in such circumstances, were not supposed to be demolished or reutilized. Unlike other major regions of the USSR, among churches not closed officially, Ukraine had more non-functioning churches than functioning ones (75 percent versus 27 percent in the RSFSR, for instance).[21]

Most likely it was not a preventive strategy to help save churches, but rather the opposite, an attempt by local authorities to prove their loyalty to Moscow and find ways to close churches without the required approval of the federal Cult Commission.[22] Paradoxically, this may have helped many such churches to survive: churches officially not closed (e.g., with the approval of the Commission) could not be demolished or their demolition was given second priority. More than that, invoking the laws and decrees of the time, the Chair of the All-Union Cult Commission Krasikov warned the Ukrainian VTsIK that eventually "these churches must be returned to believers." He stressed that in Ukraine the numerous non-functioning churches (together with the officially closed but unused ones) possessing the "church's look," provide a fruitful ground for the "anti-Soviet elements" and stimulate the agitation for the churchs' return to believers.[23] Many churches were initially closed on a seasonal basis, to ensure the storing of wheat harvests, while the parish was still taxed as if the church were functioning.[24] Of all the republics of the USSR, the Commission received the most requests for permission of home services from Ukraine, surely a result of "the great percentage of closed churches in the republic."[25] The sketchy archival data available on church closures in Ukraine's settlements of different size[26] allow us to suggest the following generalization: in the smaller and more peripheral places, church demolitions started later and were less significant.

The third major wave of church closures between 1936 and 1938 coincided with other great totalitarian purges. What mattered to the state was the extinction of all religion, and, since 1936, state statistics had often started to combine not only all strands of Orthodoxy, but also all types of denominations. The year 1939 was the worst in the history of the Church. Some scholars believe that in this year, in the whole of the USSR, there were only 200-300 open Orthodox churches (Davis 1995: 13) or just above 100 functioning Orthodox churches (Chumachenko 1999: 10). In the diocese of Kiev, for instance, of 1,600 churches in 1917 only two were functioning at the time of the German occupation in 1941 (Mykorskiy 1951).[27] Meanwhile, the 1937 population census indicated that at least 42.3 percent of the population of the USSR still considered themselves Orthodox.[28]

Land Acquisitions, German Invasion, and the Church's Survival (1939-43)

Despite the disastrously low number of open churches by 1939, on the eve of Hitler's attack in 1941, the number of functioning churches in the USSR had already grown to 4,225. These statistics were released by the Soviet embassy in London to counter criticism of Soviet religious suppression voiced by their newly acquired allies, the British (Davis 1995: 17). This seemingly incredible increase was actually a result of the territorial acquisitions of the Soviet Union: over 90 percent of the churches were in the western borderlands annexed in 1939-1940 (western Ukraine and Belarus, Moldova, and the Baltics). As the discussion of pre-revolutionary property distribution has shown, these areas always had a relatively high proportion of churches of all kinds.

Paradoxically, the Church was saved from total extinction by the Germans who, in 1941, opened their eastern front against the USSR. The new priorities distracted the state's attention from religious matters, and (after 1939) anti-religious assaults began to ease. In addition, the new authority allowed an Orthodox revival in the areas of German occupation in the western European part of the country, and many closed churches were reopened (see Alexeev and Stavrou 1976, Fireside 1971). An inspector for the Council for the Russian Orthodox Church Affairs gave the figure of 7,547 churches opened in the occupied territories between 1941 and 1945 (Davis 1995: 22).

First Revival in 1943-48

The final impact of the German invasion was Stalin's own decision to regain the support of Orthodox believers. A revival of the Church (in the post-war period the main Church was known as the Russian Orthodox Church, hereafter the ROCh) was allowed after 1943. In this year the formerly occupied areas began to be reincorporated into the USSR and Stalin had to decide how to proceed with the reopened churches there.[29]

Yurii Degtiarev, in his provocative article "Did Stalin open churches?" notes that the local authorities of the frontier regions started church returns as early as 1941 (Degtiarev 1995: 130-43). According to Degtiarev, Soviet government Head Molotov, suggested to the Chair of the Council for the Affairs of the ROCh, Karpov, that he rely on "expediency" and "necessity," rather than laws and juridical acts in making decisions about church returns. Degtiarev cites many examples of inconsistencies and contradictions among the actions of national and local authorities; "local authorities in some regions were more active in closing than opening churches." In 1946-47 deconstructions of empty churches for building materials without official approval of the Council for ROCh Affairs were indeed a widespread practice (Chumachenko 1999: 73). Unfortunately, Degtiarev has not provided geographical particulars, only mentioning that the number of Orthodox communities declined in the Baltics, Moscow, Volyn', Brest, Grodno and other oblasts. These were all areas of German occupation and/or warfare, and, consequetly, of post-war shortages of building materials.

My archival findings allow a clarification of the geographical pattern of church return in the post-war period. Table A4.3 and Figure A4.14 show the change in church density between 1946 and 1948 (Sidorov 1998: 285). If Stalin's revival of the Church was a reaction to the German invasion, then different trends in the formerly occupied territories should not be overlooked. While Ukraine, Belarus, and Moldova had the highest increase in the number of churches in this period, the western Russian lands adjacent to them were the only areas losing churches. This pattern most likely was a result of the church imbalance on the western margin (it simply had remaining buildings to be reopened); yet the fact that the number of churches in the westernmost Russian regions were not stagnant, but *declining*, warrants further investigation into Stalin's religious "revival."

My hypothesis is that this pattern reflects Stalin's ambivalence about the ROCh (Molotov's "expediency" and "necessity"). On the one hand, he needed support, especially in the non-Russian republics (and these republics were leaders of the revival, with the exception of Latvia). On the other hand, he still wanted to punish the formerly occupied areas for any cooperation with the Nazis (this was most certainly the case with Latvia). Ukraine was again relatively privileged in this period of "playing chess with churches" — whereas the adjacent Russian territories were losing churches, it was gaining them. Certainly this trend had variations at the level of oblasts in Ukraine (in western Ukraine, the growth in church numbers could, in part, be attributed to the forcible incorporation of the Uniate — Greek Catholic — Church into the ROCh in 1946), yet a growing difference between Ukraine and western parts of the Russian Federation is visible.

1949-66: New Assault

In the period 1949-1957 (Table A4.4., Figure A4.15) the total number of churches declined again (from 14,457 to 13,381 churches).[30] This trend started when Stalin was still in power and continued after his death in 1953. This time the western republics were losing churches yet, again, not in the westernmost areas, which were to be fully incorporated into the Soviet Union with the Russification of their residents. This decline was minor, however, compared to Khrushchev's 1958-66 assault, when the Church lost about 40 percent of its buildings (Table A4.5) (Sidorov 1998: 287-88). Figure A4.16 shows the density of churches in 1958, before the attack. Clearly the western areas of Ukraine and Moldova, as well as Estonia, were leaders. Although these countries seemingly were the prime victims of the assault (Figure A4.17), the west of European Russia was also targeted. Nevertheless, in the end the western areas, including Ukraine, still had the highest church density in 1966 (Figure A4.18).

1966-86: Period of Stagnant Oppression

In the Brezhnev period of stagnation this declining trend continued until the beginning of *perestroika*. Historically, the era with the second lowest total number of churches in the USSR was reached in 1986-88, when there were only about 6,740 registered communities. However, this figure almost doubled in succeeding years, reaching 12,800 in 1994 (Table A4.5) (ibid.). The territorial imbalance in church distribution in favor of the western margin (especially Ukraine) again, paradoxically, allowed it to remain the main victim as well as the final beneficiary of the process (Figures A4.19 and A4.20).

1986 and after: Uneven Revival

With the rise to power of Mikhail Gorbachev, the growth in the number of parishes in 1986-91 was characteristic of most Slav-dominated oblasts of both the Russian Federation and Ukraine (Figure A4.21). The western parts of Ukraine (and Moldova) were, again and again, the leaders, even in contrast with the eastern parts of Ukraine. Clearly it was a legacy of the previous uneven "play with churches."[31] Despite their relatively high number of parishes in the post-war period, and because of the relatively "mild" nature of Khrushchev's assault on churches (most of them were perhaps only closed, not destroyed as in the 1930s), these borderland areas had the greatest potential for growth at the time of *perestroika*.

It is interesting to note that in the areas which did not experience the process, Kazakhstan and Central Asia, there was no significant increase in the number of Orthodox churches during this period. The presence of Estonia and Latvia in the same category is somewhat unexpected. As mentioned earlier, the Baltics, very much like the western parts of Ukraine, were late-comers to the USSR and escaped the purges of the 1930s (as well as Khrushchev's assault). Perhaps they did not have many "church resources" left for *perestroika*-inspired growth. In addition, certain political and personal reasons were important for the *perestroika* pattern. Whereas nationalism and associated constraints on the development of Orthodox communities were characteristic of the Baltics well before their final independence (after 1991), the ROCh was more fortunate in Lithuania, perhaps because of the role of their charismatic bishop, Khrisostomus, and some local Communist Party leaders. Finally, the relative lagging of such areas as Moscow and the European North (including Leningrad-St. Petersburg) in the process of Orthodox revival during *perestroika* is remarkable. Most likely it was a result of their somewhat privileged position during the post-war period; they might not have sufficient "church resources" left to exhibit a growth in the number of parishes equal to other areas of the country. On the other hand, the Baikal and Far East dioceses, have never had many churches, and for these areas the establishment of new communities meant construction of new churches. Also, their remote position within the country should not be overlooked.

By 1991 the westernmost parts of Ukraine, Moldova, and the Baltics (with the exception of Latvia) retained their status as strongholds of the ROCh. In the Russian Federation as well the western European sectors had relatively more parishes (Figure A4.22).

The pattern of parish dynamics described for the *perestroika* period (1986-91) continued in 1991-94, although in exaggerated form. Areas of loss for the ROCh included not only the Uniate western Ukraine, but also Estonia and Latvia (in notable contrast to growth in the former Communist-governed Lithuania) (Figure A4.23). There was also a decline in the number of parishes in the central European oblasts west of Moscow; a likely result of registration and check-up of already existing communities. Yet this pattern warrants further investigation. Another noteworthy development was the leading position in this post-*perestroika* growth of some Siberian oblasts. The overall density pattern, however, remains the same; the western edge of the former USSR has a higher density of parishes than the rest of the country. The legacy of the Soviet "playing chess with churches" is still present within the former Soviet space (Figures A4.24 and A4.25, Table A4.6).

LEGACIES OF THE SOVIET RE(LI)GION

Church property distribution possesses not only a certain geographic inertia, also has its own power potentialities. Some geographic characteristics of the ROCh regarding its ruling elite and schismatic fractures reveal political legacies of the uneven distribution of church holdings in the realm.

Safronov has compiled data on the areas of origin of the ruling elite (bishops) of the Church in 1916 and in 1943-97 (Safronov 1998: 116-128; see also Mitrokhin and Timofeeva 1997). The contrast between the two periods is striking. Not dominating before 1917, Ukraine and Belarus (together with Moscow) formed the three leading regions of origin of bishops in the ROCh in the Soviet time. The most important change during the Soviet era was the significant increase in the number of bishops from Western Ukraine. In the 1950-70s, the number of bishops from Ukraine as a whole was disporportionally high in the ROCh, constituting 25-30% of the total. Even now the proportion of "Ukrainian" bishops of the ROCh on the territory of the Russian Federation is about 10%. Safronov offers three explanations for this dramatic dominance of Ukraine, especially western Ukraine: traditionally high religiosity of people, the forced transfer from the jurisdiction of the Roman-Catholic Church after 1946, and location of the majority of still open churches in the USSR there.

The collapse of the former Soviet Union had an important immediate implication for the ROCh: many, if not the majority, of its parishes turned out to be located abroad — outside of the Russian Federation. Nationalistic dimensions notwithstanding, the relative surplus of churches could be suggested as one of the factors explaining the resurgence of Ukrainian religiosity. Whereas in the Russian Federation most churches had been closed before the war and never reopened, with many being simply demolished or in a state of ruin, most church closures in Ukraine were a postwar phenomenon still in the memory of living generations. In addition, relatively few churches were demolished after the war, with closed yet physically extant churches serving as a constant reminder of the brutalities of the Soviet ("Russian") power. In short, the prevalence of churches could be one factor explaining relatively high post-Soviet religiosity and, eventually, nationalism in Ukraine.

The relative surplus of church buildings could also be one of the factors behind the diversity of Orthodox Churches in Ukraine (currently, four Orthodox Churches function there). First, the majority of Orthodox parishes keep a juridical affiliation with the ROCh under auspices of the Ukrainian Orthodox Church-Moscow Patriarchate (UOCh-MP) with about 7,000 parishes (*Religioznye Ob'edineniia* 1996: 82) (Figure A4.26). The Ukrainian Orthodox Church-Kievan Patriarchate (UOCh-KP) (Figure A4.27) is a second major Church, with 1,300 parishes (ibid.).[32] Third is the Ukrainian Greek Catholic Church (UGCCh), or the Uniate Church (no parish statistics available) (Figure A4.28).[33] Fourth is the Ukrainian Autocephalous Orthodox Church with 1,200 parishes (*Religioznye Ob'edineniia* 1996: 82).[34]

Due to their respective historical complexities, discussion of religious and political differences between these churches is beyond the frame of this study and can be found elsewhere (Markus 1995: 163-181). However, their geographies are relevant. According to Khmilevsky, the competing Churches tend to dominate in different areas of Ukraine; the Moscow-affiliated branch in the east, the Greek-Catholics in the west, and the Kievan Patriarchate in between, in Kiev and southward (separate data for the Autocephalous Orthodox Church are not available) (Khmilevskii 1993). Most likely, this estimation is based on qualitative data. Statistics about churches (Markus 1995: 175), summarized in Table A4.7, however, do not confirm this model. Contrary to Khmilevsky's conclusion, all three Churches are dominant in the west of Ukraine (Figures A4.26, A4.27 and A4.28). This pattern is clearly a continuing legacy of the Soviet past, with its extremely uneven church distribution.

The imbalance of church property is also an important factor for international relations within the former USSR. Table 4.2 shows the number of Orthodox communities in the republics of the former USSR in post-*perestroika* years. In 1993 and 1994, the Ukrainian part of the ROCh (the Ukrainian Orthodox Church-Moscow Patriarchate, or the UOCh-MP) was numerically larger than the ROCh (5,701 parishes vs. 5,290 respectively). If other Orthodox Churches in Ukraine are added, Orthodoxy in Ukraine would become numerically larger than in any other part of the former USSR (about 60 percent of all Orthodox parishes in the former USSR would be located in Ukraine).

Table 4.2. Status of Orthodox Churches in the successor states of the USSR, 1993 and 1994, number of parishes.

Orthodox Church	Jan. 1, 1993	Jan., 1994	% of Total
UOCh-MP (Ukraine)	5,490	5,701	31.9
ROCh (Russia)	4,566	5,290	29.6
UGCCh (Ukraine)	2,807	2,897	16.2
UOCh-KP (Ukraine)	1,763	1,892	10.6
UAOCh (Ukraine)		281	1.6
ROCh (Minsk diocese)		850	4.7
ROCh (Kishinev diocese)		650	3.6
ROCh (Alma-Ata diocese)		102	0.6
ROCh (Riga diocese)		87	0.5
ROCh (Vilnius diocese)		82	0.5
ROCh (Tallinn diocese)		63	0.4
Total:	14,626	17,895	100

Sources: *Nauka i Religiia* (1993 (6): 14-15); the Ukrainian Committee on Religious Affairs, unpub. data, 1983; Markus (1995: 170); Davis (1995: 111).

The current numerical lead of Ukrainian Orthodoxy has a long pre-history (Sidorov 1998: 290). Throughout the post-Soviet period, the gap between Ukraine and the rest of the country was as significant as it was in 1993. With minor variations, the proportion of Ukrainian parishes in the former USSR stayed at approximately 60 percent; with a maximum of 63.7 percent in 1953 (Table A4.8). This continuity serves, perhaps, as an example of how the territorial dimension of the Church, its building distribution, shapes socio-historical processes.

The imbalance in distribution of church property makes Ukraine a highly important part of the ROCh. In a certain sense, ROCh's property in Ukraine often serves as a hostage in bilateral politics between Ukraine and Russia. To illustrate this point, it is enough to see the special position the UOCh-KP occupies among all Churches alternative to the ROCh. The UOCh-KP conducts a policy of opening parishes on the territory of Russia, with three bishops currently residing in Russia. Although not yet widespread, this Ukrainian alternative to Russian Orthodoxy is significant. The UOCh-KP serves as a last refuge for many alternative priests. For instance, the famous human rights activist father Gleb Yakunin, expelled from the ROCh, has since joined the UOCh-KP. If this trend continues the UOCh-KP may be perceived as an annoying alternative to the ROCh in Russia over time. Backed by the Ukrainian authorities (especially when Leonid Kravchuk was the Ukrainian president), the position of the UOCh-KP is also strengthened by the church imbalance, because the significant property of the ROCh in Ukraine serves as a "hostage" in periods of attacks on the branches of the UOCh-KP in the Russian Federation.

The Soviet-era pattern of church-density, with the western regions dominating, is gradually being eroded. Since relatively high growth has occurred over the last few years in Russia and not in Ukraine alone, one might expect that the legacy of this density gradient will gradually diminish. At this point, however, the numerical dominance of Ukrainian Orthodoxy still has an important geopolitical potential underestimated by analysts. Two poles, the patriarchates of Moscow and Constantinople, determine the current balance of interests in world Orthodoxy. If the Ukrainian Churches were united, the number of parishes of all Orthodox Churches in Ukraine would make it the leading Orthodox country in the world.

The legacy of the imbalance of church property distribution is again clearly visible here. These themes certainly require further investigation.

Conclusion

Despite the central importance of church buildings for Orthodox life as well as for state religious politics before, during, and after the Soviet era, the issue of church property remains a neglected topic in studies of the Russian Orthodox Church. Despite the dominance of historians in the field, no major survey work is available on state-church relations that covers the late-Imperial, Soviet and post-Soviet periods. This chapter contibutes to previous historical studies by providing a wider and more detailed periodization of the SCR with regard to its property dimension.

As some previous studies have shown, church manipulation by the Soviet state was much more historically nuanced than is widely known. Historically, the Soviet authorities not only closed church buildings but also opened them at certain times. This chapter adds a regional dimension to these new findings. At the risk of exaggeration, one may even say that throughout much of the post-war period the Church was a *regional phenomenon* because the majority of its churches concentrated in the lately acquired, westernmost borderlands of the

USSR (Moldova, Ukraine, Belarus, and the Baltics).

A geographical account of this historical match between religion and region ("re(li)gion") is long overdue. Both closures and returns of churches were affected by the regional political aspirations of the state. The legacy of this territorial imbalance in the geography of remaining church property exercises a continuing, yet not well known impact on the Church. This geographical imbalance manifests itself, for example, in certain regional imbalances existing among the ROCh' elite. Another example is the internal and external religious status of Ukraine where the imbalance of property distribution contributes to domestic and foreign religious conflicts. This legacy is still alive, even as leaders are chosen and pass away and churches disappear and return. Entanglement with the state remains the Russian Orthodox Church's strongest and yet its weakest feature. This most important unresolved problem of the Church (Odintsov 1994) suggests the real possibility that the post-Soviet reversal of Communist anti-religious practices could justify previous practices and also produce new injustices.

Chapter 4: Notes

1. A version of this chapter was presented at the Annual Meeting of the Association of American Geographers in Charlotte, North Carolina, in April 1996. The author is grateful to the participants at this convention for their useful criticism. Professor Ihor Stebel'sky (Canada), for instance, should be credited for an insight into the correlation between the church property's regional prevalence and the settlement pattern. A version of this chapter was also published in *Historical Geography* (Sidorov 2000a), and I am grateful to the anonymous reviewers for their comments.

2. Lenin (1933, 14).

3. The Russian Orthodox Church is still by far the largest organization in the realm with about 50% of all organizations registered. In absolute terms, its loss of church property was far greater than that of all other religions in the realm combined. For example, in 1926 in 29 provinces of the Russian Federation there were 1,003 closed Orthodox churches (or 5.4 percent of the total). For other religions these figures were smaller: Orthodox Old Believers — 27 (2.8 percent), Catholics — 6 (6.8 percent), Lutherans — 6 (3.6 percent), Muslims — 29 (3.1 percent), Judaists — 10 (4.3percent), Evangelicals – none closed, Baptists — 5 (6.4 percent), others — 2 (1.5 percent) ("Statistika Religioznykh Ob'edinenii" 1926: 61-62). Comprehensive comparative statistics are not available at this point, allowing us to ignore the interconfessional dimension of the topic.

4. For the first truly analytical approach to the study of the specifically anti-religious campaigns, see Pospielovsky (1988).

5. For example, Smolitsch (1964-91).

6. For simplicity, the contemporary Russian Orthodox Church is considered here as a successor of the pre-revolutionary Church, although the issue remains subject to debate among the many Orthodox Churches in post-Soviet Russia (see Sidorov 1998).

7. The density pattern reflects different settlement size. One settlement usually had one church, and the rural settlements in northern European Russia were generally much smaller than those in the south.

8. The data on Trans-Caucasia does not include Armenian churches.

9. As noted, the geography of cemeteries reflects not only the current status quo, but rather the cumulative effects of all previous periods. Therefore, this map could be more accurate even if the churches

are related not to the contemporary (ca. 1913) population, but to territory.

10. Unfortunately, no authoritative source of statistics exists for 1917-1957. In this chapter, this gap is filled by my own findings in the Russian archives. The State Archive of the Russian Federation (GARF) has several collections of relevant documents (f.5263, op.1; f.6991, op.1-7). As a result, this period is considered in greater detail than the better known period of 1957-91.

In reporting these statistics, it is important to note that church density for the pre-revolutionary years was calculated relative to the regional Orthodox population and, for the Soviet period, due to lack of religious statistics, to the Slavic population (defined as Russians, Ukrainians, Belarusians, and Moldovans). This gives somewhat distorted figures for areas such as the Baltics or the Volga region. Yet, in a country like Russia, with its enormous territorial, ethnic and religious discrepancies, it would be a mistake to utilize such common measures of density as per capita of total population or per unit area.

Second, for most of the Soviet period, data on church buildings almost always coincide with registered communities of the Russian Orthodox Church, because availability of a church building was an important pre-condition for a community's registration. Lack of buildings frequently led to communities existing without registration. In *perestroika* times this situation has been reversed: many communities are registered without any present building. Still, the "church imperative" (meaning the registration requirement of obtaining a church) is important for Orthodox believers. In general, the Russian Church's glory is its rites, and liturgy in a physically extant church is essential in Orthodoxy (Chapter 2).

11. As in some other countries, the army of the Russian Empire had Orthodox chaplains.

12. A full collection of documents pertaining to the separation of the state and the Church can be found in Gidulianov (1926).

13. Another indirect result of this first major assault on churches was the rapid initial success of the Communist-backed Renovationist schism in 1922. The main Church was certainly weakened by the attack on its property, although the quick transfer of about 70 percent of all Orthodox churches to the Renovationists could be considered a lesser evil than closure and eventual decay. By 1925 most parishes abandoned Renovationism, and it became a minor branch within the Church (see Sidorov 1998: 284; Chapter 3).

14. The RSFSR at that time was significantly larger than its cur-

rent successor, including such areas in Central Asia as Kazakhstan (see Sidorov 1998: 284).

15. RTsKhIDNI f. 17, op.112, d. 443a, l.3ob.

16. RTsKhIDNI f. 17, op. 113, d. 871, l. 33. Notes of meeting on May 18, 1929.

17. RTsKhIDNI f. 17, op. 113, d. 871, l. 36. Notes of meeting on May 29, 1929.

18. For further reading, see Lypkivsky (1959), Mydlowsky (1962), *First Victims* (1953), Mykorskiy (1951).

19. A report of the Cult Commission of the VTsIK, GARF f. 5263, op.2, d. 10; the author's calculations. Data for the RSFSR, Armenia, and Georgia are not complete (see also Odintsov 1994: 36). Significant regional variations observable within the RSFSR: only about 1 percent of all pre-revolutionary churches functioned in Yakutia and the Far East, while 61 percent — Ivanovo oblast, above 50 percent – in Gorky oblast, Tatarstan, and Moscow oblast (GARF f. 5263, op. 2, d. 10, ll. 41-42).

20. In the USSR as a whole, by April 1, 1936, of the 41, 868 churches closed 35 percent were reused for educational and cultural purposes, 33 percent – as storage facilities, 10 percent were demolished, and 22 percent were not used at all (GARF f. 5263, op. 2, d. 10; the author's calculations). On May 1, 1937, in 70 cities of the USSR 22 percent were used for educational and cultural purposes, 16 percent – as housing, 16 percent – for economic purposes, 10 percent – as storage facilities, 11 percent were not used (ibid., l. 34).

21. GARF f. 5263, op. 2, d. 10, ll. 41-42.

22. A local Ukrainian representative of the Commission, for example, cynically commented that it was easier to get approval if the churches were transferred to the Renovationists for this was how he had managed to have several churches closed (GARF f. 5263, op. 2, d. 13, ll. 10-11).

23. GARF f. 5263, op. 2, d. 13, ll. 21-21ob.

24. GARF f. 5263, op. 2, d. 13, ll. 10-11.

25. GARF f. 5263, op. 2, d. 13, ll. 10-11.

26. Some data on Kiev, Dnepropetrovsk, Kharkov, Poltava, and Kamenets-Podol'sk is available in GARF f. 5263, op. 2, d. 13.

27. Again, Kiev may not be very representative of Ukraine as a whole.

28. *Vsevoiuznaia Perepis' Naseleniia 1937* (1991: 106-7); the author's calculations. The category for "Orthodox" included the Old Believers, Ukrainian, and Georgian Orthodox Autocephalists, Ioannites, etc.

29. Notably, as under the Germans, the Renovationists and other

Orthodox schismatic Churches were denied the privilege of revival. In direct contrast to the 1920s, the state's policy of religious diversity was to have one Orthodox Church, since what the state needed was legitimization and popular support of its post-war efforts (Chapter 3).

30. GARF f.6991s, op.2, d.180, ll.22-25; f.6991s, op.2, d.263, l.2.

31. The ROCh, however, experienced a dramatic decline in the number of parishes in the westernmost parts of Ukraine. This was a result of the re-emergence of the Uniate (Greek Catholic) Church, or the Church of the Eastern Rite. It is formally under the Pope of Rome, yet its ritual is Orthodox. Its churches were forcefully transferred to the ROCh after the war, therefore this post-Soviet drop in the number of ROCh churches there represents the only movement of the pendulum in the opposite direction.

32. For further readings, see Bilokhin (1995).

33. For further readings, see Markus (1995).

34. For further readings, see Sysyn (1993: 191-81).

CHAPTER 5. POST-IMPERIAL SPACES:
THE RUSSIAN CHURCH AS THE MOSCOW PATRIARCHATE

The True Church is one, and one is the God's blessing residing in it. There cannot be two Churches and two blessings.

Metropolitan Petr, locum tenets of the Church[1]

THE END OF COMMUNISM AND THE QUEST FOR THE RETURN OF CHURCH PROPERTY

Several closely related events in 1988-89 serve to identify a line separating the Soviet and post-Soviet periods of Russian history. These developments during the rule of Mikhail Gorbachev (1985-91) affected the state, society and the country as a geopolitical whole. At the same time, they dramatically changed the destiny of the Russian Orthodox Church in the 20th century.

First, in 1988 the state allowed a ROCh-wide celebration of the millenium of the Russian conversion to Christianity, thus propelling religious issues to the center of society's attention. For the first time in decades the ROCh not only became publicly visible, but also seemed respected by the state. A growing number of Orthodox church societies were newly registered, and the ROCh was granted unprecedented permission to build its main cathedral. More than anything else, this proposed Millennium Trinity Cathedral exemplified a new direction for state religious policies. Located far from the Kremlin, at the outskirts of Moscow in Tsaritsyno (Figure 6.3), construction was to symbolize the final fulfillment of the decree ordering separation of the state and the Church, both in the sense that the state would not intervene in the religious domain, and also in the sense that the state would not support the Church. It is noteworthy for later discussions in Chapter 8 that the Millennium Cathedral has not yet been built.

Second, Soviet society embarked on a critical reconsideration of its Communist foundations. Not surprisingly the previous persecution of religion was widely criticized. *Perestroika's* most famous film (*Repentance* by Tengiz Abuladze) coined the popular expression that "there is no need for a road, that does not lead to a church." The return of the pre-revolutionary dominant Orthodox ideological foundations of society was gradually becoming a topic of public discussion.

Third, the geopolitics of the Soviet Union were dramatically altered. Under Gorbachev, the Iron Curtain, symbol of the self-seclusion of the Soviet empire, was dismantled, opening new industrial and ideological markets for the West. Although the new situation provided a number of opportunities for the ROCh in the field of international cooperation, this also meant that weakened by decades of Soviet repression, the ROCh suddenly had to compete with foreign alternatives, and with traditional and non-traditional Russian religious organizations. Orthodox alternatives, such as the Foreign Russian Orthodox Church or the Synod of the Estonian Church in Exile, separated for decades from their places of origin by the Iron Curtain, were now back again.

In short, *perestroika* prepared both society and the state for the idea that past Communist injustices towards religion should be reversed. In practical terms this meant reopening nationalized churches and easing juridical constraints on religious life. However, church property return only became a large-scale phenomenon after 1991, in the post-Gorbachev and post-USSR era. The transformation of the USSR also brought a number of new problems for the Church and society in general. Three developments during this period are important in this regard.

First, civil society was dramatically restructured. Atomized by the breakdown or corruption of all major Soviet societal institutions, the collapse of the USSR, and the economic difficulties of the transition to a market economy (both in the Russian Federation and outside of it), Russian society increasingly identified itself with the ROCh as the only trustworthy social institution. Second, dismemberment of the Soviet Union dramatically altered the state. The ideology of internationalism under Gorbachev was replaced by growing nationalist sentiments and policies under Yel'tsin and other leaders of the new independent republics. The ROCh became a vital element of this new nation-building (and/or empire-saving) system in the post-Soviet world (Dunlop 1995). Third, the balance of power between the previously all-mighty central (federal) state and powerless local authorities ("subjects of the federation"[2]) shifted dramatically in favor of localities and independent republics. It remains to be seen if the competition between the central state and local authorities, between the Russian state and the newly independent republics, will eventually be beneficial for the ROCh's desire to regain closed churches. These issues will be addressed in this and the following chapters.

This chapter has a four-fold agenda. First, it considers the process of church property denationalization in two republics of the former USSR, Estonia and the Russian Federation (Chapter 6 considers the same process at the local level of Moscow). Second, it provides a necessary link between the previous discussions of processes at the national level and subsequent considerations of situation at the local (Moscow) level. The section on Estonia in this chapter has significant commonalties with the analysis of the Ukrainian situation in Chapter 4, and discussion of the Foreign Church in Russia will be continued in Chapter 6.

Third, this chapter is tied together by consideration of another mismatch, caused by the collapse of the Iron Curtain: that between the state, society and the Church. The fourth goal of this chapter is to analyze how this new mismatch brought alternative foreign Orthodox communities in exile into conflict with the main Church.

Whereas previous chapters have examined such facets of the Church as its believers, clergy and property, the focus of this chapter is on its name, more specifically, its juridical name, because it is an issue of primary importance for the failure or success of different Orthodox communities in obtaining the denationalized church property.

The main Church, known as the Russian Orthodox Church-Moscow Patriarchate, emerged in 1943 after Stalin permitted its revival. Although "the Russian Orthodox Church" and "the Moscow Patriarchate" are interchangeable names for the post-war Church, certain differences still exist. The Russian Orthodox Church (ROCh) is a somewhat more official name, while "the Moscow Patriarchate" (MP) is often used as its informal synonym or to differentiate it from Churches with similar names. "The MP" connotes a more limited historical (Soviet period) and geographical (at the top of the hierarchy) scope. Lay believers, for example, are more likely to identify themselves with the ROCh, treating the MP as an obvious yet unnecessary subtitle. Opponents of the Church also often prefer to call it "the Moscow Patriarchate" to highlight its dependence on central Moscow.

THE ESTONIAN CONFLICT: AN ORTHODOX "COLD WAR"?

Introduction

On February 23, 1996, during the holy liturgy in the Patriarchal Cathedral of the Epiphany, the Patriarch of Moscow and All Russia, Alexii II, omitted the customary commemoration of Bartholomew I,

Figure 5.1. Archbishop of Constantinople, New Rome, and Ecumenical Patriarch Bartholomew I (left) and the Patriarch of Moscow and All Russia, Alexii II, in the Kremlin, Moscow, 1993, photo by the author.

Ecumenical Patriarch of Constantinople. This happened for the first time in the thousand-year long history of the Church and signified the ROCh's formal break of all relations with the Patriarchate of Constantinople ("Vpervye za Tysiacheletie," 1996).[3] Historically and canonically, the Patriarchate of Constantinople, also known as the Ecumenical Patriarchate, is the prime spiritual center for Russian Orthodoxy; its Patriarch is "the first among equal" patriarchs (Figure 5.1).

The conflict had been in the making since 1993, when the Estonian government recognized an exiled Church as the legal successor of the pre-World War II Orthodox establishment. The suspension of relations with Constantinople was a quick and perhaps emotional reaction by Alexii II to the February 20, 1996, decision of the Patriarch of Constantinople, Bartholomew I, to place the new Estonian Church under its jurisdiction together with all newly obtained Orthodox property in Estonia. Thus, Russian Orthodox parishes, which had been under the auspices of the ROCh since 1940, formally lost all their property. In short, the conflict emerged due to differences over control of Orthodox churches in independent, post-Soviet Estonia, part of a profound conflict between the Russian population in Estonia, the Moscow-based Church and the Estonian state.

Three dimensions of this conflict are particularly important for our geographical analysis. First, against the Orthodox canons, two Orthodox Churches appear on the same territory. Second, there is the possibility of extinction of the Moscow-based Church in Estonia. Third, the two sides are backed by the most influential patriarchates in world Orthodoxy. This gives the conflict global dimensions, causing some observers even talk about an "Orthodox Cold War."

Orthodoxy in Estonia before the 1940s

Because Church members were drawn from the Estonian and other ethnic communities, Estonia is the only country of the three Baltic republics in which "Orthodox" does not in effect mean "Russian" (Uzzell 1996b). At the same time, the role of Russia in Estonian Orthodoxy is critical; Orthodox Christians have existed in Estonia from the 11th century, brought there by missionaries from Kievan Russia (Rus'). In the 17th century some of the Old Believers fled to Estonia from Russia. During the 19th century, Estonian peasants were encouraged to convert to the Orthodox faith with promises of land and socio-economic improvement. The Orthodox Church was also used as an important tool in the Russification campaigns of the late 19th century that attempted to break German dominance of Baltic local life. This increased the number of Orthodox believers in Estonia. In the 19th century the majority of Orthodox Christians here were ethnic Estonians, but the Orthodox have always been heavily outnumbered by Lutherans. By 1935 approximately one-third of the total Estonian population was Orthodox Christian.

In 1917, the Orthodox Russian-State Church held more than 5 percent of Estonian territory, excluding a great number of buildings constructed by donated funds of believers or by the Russian tsarist state. Although this property was partially nationalized by the Estonian Republic after 1919, it still remained partly in the hands of Orthodox communities. For instance, the biggest Pyukhtitskii monastery and its land had *stavropigial'nyi* status, meaning it was under the direct jurisdiction of the Patriarch of Moscow and All Russia, and not of the local bishop (Shevchenko 1996).

During WWII, twelve Orthodox churches were ruined. Of the

remaining 162 churches, 62 were closed in the period from 1944 to the late 1960s, 57 of which held services in Estonian. Most closures occurred in the 1960s; of the 34 closed churches, 31 had used the Estonian language (Novikov 1996a, 1996b). Before its occupation by the Soviet Union in 1940, Estonia had 156 Orthodox parishes,[4] nearly half of which were closed by Stalin and Khrushchev.

History of the Estonian Church

No ecclesiastical structure or autonomous diocese existed in Estonia until 1919 (it was part of the Riga diocese) (Figure A2.2). The Estonian Orthodox Church was formed on March 18-22, 1919, by the General Council of the Estonian Orthodox Congregations, in which almost all local parishes participated. However, by that time Estonia had become a sovereign state and the Church in Russia was in its deepest crisis so it is not surprising that in 1923 the new Church placed itself under the jurisdiction of the Patriarch of Constantinople (Romanov 1996). An independent Church was able to avoid the destruction and pillaging of church property that occurred in Soviet Russia.

The jurisdiction of Constantinople over Estonia was short (1923-40). After 1923 the Church in Estonia became known as the Estonian Orthodox Metropolitanate in the jurisdiction of the Constantinople Patriarchate, successor of the Reval diocese of the Orthodox Russian-State Church. In 1935-40 the Church was renamed the Estonian Apostolic Orthodox Church. The Soviet occupation of Estonia in 1940 eventually resulted in a split within the Church: because Estonian Orthodox parishioners were forcibly subordinated to the ROCh, some clergy fled Estonia and established themselves at the Stockholm-based Estonian Church in Exile (or the Synod in Exile). The latter group maintained affiliation with Constantinople. It is noteworthy that in 1978, during the Cold War years, Constantinople suspended even its formal claim to spiritual leadership of the increasingly Russified parishes of Estonia.[5]

According to the Associated Press, after the Soviet occupation the number of ethnic Estonian Orthodox believers dwindled from 200,000 to 10,000, yet Soviet-era immigration brought to Estonia more than 100,000 new Russian believers. Until April 11, 1992, the Estonian Church was only a bishopric of Moscow. Afterwards the Moscow Patriarchate granted juridical, financial and property autonomy to its parishes in Estonia. Only formal canonical relations remain in place now (Komlev 1996, Shevchenko 1996).

The only exception to this post-war, Moscow-based Church was a handful of parishes and priests, 23 clergymen, and 7000 lay people[6] who had fled Estonia in 1944 and established the Church in Exile. However, most members of this Church were reportedly elderly and of Swedish citizenship, the Synod itself was not registered anywhere, including Sweden, and it had no bishop (Shevchenko 1996). By the 1980s, even the Church in Exile was in decline as larger Orthodox jurisdictions or Western secular culture absorbed the grandchildren of the tiny Estonian diaspora living in Sweden (Uzzell 1996a).

The Dismemberment of the USSR and the Estonian Schism

The sudden collapse of the Soviet Union put the state, society, and the ROCh at geographical odds. It also brought two immediate juridical problems to the fore: 1) the location of the ecclesiastical center for Estonian Orthodox parishioners, and 2) the restoration of church property under Estonian law (*Estonia Today* 1996).

With the restoration of Estonian independence the Stockholm-based Estonian Church in Exile suddenly re-emerged from obscurity. The new Estonian authorities require that all religious organizations operating in Estonia reregister with the Ministry of Internal Affairs. This is a normal practice in many countries, however, what makes this new registration a political issue in Estonia is the fact that the state used this formal, "democratic" procedure to conduct a religious coup. Of the two contenders for the status of successor to the pre-Soviet Church in Estonia, the Estonian authorities clearly privileged the Church in Exile, which after its new registration changed its name to the Estonian Apostolic Orthodox Church (EAOCh).[7]

The reemergence of the Church in Exile as a successor to the pre-war Church is seen by some analysts to be a result of the active efforts of just one person. Henn Tosso, a trained economist and a former economic advisor to the bishop of Tallinn, secretly established relations with the Synod in Sweden and arranged to become its representative in Estonia. Supported by 21 parishes, on August 11, 1993, he submitted an application for the re-registration of the statute of the pre-war Church. Despite the fact that the unregistered Synod in Exile was located outside the country, the state approved the application, and Tosso *de facto* became the sole supervisor of all Orthodox church property in Estonia (Romanov 1996).

On November 5, 1993, the Moscow-based Church applied for registration in Estonia under the same name of the EAOCh, also supplying a copy of the registered statutes. This application was refused by the Estonian authorities on grounds that it violated the Law on Churches and Congregations. The name proposed was identical to the name of an already existing registered organization. Despite challenges to this decision, it was repeatedly upheld. The Estonian authorities wanted the Moscow Church to register under the name of the Russian Orthodox Church because this would limit its property rights. For instance, it already had to pay rent for its property and has had to vacate some buildings as a result (Shinkin 1996). As of July 1995, the Moscow-based Church in Estonia has refused to submit the statutes of its operations in Estonia (*Estonia Today* 1996).

The Split among Believers

There are some 40,000 Orthodox believers in Estonia; about 25,000 belong to the ROCh and the rest to Constantinople (Reuters News Service 1996, *Estonian Review* 1996). Of the 80 parishes, approximately 53[8] have indicated their preference for Constantinople (Uzzell 1996b), and 27 for Moscow. These 53 parishes are served by only 11 priests, while many parishes are just barely alive and/or not firmly pro-Constantinople. Forty-five parishes have only 9 priests and 3677 parishioners (Shevchenko 1996). There are mainly large parishes among the 27 pro-Moscow communities and primarily small parishes in the 53 pro-Constantinople parishes. In several cases, the parish and the priest have differing opinions. By early 1994, 21 parishes had registered with the EAOCh, and stated their desire to be under Constantinople's ecclesiastical jurisdiction. According to the Memorandum of the World Council of Churches,[9] "the division is not simply Estonians versus Russians. There are Estonians [e.g., congregation of Alexandr Aim] who want to stay with Moscow and Russians [e.g., community of Simeon Kruzhkov[10]] who favour Constantinople." The church crisis in Estonia is not merely an ecclesiastical version of ethnic politics. At present there are 80 Orthodox parishes in Estonia,[11] of which 40 are Estonian, 30 are non-Estonian, and 10 are mixed congregations.

The Property Dimension of the Crisis

Given developments during the last fifty years of Soviet occupation and the value of the property involved, many controversial issues, both canonical and legal, have been raised. For local observers, concerns over registration appear to revolve mainly around the issue of property. The re-registration process is very important for the return to rightful owners of the property that was confiscated by Soviet authorities. These property holdings extend beyond the basic properties that are currently in use. The Moscow-based Church refused to register under a new name for the obvious reason that this would mean forsaking all claims to pre-1940 properties, including Archbishop Kornilius's own office in Tallinn's historic Old Town (Uzzell 1996a, Babasian 1996).

No one Church involved in this conflict is absolutely legitimate in its claims (Krotov 1996). Both the pro-independence and pro-Moscow parties in the conflict are relatively recent formations, and this fact is often used by each side's opponent in conflicts over property. For instance, although the diocese of Tallinn of the Moscow Patriarchate was present in the republic for decades, it emerged in 1944 as a new organization. It did not own any property since Soviet law did not grant juridical rights to religious organizations (Novikov 1996a, 1996b).

However, both the pro-independence and pro-Moscow parties of the conflict have strong arguments in support of their claims for property rights. On the one hand, the independence of Estonia from Communist Russia in the 1920-30s saved it from Stalin's assault (Chapter 4). On the other hand, those clergy members who did not leave the country after 1944 and stayed in Estonia under the Moscow Church, together with their parishioners, saved the property from the Khrushchev assault in the 1950s (Chapter 4) (Alexii II 1996, Soldatov 1996). The current head of the ROCh, Patriarch Alexii II, was for 25 years the head of the Estonian diocese (Korolev 1996b). As the bishop of Tallinn, he greatly contributed to saving many churches in Estonia from closing during the Khrushchev anti-religious campaign (Shevchenko 1996). Some observers believe that the current property of communities of the Moscow Church should be left intact and considered compensation for the preservation of all church property. As the argument goes, the right of church property possession should be granted to communities, and not to administrative church organizations (Soldatov 1996).

The Geographical Factor

This Estonian conflict has several important geographical dimensions at different scales. First, the conflict has expanded beyond the local level. The Estonian state does not formally intervene in the internal affairs of Churches functioning in Estonia and in the debate between Moscow and Constantinople. Yet, Estonian President Meri Lennart reportedly stated at a meeting with Estonian clergymen that: "We advise you to be under the jurisdiction of Constantinople." This "advice" was important in the final decision of many priests to join the Constantinople jurisdiction (Alexii II 1996). In contrast, the involvement of the Russian state in backing the ROCh's local branch is openly stated at the highest level. On December 9, 1995, the Russian Foreign Ministry, in a strongly worded statement, said that the dispute over property rights among Orthodox Christians in Estonia could have an adverse impact on Estonian-Russian relations in the future (*Eesti Ringvaade* 1995). On February 29, 1996, President Yel'tsin sent a letter to President Meri Lennart about the Orthodox Church dispute ("Tserkovnyy Konflikt v Estonii" 1996), that openly backed one of the two rival churches.

Second, other countries are also involved in the conflict. The involvement of Finland (the registered EAOCh is temporarily governed by Archbishop Johannes of Karelia and Finland) may have some geopolitical foundation. Governance of the EOACh has made the small Finnish Church more powerful politically and economically. The geopolitical reality is that Finland and Estonia compete for the transit of Russian exports and imports; the conflict over church property negatively affects general Russian-Estonian economic relations and, in turn, could redirect part of Russian trade to Finland and other states in the region. According to the Estonian newspaper *Aripaev*, President Yel'tsin has signed a decree to decrease Russian transit via Estonia in retaliation for the lost monopoly on Orthodoxy ("Interesnoe Nabliudenie" 1996). Although this information sounds doubtful (for Russia the cost of transit via Finland is higher than via Estonia), the conflict certainly has serious geopolitical implications. The ROCh suspended its relations with the Finnish Orthodox Church because of the involvement of the Archbishop of Finland Johannes in the conflict ("Separatizm Ne Po-Khristianski" 1996). On February 23, 1996, the Patriarch of the ROCh and the President of the Russian Federation discussed the crisis "behind closed doors" ("Patriarkh Alexii" 1996).

Third, Estonia has become an arena for the first open clash between the two most influential patriarchates in the world, perhaps even leading to what some have called the "Orthodox Cold War." Canonically, two autonomous Orthodox Churches may not co-exist on the same territory; the Constantinople Council of 1593 determined the canonical territory for the ROCh as "Moscow, Russia and northern countries" (Korolev 1996a). On the other hand, the Patriarchate of Constantinople has had traditional jurisdiction over Orthodox parishes in Europe, and Estonia is "European now more than ever" ("Moskva i Konstantinopol'" 1996). Some observers already claim the emergence of a "Baltic Orthodoxy," more western than eastern (Cleman 1996).

The conflict between the two patriarchates can have implications in areas far away from Estonia. For example, it may change the Moscow Patriarchate's policy of non-involvement in the Orthodox matters of Greece, where some believers (especially since the 19th century) (Klenskii 1996) are reportedly interested in transferring their allegiances to the Moscow Patriarchate. Moreover, as far back as 1943, Stalin had plans to use the ROCh for possible incorporation of the Balkans (including Greece) into the sphere of Soviet influence (Novikov 1996b). But even today, the state television in Greece represents only the position of the Moscow Patriarchate, ignoring the other side ("Nevidimye" 1996). The General Secretary of the UN, the World Council of Churches, and the Conference of Churches of Europe have also supported the Moscow-based Church in this matter (Shinkin 1996).

Second, the transfer of the Estonian parishes to Constantinople may cause similar actions in other republics of the former USSR, such as Ukraine, Moldova (BNS 1996) and Latvia (Cleman 1996). In Ukraine, both the Ukrainian Orthodox Church-Kievan Patriarchate and the Ukrainian Autocephalous Church of Patriarch Dmitri Yarema are possible candidates for such a transfer (Babasian 1996). Finally, some rebellious communities within Russia itself may in the future seek the jurisdiction of Constantinople (ibid.); some are already under the jurisdiction of the UOCh-KP (Lebedeva 1996). For instance, the famous human rights activist, former priest of the ROCh and currently of the UOCh-KP, father Gleb Yakunin, totally approved the position of the Patriarchate of Constantinople with regard to the Estonian conflict (Sh. 1996).

Conclusion: Future of the Conflict

In sum the conflict between the ROCh and the Constantinople Patriarchate is still not resolved, but rather postponed. In May 1996, the two patriarchates issued statements saying that they agreed to restore full communion between them, and that Constantinople had agreed to a four-month moratorium on its February 20, 1996, decision to extend its jurisdiction to Estonia ("Orthodox Churches Avoid Schism" 1996). During this period, local parishes were to make their decisions about jurisdictional affiliation with one of the two patriarchates. This means that the most likely outcome of the conflict is the emergence of two Orthodox Churches on the same territory. On August 23, 1996, *Estonian Review* reported that delegations from the Ecumenical (Constantinople) Patriarchate and the Russian Orthodox Church had reached a preliminary agreement on the division of the Orthodox congregations in Estonia. A communiqué issued after these meetings stated that a list had been drawn up designating the subordination of most Orthodox congregations in Estonia. According to Tosso, representative of the Church subordinated to the Ecumenical Patriarchate, "of the country's 84[12] Orthodox congregations, about 30 will be under Moscow." However, according to pro-Russian sources, in July 1996 the number of communities supporting Constantinople dropped to 39 (Petrov 1996). The talks on property division were to continue, and a joint commission was to be established to determine the property split (*Estonian Review* 1996). The Estonian state has also taken a more realistic position. The Board of Religious Affairs has said that "if those who wish to remain under the Patriarch of Moscow register under a different name from the existing EAOCh, then those parishes will have the right to retain all properties that they are currently using, essentially church buildings and housing for priests."

THE COLLAPSE OF THE IRON CURTAIN
AND CHURCH PROPERTY RETURNS IN RUSSIA

Introduction

Though the process of church property returns in the Russian Federation has been underway locally since 1988, in 1993-4 the federal authorities made an effort to establish control over the process. Three major federal agencies were supposed to determine the particulars of religious property denationalization: the President, the government, and the parliament. On April 23, 1993, the President of the Russian Federation, Yel'tsin, issued decree no. 281-rp "On return of spiritual buildings and other property to religious organizations." A year later, on May 6, 1994, in its official statement, the government specified the way this return should be handled. Finally, in July of 1994 the parliament considered, but then rejected, a proposed law defining property rights for Russian religious organizations. All these documents were subject to public criticism.

The Presidential decree expressed only the intention to de-nationalize church property, it did not explain the actual process whereby church properties were to be returned. The government's statement, which was intended to provide these particulars, turned out to be poorly prepared. For instance, it was supplemented by a listing of 343 churches (238 of which were Orthodox) earmarked for return from the state. Unfortunately, these were located in only 13 of the 89 units of the Russian Federation.[13] To make the listing look more impressive the federal authorities are reported to have included churches that were to be nationalized at the local level. More than anything else, this incomplete listing demonstrated the chaotic nature of the church property return process which was caused by an unclear demarcation of federal and local rights and responsibilities (Stepanova 1995).

This governmental provision also failed to address more general questions. As a priest of the ROCh noted, this is a return (of some buildings) and not a restitution (general restoration of property rights). This kind of return without restitution has, in fact, under way since 1943, when Stalin changed his severe anti-religious stance. The governmental resolution thus did not alter the process that was already underway, but it did allow the state to restore its control over religious matters, re-creating, in fact, the notorious Council on Religious Affairs (Pavlov 1994b).

The truly revolutionary law developed in collaboration with major religious groups in Russia governing property rights of Russian religious organizations was rejected by the Parliament (Duma). This legislation would have ensured the right of repressed religious organizations to claim compensation and restitution of their property rights, describe successor organizations, the property itself, and land return (Rodin 1994). It is noteworthy that both the Communist and reformist parties rejected the proposed law (Kirpichnikov 1994), reportedly because many deputies were concerned that it would create a precedent for other communities repressed by the Communist state, e.g., the Cossacks and peasants, to also claim rights to land and property.

Finally, a number of historical questions remain unanswered. For instance, as writer Mikhail Chulaki has noted, after the Church Reform by Peter the Great, the Russian-State Church became just a department of the state. Consequently, churches were state property. Therefore, only pre-Petrine constructions (such as the Kirillo-Belozerskii monastery or Trinity-St.Sergii Lavra [Figure 2.3]) could be reclaimed and returned as nationalized church property. The church property built after the Church Reform could only be "donated" or "given for free use," an arrangement that would eventually benefit the ROCh because state funding for maintaining the buildings would continue after the return (Chulaki 1994).

In short, the federal state has failed to properly address the process of church property return. Instead, local governments have administered this process, despite both the absence of federal laws on the matter and the considerable controversy surrounding the question of who should receive the property.

Controversy over the Beneficiaries of the Return:
The Legacy of the Soviet Past

Returns of church property were often justified on the grounds of reversing the injustices of the Soviet past with regard to the physical embodiment of Orthodoxy (church buildings). Yet these returns, paradoxically, strengthened another unjust Communist practice – i.e., the privileging of the ROCh as the only legitimate successor of the pre-revolutionary Orthodox State-Russian Church. As a result of previous schisms, the current ROCh was not the only claimant for the property.

First, the Old Believers claim all pre-Nikonian (pre-1666) Orthodox property as their own, especially with regard to books and icons. Concerning the closed churches, the Old Believers not only wish to get their buildings back, they also need help assisting in their restoration. But, because the Old Believers were disenfranchised in the past, their alienation continues to be the basis for their current disadvantage in the process of church property returns; one injustice creates another, and the strong get full state support, while the weak and unprivileged go unheard. Since the current return is in fact the final one, it is important for the public to be informed about all significant returns in advance. Justice is not equal to "restoration of the situation before 1917" since a chain of injustices were committed long before then (Shakhov 1994).

Second, the Church unrest of the 1920s caused another series of schisms. The traditional Russian-State Church split into several fractions, of which the modern ROCh is only one (although by far the biggest). The remaining alternative Churches are now voicing claims that the ROCh is not a legitimate successor to the pre-revolutionary Church, which they argue ceased to exist in 1927 (Rybakov 1993). These serious claims will be considered here.

The Main, Foreign and Catacomb Churches: Conflict over *Sergianstvo*

Besides the short-lived Renovationism, throughout the rest of the Soviet period, Russian Orthodoxy consisted, *de facto*, of three branches: 1) the main ROCh which, despite Communist oppression, remained part of society in exchange for collaboration with the state; 2) the Russian Orthodox Church Abroad (also Karlovci Church, but hereafter the Foreign Church) which preserved its "purity" by staying away from both the state and most of society; and 3) the True Russian Orthodox Church (hereafter the Catacomb Church), which went underground in the Soviet period, remaining essentially a sectarian movement isolated from both the state and society.

Consideration of the juridical, canonical and historical claims to supremacy of these three branches are beyond the frame of this study and, besides, are not truly germaine to the critical fourth agent in this dispute — the state. Disregarding all their differences, both the Soviet and post-Soviet states have preferred to privilege the ROCh. This is not surprising, since only the ROCh had wide popular support and could serve either as a means of control, or provide of legitimation for the state. In addition, the two other Orthodox Churches were banned from legal existence during the Soviet period, only formally allowed to operate in Russia during the post-Soviet era. This chapter accepts the position that all these organizations have some legitimacy and certain historical merit behind their claims for church property, focusing on the *mechanism* of post-Soviet church property return and its spatial context.

Origin of the Split: 1927

The pre-revolutionary Church's final subordination to the Soviet state is often traced to one person and a precise date. Although a softening of the Tikhonite Church's anti-Communist position could be traced to some actions of Patriarch Tikhon before his death in 1925,[14] it was his successor's manifesto which marked the watershed in subordination to the new authorities. On July 20, 1927, Metropolitan Sergii published a declaration of loyalty to the state. This action is often considered the decisive step toward the ROCh's policy of servitude to the state. This subordination to the state became known as *sergianstvo*, after Sergii. Sergii's declaration was obviously a highly controversial act. On the one hand, it helped the Tikhonite Church gain state support to survive in general (Chapter 4) and fight the Renovationist schism in particular (Chapter 3). On the other hand, it created several other schisms within the Church.

First, the declaration was totally unacceptable to those clergy and believers in exile who then formed the Foreign Church (also known as the Karlovci Church after the place of its founding council).[15] As a result, in the fall of 1927 the schism was formalized (Dvorkin 1994: 233). Second, the declaration caused domestic dissatisfaction among clergy and believers in the Soviet Union who refused any compromise with the "Godless" Communists. The Church, already fractured by Renovationism and several other short-lived schismatic movements fighting for power after Tikhon's death,[16] was propelled by Sergii's declaration into deepened differences that drove some clergy into final excommunication and internal exile. This loosely structured but connected network of underground Orthodox communities is collectively known as the Underground (Catacomb) Church. It includes the groups known as the True Orthodox Church and the True Orthodox Christians.[17]

Geographical Distribution of the Alternative Churches

According to an expert of the ROCh, the Foreign Church has about 280 parishes in the world, many of which (in Morocco, Ethiopia, Iran and the Middle East) are fictitious. Of 140 real parishes about 90 are in the US. More neutral state experts give higher estimates for the Foreign Church — about 350 parishes and up to half million believers in 30 countries (mainly the US, Germany, Canada and France plus Belgium, the Netherlands, Lebanon, Turkey, Australia, New Zealand and others) (*Religioznye Ob'edinieniia* 1996: 65). This is a relatively small number (the Greek archbishopric in America has close to 700 parishes, the Autocephalous Orthodox Church in America, almost 600 parishes) (Dvorkin 1994: 218). Since 1981, the Foreign Church has also succeeded in bringing under its jurisdiction some Catacomb communities in Russia (ibid., 70-71).

The Catacomb Church is known as a highly clandestine organization. During the Soviet period, its members refused to deal with the state in any way; often refusing to join collective farms, serve in the army, participate in elections, hold passports, or even use electricity and radio (regarded as "the Bolsheviks' innovation"). It is no surprise then that the Soviet state used all its repressive means to eradicate this Church.

Catacomb bishop Amvrosii (von Sivers) identifies several state campaigns to eradicate the Catacomb Church. 1) 1928-34 — deportation, incarceration and killing of clergy and active parishioners, culminating in the destruction of all church buildings in the USSR in 1930-33. The order to dynamite *all* church buildings belonging to the True Church means that very few have survived to the present day and are thus unable to be claimed.[18] 2) 1937-38 — revealing of Catacomb believers in hiding and execution of already imprisoned anti-Sergians; 3) 1943-46 — revealing and deporting, in 1944 and 1946, Catacomb communities existing during the war on German-occupied territories (they were allowed to operate everywhere with the exception of Pskov oblast'); 4) 1950-53, 1958-63, and the early 1970s — repression of the True Catacomb Church and in an attempt to bring clandestine believers into the open creation of a pseudo-Catacomb Church; and 5) 1980-84 — attack on the new generation of young Catacomb believers (Sivers 1994; 1996: 99-101).

The Catacomb Church is reported to currently have more than 250,000 followers in republics of the former USSR (von Sivers 1996: 102). The Ministry of Justice of the Russian Federation lists the following groups within the Church.[19]

1) Those under the jurisdiction of the Russian Orthodox Free Church (see above); with parishes in southern European Russia (Kuban' and North Caucasus), Belarus, and Ukraine.

2) Those under the jurisdiction of the archbishop of Athens Avksentii (old-style calendar Greek Church): multiethnic parishes, many with Povolzh'e and Arctic peoples.

3) Those under the jurisdiction of the Synod of archbishop Andrei (the True Orthodox Church of Greece).

4) The True Orthodox Church, Siberian Metropolitanate. This

Church is autonomous, yet its head is appointed by the Ukrainian Orthodox Church-Kievan Patriarchate (Chapter 4). It has 26 parishes (only 6 are registered).

5) Followers of Metropolitan Gennadii (Sekach). This is the most popular strand of the True Church, but because its canonicity is questionable it is ignored by other communities.

6) Followers of Lazar' of Kashira[20] (Moscow oblast), 5 communities, 1 monastery.

7) Followers of Alexei Vlasov (Moscow, Bibirevo neighborhood), dissident intelligentsia, bishop-less (acephalous) communities.

8) The Russian True Orthodox Church — Metropolitanate of Moscow and all Russia (5 Moscow communities).

9) True Orthodox Eastern Heavenly Apocalyptic Church of Ioann the Theologian's Revelation (Lipetsk oblast).

The geographical prevalence of the Catacomb communities remains an understudied topic because of its illegal status, highly conspiratorial character and loose structure. Fletcher states that only the True Orthodox Church was geographically widespread (Fletcher 1971: 183), and that the True Orthodox Christians were widely dispersed throughout the Soviet Union (ibid., 200). He cites Soviet scholars' data concerning their activities in sixteen separate localities, ranging from "the Donbas and the Kiev-Kharkov areas in the Ukraine, to the Moscow and Kirov areas in European Russia, to Novosibirsk in Western Siberia, and to Alma-Ata [in Kazakhstan] near the Sinkiang border and the Tashkent area" in Uzbekistan (ibid.).

The materials of the secret services are perhaps the only source of insights into the Church's geography in the former USSR, since it was denied the right of registration. Table A5.1 and Figure A5.1 describe the prevalence of Catacomb communities in the USSR, according to data of the All-Union One-Time Survey of Religious Organizations on January 1, 1962. These data are based on reports from local representatives of the Council for Religious Affairs. One may observe that the Church was prevalent in areas with some experience of sectarianism (southern areas of the country).

Impact of the Iron Curtain's Collapse

The end of Communist rule, marked by the collapse of the Iron Curtain in the late 1980s, paradoxically brought the Foreign Church and the ROCh into a direct confrontation. *Sergianstvo*, or the policy of collaboration with the Communist state, was not the only stumbling block to normalizing relations between the ROCh and the Foreign Church. There are three other disagreements concerning a) the large numbers of the ROCh's current highest personnel appointed during and by the Communist state, b) the ROCh's refusal to canonize the new martyrs of this century (primarily, the last Russian tsar), and c) the ROCh's participation in the modern ecumenical movement (Osetrov 1994).

In May 1990, the Archbishop's Council of the Foreign Church decided to open parishes in Russia (Iashunskii 1992: 243). This meant that it would accept jurisdictional transfers of communities from the ROCh. Russia having been labeled "missionary territory," all three bishops of the Foreign Church in Russia were given the right to accept any willing parishes (regardless of their geographical location). By 1992, the Foreign Church had three dioceses in Russia: Suzdal' diocese with over 70 parishes in Suzdal' (Vladimir oblast'), Moscow, St. Petersburg, Nizhniy Novgorod, and Siberia; Tambov and Oboyan' diocese with about 50 parishes of the Catacomb Church;[21] and the Black Sea (Krasnodar) diocese with 7-8 Catacomb parishes (ibid., 69-70).[22]

This quick growth and unrestrained proselytism was eventually harmful for the Foreign Church. Several schisms fractured the Foreign Church's community in Russia (registered, it is worth noting, as the *Russian-State* Orthodox Free Church). This could be, in part, a result of the diversity of its adherent. Four groups of clergy and parishioners in Russia initially joined the Foreign Church: 1) liberal dissident intelligentsia who saw the ROCh as a "KGB agency", 2) conservative monarchist priests of the ROCh, opposed to its ecumenical activities, 3) clergy and parishioners who left the ROCh because of administrative and financial conflicts, and 4) some Catacomb communities. This heterogeneity led to schisms. First, the Foreign Church lost some of its Catacomb communities in Russia. In 1993 the Catacomb Church broke this affiliation in protest against the Foreign Church's acceptance of former priests of the ROCh (the Catacomb Church is strictly opposed to any contacts with the ROCh) (ibid., 68-69).[23] Second, a series of conflicts took place between the predominantly conservative, nationalistic and monarchist Foreign Church and the mostly liberal Free Church.[24] In the summer of 1993 about 65 parishes of the Free Church in Russia broke with the Foreign Church and formed an independent Russian Orthodox Free Church (hereafter the Free Church) (Pospielovsky 1995b: 210; Vershillo 1993). The final schism occured on March 12, 1995 (*Religioznye Ob'edineniia* 1996: 72).

In short, the Foreign Church's community within Russia can
currently be characterized as split into three parts: 1) the Free Church;
2) two bishops still under the Foreign Church; and 3) independent parishes (such as that of Alexei Aver'ianov who was expelled by the Foreign Church for his damage to its image in Russia).[25] Some clergy returned to the ROCh and, as mentioned, to the Catacomb Church.

The first Catacomb community was registered in the Russian
Federation as early as 1991. Since then, 25 Catacomb communities have
been recognized as legal religious organizations (Table A5.2), but a significant number of communities still refuse legalization.

Figures A5.2 and A5.3 show the geographical prevalence of communities of the True (Catacomb) and Free/Foreign Churches in Russia.[26] As of January 1, 1996, the Free/Foreign Church was present in 36
of the 89 units of the Russian Federation. Communities of the True
Church are registered in 14 units of the Russian Federation. However,
these data are not complete since many communities still avoid all contact with the authorities. Two centers of True Church prevalence can
be identified; around Moscow and in Kurgan oblast'.

In short, legal off-springs of the Foreign and Catacomb Churches
in post-Soviet Russia (the Free and True Churches respectively) have
created two alternatives to the undisputed rights of the ROCh to the
property of the pre-revolutionary Orthodox Russian Church. Although
it would be unrealistic, and perhaps unjust, for society to transfer all
church property to these relatively small communities, it is also obvious that, having recognized them legally, the state should also respect
their right to some church property. It remains to be seen if current
practices of church property return will realize this.

In the absence of an agreement between the three Churches split
by the Communist heritage, it is the state, and specifically the local
state, which is the *de facto* judge to finalize its own vision of the solution through allocation of returned church property. The case of Moscow (Chapter 6) is particularly telling in this regard.

Property Restitution and the Juridical Succession of the Church and State

The alternative, anti-Sergian Orthodox Churches are not the only
ones questioning the rights of the ROCh as sole juridical successor to
the pre-revolutionary Church. Within the ROCh there are also voices
challenging its right. The opinions of a well-known Orthodox publi-

cist, father Innokentii (Pavlov), is particularly important, because they elevate the whole discussion to a higher level. In the end, he believes (or hopes), the problem of church property return is about a series of historical, psychological, and juridical gaps, mismatches and discontinuities which apply not only to the Church, but to the post-Soviet state and to society more generally.

Father Innokentii insists that that neither the state nor the current ROCh have a right to claim continuity with the tsarist state and Church. The former was overthrown in March 1917, the latter ceased to exist in 1922, when Patriarch Tikhon failed to gather the Local Council of the Church. The current Church, the ROCh-Moscow Patriarchate was registered in May 1927, in the Internal Affairs Commissariate (NKVD) by the deputy of *locum tenens*, a position which is not recognized in any Church juridical acts. Yet father Innokentii argues that these are minor reasons for the juridical discontinuity between the pre-revolutionary and current Church and state (Pavlov 1996).

What makes the two current institutions truly discontinuous with their pre-revolutionary analogs is the continuing disrespect for property rights (other rights were either partially acknowledged or restored). The above-mentioned law on the restitution of property rights of religious organizations was rejected by the parliament in 1994 because fears were raised that it would create a precedent for the return of all kinds of property (e.g., private property of peasants, nobility, etc.). Similarly, while claiming church property for itself, the ROCh does not argue for the restitution of the property rights of other religious and social organizations. To bridge the gap and solve the problem of juridical continuity, in f. Innokentii's opinion, the state should recognize the property rights of all individuals and organizations who suffered from the Bolshevik tyranny. Similarly, the ROCh should return to canonical and juridical decisions of the last legitimate Council of 1917-18 (including its stance on property) (ibid.).

In short, according to f. Innokentii, the property question is the key issue to solving the problem of legal discontinuity between the pre- and post-Soviet institutions, a kind of domestic equivalent to the problem of Tsarist Russia's international debt.

Conclusion

Soviet rule largely separated Russian Orthodoxy from its physical embodiment, its church buildings, and altered both its institution

and its churches. Most church buildings were changed through closure, demolition, reutilization or usage by the state, as a bargaining
tool to control Orthodox believers (Chapter 4). Chapter 3 discussed the
short-lived Renovationist schism of the 1920-30s. The Church was altered by the schism and persecutions of the 1930s, and eventually subordinated itself to the state. This subordination resulted in another
schism within the Church, a schism over collaboration with the state.
Its main remnants were the clergy who escaped the country to form
the Church in Exile and the main Russian Orthodox Church. The former
claim moral purity, because they did not collaborate with the Communist authorities, as their main argument for succession to the pre-revolutionary Church. Meanwhile, the latter have the advantage of popular and often (but not always) state support. The two sides were divided for decades by the "Iron Curtain," or the policy of self-seclusion
by the USSR. However, with its collapse, the two competing agents are
facing one another again. Their dispute has been magnified by the
new post-Soviet opportunities of acquaring denationalized church property.

This chapter has looked at two returns: first, the return of church
property (denationalization) and second, the return of the foreign
Church(es) from exile. Two cases, Estonia and the Russian Federation,
have been considered in depth, because here the conflicts between domestic and foreign branches of the Church have been particularly intense there.

Although many classes/ommunities were expropriated by the
Communist state (e.g., nobility, peasants, various ethnic groups), closed
churches in fact have become the key symbol of the state's domestic
debt. Several other factors are also important. First, most other unprivileged groups (e.g. the Cossacks, ethnic groups, even the peasants)
are of only regional importance, whereas closed churches are almost
ubiquitous. Second, churches can be returned, in general, without corresponding return of church land, whereas this is not the case for the
other unprivileged communities. Third, of all of these, the Church was
most successful in preserving itself as an institution as well as in its
physical embodiment (although the inappropriateness of secular usage of churches is obvious). Finally, and most importantly, the state
would benefit most from this kind of denationalization. In addition to
ideological returns, church property return can be financially rewarding: unlike other forms of nationalized property, many closed churches
(unlike the demolished ones) were a monetary burden for the state,
often requiring restoration and maintenance costs. The restoration of

returned churches can also be highly rewarding, especially for local states such as Moscow where there is strong involvement with the construction industry.

This chapter argues that the rhetoric of church property return as a means to match the pre- and post-Soviet states is problematic. The goal of bridging the Communist gap through denationalization has undermined the goal of restoring justice (in fact, the very word "justice" has arguably almost disappeared from the post-Soviet political lexicon). Moreover, this rhetoric gives the illusion that it is possible to deny the past and/or the legacy of Soviet history. Finally, this rhetoric maintains the understanding of space as a neutral container which can be filled in in one way or another. It is especially noteworthy that f. Innokentii cites the Soviet state's respect for tsarist international boundary agreements as an example of its only partial disregard for law. This belief in Soviet respect for the stability of space is totally unfounded: most external and almost all internal boundaries were changed during Soviet rule.

The historical gap is not the only mismatch, which must be considered with regard to overturning the Communist anti-religious policies. Geographical mismatch between the pre- and post-Soviet state, society and the Church must be also taken into account in order to understand how church property return in the post-Soviet world creates new injustices for the ROCh itself, for other Orthodox organizations, and for societal institutions as well. But to illustrate this, it is instructive to examine the process of church property return at the local level, using the example of Moscow.

Chapter 5: Notes

1. Tsypin (1994: 75). This was said with regard to the Renovationist schism.

2. The city of Moscow and Moscow oblast' are separate administrative subdivisions of the Russian Federation.

3. Babasian (1996) cites three suspensions: in the early 11th century, 1051, and 1448.

4. According to Novikov (1996a), 158; of them, 23 used the Russian language.

5. Letter of Patriarch Dimitri, May 3, 1978, protocol No. 207 (Romanov 1996).

6. Bartholomew I (February 24, 1996).

7. Its registered name in Estonian is "Eesti Apostlik-Iigeusu Kirik," which is unofficially translated into English as "The Estonian Apostolic Orthodox Church." The registered English name for the Church is the Estonian Orthodox Church.

8. Other sources indicate that there all together 84 Orthodox communities, of them 54 are under Constantinople.

9. Memorandum of the World Council of Churches (February 23, 1994).

10. According to Klenskii (1996), the position of Simeon Kruzhkov is not supported by his parishioners.

11. The largest Churches in Estonia are the Estonian Evangelical Lutheran Church (170 congregations), and the Association of Estonian Evangelical Christian and Baptist Congregations (90) (*Estonia Today* 1993).

12. See Note 8.

13. The listing has the following geographical distribution: Altay – 3 churches, Bryansk 11, Vladimir 124, Volgograd 21, Ivanovsk 114, Kaliningrad 7, Kaluga 14, Murmansk 5, Omsk 2, Ryazan' 6, Tomsk 18, Ul'yanovsk 4, Chita 14. The following confessions were included: Russian Orthodoxy (ROCh) – 322 churches (238 in two oblasts'); Lutheran 14 (mostly in Vologda and Kaliningrad oblasts), Muslim 5, Catholics 2, Old Believers 1, Judaism 1 (Stepanova 1995).

14. For example, in April, 1925, the Patriarch published "Zaveschatel'noe Poslanie" with sentiments of loyalty to the Communist regime.

15. Other names include the Russian Church in Exile, the

Synodal Church, the Foreign Church, the Free Russian Church, the White Church (Dvorkin 1994: 217-8). The founding council met in Sremski-Karlovtsy, Serbia, in November, 1921.

16. The best account of these schisms can be found in Snychev (1993). See also Fletcher (1971), Pospielovsky (1984: 113-162).

17. The two were cognate movements differing primarily in the degree of their organizational flexibility. True Orthodox Christians maintained few organizational encumbrances, instead relying on an exceedingly flexible, almost spontaneous form of underground religious activity (Fletcher 1971: 198).

18. Sivers (1996: 100); *Religioznye Ob'edineniia* (1996: 77). The best (and only) known case is the famous beautiful Spas-on-Blood cathedral in St. Petersburg, which was not dynamited only for site-specific reasons — it is located on the banks of a channel (*Religioznye Ob'edineniia* 1996: 77).

19. *Religioznye Ob'edineniia* (1996: 77-82). Ierodiakon Iona (Iashunskii) (1992: 243-260) gives somewhat different classification.

20. For a detailed profile of the tragicomical figure of Lazar, see Pozdniaev (n. d.)

21. In 1981-93, about 50 parishes of the Catacomb Church (communities under Tambov and Oboyan' bishop Lazar' (Zhurbenko)) were in the jurisdiction of the Foreign Church (*Religioznye Ob'edineniia* 1996: 68).

22. Also, interview with father Valentin, archbishop of Suzdal' and Vladimir (Rusantsov 1994).

23. According to the press-secretary of the Russian Free Church f. Andrei (Osetrov), hundreds of Catacomb believers are still affiliated with his Church (Osetrov 1994).

24. A chronicle of relations between the two Churches in 1990-94 is published in *Suzdal'skii Palomnik* (1994). For materials related to contacts between the Foreign Church and Russian nationalist society Pamiat' see Babasian (1992), Shusharin (1992), Kolpakov (1993), Goriacheva (1994).

25. Protoierei Alexei Aver'ianov was secretary to the Foreign Church's main representative in Russia, bishop Varnava (Prokof'ev) of Cannes. The two established close relations with the notorious ultranationalist and anti-Semitic *Pamiat'* society, which led to the conflicts with the Free Church (Babasian 1992).

26. The Russian Federation's Ministry of Justice, the principal source of statistics on registered religious organizations in post-Soviet

Russia, combines data for the Foreign and Free Churches because of the former's insignificance and the close links between the two. The Foreign Church's two remaining dioceses are centered in Ishim (Siberia) (includes temporarily the Moscow, North Russian, and St.Petersburg dioceses) and Kuban' (Krasnodar) (*Religioznye Ob'edineniia* 1996: 72).

Chapter 6. Local "Iron Curtains" in a World City: The Case of Moscow

I have said enough, I hope, to impart to the reader a portion of the surprise which the first view of Moscow produced in me. To add to that surprise he must recollect, what he will have often read, that this city is a country within itself.

Astolph de Custine, French marquis, 1839[1]

Since, unlike other former Soviet republics, the federal government of the Russian Federation did not fully control the process of church property denationalization in the 1990s, it is especially important to examine this process at the local level. Following the aforementioned statement by the Russian federal government, the Mayor of Moscow issued his own decree on August 12, 1994 (*Vestnik Merii Moskvy* 1994c). By that time, the city had already moved far along the way toward denationalizing churches.

The harbinger of change was the easing of registration procedures for religious communities. Tables A6.1 and A6.2 show tendencies in the post-Soviet registration of Orthodox communities. From this data it is evident that the diversity of confessions and types of churches have increased. In addition, it is also obvious that the boom of the early years is over and the current status is close to a saturation level, a condition determined for Orthodox communities by the limited number of available church buildings. However important these formal registration statistics may be, they are misleading if not complemented by some data on the actual presence of religious groups in the city, i.e., primarily some information about the access which different Orthodox communities have to church property.

For the city as a whole, the following figures on current church property were available. In 1985, Moscow had only 54 functioning churches. As of September 1995, the city of Moscow had 7 cathedrals and churches in the Kremlin, 5 monasteries and 2 nunneries with 34 churches; 233 parish churches (178 functioning, and 55 still without services); 7 churches of the Moscow Patriarchate; 24 churches in state institutions (10 of them functioning); 5 baptismal churches; 10 churches

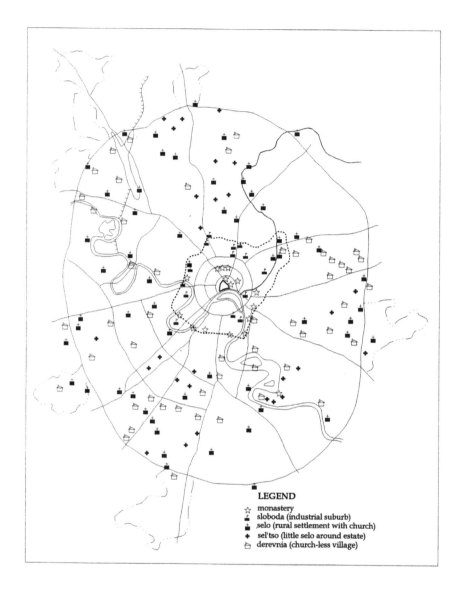

LEGEND
☆ monastery
⚑ sloboda (industrial suburb)
◼ selo (rural settlement with church)
✚ sel'tso (little selo around estate)
⌂ derevnia (church-less village)

Figure 6.1. Types of 17th century settlements on the territory of contemporary Moscow. Source: NIiPI Genplana Moskvy, unpub. data compiled by V. S. Kusov; Sidorov (1998: 154).

under construction by parishes; and 6 chapels (*Pravoslavnaia Moskva* 1995: 8).[2] As a Moscow City Duma coordinator in charge of cultural affairs and relations with religious organizations put it, "we want to return all the church property that is neither currently lived in, nor to be privatized."[3]

Although these property statistics are an important addition to the data on registration of religious communities, they also need specification along two lines. First, it is important to specifically analyze the three main dimensions of the church property transfers in post-Soviet times, namely return of nationalized churches, reconstruction of demolished churches, and new church construction. Second, it is also important to analyze the geographical particulars of church property distribution at the local level, with particular regard to changes brought by the Soviet rule that caused the mismatch between the new expanded city of Moscow and the unchanged Church.

The first aim of this chapter is to analyze the two processes of church property transfers in post-Soviet Moscow. In doing so, this chapter pursues the second goal of continuing the discussion of territorial mismatches, this time, between the local (Moscow) state, the local society (Muscovites), and the Church in its Moscow diocese. These agents are framed by or, in turn, contribute to the mismatches. The third aim of this chapter is to discuss the implications of these mismatches for issues of power and difference, examining the exclusion of alternative Orthodox communities from access to denationalized church property.

PROPERTY RETURN AND THE CENTER-PERIPHERY DISCREPANCY

The Church and the City before 1917

When French nobleman marquis Astolph de Custine in 1839 visited Moscow for the first time he saw a cityscape which produced

> "an impression that cannot easily be forgotten. Before the eye, spreads a landscape, wild and gloomy, but grand as the ocean; and to animate the dreary void, there rises a poetical city, whose architecture is without either a designating name or a known model" (de Custine 1989: 394-5).

De Custine attributed the peculiarity of this image to the architectural features of Orthodox church buildings. For instance,

> "[b]right chains of gilded or plated metal unite the crosses of the inferior steeples to the principal tower; and this metallic net, spread over an entire city, produces an effect that it would be impossible to convey, even in a picture. ... a phalanx of phantoms hovering over the city. ... The play of light, in the aerial city, produces a species of phantasmagoria, in broad day, which reminds one of the reflected brilliance of lamps in the shop of a lapidary. These changing hues impart to Moscow an aspect altogether different from that of the other European cities. The sky, when viewed from the middle of such a city, is a golden glory, similar to those seen in old paintings. Schnitzler states, that, in 1730, Weber counted at Moscow 1500 churches. Coxe, in 1778, fixes the number at 484. As for myself, I am content with endeavouring to describe the aspect of things, I admire without counting; I must, therefore, refer the lovers of catalogues to books made up entirely of numerals" (ibid.).[4]

De Custine's comments are important because he verifies that churches were relatively evenly distributed over the territory of the city. Figure 6.1 shows the 17th century rural settlements of different types around 19th century Moscow, superimposed on the territory of the 1960 city. On this territory (bounded by the ring road) there were 157 settlements with their own places of worship (NIiPI Genplana Moskvy 1991a). It is noteworthy that already at that time (17th century) some monasteries had been closed by the state. The largest number of monastery closures happened in the 17th and 18th centuries (19, more than 30 percent of the 62 known monasteries on the territory of contemporary Moscow) (Burakov 1991: 16) as a result of the state acting to limit the Church's land ownership. Despite changes of this kind, in general the number of churches continued to grow. By 1917 there were in Moscow close to eight hundred Orthodox churches and about seventy chapels (Table 6.1).[5]

The density of churches most likely declined from the center towards the margins of the city, yet no significant part of the city was without churches. Even suburban areas of the city had churches at cemeteries. Thus, the spatial extent of the city and the Church were the

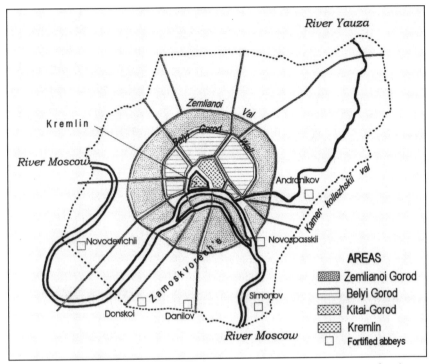

Figure 6.2. Historic areas of downtown Moscow. Source: author's adaptation of Colton (1995: 17).

same (Figure 6.2).[6] As a result of three processes, this situation changed dramatically during the Soviet period (Figures 6.3 and 6.4).[7]

First, Soviet Moscow, once again the capital city since 1918, was most obviously reshaped by the intense *Soviet politico-architectural reconstruction* of its historical downtown, including the ruthless demolition of many churches. This began in 1922, with the Alexandr Nevskii Chapel on Manege Square (Palamarchuk 1992: 13; *Sviatyni Drevnei Moskvy* 1993: 9). This campaign to "clear historical trash" included, for example, the humiliating location of more than two dozen public toilets on former church sites, including the site of the Church of Kazan' Icon of the Holy Virgin on Red Square (Palamarchuk 1992: 15) (Figure 6.3). Similarly, the country's major Cathedral of Christ the Savior, in downtown Moscow, was dynamited to clear space for the most ambitious of all Communist architectural projects, a gigantic Palace of the Soviets (Chapter 7). Finally, several churches with tall bell-towers were dismantled at the beginning of the war, in 1941, for fear that they could serve as landmarks for German artillery. Several churches were also

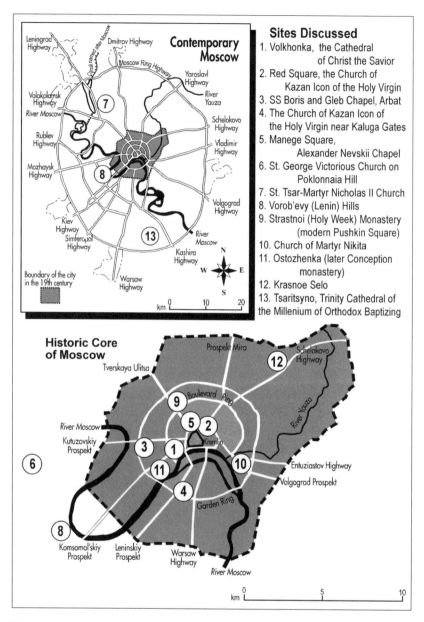

Sites Discussed

1. Volkhonka, the Cathedral of Christ the Savior
2. Red Square, the Church of Kazan Icon of the Holy Virgin
3. SS Boris and Gleb Chapel, Arbat
4. The Church of Kazan Icon of the Holy Virgin near Kaluga Gates
5. Manege Square, Alexander Nevskii Chapel
6. St. George Victorious Church on Poklonnaia Hill
7. St. Tsar-Martyr Nicholas II Church
8. Vorob'evy (Lenin) Hills
9. Strastnoi (Holy Week) Monastery (modern Pushkin Square)
10. Church of Martyr Nikita
11. Ostozhenka (later Conception monastery)
12. Krasnoe Selo
13. Tsaritsyno, Trinity Cathedral of the Millenium of Orthodox Baptizing

Figure 6.3. Location in contemporary Moscow of the areas discussed in Chapters 6 and 7. Sources: Sidorov (1992, 2000b: 549); the author. Notes: Vitberg's construction site (near modern Moscow State University): 2. Ton's variants of the original Cathedral's location: 1 (final) 3, 4. Locations of the convent of Alexius the Man of God: 1, 5, 6. Open-air swimming pool Moskva: 1. Major contemporary cathedral construction projects: 1, 8.

Figure 6.4. Okhotnyy Ryad, downtown Moscow, 1930s. Source: Kirichenko (1992: 229), used by permission. Note: This was one of the sites considered for construction of the Palace of the Soviets. With the exception of the 6-storey building in the background (National Hotel), all buildings in this picture have been demolished, including Alexander Nevskii Chapel.

demolished under Khrushchev in the late 1950 and early 1960s for purely propagandistic purposes.

Second, Moscow's cityscape has been affected by *urban modernization*. This profound restructuring of the city resulted in the demolition, closure, and re-utilization of many churches for secular purposes. For example, the construction of Moscow's first underground railway in the late 1920s by the cut-and-cover method resulted in the demolition of many churches and other architectural landmarks, despite the fact that many of them had been restored only a few years earlier (Palamarchuk 1992: 14). In the late 1920s, while the city population was rapidly growing, 23 churches were demolished to clear places for new school construction because at that time 80 percent of pre-revolutionary school buildings in Moscow were occupied by other new organizations. Another 80 downtown churches were demolished in favor of residential and office construction (ibid., 14-5).

Whereas before the 1917 revolution the city had more than 650 functioning Orthodox churches (ibid., 7; Palamarchuk 1989: 8), by January 1, 1933, this figure was just 112 and, by April 1, 1936, just 75 (GARF f. 5263 op.2 d.10). In 1985, only 42 churches (or seven percent of the 1917 total number) remained open on the territory of ca. 1917 Moscow (Palamarchuk 1989: 8). By that time, half of all the 1917 churches had been demolished while the remainder were simply closed or reutilized. It is difficult to cite examples of other major world cities with a similar dramatic secularization of the urban landscape.

Table 6.1. Status of Moscow churches in 1917, 1985, 1990 and 1995.

Part of city	1917 Open	1985 Open	1985 % of 1917	1990 Open	1990 % of 1917	1990 Closed	1990 % of 1917	1990 Demolished	1990 % of 1917	1995 Sept Open	1995 % of 1917
Kremlin & monast.	145	8	5.5	47	32.4	33	22.8	66	45.5	41	28.3
Kitai gorod	27	0	0.0	1	3.7	12	44.4	14	51.9		
Belyi gorod	76	4	5.3	5	6.6	24	31.6	47	61.8		
Zemlianoi gorod	101	5	5.0	10	9.9	34	33.7	58	57.4		
Zamoskvorech'e	50	3	6.0	12	24.0	16	32.0	23	46.0		
Center, total	399	20	5.0	75	18.8	119	29.8	208	52.1	41	28.3
Margins of 1917	278	22	7.9	38	13.7	109	39.2	141	50.7		
Margins of 1960	87	12	13.8	42	48.3	14	16.1	32	36.8		
Total Moscow	764	54	7.1	155	20.3	242	31.7	381	49.9	219	28.7
Moscow oblast'	1174	133	11.3							551	46.9
Non-Orthodox	84	13	15.5	16	19.0	21	25.0	52	61.9	0.0	
incl. Old Belief	57	5	8.8							6	10.5
Old Belief in Moscow oblast'	36	11	30.6							14	38.9

Sources: Palamarchuk (1989: 8; 1992: 7), *Pravoslavnaia Moskva* (1995), the Committee on Relations with Religious Organizations of Moscow Oblast', unpub. data. Note: Data for Moscow oblast' is for 1917, 1980, and 1.1.1995. Old Believers are included in "Non-Orthodox." For location of the historic areas of the city, see Figure 6.2.

A third force altering Moscow's Orthodox cityscape during the Soviet era was an *urban expansion*, that produced a large-scale residential mismatch. In 1897 Moscow was a city of slightly more than one million inhabitants (*Pervaia Vseobschaia* 1903), but by the 1990s its total population was close to nine million, and the daytime population (including commuters and tourists) exceeded ten million (Table 6.2). The territorial extent of the city had also expanded well beyond the original pre-Soviet 1917 city boundary. While Moscow's population quintupled and its territory quadrupled (Colton 1995), the city is certainly different from its pre-revolutionary predecessor. The main Church was not allowed to respond to these changes, however, so the typical residential land-

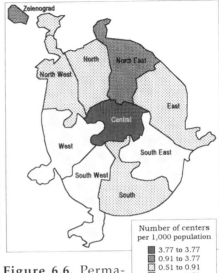

Number of centers
per 1,000 population
- ■ 3.77 to 3.77
- ▦ 0.91 to 3.77
- ▧ 0.51 to 0.91
- ☐ 0.32 to 0.51

Figure 6.5. New temporary chapel in a typical Moscow residential neighborhood (Otradnoe) characteristically church-less during the Soviet period. Photo by the author, 1998.

Figure 6.6. Permanent religious centers in Moscow okrugs related to population, 1991. Source: Table 6.3, Sidorov (1998: 160).

scape of modern Moscow is either churchless, or includes small, originally rural churches, which geographically and architecturally seem out of place in their new urban setting (Figure 6.5).

A profound territorial mismatch, thus, has emerged between the church-packed downtown (the city of the 19th century), the official city (within the administrative boundaries), and the actual city (metropolitan area[8]). It is common among specialists of Moscow church geography to divide the territory of the contemporary city into three zones: 1) an historical center of the city, encircled by the Garden Ring, with five traditional districts [the Kremlin, Kitai gorod (China town), Belyi gorod (White town), Zemlianoi gorod (Earth town), and Zamoskvorech'e (Trans-river)]; 2) the rest of the 1917 city (between the Garden Ring and Kamer-kollezhskii val); and 3) the margins of contemporary Moscow (between the 1917 city boundary and the latest, 1984, boundary with annexes. For convenience, some authors prefer to use the 1960 Ring Road as the city boundary because it is more clearly defined) (Figure 6.3).

Table 6.2. Structure of daytime population of Moscow, 1986-92.

Composites of population	Unit of analysis	1986	1989	1992
1. Present population	mln people	8.7	8.97	8.96
Permanent population		8.6	8.88	8.87
Difference		0.11	0.09	0.09
2. Temporary population,	mln people/day	1.66	1.8	1.8
incl. daily commuters		0.6	0.7	0.7
occasional commuters		0.59	0.6	0.6
tourists, businesspeople		0.47	0.5	0.5
3. Total daytime population	mln people/day	10.3	10.8	10.8

Source: NIiPI Genplana Moskvy 1992: 80. Compiled by V. G. Glushkova.

According to incomplete data from the Institute for General Planning of Moscow (NIiPI Genplana Moskvy 1991), in 1917 there were about 520 Orthodox and Edinoverie churches in Moscow.[9] By 1991, only 138 of the 280 churches located outside the historical center of the city (bounded by the Garden Ring) had survived, and of these only 22 were functioning.[10] On the territory between the 1917 and the 1984 city boundaries, 64 churches survived, only 22 of which were functioning.[11] Altogether, outside the historical center of Moscow, 202 churches survived, only 44 of which were functioning (NIiPI Genplana Moskvy 1991: Ch. 3). Similar data are included in Table 6.1, showing the status of churches in Moscow in 1917, 1985, 1990, and 1995 (Palamarchuk 1989).

Modern Moscow has been divided into three zones for planning the allocation of churches, with different goals for each area. The historical center of the city, with its relatively numerous preserved churches, primarily needs only the restoration of the buildings' religious functions, i.e., to begin services. The middle zone (the margins of 1917 city) has fewer churches but many fortress monasteries; the environment here has been significantly altered by urbanization, and policy should be aimed at adaptating surviving churches to their new urban context. The rest of the modern city, between the 1917 and 1984 boundaries, consists primarily of new residential neighborhoods built on former rural lands that are often church-less. Therefore, new church constructions are more important here.

During this time not only did the total number of churches in the city decline disastrously, the urban geography of churches was also altered. Table 6.1 shows that the margins of the city were relatively more fortunate in preserving functioning churches; here 13.8 percent of all churches in 1917 were still functioning in 1985 (twice the 7.1 percent average for the city as a whole). Yet this is somewhat misleading since these areas were rural in 1917 and have since been absorbed by the expanding city. It is here that the majority of Moscow's population now resides.

According to father Vladimir (Divakov), the dean of the Central church district (*blagochinie*) of Moscow diocese, as of September 1996 Moscow had 228 parish churches. The total number of churches of all types (including chapels) was 307; of them, 162 were in the center of the city and 145 in other districts (Divakov 1996).

Table 6.3 contains data on the distribution of permanent religious centers in Moscow okrugs (prefectures) in 1991. Figure 6.6 maps these data showing the number of religious centers related to population. On the map, Central Okrug is clearly leading, while the average density of the centers for the city as a whole is 0.83 per 1000 people and 0.07 per sq. km. The same parameters for the Central Okrug are 4 times higher (3.77 and 0.30 respectively). Overall, the southern half of the city has lower densities for church centers than the northern part. In particular, the north-eastern part of the city has a relatively high density of centers.

Table 6.3. Permanent religious centers in Moscow by okrug, mid-1991.

Okrug	Functioning centers, number	Area, sq.km	Population, thousand	Center's areal sq. km per center	1000 population per center	Centers' density centers per 1000 population	center per sq. km
Central	26	87	690	3.35	26.5	3.77	0.30
North East	10	102	1095	10.20	109.5	0.91	0.10
Eastern	9	151	1255	16.78	139.4	0.72	0.06
South East	3	112	833	37.33	277.7	0.36	0.03
Southern	7	131	1360	18.71	194.3	0.51	0.05
South West	3	107	952	35.67	317.3	0.32	0.03
Western	4	133	1030	33.25	257.5	0.39	0.03
North West	4	107	602	26.75	150.5	0.66	0.04
Northern	6	87	970	14.50	161.7	0.62	0.07
Zelenograd	2	36	169	18.00	84.5	1.18	0.06
Total	**74**	**1053**	**8956**	**14.23**	**121.0**	**0.83**	**0.07**
incl. urban parts	72	994	8956	13.81	124.4	0.80	0.07

Source: NIiPI Genplana Moskvy (1992: 71, 81). Comp. by V. G. Glushkova.
Note: Central Okrug's 26 centers include 3 synagogues, 2 mosques, and 2 Roman-Catholic churches.

Table A6.3 shows the profile of registered religious organizations in Moscow oblast' in 1994. Figure A6.1 depicts the geographical distribution of Orthodox communities in Moscow oblast'. The gradient of Orthodox parish density outside of Moscow is almost the opposite of that in the inner city. While the highest density of religious centers in the latter is in the downtown, and density decreases with distance from the center, in the peripheral area the density of registered communities increases with distance from the city. This pattern is most likely a result of the metropolis' attractiveness to the population of neighboring districts of the oblast' that not only used to commute to Moscow for jobs, but also to practice their religions.

Denationalizing Churches: Cult/Culture Conflicts

Denationalization of church property has been accompanied by conflicts, primarily between communities of believers and the current occupants of the formerly religious buildings. Such current occupants of former churches as Dental Clinic no. 1 (Katys 1995), Moscow school no. 1216 (Aksenov 1994), Soiuzmul'tfil'm cartoon studios (Mikhailov 1994, Vasil'ev 1994), the Moscow Institute of Architecture (Tyssovskaia 1994), the Russian Literature Museum and Beryozka dance group (Melikiants 1994), the old building of Moscow State University (Lobacheva 1994, Filonova 1994, Nikol'skaia 1994a, Kozlov 1994, "V MGU Budet" 1993, Beglov 1994, *Rossiiskaia Gazeta* 1994), the Tret'iakov Gallery (Strel'chik 1993, G. Dmitriev 1994) and the 1812 Patriotic War Museum in Fili (Arpishkin 2000, Revzin 2000a) were all suddenly involved in conflicts over former church property which had been recycled for secular purposes. In Moscow oblast' many museums are located in former churches and monasteries, so denationalization poses a threat to culture equal only to the Bolshevik aggression (Savostiuk et al. 1994). For example, two unique museums of religious art, in New Jerusalem monastery in Istra (Vystorobest 1994, Kulakova 1994, Charondin 1994) and Trinity-St.Sergii Lavra in Sergiev Posad (Kuprach 1993, Sorokin 1993, Krestnikov 1993, "Paskhal'nyi Podarok Patriarkhu" 1994, Vaneeva 1992), have lost their juridical battles for buildings and must vacate them. Since no alternative locations are immediately available, these museums feel threatened with extinction.

As some authors insist, the generosity of the Moscow City Government (and personally Luzhkov) in transferring denationalized church property to the ROCh could, in fact, be part of a latent redistribution of rent revenue currents in favor of its protégé-businesses. The transfer of property from the City Government to the Church and further, to new commercial renters, would shield them from state control because various bureaucratic controlling agencies prefer to avoid touching the Church. The Church would benefit too: many religious organizations have, for a long time, been successful money laundering institutions (Komarov 1999).

NEW CHURCH CONSTRUCTION

Allocation of Places for New Church Construction

In 1997 the Institute for General Planning in Moscow has completed a unique project which provides a scientific rationale for allocation of sites for cult buildings of different major religions in Moscow (NIiPI 1997, Konovalov 1999, Figures 6.7 and 6.8). Characteristically, as of 2000, the Mayor of Moscow has not officially signed and approved the scheme, reportedly because he has lost interest in the topic (perhaps because of the reconstruction of the Cathedral of Christ the Savior, Chapter 7). In the absence of such a comprehensive and objective rationale, permission for church buildings is given on a case-by-case basis – a fact which provides a fertile ground for different injustices and complaints.

In the mid-1990s, there were 10 new churches under construction in Moscow (*Pravoslavnaia Moskva* 1995: 8) (one of them, the Cathedral of Christ the Savior, was strictly speaking a case of reconstruction, rather than new construction). In addition, 73 sites had been reserved for new construction in the future (Figures 6.7 and 6.8; Sidorov 1998: 316). Clearly, most of these new sites are located outside the downtown, in the best focal points of new residential districts of the city; together with the sites of demolished and closed churches, they create a relatively dense network of new churches. This pattern would apparently challenge my hypothesis that post-Soviet property return in all its forms reinforces the Soviet mismatch between the Church and the city. In this section of the chapter, I intend to provide arguments against this conclusion. My main idea is that the network of new church construction sites preserves the best sites in the city for the main Russian Orthodox Church (the ROCh), providing it with some additional advantages over competing alternative communities and congregations. For instance, according to specialists at the Institute of General Planning of Moscow (1997), there is a convention that no alternative Ortho-

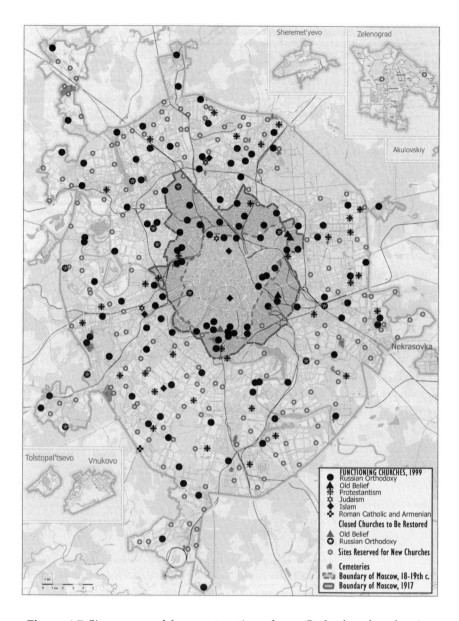

Figure 6.7. Sites reserved for construction of new Orthodox churches in Moscow, 1999. Sources: the author's adaptation of Konovalov (1999: 59); Sidorov (1998: 164, 316).

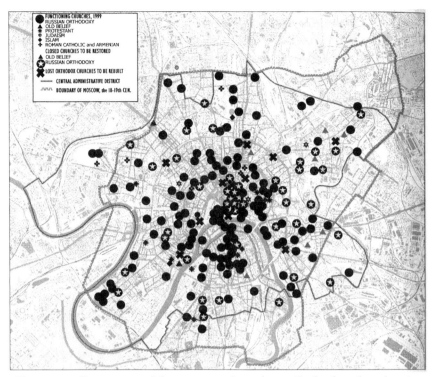

Figure 6.8. Sites reserved for construction of new Orthodox churches in downtown Moscow, 1999. Sources: the author's adaptation of Konovalov (1999: 59, 60); Sidorov (1998: 164, 316).

dox churches or other religious buildings be permitted to be built within sight of ROCh churches because of possible conflicts. Therefore, the denser the network of these reserved potential sites outside the downtown area, the less chance other communities have to erect their own religious buildings. Paradoxically, this network may not decrease the mismatch because it could work to *prevent* new church constructions outside the downtown. Proposed memorial symbols (plaques and signs) at the places of lost churches (Table 6.4, Figure 6.13) can serve a similar purpose. While the ROCh is preoccupied with restoration of its already-existing buildings, the plaques and signs will implicitly prevent any alternative church construction in their vicinity. In addition, most cases of actual, as opposed to possible, construction sites are located primarily in the center of the city.

Figure 6.9. The restored Church of Kazan' Icon of the Holy Virgin on Red Square (photo by the author, 1996).

Figure 6.10. Plaque inside the Church of Kazan' Icon of the Holy Virgin on Red Square (photo by the author, 1996).

Church of Kazan' Icon of the Holy Virgin on Red Square

Perhaps the first church restored in Moscow during the 1990s was the Church of Kazan' Icon of the Holy Virgin on Red Square (Kazanskii Church) (Figure 6.9). From the very beginning, it served as a trial test for the restoration of the Cathedral of Christ the Savior (and other reconstructions), and can be treated as its small version and a pioneer of some of its features (Chapter 7).

Kazanskii Church was first built in 1626 by Tsar Mikhail Fedorovich Romanov and Count Pozharskii, the liberator of Moscow from Polish-Lithuanian invaders. The church was rebuilt in 1636 after it was destroyed by fire. Here, in 1812 the Commander-in-Chief of the army, Mikhail Kutuzov, received a blessing for his victory over Napoleon's troops. The church was demolished in 1936, yet in 1927-32 Petr Dmitrievich Baranovskii undertook the heroic task of measuring the building and preserving the church's original design for future restoration (Beliaev and Pavlovich 1993, Trofimov 1993).

Table 6.4. Proposed memorial symbols (plaques and signs) at the places of lost churches.

Area	churches	plaques	signs
Kremlin			
demolished churches	10		
suggested symbols	10	7	3
Kitai-Gorod			
demolished churches	27		
suggested symbols	8	3	5
Belyi Gorod			
demolished churches	63		
suggested symbols	38	24	14
Zemlianoi Gorod			
demolished churches	53		
suggested symbols	58	29	29
Between Garden Ring and Ring Road			
demolished churches	130		
suggested symbols	72	52	20
Total			
demolished churches	283		
suggested symbols	186	115	71

Source: NIiPI, unpub. data, 1991-92. Note: These figures are only a rough estimate. For location of the historic areas of the city, see Figure 6.2.

The decision to reconstruct this historically remarkable church was made as early as 1988 (ibid.). Small, yet prominently located on Red Square opposite St. Basil's church, it promised to become a definite success. The city government under Mayor Luzhkov finally undertook the project. The church was officially reopened in November 1993, after a year and a half of construction work.[12]

The following practices tested during this restoration were repeated in the restoration of the Cathedral of Christ the Savior (Chapter 7) and are worth summarizing:

1) This church was rebuilt in speedy fashion.

2) The Moscow Patriarchate helped little in the restoration and had conflicts with the church's community (Armeev 1994).

3) Expenses have been paid mostly by the Moscow government, not the federal one (and certainly not by public contributions).

4) The public was offered only negligible participation in the

reconstruction. Utilization of their donations was doubtful,[13] and public participation in the church's formal opening had been refused (Zavrazhin 1993) or strictly limited.

5) The relative disregard for other Churches was illustrated by the fact that the largest bell in the new church belonged to a different Orthodox Church (the Old Believers)[14] (Korolev 1993b). The Moscow Patriarchate reportedly knew this (Nezhnyi 1993a).

Most importantly, the restored church on Red Square openly symbolizes state power. In its entrance hall, the new church has a golden plaque with lighted candles below. It states, among other things, that "this church was restored by the order of the first Russian President B. N. Yel'tsin and the efforts of Moscow Mayor Yu. M. Luzhkov and his deputy A. S. Matrosov" (Gronskii 1994; Palishin 1994) (Figure 6.10).

As will be shown in the next chapter, the reconstruction of the Cathedral of Christ the Savior has been characterized by similar processes. This pattern was replicated in other places in Moscow too, such as SS Boris and Gleb Chapel on Arbat Square.

SS Boris and Gleb Chapel near Arbat Gates

SS Boris and Gleb Chapel was one of the oldest churches in the area near Arbat Gates in Moscow. The chapel and the area were first mentioned in 1453 (Kozlov 1997). However, according to *The Journal of Moscow Patriarchate*, the chapel was initially built in 1527. In any case, in the style that we know it today the chapel has existed since 1764, when the original chapel was profoundly altered and restored in western European Baroque style (architect K. I. Blank). The second half of the 18th cen. was a dramatic period for ancient churches in Moscow: many were ruined and replaced by more trendy, western-style churches reminiscent of Paris, Vienna or Rome more than the ancient Orthodox Moscow (Kozlov 1997).[15] Despite a serious conflict among nobility who traditionally used to live near the Arbat Gates area, the chapel was "westernized" too (ibid.).

In 1922[16] the new city authorities issued a decree for demolition of the chapel because "it constrained traffic" and "due to new city planning" (K. 1997). Citing the architectural uniqueness of the chapel (one of the best examples of the Baroque style church in Moscow), the intelligentsia managed to keep postponing the implementation of the decree for some time (Kozlov 1997). In 1929, "the first tragic year for Orthodox Moscow" (Kozlov 1997), many churches in the area were closed

Figure 6.11. The restored SS Boris and Gleb Chapel near Arbat Gates in front of the Ministry of Defense (photo by the author, 1998).

Figure 6.12. Plaque inside the restored SS Boris and Gleb Chapel near Arbat Gates, photo by the author (1998). It says, among other things, that this chapel was restored in 1997 "with support of the President of the Russian Federation B.N.Yel'tsin and efforts of Moscow Mayor Yu.M.Luzhkov." The chapel is restored at the site of a previously ruined church. Site of the original SS Boris and Gleb Chapel is actually several dozen meters aside.

Figure 6.13. Memorial sign on the site of the original SS Boris and Gleb Chapel (photo by the author). Only the cupola of the restored chapel is visible at the background (behind the metro entrance building).

and replaced by proletarian dormitories. In this way the new authorities demonstrated their desire to alter the traditional social profile of the neighborhood dominated by old Moscow intelligentsia and nobility (Kozlov 1997). In 1930, the chapel was ruined (K. 1997).

Resurrection of the chapel in post-Soviet Moscow was carried out with remarkable speed. The Patriarch of Moscow and All Russia, Alexii II, blessed the foundation stone for SS Boris and Gleb Chapel on May 8, 1997. Three months later the chapel was opened (Figure 6.11). It is noteworthy that the foundation ceremony for the chapel was attended by the highest political figures, President of the Russian Federation Boris Yel'tsin, Prime-Minister Viktor Chernomyrdin, and Moscow Mayor Yurii Luzhkov (K. 1997). The restoration had gone remarkably smoothly and a plaque inside informs that this chapel was restored in 1997 "with support of the President of the Russian Federation B.N.Yel'tsin and efforts of Moscow Mayor Yu.M.Luzhkov" (Figure 6.12).

At the same time, it is not well-publicized that SS Boris and Gleb Chapel has been restored on the site of another 17th cen. church ruined by the Soviet authorities in 1933, the Church of Holy Hierarch Tikhon, the Bishop Amafutinskii (Figure 6.13). Being initially situated next to one another, both churches witnessed the same historical events and therefore should be equally revered, even if they are not equal in all other respects. The reason for replacement of one sacred structure by another could be better understood if the changed geographical and political context of the place were taken into consideration.

The chapel re-emerges now not as a major church of the area but rather as a main church of a powerful ministry. During Soviet times the area of Arbat Gates has been dramatically transformed by construction there of the headquarters of the Ministry of Defense. SS Boris and Gleb are traditionally protectors of the men with arms. The restoration in front of the major military complex of the chapel devoted to the military seemed for the authorities highly appropriate, even if it now occupies the site of another church. Despite that, at the foundation ceremony Yel'tsin expressed his hope that the reconstruction would contribute to reconciliation and accord in the country (K. 1997). Indeed, this was an important goal at the time of the Chechen unrest. Ironically, according to legend, Boris and Gleb were victims of an internal quarrel between ancient Russian princedoms. In any event, the reconstruction of the chapel itself was remarkably without conflict and not widely publicized. Rumors suggested that the flawless reconstruction was personally and discretely backed by Boris Yel'tsin whose only grandson's name is Gleb.

Figure 6.14. The new Church of Kazan' Icon of the Holy Virgin near Kaluga Gates (October Square) in front of the headquarters of the Min istry of Internal Affairs (photo by the author, 2000).

The Church of Kazan' Icon of the Holy Virgin near Kaluga Gates

The SS Boris and Gleb Chapel is not the only "show-case" church of key power groups in Russia. In 2000, the Ministry of Internal Affairs of the Russian Federation has also built its own church. The two cases share a number of remarkable similarities.

The restored Church of Kazan' Icon of the Holy Virgin near Kaluga Gates was first built in 1627 of wood (Sigida 2000) and, in 1694, restored in stone in the Byzantine style (Dorovskikh 2000). In 1927 the church was closed[17] but, in 1929, reopened as museum of the Mining Academy; in 1933 the belfry was partly deconstructed and the church was again opened as a cinema (Dorovskikh 2000). In 1972 the church was dynamited to clear place for headquarters of the Ministry of Internal Affairs (Sigida 2000). In the late 1990s, the Minister of Internal Affairs, Sergey Stepashin, proposed restoration of the church and it was built (under a new minister) not far from its original site in front of the ministry (Figures 6.14 and 6.15).

The consecration ceremony in 2000 was attended by all the highest politicians in the country. The ex-president Boris Yel'tsin in his

Figure 6.15. Plaque on the new Church of Kazan' Icon of the Holy Virgin near Kaluga Gates (October Square), photo by the author, 2000. The plaque states, among other things, that "this church was built in 2000 to honor the died defenders of social order [policemen]" and "is built with voluntary donations. Names of the donors, Our Lord, You know yourself."

speech referred to the symbolism of the Kazan' Icon of the Holy Virgin which is traditional protector of Russia from disasters and invaders. At the same time the new president, Vladimir Putin, paid respect to "our comrades [policemen] who fell for the interests of Russia" (Sigida 2000). Putin may have some personal attachment to the church since his close friend and classmate has been appointed as its senior priest (Rosbizneskonsalting 2000). There were complaints that this ceremony continues the policy of privileging Orthodoxy over other religions in Russia (Babaeva 2000, Ovrutskii 2000). It is too early to say if the conspiratory and technocratic-minded Putin will follow the religious policies of the emotional Yel'tsin or the flamboyant Luzhkov.[18]

In any case, the reconstruction followed the trend – the restored churches of Moscow downtown often re-emerge with newly added political meanings. The ministries of Defense and Internal Affairs are likely to be followed by other powerful organizations such as the Ministry of Railroads. Even shopping malls may have their own churches, as the case of Alexandr Nevskii Chapel on Manege Square reveals.

Alexandr Nevskii Chapel on Manege Square

The Chapel of Aleksandr Nevskii was the first Moscow victim of the Bolshevik anti-religious assault in the 1920s (Palamarchuk 1992). Not only has it been demolished, but the buildings around it, too, have

Figure 6.16. The three-level underground shopping mall on Manege Square photo by the author, 2000).

been totally ruined during the Soviet period (Figures 6.04). The current Manege Square did not exist before the Bolshevik revolution. Located in the very heart of Moscow, this square was considered an alternative site for the Palace of Soviets (Chapter 7; Figure 7.13). Eventually, the square was created as a result of clearing space for a wide prospect leading to the Palace of the Soviets. This square has again ceased to exist in the 1990s with completion of a cultural-business center underground.[19] It is now occupied by a park with pedestrian sidewalks, skylights and plazas set amid numerous monuments to all past Russian tsars.

Initially, the underground complex on Manege Square was planned at six or seven underground levels with a total space of 140,000 sq. m., at an estimated total cost of $150 million (Shimanskii 1996). This plan included a concert hall, a historical theater, an archeological museum, and a portrait gallery of Moscow's most prominent figures. The first three stories (counting from the top) will be given over to the museum of the History of Moscow and the Russian State, stores, offices, restaurants and casinos. The fourth story is designed for technical support, and the fifth and sixth are intended for garages. Britain's Bovis company and Lambert Scott Inns developed another design providing

Figure 6.17. Architect's model of the proposed Alexandr Nevskii Chapel on Manege Square (photo by the author, 1998). The building at the background to the left is Moskva Hotel, and to the right – the Historical Museum.

for 70,000 sq. m. in three levels. Construction costs were supposed to be raised from investors interested in retail space. The third design, currently implemented, was presented at the end of 1995. The architects proposed to emphasize the content on the ground, laying out three terraces. Only three levels are underground — housing a museum, restaurants and stores, a section of the underground Neglinka River and parking-lots. Each level has a different architectural theme. The first brings the Kremlin palaces to mind; the second is reminiscent of Russian architecture in *le style moderne*; while the third is classical. This proposal drew sharp criticism from the Moscow Architectural Council, however. An art historian remarked that, in its design, the "pompous" complex reminded him of the declining years of the Roman Empire, "it is eclectic in the worst sense of the word" (Figure 6.16) (Andriiasova 1996).

    With the gradually eroding nature of the project and increasing criticism, a major addition to the project has been suggested – a little Chapel of Alexandr Nevskii (Figure 6.17). The "crystal crown" of the chapel would shield the Manege underground complex from potential criticism. The chapel would become a part of the secular amusement complex and its restoration would be only symbolic. As of 2000, the chapel has not yet been restored. Perhaps with growing popularity of the Manege shopping mall, the urgency of the chapel's restoration diminished.

Figure 6.18. "Tragedy of People." Sculpture in the Victory Complex on Poklonnaia Hill (author Zurab Tsereteli). Photo by the author, 1998.

St. George Victorious Church on Poklonnaia Hill

The competition between the ROCh and alternative *Orthodox* communities is analyzed in the last part of this chapter. This section, in contrast, considers the role of the new church constructions in the ROCh's competition with *non-Orthodox* alternatives.[20] The disputed construction of St. George Church on Poklonnaia Hill is particularly noteworthy in this regard.

The Memorial on Poklonnaia Hill was built in 1995 to commemorate the Victory in the Great Patriotic War of 1941-45. It took the country 50 years to design the complex, perhaps as a result of changing ideological context and, in part, because of the disastrous WWII casualty list for the former USSR. The image of countless people falling like dominos (Figure 6.18) reflects this theme. Initially placed near the entrance to the park complex, the monument was later moved to the interior, reportedly because of complaints by local residents that the proximity of such a dark image has negatively affected the value of their property (Klin 2000).

Figure 6.19. "Bayonet" obelisk, the main monument of the memorial complex on Poklonnaia Hill, built in 1995 to commemorate Victory in the Great Patriotic War of 1941-45. The 141.8-meter obelisk (a reference to the 1418 days of the war) is topped by a winged statue of Nike, the Greek pagan goddess of Victory. Photo by the author, 1998.

Figure 6.20. The bottom part of the obelisk at the Victory Memorial Complex on Poklonnaia Hill with a monument to St. George Victorious killing an enemy-snake. Photo by the author, 1998.

The very location of the memorial even raised questions. The Hill is historically significant primarily in the context of the first, not the second, Patriotic War,[21] creating some doubts about the ethicalness of constructing a war memorial on the historical site of another war (Korneev 1993). This geographical juxtaposition perhaps improved the image of the second, Great Patriotic War with its disastrous casualty list. While the image was improved, the actual Hill was flattened by the construction and ceased to exist as a landform (Kusov 1995). The erected 141.8-meter obelisk,[22] the Memorial's central symbol, could not substitute for the loss of this landmark hill (Figure 6.19). The black obelisk unwelcomely imitates the shape of a three-edged bayonet which has been banned everywhere as a barbaric weapon. The obelisk is topped by a winged statue of Nike, the Greek goddess of Victory (sculptor Tsereteli). The obelisk could perhaps be justified as an engineering

Figure 6.21. The Church of St. George Victorious, the patron saint of Moscow, stands near the central pathway of the Victory Memorial Complex on Poklonnaia Hill (1993-95, architect Polianskii). Photo by the author, 1998.

Figure 6.22. Bas-reliefs on the Church of St. George Victorious on Poklonnaia Hill (sculpture by Z. Tsereteli). Photo by the author, 1998.

masterpiece and the tallest construction in the world, having a proportion of height to width of 20:1 (architects Budayev, Vavakin and others) (Zubtsova and Lutskii 1995), however, some Orthodox find the pagan imagery of the obelisk inappropriate for such a memorial.

In its grandiose style, the design of the Memorial is characteristically totalitarian yet mass-cultural in its eclecticism (Figure 6.20). Designed in the late-Soviet period, it looks strangely as though it was completed in the style of a completely different aesthetic epoch (Tumarkin 1995). Mayor Yu. Luzhkov has publicly acknowledged the aesthetic shortcomings of the project, yet still argues that this was a noble burden to be carried for the sake of giving recognition to the 50th anniversary of the Victory. It is worth mentioning that the actual construction was subsidized with a loan from the local Moscow authorities. A year later the federal government still owed this debt to the local government of Moscow. The final stage of construction was quite rapid, carried out with great dispatch and a rush to meet the deadline of May 1995. In the last stages of the design, the project was saved (or at least significantly upgraded) by adding a modern Orthodox church[23] named

Figure 6.23. Mosque at the Victory Memorial Complex on Poklonnaia Hill (opened in 1997). Photo by the author, 1998.

after St. George the Victorious (Figure 6.21).[24] Initially designed as a small church (15x15 meters, 40 meters to the cross) for 30-50 parish believers, or as a place for special events (*Moskovskii Komsomolets* 1993b), it has become one of Moscow's most popular churches, constantly packed with visitors. This despite the fact that against the canons of Orthodoxy the church has been decorated not with icons, but with bas-reliefs, both inside and out (Rokhlin 1995) (Figure 6.22).

The Memorial's association with Orthodoxy has resulted in a controversy over religious tolerance which has not yet been resolved. The project could become an undemocratic model for other projects in the city, especially since, obviously, not only Orthodox faithful died in the war. Mayor Luzhkov has had to allow construction in the Memorial of churches of other "historically significant" religions in Russia, i.e., a Catholic church, a mosque and a synagogue (Figures 6.23 and 6.24).[25] An area of 0.5 hectare has been rented out for 49 years to erect the synagogue and mosque in the western portion of the Park. A place for the Catholic church has also been assigned, as well as for other confessions (Korneev 1993), but as of 2000, any further church constructions in the park are not likely. No land assignments have been made to other confessions. Some critics have, as a result, begun asking whether the war monument is to become a museum of religions.[26] If so, interconfessional conflicts are possible. For instance, the Mayor's per-

Table 6.5. Prospective religious composition of Moscow population.

Religion	Official account		Expert estimation		Expert forecast	
	1970	1979	1989	1992	2001	2011
Orthodoxy	93.4	94.6	94.8	89.5	84	82.2
Judaism	3.5	2.8	2	4.5	6	6.2
Islam	1.9	1.9	2.4	5	8	8.5
Catholics	0.3	0.5	0.4	0.5	1	1.1
Other	0.8	0.2	0.4	0.5	1	2
Total	100	100	100	100	100	100

Source: NIIiPI Genplana Moskvy (1992: 87). Compiled by V. G. Glushkova.

mit for construction of the synagogue has ignited criticisms from very different positions. On the one hand, some existing local Jewish organizations[27] refused to accept that a foreign-based charity organization can build a Jewish monument (Korneev 1993). Instead, they insisted on building their own alternative memorial building in memory of Jewish citizens who died in the war (*Segodnia* 1993). On the other hand, there are critics claiming that only the Orthodox Church has the historical right to be in this place, for in Russia national monuments only contain Orthodox churches (Alexeeva 1993; Korneev 1993).

In light of this debate, it is interesting to mention that according to specialists of the Institute of General Planning of Moscow Orthodox

Figure 6.24. Synagogue at the Victory Memorial Complex on Poklonnaia Hill (photo by the author, 1999).

dominance in the city will gradually decline, although not significantly. In the early 1990s, Institute researchers conducted a study into the religious situation and its relation to the needs of the city in the near future (NIiPI Genplana Moskvy 1991; Table 6.5). According to Table 6.5, by 2001 the proportion of Orthodox believers in Moscow will drop almost 10 percent in comparison with 1989 (84 percent and 94.8 percent respectively). Islam and Judaism are expected to gain in this period of "religious restructuring." Although their proportion is expected to stay significantly lower than that of Orthodoxy, the general tendency of non-Orthodox beliefs to grow questions the policy of privileging one religion in places like Poklonnaia Hill.

Before the remainder of this chapter focuses on specifically Orthodox competition for church property, I would like to link the projects discussed so far to the restoration of the Cathedral of Christ the Savior discussed in Chapter 7. Like the project to restore the chapel on Manege Square, the "successful" Memorial complex on Poklonnaia Hill has shown the potential of even a "touch of Orthodoxy" for improving public perception of a project in motivating similar actions in subsequent projects. The idea of using Orthodox church constructions as trendy, efficient, and legitimizing additions to the risky public projects of local Moscow officials is becoming a common practice and deserves further investigation.

Erection of the church on Poklonnaia Hill created the conditions that facilitated and led to the restoration of the Cathedral of Christ the Savior (Chapter 7). The Memorial's construction served to preserve an ambitious team of well-organized construction workers and architects, who came here after finishing the Church of Kazan' Icon of the Holy Virgin on Red Square (Korolev 1993b) and eventually went on to the work of reconstructing the Cathedral. Working under deadline pressures became the norm, creating a major justification for reversing the traditional hierarchy of decision-making; now architects largely followed a construction process dominated by engineers, technicians, and managers. Indeed, technical innovations are widely publicized to hide aesthetic or even moral blunders.

The Memorial represents one of the first manifestations of what could become a unifying "grand-style" for Moscow's newest generation of projects. This "grand-style" is characterized by the dominance of monumental decorations made by one artist, Zurab Tsereteli (Shimanskii 1996). Although initially viewed as a last, beautifying remedy for a failed complex, they have subsequently come to dominate the design process.

EXCLUSION OF ALTERNATIVE ORTHODOX COMMUNITIES

Although as is evident from their formal registration alternative Orthodox communities have been legalized by the state, their actual functions in the city are constrained by denial of access to church property. The mechanism of denial is strikingly reminiscent of that utilized in Estonia: the priority of registration is the primary means of privileging the main ROCh.

The True (Catacomb) Church

There are several Catacomb communities in Moscow. After being denied access to property, many again returned to a semi-underground status, functioning out of the homes of believers. Only one of these communities agreed to be interviewed, only by telephone. This interview merely revealed the vulnerable condition of the community and its lack of entrepreneurial energy in acquiring church property. As at the national scale, the local geography of these True Orthodox communities in Moscow remains an understudied area.

Figure 6.25. St. Tsar-Martyr Nicholas II Church (under jurisdiction of the Russian Orthodox Church Abroad) in a Moscow cemetery located in a converted morgue building. Photo by the author, 1997.

The Foreign (Free) Church

The case of Foreign Church communities is better documented, although primarily by their representatives. Father Mikhail Ardov, son of a prominent writer and a gifted author himself, is the most outspoken advocate of the Foreign Church. For instance, he has widely publicized the answer of the Moscow Mayor to the question of why the Foreign Church in Russia is being persecuted. Mayor Luzhkov is reported to have said that he would not allow schisms [in Orthodoxy] and that the Foreign Church would receive no buildings in Moscow (Ardov 1996a: 112).

It is important to note the ways in which this juridically weak stand of the Moscow Mayor is realized in practice. The case of one Foreign Church community is important in this regard (Ardov 1996a: 118-119; 1996b, 1994). In 1991, after a long delay, legal authorities in Moscow registered the Brotherhood of Job Pochaevskii. The chairman of the Brotherhood, A. V. Mikhal'chenkov, thereafter immediately began the process of obtaining a church building. By that time, however, almost all existing and closed Orthodox churches in Moscow (with the exception of Old Belief ones) had already been claimed by the ROCh.

Previously the Patriarch of the ROCh had submitted a listing of these churches to the Moscow authorities. If a church was not on this "Patriarch's list" and the brotherhood submitted a formal request for it, the Moscow authorities would immediately contact the ROCh, hinting that they should create a formal parish community for this church. Finally the Brotherhood would be notified that this church had already been assigned to a community of the ROCh. Similarly, to prevent transfer of the unlisted bell tower of the demolished church of the nativity of St. John the Baptist (Pokrovka Street and Garden Ring), the authorities, Mayor Luzhkov and the governor of the Central district A. Muzykantskii, transferred the whole block of old buildings together with the bell tower to the Theater of Satire and the ROCh.[28]

In light of such repeated official actions, Mikhal'chenkov took an unusual and bold step: he asked the Old Believers to transfer to the Brotherhood one of the six or seven closed churches which were to be returned to them by the state. Since the Old Belief has been in decline for a long time and has limited resources to maintain even the churches available to them in Moscow, the Church leaders agreed to help the Brotherhood. They chose a former church which is currently occupied by a club of a plant. The Old Belief Church (under Metropolitan Alimpii) then officially requested that the Moscow City Council not prevent transfer of the building to the Foreign Church. While postponing the transfer by all bureaucratic means, the authorities exercised a certain pressure on the Old Believers: they were threatened with the possibility that they would not receive any churches unless they withdrew the letter. Despite this Metropolitan Alimpii wrote a second letter "persistently recommending" the transfer of the church. Moreover, in this letter he reportedly likened the situation of the Foreign Church in Moscow to the past persecutions of the Old Believers themselves. In the end, even in this seemingly clear-cut case, the authorities finally simply refused to approve the transfer.

Similar conflicts have occurred in places outside of Moscow and have been documented not only by father Mikhail Ardov but by others. They include locations as distant as Suzdal' (Vladimir oblast'), Zheleznovodsk (Stavropol' Kray), Shadrinsk (Kurgan oblast'), Trubchevsk (Bryansk oblast'), Kuibyshev (Kainsk) (Novosibirsk oblast'), settlement Poselki (Penza oblast') (Ardov 1996a: 119-120), Novgorod oblast' (Schipanova 1994). The case of the violent closure of St. Trinity Church in Oboyan' (Kursk oblast') became especially widely cited. This parish changed its original catechism and joined the Free Church because of a conflict with the diocese's ROCh bishop. In retaliation, in August 1993, the bishop succeeded in getting a special police unit force (110 people) to empty the church of this parish. In this city of 15,000 residents and four churches, up to 1,000 people now had to pray outside the occupied church (Nezhnyi 1993b, 1993c, 1994; Scherbina 1993, Ioasaf 1993, "Khozhdenie vo Vlast'" 1994).

Having failed in downtown Moscow and at the city-wide level, alternative communities are now trying to carve out niches in less prestigious, peripheral places. The community of father Mikhail Ardov, for example, succeeded in buying a morgue and converting it into a church (Figure 6.25). Another community succeeded in establishing good relations with the administration of a cancer hospital and plans to build a new church on its territory despite protests from the main Church (Makeev 1994). In sharp contrast to the Catacomb Church, the Foreign Church's representatives have proven to be able entrepreneurs and persuasive propagandists.

Another example of using the peripheral places in the city is offered by the independent community of the extremely nationalistic priest, Alexei Aver'ianov. Aver'ianov, who was expelled from several Churches and now acts autonomously, is of interest because of his current geographical "niche." Having lost Marfo-Mar'inskaia Cloister in central Moscow and other locations in Moscow oblast', father Aver'ianov settled near the city of Podol'sk, between Moscow city and Moscow oblast'. Having been "ignored" by the local authorities of both city and oblast', he finally obtained the support of a local Cossack community around a very large cement plant and received from them a building for his church. This despite protests from priests of the main Church's Podol'sk church district (*blagochinie*) ("Nadeemsia, Chto Nash Golos" 1993).

Conclusion

This chapter has attempted to provide geographical insights into the particulars of church property de-nationalization. Such local characteristics of Moscow as the territorial mismatch between the state, society, and the Church are important for an analysis of the divergent tendencies of the church property return process.

The Orthodox Churches in Moscow are now re-emerging into a city which was radically altered by Soviet rule; altered in ways which have profoundly affected the city's distinctive churchscape. The visible abuses of church buildings as a result of reconstruction and modernization have attracted the attention of scholars, politicians and Muscovites in general (Palamarchuk 1992). In fact, these alterations of Moscow's traditional cityscape were so crude and unacceptable that popular demands to restore the "lost city" became one of the first, and politically most significant, post-Soviet popular demands. By contrast, the territorial mismatch between the location of Moscow's churches, the extent of city governance, and residential patterns has been only cursorily acknowledged and remains an understudied phenomenon. This chapter has attempted to reveal the significance of the mismatch for the politics of church property returns.

The current renaissance in Russian Orthodoxy exhibits divergent tendencies both at the large scale of Church politics and at the local scale of religious communities. While the federal state often acknowledges the existence of many other Churches at the large scale, including other Orthodox communities, local states have often successfully resisted trends toward diversification through their control of denationalized church property. The success of newly emerging alternative Orthodox communities has thus been blocked by local constraints on the allocation of religious property and space which remain primarily in state hands. Facing opposition from a new coalition between the main Church and local authorities, many alternative communities have already ceased to exist, while others continue to struggle to survive.

There are striking similarities and differences in this process in Estonia (Chapter 5) and Moscow. In both cases the dispute over property involves the ROCh – which is accused of collaboration with the Soviet regime – and Churches in exile which lack popular support. Although the states in Moscow and Estonia support different Churches, they are in agreement over their utilization of similar respective policies to achieve their political goals. Moreover, both formally allow the alternative communities to function while effectively marginalizing them through constraints on access to property.

Although a geographically nuanced account helps to reveal the unjust and hypocritical nature of current state policy towards alternative Orthodox communities, this chapter tries to go beyond merely arguing for a more consistent religious policy across all state levels. It is argued here that the religious practices of the (local) state are unjust not only because they are judicially controversial, but because they work against the city's needs. All dimensions of the post-Soviet church property transfers (denationalization; reconstruction of demolished churches; new construction) being intrinsically affected by the policy of privileging the main ROCh has resulted in the paradoxical situation whereby, because because in their current forms they increase the center-periphery discrepancy and create new, "local Iron Curtains," Communist era religious policies are continued and extended.

Chapter 6: Notes

1. Marquis Astolph de Custine (1989(1839): 395).
2. For December 1993 statistics, see "Sluzhenie Tserkvi"(1994).
3. Mikhail Moskvin-Tarkhanov, quoted in Dunaev (1994).
4. In contrast to de Custine's concluding remark, not only images of the lost Orthodox glory but also the question of "numerals" (the number of church buildings) is of vital importance for the ROCh. Both are essential elements of the politics of Orthodox property transfer in post-Soviet Russia. While proliferation of the former has helped create the necessary popular approval for de-nationalization of the property of the late Imperial Church, the latter is of vital importance for the actual politics of this transfer.
5. Different sources give different figures. *Sviatyni Drevnei Moskvy* (1993: 3) gives 677 as the number of all churches and chapels in pre-revolutionary Moscow.
6. A description of Moscow's churches and their history in English can be found in Colton (1995: 19).
7. In 1991, Vladimir Kozlov published a series of articles in *Moskovskii Zhurnal* documenting the sad destiny of Moscow churches during the Communist rule. He describes the expropriation of the churches' possessions in the 1920-30s, documenting the demolition of some Moscow churches in the 1930s, or detailing the demolition of Moscow monasteries (Kozlov 1991b, 1991c, 1991d). This study is not principally concerned with monasteries but it is worth mentioning that, as with the country as a whole, Moscow's monasteries have suffered three waves of assault: 1918-21 - the nationalization of monasteries and their reutilization as workers' dormitories, kindergartens, schools, prisons and concentration camps; 1929-31 and 1931-36 - the demolition of 10 out of Moscow's 25 monasteries.
8. Unlike in the US, metropolitan areas are not formalized statistical-administrative units and are rarely the basis for scholarly analysis or considered a part of public discourse.
9. This figure (520) contradicts to Palamarchuk's count of more than 750 churches (Table 6.1). The NIiPI Genplana Moskvy most like meant the city within 1917 boundary, while Palamarchuk considered the territory within 1960 boundary (the Ring Road).
10. These 116 closed churches initially were of the following types: 5 - army garrisons and prisons, 12 - shelters, 27 - clinics and hospitals; 44 - parish, 16 - charity centers, 8 - schools and institutes; 4 - town churches (NIiPI Genplana Moskvy 1991, Ch. 5).

11. Of these 64 churches, 39 were parish churches of rural settlements (15 are still functioning), and 25 were parish churches on estates (7 still functioning).

12. The cathedral might not have been immediately opened to public.

13. The initial cost of the Kazanskii Church's reconstruction was expected to be 6 million rubles. In the first year people donated 2 million. Later inflation lowered this amount (Korolev 1993a). Authorities did not even see the people's donated money. The priest of the cathedral insists that the donated money has been used carefully (Armeev 1993).

14. The bell was made in 1908 for the bell-tower on the Rogozhskoe cemetery and stored until recently in the Kremlin Congress's Palace' storehouse. It has an engraved message confirming its origin (Nezhnyi 1993a).

15. For an example of the ancient Orthodox Moscow style characterized often by hipped-roofs and five coupols, see Figure 7.6.

16. According to the most reliable source, Kozlov 1997, the decree was issued in 1929.

17. According to Sigida (2000), in 1922.

18. Putin has already been criticized for transferring, just after the politically important time of elections, an old church to the ROCh. The previous owner of the church, a state museum, would be a better preserver of the fragile edifice (Arpishkin 2000, Revzin 2000a).

19. The construction's total estimated cost is $800 million (M. 1995).

20. For an overview of non-Orthodox religious organizations in Moscow, see, for example, Cherkasov-Georgievskii (1992).

21. It was on this site that, on July 11, 1812, Muscovites met Tsar Alexander I coming to Moscow. This was a historical moment, since after that the war with Napoleon became "Patriotic" (meaning wide public participation). On August 31 Kutuzov discussed here his further plans after the decisive Borodino battle. On September 2 Napoleon waited here (in vain) for the symbolic keys from the defeated Moscow (Korneev 1993).

22. The obelisk's height, 141.8 meters, corresponds to the number of days of the Great Patriotic War of 1941-45.

23. The idea of architectural design is by Anatolii Polianskii, the author of design for the cathedral in Tsaritsyno.

24. George and Yurii are interchangeable names in Russian.

25. The death rituals differ in different religions and, with ex-

ception of Christians, are not linked to church-buildings (Kliuev 1993).

26. A better solution could be a modest wall or obelisk of common memory where everyone could bring flowers, light a candle and pray.   Common Victory, common memory, common prayer (Kliuev 1993).

27. Moscow synagogue and the Congress of Jewish Religious Communities and Organizations of Russia.

28. The bell tower was to be used by the theater together with the ROCh's Patriarchal Epiphany cathedral.

Chapter 7. National Monumentalization and the Politics of Scale: The Resurrection(s) of the Cathedral of Christ the Savior in Moscow

I am sure that no church was closed without God's will.... . Certainly, we feel pity for the Cathedral of Christ the Savior which was demolished. Yet we understand that there was something in our Christian life that allowed it to be ruined.

Father Alexandr Men',
prominent Russian Orthodox priest[2]

A highly visible architectural phenomenon has altered the cityscape of Moscow. In the very heart of the city, in the area known as Volkhonka two blocks southwest of the Kremlin (Figure 6.3), on a high curved bank of the Moscow River, a 103-m-high church has been re-constructed in a single year (Figure 7.2). Officially opened in September 1997, two years later the Cathedral[3] of Christ the Savior (hereafter the Cathedral) remained only partially accessible to the public due to continuing interior work. Yet Cathedral's immense scale has already established its presence on the cityscape.

As with many preeminent national monuments, scale has always been an essential element of the Cathedral's story (Table 7.1). The initial nineteenth century plan, later abandoned, was to create the world's largest church in commemoration of the victory over in the 1812 war with Napoleon. As eventually constructed over several decades (1831-81), the first Cathedral on this site was Russia's largest church. This building was demolished by the Bolsheviks in 1931 to clear space for a new monument, the 415-m Palace of the Soviets. But this structure never was completed, and the foundation pit later became one of the world's largest outdoor swimming pools (1960-93). In recent years, this pit has arguably become Russia's most famous geographical symbol for the failed Communist endeavor. The new Cathedral has replaced the pit.

This architectural reversion corresponds to the intended symbolism of the project. The new Cathedral is publicized as a reversal of

Table 7.1. Summary of Uses and Historical Context of the Sites of the Cathedral of Christ the Savior

Use	Context					Cultural Forms	
	Dates	Founder	Political Status	Ideology	Position of the Russian Orthodox Church	Functions	Status of Construction
Convent of Alexius the Man of God	1360/1514–1837	Alexii	Metropolitan of Moscow and all Russia	Orthodox Christendom	primary political power	religious	completed
Vitberg's cathedral	1817–1825	Alexander I	Russian Emperor	spiritual leadership in post-Napoleonic Europe	department of the State	war memorial; ecumenical church complex	abandoned
Ton's cathedral	1831/1881–1931	Nicholas I	Russian Emperor	strong empire	department of the State	a major cathedral; war memorial	completed
Palace of the Soviets	1937–1941	Stalin (early)	Leader of the USSR	global communist union	subject to harsh repressions	gathering and monument to the USSR	abandoned
Pit	1941–1960	Stalin (late)	Leader of the USSR	recovery of the USSR	limited revival		
Open-air swimming pool Moskva	1960–1994	Khrushchev	Leader of the USSR	strong USSR	marginalized; subject to repressions	recreation	completed
Restored cathedral	1994/1997–present	Luzhkov	Mayor of Moscow	strong position of Moscow power group in post-Soviet Russia	formally independent; weakened by Soviet persecutions; depends on state support	main cathedral; historical memorial; headquarters of the Russian Orthodox Church; gathering/retail/parking	completed

Source: Sidorov (2000b: 551), used by permission.

Figure 7.1. Demolition of the Cathedral of Christ the Savior, 1931, shown in stills from a documentary film by V. Mikosha. Source: Kirichenko (1992: 260-62), reproduced by permission, the author's compilation.

Figure 7.2. Reconstruction of the Cathedral of Christ the Savior (photos by the author: top: 1995, middle: 1996, bottom: 1997).

the Communist practice of eradicating religion (and traditional national consciousness in general) through such place-specific actions as nationalization, closure, demolition, and juridical transfers of churches (Sidorov 1998). Thus, the reemergent Cathedral is a powerful symbol of the presumed break with the Soviet past and the beginning of yet another epoch for Russian society.

One way to explain the remarkably changing forms of national monumentalization in this place is to look at the corresponding spatial and social changes of the nation. It is an irony of history (and geography) that, coincident with the Cathedral's reconstruction, the territorial scale of the country it was meant to represent has shrunk dramatically. With the dismantling of its territorial successor, the Soviet Union, and the formation of the independent Russian Federation and other republics, in 1991 the Russian Empire finally ceased to exist as a cultural realm. As will be shown, the Cathedral's design, especially its architectural scale, reflects shifts in the scale of Russia's national identity.

The social changes in the nation have also affected the project that was meant to represent it. This book treats the nation as a threefold, politico-socio-religious construct. In addition to considerations of the state and society, the Russian national identity has been shaped by the Russian Orthodox Church (hereafter the Church) or, paradoxically, the rejection of it. For example, as mentioned previously (Chapter 2), it was a common belief in the pre-revolutionary Russian Empire that the key elements of the country's identity were its main Orthodox religion, its autocratic state system, and its distinctively unselfish compliant society. To convert to Orthodoxy meant to become Russian. Russia was said to be "Orthodoxy, Autocracy, Nationality." As the history of the Cathedral attests, the relative importance of these three entities, as well as their spatialities, were fluctuating. The interplay between the politically and spatially changing state, society and Church can explain the often peculiar forms and ways of Russian national identification.

This chapter has a threefold agenda. First, it examines the evolving process of national monumentalization as a result of conflicting political interaction and spatial non-correspondence between the state, society, and Church. Their interplay in each historical period produced the different forms that the national monument would take. The second goal is to demonstrate, within the context of the new Cathedral, that the underestimated pre-Soviet and post-Soviet practices of place manipulation are a continuing legacy. Third, by examining the politics of scale that have shaped the monument's meaning at different historical periods, including the current phase, the chapter contributes to an understanding of the importance of scale in politico-geographical studies.

Following a conceptual introduction, the body of the chapter is organized chronologically. The first chronological section describes five predecessors of the restored Cathedral: the first unrealized project; the Convent of St. Alexius the Man of God in the area of the later Cathedral (Volkhonka); the Cathedral as originally built; Stalin's unfinished Palace of the Soviets; and the derelict pit/swimming pool left after the failure of the previous project. The second examines the current restoration of the Cathedral: the relative roles of society, the Church, and the state, as well as the project's scale and funding, public perceptions, and the meaning of the added underground basement. The conclusion discusses the role of geographical scale in the project and its implications for post-Soviet Russia.

GEOGRAPHICAL STUDY OF RELIGIOUS/NATIONAL MONUMENTS

Many analysts have seen the current renaissance of the Russian Orthodox Church, after years of harsh Communist rule when literally thousands of church buildings were closed, priests were killed or imprisoned, and the Church was brought close to extinction (Pospielovsky 1984; Davis 1995), as a sign of a long-awaited religious freedom in the country (e.g., Hill 1991). Indeed, many nationalized churches were returned to believers, religious presses are now booming, and the denominational landscape is increasingly diversified. In this view, the restoration of the Cathedral, Russia's preeminent Orthodox church, is a sign of the final dismantling of the antireligious Soviet system. At the same time, the Cathedral is a major national monument, and its reconstruction signifies the beginning of a new epoch in Russian history. This coupling of secular and Christian dimensions is very typical of Eastern Orthodoxy. From the very beginning, the Cathedral had a complicated double symbolism. It was built as a national war memorial, yet designed in religious form. The Russian Orthodox Church, throughout its history, has had very close ties with the state (e.g., Ware 1963): the Communist policies of manipulating religious monuments have roots in earlier tsarist practices.[4]

Outside Russia, geographers have examined the meaning of prominent public monuments. Harvey (1979), for example, revealed the politics involved in the construction of the Basilica of the Sacred Heart in Paris; Duncan (1990) studied the politics of landscape interpretation in the Kandyan kingdom; Peet (1996) explained the political significance of Daniel Shay's Memorial in Petersham, Massachusetts; Loukaki (1997) contrasted interpretations of the Sacred Rock of the Acropolis; and Atkinson and Cosgrove (1998) examined various attempts by the Italian state to define national identity through the Vittorio Emanuele II Monument in Rome. These studies demonstrate that the construction of religious/national monuments typically involves complex political manipulations of their meanings.

The case of the new Cathedral is, however, unusual in three respects. First, this reconstruction, being an architectural "second take," self-consciously addresses the politics (i.e., the Soviet ideology) involved in a prominent landscape. At least superficially, the project is driven by critical and ethical motivations (to restore justice to the place). It will be argued here, however, that this process is only partially successful: not all historical injustices have been addressed, and some new ones have been added. Second, the case of the Cathedral has been shaped by unusually dramatic sociospatial transformations taking place in the state, society, and, especially, the Church. The result was that, in addition to the monument itself, the vacant space left after its demolition and the process of reconstruction are equally important for national identity. Third, while most monuments experience changes at different scales, the story of the Cathedral is unusually representative of the fact that scales themselves change, especially the national scale.

The traditional fixity of scale in human geography has been challenged recently by the so-called "constructionist" approach to scale advanced by Herod (1991, 1997), Smith (1992, 1993, 1994), Swyngedouw (1992), Meyer (1992), Johas (1994), Leitner (1997), Delaney and Leitner (1997), and Marston (2000). The common ground of this body of research is the assertion that geographic scale is socially constructed rather than ontologically predetermined, and that geographic scales are themselves implicated in the construction of social, economic and political processes (Leitner 1997). The traditional understanding of scale as "neutral," "objective," and "fixed" is therefore challenged (Smith 1992; Agnew 1993; Agnew and Corbridge 1995), and there is a growing understanding that the concept is period-specific (Smith and Dennis 1987; Herod 1991) and political (Taylor 1982; Staeheli 1994). Some scholars have focused on examples of "jumping scales," breaking imposed scales as part of social movements' resistance to "scalar territoriality" (Smith 1992, 1993, 1994; Staeheli 1994; Miller 1994; Adams 1996). Since scale is socially produced, there is a politics involved in its production (Herod 1991: 82), many facets of which are increasingly attracting the attention of scholars. For example, geographers have addressed the implications of a scale dissonance between the globalized economic processes and still primarily national forms of organization of political and social life (e.g., Cox 1997). Similarly, scholars have become more aware of cultural globalization and its discontents (e.g., Appadurai 1996), although the connection between the political and cultural spheres in scalar processes needs further attention.

This chapter studies mismatches in the extent of scales of the state, society, and the church in the case of the Cathedral. For instance, the cultural and political domains of the Russian national state had a different territorial extent (e.g., European, Russian, international, local) in different historical periods, and the Cathedral's evolving design reflects these shifts, despite being still formally considered as national monument. Initially a monument for the whole Russian Empire, the Cathedral reemerges today as a local endeavor. Effects of this "localization" of the national monument would arguably not be clear without incorporating the construction of scale into the analysis. Although nominally the intended scope of ideological influence ("ideological scale") of the Russian state remained "national," history shows that its effective borders have varied dramatically. The changing architectural scale of the "national" monument not only helps to reveal the significance of variations in ideological scale, it affects processes at the "national" scale as well, as happens, for instance, in the current phase of the Cathedral's reconstruction. By focusing on the link between the architectural scale of a monument and the ideological scale of the state, the following analysis of the Cathedral as monument also draws attention to themes that have been omitted from the current debates about geographical scale.

The Original Cathedral

The 1812 Patriotic War and Vitberg's Cathedral

In the short summer night of June 12 (24), 1812, troops of the world's mightiest power at the time, Napoleon's Europe, entered the territory of the Russian Empire without a formal proclamation of war and began a long march in a seemingly illogical direction. They were heading not, as one would expect, toward the splendid Europeanized city of St. Petersburg – the official capital city of the Empire for the century since Peter the Great – instead, their goal was the old capital, the more Asiatic, unruly, and traditional, city of Moscow. Napoleon explained his reasoning in the following way: "If I occupy Kiev, I would embrace Russia's legs, if I conquer St. Petersburg, I would grasp its head, but having taken Moscow I would strike its very heart" (Kirichenko 1992: 7).

The smaller Russian army, one third the size of the French army, scattered along the extensive western border of the empire, could not immediately consolidate its forces and engage in a major fight with the invaders. Instead it allowed them to march into the seemingly endless interior of the country. One month after the invasion, in a manifesto to his nation, Tsar Alexander I had to call on his people for popular support, although the formation of people's militias and guerilla warfare were already underway. Still, the boldness of the tsar's step cannot be underestimated, for at the time Russia was a largely fuedal country. A similarly daring step was taken by Army Chief M. Kutuzov in his decision, after the exhaustive battle of Borodino, not to fight further for Moscow but instead to keep consolidating the Russian army forces nearby. When in September 1812, Napoleon entered undefended Moscow, most of its 270,000 residents had left the city. The capture of Moscow eventually turned into a failure for the victorious emperor: the army, demoralized by sacking, purposelessness, and drinking, was trapped in a desolate city and almost completely surrounded by regular Russian troops and people's militia. In addition, Moscow was devastated by the greatest fire in its history, perhaps as a result of both guerilla actions by remaining residents and the invaders' acts of barbarism. The fire ruined more than two-thirds of Moscow's buildings, especially in the city center. A month after his invasion into the city, Napoleon was forced to leave Moscow, retreating along the only road not blocked by Russians. Just over a year later, in 1813-14, Russian troops liberated Europe from Napoleon and entered Paris.

All commentators, from the tsar himself to Leo Tolstoy in his monumental novel *War and Peace*, agreed that the Russian success was largely a result of popular resistance. The name of the 1812 campaign, the Patriotic War, is thus very appropriate. Judging by the scale of general destruction, the role of civilian heroism, and the consequences for Russia's national consciousness, the war could only be compared to one other milestone period in Russian and European history – the events following the Nazi invasion on the night of June 22, 1941, known in the former Soviet Union as the Great Patriotic War.

The first Patriotic War was also perceived as a holy war. The disaster and triumph of 1812 was not considered accidental by many in Russia. For the deeply religious majority of the country, the invasion was God's punishment for Peter the Great's policy of westernization of the country in the eighteenth century, and for the consequent betrayal of the national values that are crystallized in Russian Orthodoxy. Accordingly, the spectacular victory in the war was also largely received as divine salvation. In short, the victory was associated less with the state than with the people themselves and their religion. To immortalize both the nation's "unprecedented zeal, loyalty to and love of the faith and Fatherland" and "to commemorate Our gratitude for God's Providence" (Butorov 1992: 4), on Christmas Day 1813, Tsar Alexander I issued a decree to construct a cathedral-monument to Christ, the Savior of Russia. It is noteworthy that this structure was to be erected not in the official capital of the empire, but rather in Moscow, the traditional core of Orthodox society. Moscow sacrificed most for the victory, literally burning itself, and its post-war reconstruction was a major patriotic effort.

Although the winning project (selected in a competition in 1816) was never fully realized in its original form, the architectural competition was a critical first stage in the creation of this church-monument (Figure 7.3). The project was designed by a young architect of Swedish Lutheran descent, Alexander Vitberg, a deeply religious idealist. Being close to Russian Free Mason circles (which, in the local context, meant being sympathetic to westernization), Vitberg intended to interpret the monument beyond "exclusively the canons of the Greek-Russian Church ... since its very dedication to Christ shows its belonging to all Christianity" (Kirichenko 1992: 29). Vitberg's understanding of Christianity originated within the philosophical tradition of romanticism so it is not surprising that his project emphasized freedom of personality and belief in the people as creators of history. Vitberg proposed commemorating the names of every dead soldier, which, in a serfdom-based class society, was a revolutionary idea. His project venerated the individual over the state.

It is also remarkable how little the winning project's design and location in the city had to do with the nation. For instance, the project's location on the Vorob'evy Hills, at that time the extreme southwest margin of Moscow beyond the river (Figure 6.3), did not pretend to establish symbolic links with the historical center of Moscow and the city as a whole. The location lay, instead, between the two roads Napoleon's troops used to enter and leave the city (Kirichenko 1992:

Figure 7.3. Architect's drawing of the proposed cathedral-monument for Victory in the Patriotic War of 1812 (never built). General view from the river, Vorob'evy Hills, 1825. Architect A. Vitberg. Source: Kirichenko (1992: 28), used by permission.

33). Since most Muscovites were pedestrians and no bridge existed nearby at the time, the large, distant building would most likely have been occupied only a few times a year, as historian N.M. Karamzin and others feared (Kirichenko 1992: 43).

Architecturally, the project had few distinctive Russian influences, mainly because it combined elements of internationally popular classicism and romanticism (Figure 7.3). The architect himself summarized his ideas on the project: "[f]irst, its colossal scale should reflect Russia's grandeur, second, ... it must have in character ... strictly original architectural style, third, its parts should reflect the spiritual idea of a living church — man in body, soul and spirit" (quoted in Kirichenko 1992: 29). Accordingly, ideas of the Trinity dominated the project, which consisted of three churches: an underground church was dedicated to Christ's birth, a ground-level church to the Transfiguration, and the upper church to the Resurrection. This Trinitarian symbolism was also intended to emphasize the ecumenical, European meaning of the monument; the three main branches of Christianity would unite here (Sirotkin 1995).

The total projected height of the structure was 237 m, 170 of which were above ground. Further elevated by the hill on which it was to be built, this edifice would compete in scope with St. Peter's cathedral in Rome. In short, the architectural scale of the project was to signify the spiritual leadership of Russia in the post-Napoleonic world. At the same time, it was perhaps the first attempt to build a national cathedral-monument: through the added functions of national museum and monument, the church expressed the new national values of the nineteenth century earlier than other architectural forms (Kirichenko 1992: 29).

Realization of the project began in 1817 with a foundation ceremony, which turned into a popular festival. By 1821 the Commission for the Cathedral's Construction had acquired 11,275 serfs and begun foundation work (Kirichenko 1992: 37). The sudden death of Alexander I in 1825 interrupted construction, which was finally discontinued three years later by the new tsar, Nicholas I, at least partly due to Vitberg's amateurish management and consequent financial corruption. Doubts also existed about the durability of such a large construction on the sloping terrain. However, the real reason for the failure of Vitberg's project was to be found in a profound ideological shift exemplified by the new tsar's belief that the cathedral-monument could be meaningful only if built according to national (traditional Russian) architectural forms (Kirichenko 1992: 38). This meant that the focus of the Cathedral's meaning should be re-directed to the Russian state rather than to the European world.

The winner of the second design competition for the cathedral's design, in 1829, was Konstantin Ton, who stood in direct opposition to Alexander Vitberg's idealism and cosmopolitanism. A pedantic architect, a tough manager, and a widely experienced builder, Ton was able to anticipate the new ideological hegemony determining the Cathedral's meaning. While Vitberg's project was influenced by international Greek and Roman classicism, Ton's inspiration came from Byzantium and the ancient Russian church tradition (Figure 7.4). Ton called his style "Byzantine, which has been related since ancient times to elements of our nationality" (Butorov 1992: 11), and these national architectural forms were to become dominant in his lifetime. But before we discuss these themes in greater detail, it is important to look at the new location of the Cathedral.

Figure 7.4. The northern façade of the original Cathedral of Christ the Savior, 1890s. Source: Kirichenko (1992: 146), reproduced by permission.

Locating the Cathedral, and the Convent of St. Alexius the Man of God

To stress its link with the state (as well as to the historical past), the new Cathedral was to be relocated in the center of the city, near the Kremlin (Figures 6.1 and 7.5). Ton suggested sites already occupied by churches or monasteries, offering Nicholas I, besides Volkhonka, the place of the martyr Nikita's church, on the Moscow River southeast of the Kremlin, or the monastery of the Holy Week (Strastnoi) on modern

Pushkin Square, northwest along Tverskaia Street (Figure 6.3) (Kirichenko 1992: 44). Ton's persistence in recycling sites already occupied by churches was probably not a geographical attempt to stress continuity with the ancient past, but rather a response to the fact that the center of Moscow was already built over. It was also important for him to ensure the perceptual linkage between the new cathedral and the Kremlin. In any event, the tsar chose Volkhonka, which required demolition of an important Orthodox church complex.

The Convent of St. Alexius the Man of God was the oldest of Moscow's convents, founded around 1360 by the Metropolitan Alexii, initially on the site of an ancient church of Alexius the Man of God, slightly southwest of Volkhonka. The Metropolitan (formerly, the title for the head of the Russian Church) was canonized after his death and became a divine protector of both the convent and the city. After a disastrous fire in 1514, the convent was moved into the walled "White City," in Moscow's southwestern area of Volkhonka, on one of the city's seven historic hills.

The convent's demolition to clear space for the Cathedral provides an example of pre-Soviet manipulation of sacred places. Despite the significance of its location, the convent was moved to Krasnoe Selo on the opposite, northeast edge of the city in 1837.[5] The removal of the

Figure 7.5. View of the Cathedral of Christ the Savior from the Kremlin Embankment, the end of the 19th cen. Photo by Sherer, Nabgol'ts and Co. Source: Kirichenko (1992: 63), reproduced by permission.

Figure 7.6. The Convent of St. Alexius the Man of God. View of the Transfiguration Cathedral. From painting by K. Rabus, 1838. Source: (Kirichenko 1992: 52), reproduced by permission.

convent entailed sacrifice of some of its place-attached religio-geographical meanings. The convent's main cathedral of the Transfiguration, built in 1634 by the first Romanov tsar, Mikhail Fedorovich, with its three-hipped roof design (Figure 7.6) was a rare and prominent monument of Russian seventeenth-century church architecture.[6] The destruction of this and other convent buildings to clear space for a new state monument deeply injured the public consciousness. According to a persistent legend, the senior nun, offended by the demolition, pronounced a curse which would make nothing remain firmly at this place. To make matters worse, a worker who was removing the convent cathedral's crosses fell and died in front of a large crowd of onlookers (Butorov 1992: 9). The demolition represented the first major injustice in the history of the Cathedral,[7] one which is acknowledged today by the Russian Orthodox Church's executives: "[p]erhaps, in the good deed of the erection of the new Russian sacred place this was the main, never spiritually solved contradiction" (Moscow Patriarchate's "Arkhkhram" 1995: 122). In contrast, current Moscow city authorities engaged in reconstruction of the Cathedral prefer to minimize the importance of pre-Soviet manipulation practices.

The convent exemplifies the traditional universal-local domain of typical Orthodox churches. Unlike Vitberg's cathedral, the Convent of St. Alexius the Man of God had not only a universal appeal but also local significance for Moscow. It was devoted to one of the most "popular" saints in Orthodox Christianity. The convent in Volkhonka embodied the idea of "Moscow as the Third Rome," or the Orthodox capital of the world after the fall of the Byzantine capital in the fifteenth century. It was also highly important for its commemoration to Moscow's divine protector, Metropolitan Alexii (Moscow Patriarchate's "Arkhkhram" 1995: 119).[8] In short, the convent reflected what some observers described as the vagueness and weakness of the national consciousness of the Orthodox majority within the tsarist Russian Empire (Pospielovsky 1989): it was both local (provincial) and international (universal Christian). This spatiality of Russian identity was to be changed with the invented national tradition (Anderson 1983; Hobsbawm and Ranger 1983) and its propagation through national monumentalization. The role of the Cathedral in the latter should not be minimized.

Figure 7.7. Cathedral of Christ the Savior on the eve of its demolition in 1931. Source: *Khram Khrista Spasitelia* 1993 (1891, 1918).

Construction and Design of Ton's Cathedral

Despite the persistent popular distrust caused by the 1837 demolition of the convent, the construction of Ton's Cathedral began in 1838-
39. The building was finally freed from scaffoldings in 1858, and its
scale became prominent on the cityscape. Construction was completed
in 1882, and it was officially consecrated the following year. Thus, construction required about 45 years for completion. A persistent legend
attributes this to the fact that the project was funded by the Russian
people, and it took a long time to collect money in such a vast country.
In reality, although popular support of the project was strong, the expensive construction was funded mostly by the state, which altogether
provided 15,123,163 rubles and 89 kopeks (Kirichenko 1992: 130).

The Cathedral's final form in the 1890s (Figure 7.4) was smaller
than Vitberg's design, yet still enormous compared to the churches in
the Kremlin (Figure 7.5), and it would tower over the surrounding five
or six-story buildings erected in the nineteenth century (Figure 7.7).
The superhuman scale of the building was its most visible feature, serving at the time of the Cathedral's completion as a monument to Nicholas I's authoritarianism: the monstrous cubic shape of the church was
not in keeping with Moscow's traditionally modest scale (Smolkin 1994).
This scalar arrogance of the building within its setting, the cost and
length of construction, as well as the grandeur of its interior, help account for why the Cathedral captured the popular imagination.

The Cathedral was in the center of a square, allowing observers
to appreciate such external features as the Cathedral's traditional white
and golden colors and sculptural compositions. The sculptural themes
were in part determined by the directionality of the Cathedral's façades.
The sculpture of the main western façade symbolically depicted Russian troops under protection of heavenly forces. The southern façade,
facing the direction of the decisive battles of 1812, depicted events of
direct relevance to that war. The eastern façade, facing the Kremlin,
showed Russian national saints-protectors of the country, while saints
who spread Christianity were dominant in the northern façade
(Kirichenko 1992: 74-75). The cathedral was an unprecedented synthesis of religious and national-historical themes, and of architecture, sculpture, and paintings.

The interior grandeur of the Cathedral was marked by an impressive iconostasis in the unique form of a chapel (Figure 7.8), the scale
of which was comparable to that of the main Uspenskii Cathedral of
the Kremlin. The most renowned Russian artists, mostly academicians,

participated in painting the interior. The historical character of the Cathedral was reflected in the large number of paintings portraying the lives and deeds of Russian saints (Kirichenko 1992: 100). Like the external sculpture, the internal paintings were thematized according to the direction of their walls. For example, since Christianity came to Russia from the south, the southern wall paintings depicted the events before and after Russia's 988 conversion to Christianity (Kirichenko 1992: 122-23).

It is noteworthy that the Cathedral became the most popular national church in the Russian collective imagination, although among the educated elite there was strong criticism of Ton. As quoted in Butorov (1992: 12), for critic Vladimir Stasov, Ton's projects were "drawings of a writer-clerk from talented pictures"; aesthete observers such as Igor Grabar saw in the Cathedral "an example of pseudo-national style" and "the beginning of the final vulgarization and barbarization of tastes"; poet Taras Shevchenko described the Cathedral as a "fat merchant's wife in *povoinik*"[9]; Vitberg called it "a simple village church." The building's minor towers were judged too small and distant from the main one, as some modern critics note (Butorov 1992, 12). In any event, it changed Russian architectural thinking. Eighteenth-century European influences were replaced by a new ideology of national regeneration, understood largely as a return to ancient Russian architecture. The new project fully embodied Nicholas I's ideas of filling the historical gap created by Peter the Great's reforms. In contrast to

Figure 7.8. Interior of the Cathedral of Christ the Savior. Late 19th century Christmas postcard. Source: Kirichenko (1992: 178), reproduced by permission.

Vitberg's design, Ton's monument venerated the *state rather than the individual*: his project commemorated only the names of officers killed in the war (Figure 7.9).

It is important to stress that, contrary to the common perception, the Cathedral was not the official church of the empire as it was not the most expensive one (the forty-year construction of 101.5 m St. Isaac Cathedral in St. Petersburg [Figure 2.05] cost 23 million rubles [Antonov and Kobak 1994: 105-6]), nor was it the only cathedral-monument to the Patriotic War (Kazan' Icon of the Holy Virgin (Kazanskii) Cathedral in St. Petersburg [Figure 2.06] is another major example). Even in Moscow, the most respected cathedral was the oldest Assumption (Uspenskii) cathedral of the Kremlin, where enthronement of patriarchs of the Church and tsars traditionally took place.[10] It was popular support that elevated the Cathedral to a unique position in the Russian national consciousness. The same popularity, as will be shown, was the eventual reason for its demolition fifty years after its construction.

Figure 7.9. Removal of the marble plaques with texts about battles of the 1812 Patriotic War and names of the fallen, on the eve of the 1931 demolition of the Cathedral. Source: Kirichenko (1992: 259), used by permission.

Deconstruction of the Cathedral and the Palace of the Soviets

When the Bolsheviks took power in October 1917, they immediately issued a series of decrees targeting the Church (Chapter 4). Although these legal provisions formally separated religious and civil matters, the state continued its assault on the Church. In 1922 the government staged a schism within the Church, transferring about seventy percent of all Orthodox churches, including the Cathedral, to the unpopular Renovationists. In a series of anti-religious campaigns, the Communist state succeeded, by 1927, in demolishing, closing or converting to other uses forthy-eight percent of all prerevolutionary Orthodox church buildings in the territory of the former empire (Chapter 4; Sidorov 2000a).[11] The majority of priests were killed or imprisoned. In 1927, to save the Church from total extinction, Metropolitan Sergii signed a declaration of loyalty to the new Communist authorities, thus formally ending resistance. After this milestone event, the perceived threat to the state of the Church as a rival diminished in importance, and there was a concomitant decline in state support for the Renovationist schism, which became later insignificant.

While other major cathedrals survived as museums, in the case of the Cathedral, the nun's curse proved to be true. It met the same destiny as the earlier convent only forty-eight years after its consecration, for superficially similar reasons: the site was cleared for a different sort of "cathedral," the Palace of the Soviets. A major puzzle is why this Cathedral was so special that its demolition was as important for the new Soviet national identity as the construction of the Palace itself. The victory of the new state over the Church as an institution did not bring about much change in the general religiosity of society. Some believers went into external or internal exile after 1927, forming the Russian Orthodox Church Abroad and the Underground Catacomb Church. Others kept their religiosity alive through personal practice: twenty years after the revolution, the 1937 population census indicated that 42.3 percent of the population still considered themselves Orthodox (41,621,572 out of 98,411,132 respondents) (*Vsesoiuznaia Perepis'* 1991, 106-7).[12] The Communist authorities therefore wanted to strike into the very heart of Orthodox religiosity by demolishing what the people regarded as the main cathedral.

On the frosty morning of December 5, 1931, after several powerful explosions, the original Cathedral ceased to exist (Figure 7.1; details in Kozlov 1991a). The most important sculptural ornaments and precious metals had already been removed beforehand (Figure 7.9), and

Figure 7.10. The hill of debris left after dynamiting of the Cathedral of Christ the Savior, 1930s. Source: Kirichenko (1992: 263), used by permission.

the marble exterior preserved for new governmental buildings and the subway. The real treasure of the Cathedral, however, shared the building's fate, its wall paintings by Russia's best nineteenth-century artists were destroyed. Tsarist place manipulation practices, thus, continued in the Soviet period, but the Cathedral's dramatic dynamiting and the identity of its intended replacement made it a martyr in the eyes of believers and of those who disliked the new regime. The event was later compared to the Bolsheviks' brutal murder of the Russian imperial family and to the crucifixion of Christ (Smith 1997: 166).

The emptied site (Figure 7.10) was to be occupied by a new "cathedral," which would also emphasize a new ideological scale of the state. Although territorially the Soviet Union looked like a reconstruction of the previous Russian Empire, it was intending to become a global union-state. A new ideological scale required a new monumentalized incarnation.

The history of Stalin's proposed Palace of the Soviets (Figure 7.11), perhaps, began on December 31, 1922, in the Bolshoi Opera Theater, at the congress announcing the foundation of the Soviet Union. Party leader Sergei Kirov suggested the construction of a building-monument to the young country that would accommodate the growing number of delegates joining the Union and serve as a symbol of Communist global hegemony (Palamarchuk 1994: 174), or the Communist International (Smith 1997: 163). Thus, the scale of the meaning of the Palace was to be global. In this sense, the Communist replacement

Figure 7.11. Architect's drawing of the Palace of the Soviets, topped by statue of Lenin, a variant of 1933, never built. Source: Kirichenko (1992: 234), reproduced by permission.

for the Cathedral was a return to Vitberg's project of global inclusiveness (although at the time Vitberg's "global" meant merely a European scale).

Although the new state's ideas of the Union's central monument exceeded those of the tsars, the Palace's final design of the early 1930s shared a number of features with the original Cathedral (Figure 7.12). First, both buildings served the double purpose of gathering place and monument (see note 1). The 100-meter high main hall of the Palace had 21,000 seat capacity. The 6,000-ton, 100-meter statue of Lenin atop the Palace (sculptor S. D. Merkurov) was designed to have 6 meters forefinger. Second, the Palace continued the original Cathedral's stress on gargantuan architectural scale; it should not only dominate the city, but also become the highest building in the world (Figure 7.12): this monument, with Lenin's statue on top larger than the Statue of Liberty in New York, would outstrip the heights of the Empire State Building and the Eiffel Tower. Third, the Palace (architects V. Schuko, V. Gel'freikh, and B. Iofan) was to change the dominant architectural style in the country, substituting a new international modernist architecture for the traditional Russian one. Finally, it was located on the same site as the Cathedral, and was to become a new center of the city (Figure

Figure 7.12. Architectural scale of the proposed Palace of the Soviets (variant of 1938) is compared with the Empire State Building (New York), the Eiffel Tower (Paris), and the Cathedral of Christ the Savior. Sources: the author's compilation, based on Scientific Publishing Institute of Pictorial Statistics (1938), Kondrat'ev (1995), and Kirichenko (1992: 235).

7.13). The proposal included clearing surrounding historical neighborhoods, moving The Pushkin Fine Arts museum 100 meters away, massive landscaping, and laying out new avenues directed to the Palace (portion of one of them, along the Kremlin wall, created Manege Square [Chapter 6]). The Palace was to be surrounded by parking areas for 5,000 cars.

Though the Soviet government intended to build the Palace in two years, opening it at the end of 1933, the design competition alone stretched until the spring of 1933 (Smith 1997: 166). Construction of the Palace was delayed until 1937, after the debris had been removed (Figure 7.10) and a steel foundation built and, by 1939, the walls had been raised to a level slightly above the ground. The beginning of the Great Patriotic War (World War II) in 1941 changed priorities, however, and the steel foundation was reclaimed for the war effort. With that tumultuous period, the hoped-for global hegemony it was to represent died as well.

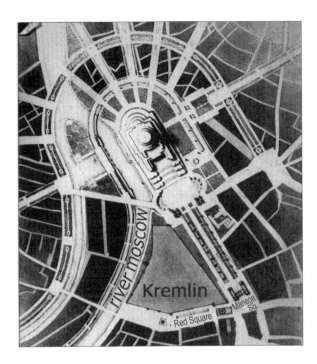

Figure 7.13. Proposed street outline around the Palace of the Soviets. Source: based on Kirichenko (1992: 231).

Postwar Pit and the Swimming Pool

In the immediate post-war period the ideological scale of the state nominally remained global, yet, unlike the pre-war period, it was directed primarily towards the Soviet Union itself. Limited by postwar shortages, the Iron Curtain, and a general loss of the revolutionary impetus of the early Soviet period, the state could declare only global intentions. The process of creating a national monument reflected this uncertainty. A new design competition for the Palace in 1957-59, this time for the Vorob'evy Hills site, but eventually the entire project was dropped. The sacred place of Volkhonka was abandoned, as was the very idea of a "cathedral." Some of the Palace's architectural ideas were eventually used in the design of Moscow State University (MSU) (1947-49) (Tarkhanov and Kavtaradze 1992: 136-37), successfully completed as the highest building in the Soviet Union almost on the original proposed site of Vitberg's cathedral, the Vorob'evy Hills.

Although MSU was the last attempt to combine architectural, communal, and spiritual symbols in major building projects, the grand scale of meaning of major architectural projects still fascinated Soviet authorities in the postwar era. The "world's highest" construction, a TV tower, was built in one area of the city, and the party's new gathering place — the Palace of Congresses in the Kremlin — in another.[13] Lacking both a spiritual dimension and a prominent location, the TV tower remained primarily a technical construction and a tourist site, while the Palace, which lacked conventional architectural value, is not a landmark. Eventually, the long-term construction and design of another war memorial, for the Great Patriotic War, on Poklonnaia Hill (Chapter 6), also distracted attention away from Volkhonka.

Why did the place of Volkhonka lose its importance for the postwar state? First, it is possible, the rulers did not want to be associated with the unsuccessful construction of the Palace of the Soviets or, after Khrushchev, with Stalin himself. Second, the new projects were very different from the Palace of the Soviets and the Cathedral, and required other locations. Finally, as a new generation of Soviet citizens came of age, the urgency of fighting popular religiosity diminished, thereby reducing the need to replace the Cathedral. Newly opened archival documents reveal that in 1949 a group of lay believers appealed to the Moscow representative of the Council for Russian Orthodox Church Affairs asking permission to build, "instead of the Cathedral of Christ the Savior, a new cathedral in memory of the historically important victory over Germany." Even they, however, did not claim the place of Volkhonka, instead suggesting in the downtown area the site of the former Petrovskii monastery.[14]

Figure 7.14. View of Moskva swimming pool, ca.1967. Source: *Istoriia Moskvy* (1967: 404).

The original foundation of the Palace of the Soviets – the "pit" – was satirized by Andrei Platonov, Russia's most prominent contemporary writer, in his novel of the same title. The timing of Platonov's writing is significant (Pavlovskii 1991). Written in late 1929 and early 1930, on the very eve of attempts to build the Palace of the Soviets, the novel describes construction of a pit for a giant building for a "new world" which was to replace the traditional city. The novel's pit is endless and seemingly purposeless, yet ever-accelerating because of random decisions to enlarge it so that the building would accommodate the growing number of ever-more contented future citizens. First published in Russia in 1987, Platonov's novel became a bestseller under *perestroika*. Thus, the place's very emptiness acquired a new meaning, as an influential geographic symbol for the failed Communist endeavor; a pit serving ironically as the "highest" and "biggest" achievement of the "new society," a paradoxical "yawning height" (Zinov'ev 1979).

In 1960 the pit was recycled as an outdoor steam-heated winter swimming pool, one of the world's largest, in the shape of a 100-m wide circle (Figure 7.14). The swimming pool, which continued to carry the popular name of the "pit," was closed in 1993 in anticipation of reconstructing the Cathedral. There was no support group for the popular pool, yet its sudden closure in 1993 was not universally welcomed (Kolpakov 1994b).[15] For years, the pool was the largest in Europe and, as such, its scale of meaning was also significant. In 1993, 207 Moscow churches were attended by 500,000 people, but, beginning in 1960, more than 5 million people used the pool annually (Baskov 1994). Only three other outdoor pools existed in Moscow, a city of nine million residents with mostly polluted rivers, and this was the only outdoor pool the general public could use. Nevertheless, no attempts were made to publicly discuss the pool's destiny.[16]

The Resurrected Cathedral

Public Perception of the Cathedral's Reconstruction

As soon as Gorbachev's new policy of openness in the late 1980s permitted some religious freedom, the idea of restoring the lost Cathedral began to gain popularity. Very much like the Cathedral itself and the empty pit left in its place, the idea was to reconstruct a new symbol of the national identity. Three initial groups of supporters can be iden-

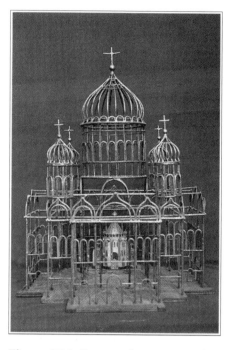

Figure 7.15. V. Balabanov *Swimmer* (1976). The upper part of the picture shows the diving tower of Moskva swimming pool with a reflection of the lost Cathedral and Tsarevich Alexii (Romanov), son of Nicholas II and heir to the throne, murdered by Red Army soldiers in 1918. Source: Balabanov (1995: 6, 66), used by permission.

Figure 7.16. Proposed reconstruction of the Cathedral of Christ the Savior, not built. Artist Yu. I. Seliverstov. Source: *Rodina* (1995: 16), reproduced by permission.

Figure 7.17. Architect's model of the Trinity Cathedral of the Millennium of the Orthodox Baptizing in Tsaritsyno, not yet built (photo by the author).

tified in the period before the reconstruction idea became widespread and monopolized by the state.

The intelligentsia of the country was at the forefront.[17] Using various media, prominent artists and writers criticized the Communist regime and campaigned for restoration of the Cathedral (Figure 7.15). The artist Yurii Seliverstov offered the most remarkable design (Figure 7.16). Arguing that exact reconstruction of the Cathedral would recall only one period of the place's history, he suggested an original way to invoke the past through the erection of a steel-contour outline of the lost building, with just the original chapel-altar inside. This relatively inexpensive project had the advantage of restoring the architectural scale of the original Cathedral, arguably its most noteworthy feature, and leaving empty space for broader interpretations that would also have allowed thousands to gather, remember the losses, and pray (Palamarchuk 1994; Pozdniaev 1994). There was also a proposal to leave the site empty for occasional gigantic holographic laser restorations of the Cathedral (Opolznev 1994; *Vecherniaia Moskva* 1994) so that an even greater number of people could gather there.

The second group interested in the idea of Cathedral's resurrection was the Russian Orthodox Church itself. Cautious too about simply replicating the lost monument, the Church planned to indirectly revive the idea of the Cathedral. During *perestroika*, to celebrate the 1988 millennium of the Russian conversion to Christianity, the state allowed construction of a new Trinity cathedral in Tsaritsyno (Figure 7.17). Designed as a reminder of the lost Cathedral, the project was nevertheless to signify the new policy of separation of Church and state, and therefore to be located not in the center, but rather in the residential outskirts of the city (Figure 6.3). This project has not yet been realized since the Church is characteristically lacking sufficient resources.

What united the two groups was the shared belief that a mere replica of the Cathedral was not only unnecessary but also unwanted – both argued for reviving the spirit of the Cathedral rather than its physical restoration. In contrast, the third group, consisting of lay believers, requested that the lost Cathedral be replaced, creating a parish community for this nonexistent church. To this end they began discrete fund-raising in public places for the project. Once reconstruction started and became politically important, however, the Church eventually dismissed this community (Smith 1997: 167).

Initially, the Moscow Patriarchate had serious doubts about the reconstruction. In November 1994, Patriarch Alexii II thought that the order of future reconstructions of churches should be as follows: the

Church of Kazan' Icon of the Holy Virgin on Red Square, St. Georgii Victorious Church on Poklonnaia Hill (the Victory Memorial), Iverskaia Chapel,[18] the Trinity Cathedral of the Millennium of Orthodox Baptizing in Tsaritsyno (Chapter 6), and (only after that experience) the Cathedral (Armeev 1993). A week later, the Moscow government's Minister had a different schedule: the government planned to restore all the demolished churches and monasteries at state expense, with 25 old churches already in the process of restoration (Zabavskikh 1993). Although the government planned to build new churches in new districts as well, the project to build the Trinity Millennium Cathedral in Tsaritsyno has been postponed in favor of the Cathedral having priority.

Eventually, the local Moscow authorities monopolized decision-making regarding construction. The Russian Ministry of Culture was totally ignored ("Spasitel' i Deputaty" 1994), and even the role of the Russian Orthodox Church was minimized. As in tsarist times, the Cathedral's construction was paid for by the state with the Church's role being merely to receive the building and legitimize the work. The public was left to debate only the narrow topics of the Cathedral's de facto reconstruction. There were several important omissions from any public discussion surrounding the project. First, the location of the Cathedral was not publicly discussed. The authorities rushed to capture the site of Volkhonka, even though other sites, such as the site of the Trinity Millennium Cathedral in Tsaritsyno, were available. Second, interdenominational justice had been dealt a blow by the privileged positioning of the Russian Orthodox Church. There are now forty-five different denominations in Moscow, half of which are popular enough to be considered major (Grigor'eva 1994), with several being historically significant. For example, a mosque was built with the blessing of Alexander I in honour of the War of 1812. The first democratic mayor of Moscow and Luzhkov's predecessor, Gavriil Popov, paved the way for the reopening of the mosque and warned about the perils of the state favoring one religion over another (Smith 1997: 168). Third, the goal of this reconstruction was not debated but officially proclaimed: to break with the Soviet past, with its antireligious and antinational practices, and to reestablish connection with the lost cultural heritage of the country. Therefore, the campaign for the project highlights the faithfulness to the design of the demolished original Cathedral, symbolizing a supposed end to the manipulation of place. As will be argued below, however, manipulation persists despite the abolition of the pit, the most notorious of Soviet geographic symbols.

In addition, the scale and design of the Cathedral were not publicly debated. While Seliverstov's arch project and the Millennium Cathedral in Tsaritsyno responded to the growing criticism of "grand scale" architectural thinking, the state-led restoration was to continue the tsarist and Soviet taste for grandiose structures (Malinin 1994, 1995). This continuation of past monumentalism would not only leave smaller, yet important churches neglected, it would also prioritize size over symbolic significance (Smolkin 1996). Finally, it was argued that the urban space of Moscow has changed considerably since the construction of the first Cathedral, making questionable the suitability of the new Cathedral to its place (Shimanskii 1994b).

As mentioned earlier, the interior of the original Cathedral was painted by the best Russian artists of the time, but with the interruption of that artistic tradition there is no one alive today capable of reproducing it (Krotov 1994). As a result of the high cost and rapid pace of the construction process, the Cathedral is also being built of ferroconcrete, an unsuitable surface for such paintings. An additional internal facing of the concrete walls by some other material is required (Krolenko 1994). The use of cheap, brick-faced ferroconcrete walls, as well as structural changes made to accommodate modern conveniences, have drawn criticism from the Church. The walls of the Cathedral will have elevators carrying spectators to a viewing platform and the belfry. As one commentator notes: "The pillars of the Cathedral, hollowed out by elevators, staircases and ventilation shafts, yet simulating massiveness and firmness, [is] the start of the lie in the revival of churches, both in a constructive and spiritual sense. May God save us from that!" (Moscow Patriarchate's "Arkhkhram" 1995: 117).

Given the sad financial fate of the first Cathedral construction (and the secrecy behind the current one), the possibility of corruption cannot be dismissed. One author compared exploitation of the idea for restoring the Cathedral to the tricks of the hero of the popular Russian satirical novel *Twelve Chairs* who successfully collected money for the "complete reconstruction of an abyss" (Shalaev 1993). To improve the image of the whole enterprise, a large-scale public relations campaign has been launched under the supervision of a former advertising agency director (Popov 1994). This included a foundation ceremony on Orthodox Christmas Day of 1995 staged to replicate the ceremony of 1839, a museum devoted to the Cathedral, publications and films (Figure 7.18). The architect of the original Cathedral, Konstantin Ton, attracted revived attention, and a special conference devoted to him was held in the official Georgievskii Hall of the Kremlin that opened with music by the Presidential Orchestra (Malinin 1995). In 1994 a public council for control of the restoration was officially established to dismiss criticism of undemocratic decision-making. This council includes politically prominent right-wing artists and statesmen (Nekrasov 1994, *Vestnik Merii Moskvy* 1994b).

One Orthodox priest conducted an unofficial opinion poll and was surprised to find, not that different people were against restoration, but that their arguments were based on the Bible, Russian history, and current realities: that to waste millions of dollars in a country with millions of homeless is a sin; that church construction in Russia is always associated with corruption, and that the Patriarch's current cathedral of Epiphany is not overcrowded even on important holidays. The priest himself is in favor of the reconstruction, but not at this "Bolshevik pace" (Pavlov 1994).[19] The gigantomania and haste typical of Soviet construction has led sceptics to refer to the new Cathedral as a "Palace of the Soviets with a cross on top" and workers to label themselves "shock workers of Orthodox (as opposed to socialist) labor" (Smith 1997: 171).

It would not be an exaggeration to conclude, after surveying press accounts, that the reconstruction has been largely irrelevant to regions other than Moscow, and that the limited public discussions (in Moscow) were dominated by local concerns. The national

Figure 7.18. Street poster inviting donations for reconstruction of the Cathedral (underway behind the fence). Photo by the author, 1997.

Figure 7.19. Headquarters of Gazprom, the Russian giant company for natural gas production (photo by the author, 1995).

monumentalization process is therefore revealed to be highly localized. In this sense, the project was a failure, since it did not become, as expected, an act of societal repentance for what was done during the Soviet time.

Scales of the Politics of Reconstruction

The new Cathedral's characteristics must be understood in the context of changes in the scale of the Russian state. The breakup of the Soviet Union and the crises caused by the politico-economic transformation of Russia have significantly weakened the state. Not only were its global ambitions relinquished, its domestic role was fragmented too. In the 1990s, the new Russian national state has largely been unable to fulfill the primary responsibilities of any state, such as provisions for basic economic, political, and cultural security of its citizens. Tax evasions, unpaid state employees, violent regional conflicts, criminalization of society, and the proliferation of foreign cultural products all became characteristic of post-Soviet Russian society. In most instances, the local state is expected to take care of these "national" problems. It is only a little exaggeration to conclude that, in many respects, the scale of the national state became local.

Figure 7.20. A three-dimensional model of the proposed business district Moscow-City with the 648-m office tower Rossiia (Russia) (photo by the author).

Moscow provides an especially noteworthy case. The city became the undisputed financial and resource-exporting center in Russia in the 1990s, in relatively good economic health and with a balanced city budget. In contrast to the country as a whole, wealth rose in the capital city. For example, in July of 1995, the average earnings of Muscovites were 3.2 times higher than the Russian average, while the cost of a "consumer basket" was only 1.3 times higher. The level of officially registered unemployment in Moscow was one-fifth the Russian average (Savel'ev 1996). The Moscow concentration of wealth has been strongest in the city's construction industry, which is patronized by the Moscow mayor Yurii Luzhkov, who is currently one of Russia's most influential politicians.[20]

By localizing a national monument, the builders enlarge the political scope of the local Moscow state, as the political context of the project attests. The early start and rapid pace of the current reconstruction came as a surprise not only to its critics, but even to those who deeply believed in the rebirth of the Cathedral. At that time there were several reasons for urgency. First, the 850th anniversary of founding of Moscow was to be celebrated in September 1997 "as a national holiday" that would provide Moscow authorities with a chance to display their achievements, of which the crowning one was to be the restored

Figure 7.21. Headquarters since 1985 of the Moscow Patriarchate at Danilov Monastery (photo by the author, 1996).

Cathedral. Second, the Parliamentary and Presidential elections of 1995 and 1996 were seen as likely to result in political destabilization, and personal attachment to this significant construction project would allow Luzhkov to secure his position as Mayor. Other factors operating at both the local and national scales may have helped Luzhkov. A costly construction of sacred significance could demonstrate the power of Moscow authorities and allow the city's government to secure control of some of the federal funds made available for the monument. Finally, there is the obvious symbolism of the second millennium of Christianity in 2000.

In addition to shifts in the balance of power, one of the main, if little-known, results of political dramas in Moscow in the early 1990s, such as the 1991 military coup and the October 1993 assault on the White House, was increased competition among power groups for local office space. The Mayoral Office, the Parliament, and the Federal Government have all changed their locations, and some other office complexes have been erected, such as the gas industry skyscraper (Figure 7.19) and the Moscow-City complex (Figure 7.20).[21] This boom in new headquarters, although imprudent in times of general social unrest, nonetheless may have required legitimation by including provisions for the holy authority of the Church. The top authorities of the Russian Orthodox Church had been presented with a new headquarters complex in the Danilov monastery in 1985 (Figure 7.21), which might have been taken as a challenge by the new Moscow government. Why could not post-Soviet authorities make a similar gift? This project would make its major agents look less "Soviet," a politically important goal since most of them were powerful insiders in the previous system.

The current phase of national monumentalization has become largely an endeavor of the local state. It was this governing body that completed the long-term construction of the Russian Victory Memorial in 1995 at Poklonnaia Hill (Chapter 6). Similarly, although Boris Yel'tsin, as early as July 16, 1992, signed the decree "On the creation of a Foundation for Moscow's Rebirth," in which restoration of the Cathedral was listed as the very first project (Nikol'skaia 1994), real restoration first began two years later, May 31st, 1994, after the city of Moscow declared its decision to construct the Cathedral (*Vestnik Merii Moskvy* 1994a). Six months later the process was in full force despite, or because of, an absence of debate about its location and general purpose.

Figure 7.22. A memorial plaque for names of corporate sponsors of the reconstruction in the basement of the Cathedral (such as a bank, a frozen foods company, and a large night entertainment club; photo by the author, 1999).

Secrecy surrounds the level and sources of funding for the Cathedral's reconstruction (Barry 1995). In the beginning, the Patriarch of Moscow and All Russia and the Mayor of Moscow announced that it would cost US$150 million (*Kuranty* 1994). This approximates two percent of the Moscow budget (Bossart 1995), and six times the budget of Russia's Federal Program for Monument Restoration.[22] The director of the Foundation of Financial Support of the Cathedral's Reconstruction believed, as early as 1994, that the final cost of the project would be US$300 million (Popov 1994), a figure also mentioned the next year (M. 1995). However, the actual construction costs remains hidden from the public. In 1999, a representative of the Foundation estimated the cost as already US$500 million with collected funds at US$320 million (Korneeva 1999). After the reconstruction the total construction cost is announced at US$650 (Tolstikhina and Mel'nikova 2001). According to the estimates of one city legislator investigating the issue, only one tenth of a day's expenditure at the site was covered by charitable donations (Smith 1997: 169).

Initial stages of reconstruction were almost certainly financed from the Moscow city budget in the form of an interest-free loan to be repaid once necessary donations had been collected (Pokrovskii 1994). Project officials argue that financing will come from the Russian Orthodox Church, the Russian diaspora abroad, and donations from Russian citizens and commercial organizations (Popov 1994). Thus far, however, this order has seemingly been reversed; Moscow banks and companies are the main source of financing (Friland 1995).[23]

Luzhkov has used his position to coax and coerce donations from private and state-run businesses (Smith 1997: 169). Special memorial plaques for sponsors' names were proposed for the Cathedral (*Kuranty* 1994) (Figure 7.22). This would amount to a listing of the rich "new Russians," replacing the listing of the 1812 heroes to whom the original Cathedral was devoted (Krolenko 1994) (Figure 7.09). The project officials insist that the Cathedral will not be built using money from the federal budget or tax revenue. Despite similar frequent public statements, however, the Cathedral's council has asked for and received federal subsidies, including tax concessions for big donors (Smith 1997: 169).

Members of the original Cathedral parish congregation, dissolved at the beginning of construction by the Moscow Patriarchate (Shusharin 1994) perhaps to avoid incorporating other voices in the process, continued collecting money on the streets, despite a lack of communication with the builders (Popov 1994). Officials even refused

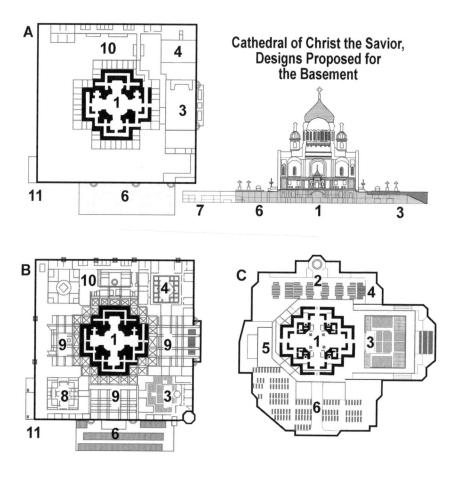

Figure 7.23. Proposed designs for the basement of the restored Cathedral.

A. "Modest" variant of the Moscow Patriarchate; B. "Extended" variant of the Moscow Patriarchate; C. Implemented variant. Functional structure: 1. the low church of the Transfiguration of the Convent of Alexius the Man of God; 2. the Holy Synod's Hall; 3. the Church Council's Hall; 4. dining halls; 5. systems of technical support; 6. garage of the Cathedral; 7. municipal garage; 8. theological center; 9. halls for exhibitions and book sale; 10. the Convent of St. Alexius the Man of God; 11. toilets.

Source: the author; based on Moscow Patriarchate's "Arkhkhram" (1995), Posokhin (1995) and Lutskii (1995). Drawn by Eric Stevens.

to deal with old women collecting money on the streets for the reconstruction (Shalaev 1993), instead, all branches of the dominant state Sber-Bank were put in charge of coordinating private donations. It was expected that with more visible success and improved publicity in the media, people's donations would increase, although there were reported cases of obligatory donations taken from lay people's salaries (Loriia 1995).

The Cathedral as a Localized National Monument

The localization of the national monument has, despite the insistence of the authorities to the contrary, affected not only the social and political outcomes of this reconstruction, but also the Cathedral itself. However accurate the current restoration could be (criticism has always been significant; see Shimanskii 1994b, Klin 2000, Revzin 2000b), a complex of new functions has been built into the basement of the Cathedral, in the 8-15 m space between the ground and the base of the Palace floor. In fact, the former Palace's pit has been recycled and filled by a three-story steelwork basement, which, because of the sloping terrain, is only partly below ground.

The significance of this underground complex goes far beyond a mere basement appendix to the restored Cathedral. It has changed its physical scale. While the total floor area of the Cathedral is only 3,980 m^2, the three-level basement has floorspace of 66,000 m^2 (P. Dmitriev 1994; Shimanskii 1994b), more than fifteen times the upper levels. The new functions added in this space are even more significant. A comparison of the various proposals for using the underground space, provided by the Moscow Mayoral Office and the Russian Orthodox Church's executive body, the Moscow Patriarchate (MP), shows that the basement reflects a political compromise between the two (Figure 7.23). The MP had two proposals for the basement (Moscow Patriarchate's "Arkhkhram" 1995: 117; Figures 7.23A and 7.23B). The more "modest" version included the restored Convent of St. Alexius the Man of God [10], with its main church of the Transfiguration [1] and halls for the Church's Councils [3] (Figure 7.23A). The design of the basement in this variant included also a dining hall [4], and a 100-car garage [6]. The MP's second, expanded, variant for the basement space (Figure 7.23B) proposed greatly increased the seating capacity for the conference-hall and dining rooms [3, 4]. To preserve some tradition, in both variants of the MP the car garage [6], together with toilets [11], were placed on the side of the basement. Major additions to this variant include a theological center [8] and spacious lobby halls [9] for exhibitions and book sales. It is understandable that the MP attempted to take this unique chance to remedy the results of both Communist and tsarist manipulation of the place. Those implementing the project were, however, more selective in their historical scope.

According to the restoration's former director and leading architect, the city authorities initially wanted only the garages and the Church of the Transfiguration in the basement (Sokolov 1994): the underground parking garage alone was regarded worth the effort (Semenov 1994). The struggle between these two parties had its victims: the director's resignation was forced following the submission of the MP's expanded version to the Mayoral Office without prior approval from the Mayor (Sokolov 1994). This was not the last politically motivated resignation. Metropolitan Yuvenalii, the chair of the interior decoration commission, resigned in 1999 for similar reasons (Revzin 1999).

The proposal that was finally accepted, and now implemented, is a compromise between the second, "expanded" proposal of the MP and the "utilitarian" aspirations of the city authorities (Figure 7.23C), but was under constant modification; 700 designers were struggling to keep pace with the construction workers (P. Dmitriev 1994). In 1995, plans for the basement included the underground church of the convent [1], the Holy Synod's Hall [2], a 1,200-seat conference hall for the Church's Councils [3], the Patriarch's office and a dining hall for 800 guests [4], recreational "chambers," and the premises of ecclesiastical educational establishments (M. 1995). Together, these will allow the complex to function as a true headquarters for the MP. A TV center will be located there as well (Shimanskii 1994a). The rest of the space will be devoted to engineering facilities [5] and the much expanded garages [6, 7], because they are expected to serve the city's needs as well [7], their capacity has grown six times compared with the original proposal (P. Dmitriev 1994).

These changes have not been accommodated by sacrificing minor functions. The dining facilities and the Patriarch's apartments and guest rooms will still be present. The most striking absence in the final project is the convent; with all the added functions, no place has been found at the Moscow Patriarchate's center for a modest female convent. Only the convent's main church of the Transfiguration will be recreated, in a limited "catacomb" version [1]. Church canons prevent the space immediately beneath a church from being used for any functions not in some way related to the service. The initial idea of locating the garage there (Krolenko 1994) has been dismissed.

Ironically, the Cathedral might be seen as standing on its head; i.e., as a reversed "pit," because the lower MP headquarters and parking garage have become the largest, most significant, and even the most politically contested parts of the project. At the same time, the newly added functions could significantly constrain its original gathering scale. The Cathedral most likely will not be easily accessible to the general public; the Russian Orthodox Church headquarters will require a security guard, and the monument seems likely to be the target of terrorists of different kinds, given its specific history. It is expected to have "the most sophisticated" computerized security complex in Moscow, with hidden video surveillance, fire detectors, and about a thousand technical and "other" specialists; the central supercomputer from a nuclear submarine is so powerful that it will be utilized to only one fifth of its capability (Nikol'skaia 1999). Even at the time of construction, security was tighter than at Moscow's banks (Vandenko 1996).

The localization of the national Cathedral described here poses questions about its future maintenance. The new Cathedral's scale may be too large for even the state to maintain it properly, let alone the city of Moscow (Kolpakov 1994a, 1994b). The desperate condition of many active churches in Moscow also makes the new construction questionable ethically. In 1993, 103 churches in Moscow were inactive, and many active churches lacked staff: fifty churches had no senior priests, and it was estimated that the number of deacons should be doubled and the number of priests tripled ("Sluzhenie Tserkvi" 1994). The Cathedral is to accommodate 10,000 people, although services in other downtown churches are less crowded than in residential margins. Downtown Moscow has more than enough churches, whereas only one-sixth of the 138 churches preserved outside the central Garden Ring are active (Grigor'eva 1994). In addition, the nouveau riche presently moving into the downtown area may be even less likely to attend services (Krotov 1994). All these factors have, paradoxically, resurrected proposals to restore the convent. The giant Cathedral will need nuns for its maintenance, and the City Mayor and the Patriarch have agreed to build a new complex for the sisterhood cloister (Pokrovskii 1994), for which nearby land has already been allocated (*Vestnik Merii Moskvy* 1994a). Yet, even if the eliminated convent is reestablished, the chance has been lost to fully resolve the long-standing conflicts over the construction of this place.

Figure 7.24. A foundation pit in the area of the proposed 648-m office tower Rossiia (Russia) at Moscow-City Complex (photo by the author, 2000).

Conclusion

Using the Cathedral of Christ the Savior as a case study, this chapter explores the uneasy process of national monumentalization in Russia (Table 1). The first attempt to build the world's largest church as a monument to victory in the 1812 Napoleonic war failed. The smaller project that was completed stretched through several decades (1831-1881), with a different design and location. The symbolic importance of the Cathedral to the national consciousness resulted in its 1931 demolition by the Bolsheviks, who attempted to replace it, both ideologically and geographically, with their own national monument, the giant Palace of the Soviets. This attempt also failed, and the foundation pit later became one of the world's largest swimming pools (1960-93) and a symbol of the failed Soviet endeavor, which in turn was replaced by new the Cathedral.

These changing forms of national monumentalization in Russia can be better understood if the corresponding spatial and social changes taking place in the nation are taken into account. Coincident with the monuments' reconstruction, the territorial scale of the country which they were to represent has changed dramatically. The

Cathedral's design, especially its architectural scale, reflects shifts in the scale of the Russian national identity as well as the interplay between a politically and spatially changing state, society and the Church. This chapter argues that the pre-, post- and Soviet religious practices should be examined more critically, as effects of political motivations associated with the national monumentalization process. As a result, the emerging religious landscape is an arena of ideological and political contestation. There is need for further research into scalar as opposed to territorial justice, and the role of scale in social and political processes in general. Meanwhile the deepest construction pit in Europe these days is in Moscow, on Krasnopresnenskaia Embankment, in the core of the proposed office complex "Moscow-City" (Figure 7.20). Though the pit is relatively idle after the economic crisis of August 1998 ("Trebuiutsia Milliardery" 2000), the Moscow government has not officially cancelled the project to build in this place the highest building in the world, the 648-m office tower Rossiia (Russia) (Nochuykina 2000) (Figure 7.24). But then this is a different story – or the same?

Chapter 7: Notes

1. I gratefully acknowledge support from the University of Minnesota for field work in 1994-95. Professors John Archer, John Fraser Hart, John Rice, Theofanis Stavrou, Trevor Barnes, and Barbara VanDrasek greatly improved earlier versions of this chapter. I am especially grateful to Professor Eric Sheppard and Valentin Bogorov. Those attending presentations at the 1997 AAG annual meeting and the 1997 European Studies Conference are also thanked for their criticism. A version of this chapter was previously published in *The Annals of the Association of American Geographers* (Sidorov 2000a) (published here with permission). I am grateful to the anonymous reviewers for their comments. I would also like to thank Eric Stevens and Professor Patricia Gilmartin for their help with graphics.

2. Krotov (1995: 21-22).

3. Although Russians most often call the Cathedral *khram* [temple], it is usually translated into English as cathedral, but does not necessarily imply an administrative center for a diocese or the seat of a bishop, as in English usage. The Russian word *sobor* may be translated as cathedral – a main or large church – but also as gathering or council, very much like the word *soviet*.

4. For example, Peter the Great ordered the closing of thousands of chapels in 1722 (Palamarchuk 1992: 11) and prohibited stone church erection to save stone resources for the construction of St. Petersburg. The Church government was changed to a state department (Synod) approved by the tsar.

5. The convent complex was repeatedly restored after various disasters. The Communist closure in 1930 was only the final action of an ongoing injustice. In 1990, one of its two remaining churches (two others having been demolished or absorbed by new construction) was returned to believers (Palamarchuk 1992: 343-349).

6. Hipped-roof churches at that time signified prominent city complexes. The cathedral was part of the hipped-roof church system along the Moscow River, which served control purposes (Moscow Patriarchate's "Arkhkhram" 1995: 119).

7. Strictly speaking, the first injustice was the replacement of the original pagan shrine in the area ("Strannoe Mesto" 1994).

8. Its location in southwest Moscow replicated that of the St. Diomid monastery in Constantinople, which was also known as "Jerusalem." Therefore, the new Moscow monastery signified continuity with

the Holy Land (Moscow Patriarchate's "Arkhkhram" 1995: 119).

9. A kind of kerchief worn by married Russian peasant women.

10. Ton's design of the Cathedral had references to the main competitors of the project. For example, the arcs of the façades were reminiscent of the Assumption Cathedral of the Kremlin.

11. Twenty years after the 1917 revolution, less than 0.5 percent of the pre-revolutionary churches remained open (Chapter 4).

12. The category "Orthodox" included Old Believers, Ukrainian and Georgian Orthodox Autocephalists, Ioannites, and others.

13. There are indications that Nikita Khrushchev considered the Pit as a possible location site for his projected television tower (Semenov 1994).

14. GARF f.6991 op. 1, d. 453, ll. 199-199ob.

15. A Siberian resident has suggested that the closed swimming pool on the site of the Cathedral was a secret monument to the chaotic and eventful Khrushchev period. While the Cathedral was a monument to bureaucratic Orthodoxy, the restored Cathedral would paradoxically serve as a monument to Stalinism: "I would prefer a morose Moscow evening, clouds of steam over the pool. And a secret sense of freedom," the author states (Poloznev 1994: 2).

16. The pool's legacy may have a tangible manifestation. The swimming pool, together with postwar subway construction, river-bed cleaning, and underground water, has further weakened the ground, which already had a poor soil texture (*"plyvun,"* or liquid mixture of clay and sand), making massive building construction at the site of the Cathedral questionable (Shebanov 1995).

17. For additional information on the intelligentsia's perception of the Cathedral's reconstruction, see Smith (1997). She, for instance, claims that Russian nationalists initially made the case for the Cathedral as a monument to military sacrifice. Several of them blamed Jews, namely the main Moscow city planner Lev Kaganovich and the architect of the Palace of the Soviets Boris Iofan, for its destruction. In contrast, all the believer-activists conceived of the reconstruction of the Cathedral as an act of repentance and insisted that the Cathedral was first and foremost an Orthodox church dedicated to the resurrection of Christ and only secondarily a historical monument or architectural landmark (Smith 1997: 167). In my opinion, Smith exaggerates the differences between the two groups, for almost all Russian nationalists are Orthodox believers at the same time, and often vise versa (see Chapter 2).

18. Voskresenskie Gates and Iverskaia Chapel, adjacent to the Church of Kazan' Icon of the Holy Virgin on Red Square, have already been restored (in the fall of 1995).

19. Arguments of the Church for the restoration can be found in Kuraev (1995).

20. As Moscow's Mayor, Luzhkov has become a leading post-Soviet politician. In 1995 he was the third most significant politician in Russia (*Nezavisimaia Gazeta* 1996), following the President and Prime Minister.

21. The most dramatic project of this sort is the proposed Moscow-City district, a business center on Krasnopresnenskaia Embankment that will include several Western-style skyscrapers (Figure 7.20).

22. This program has actually received only ten percent of the planned amount. In Moscow alone, the current funding for restoration is three to four times less than 5 years ago (Deich 1994).

23. Sponsorship could be indirect, as in the case of the Moscow Energy Company (Mosenergo) and other similar organizations (Mosvodokanal, Mosinzhproekt) which provide infrastructure for the church at no cost (*Vestnik Merii Moskvy* 1995).

CHAPTER 8. CONCLUSION

In this epoch of secularization, Russian Orthodoxy has experienced both a most dramatic decline and a spectacular current revival. Similarly, in the short period of just one hundred years, the Russian realm has undergone a number of major geopolitical transformations that have profoundly affected its state, societal and cultural institutions – including its religious ones. While these changes have attracted the attention of scholars from different disciplines, their comparative dimension is relatively underdeveloped. There is a widespread assumption in the social sciences that the state, society and cultural (religious) institutions are spatially conterminous. Most analysts view spatialities of society and cultural institutions as determined by and/or coinciding with the spatial extent of the state.

This study attempts to challenge this common approach, not because it is considered wrong, but in order to elucidate new research opportunities. To grasp the evolving geopolitics of the Russian Orthodox Church(es), this study utilizes a more dynamic and relational approach, as suggested, for example, in the writings of Michael Foucault.

By a dynamic approach I mean a focus on themes which are usually considered transitional in historical terms and marginal in a geographical sense. For example, the Russian state in this century has changed its territorial form several times: while most scholars would be interested in analyzing these forms, this study is focused more on the change from one form to another. More specifically, shifts in the geographical scale of the state prove to be decisive for understanding how different schismatic movements in Russian Orthodoxy emerged and evolved.

At the same time, this study takes a relational stand, meaning that it departs from state-determined models of politics. The argument is not only that power is an outcome of the interaction *among* the state, society, and its cultural institutions (such as the Church). I wish to go further and assign a greater role to the *spatial context* of these relations. Space, often considered a neutral arena by historians, reveals its shaping role at times of disjuncture, during periods of rupture in social life when the *positionality* of the these three agents (the state, society and the Church) with regard to one another change, altering systems of power. Similarly, at times of church schisms the positionality of the main (official) Church and its opponents, i.e., their geography relative to one another, reveals best its potential for shaping power and causing difference. Therefore, the geopolitics of the Russian Orthodox Churches in this study is presented through a series of territorial non-correspondences between the state, society and Churches.

The shift from nation-state to empire in the seventeenth century resulted in the first major schism within Russian Orthodoxy, namely the Old Belief (Chapter 2). Similarly, the Renovationist schism of the 1920s can be seen as another mismatch, this time between the global aspirations of the state and the parochial, national nature of society (Chapter 3). In the late 1930s non-correspondence of the state and society saved the Church from total extinction (Chapter 4), while the collapse of the Iron Curtain posed a serious new challenge to the Church in areas such as Estonia (Chapter 5). In contrast, at the local level, for example in Moscow, the main Church itself poses a threat to other communities (Chapter 6).

Four contributions stand out from my study. First, it provides a useful perspective for understanding Church schisms, specifically the schisms in Russian Orthodoxy. Challenging the traditional rooting of power in the state, this study shows the importance of understanding the spatiality of power relations. Awareness of this issue is important for understanding the evolving geopolitics of Russian Orthodoxy in this century.

Second, at a theoretical level, this study contributes to a more dynamic understanding of geographical scales. More specifically, it demonstrates the importance of intra-scalar differences, often neglected in the social sciences.

The third contribution of this study is its data. Previously many sources have been either closed to researchers (such as Soviet archives) or not available (as many local Russian periodicals and publications). Many facts, figures, and maps are presented here for the first time. In addition, the use of many maps is innovative simply because a tradition of cartographic analysis of Russian Orthodoxy is almost non-existent.

Fourth, this study advances the understanding of the post-Soviet religious revival through its analysis of the process of in the former USSR. Among all findings, this one was the most surprising. In contrast to my original hypothesis, my study shows that the idea of is largely irrelevant to this revival. At best, it serves as no more than a rhetorical strategy of alternative Orthodox communities for preservation of diversity and difference in Orthodoxy; at worst it justifies new post-Soviet hegemonies. In many cases, such as the return of church property and reconstruction of demolished cathedrals, democratic rhetoric was used to legitimize the hegemonic power of new political groups. The majority of the people in post-Soviet Russia are increasingly dissatisfied with the democratic ideal. Indeed, it is often considered a western invention intended to weaken Russia. At the beginning of *perestroika*, to gain popular support, a new generation of politicians proudly called themselves proponents of "democracy." A decade later, after the corruption of so many people and so many values, this word has also been corrupted and deconstructed – often being used in the form "der'mocracy" (*der'mo* means "excrement") (for, example, Nikonov 2000). This conclusion may sound pessimistic, yet it is nevertheless constructive, suggesting that a search for scholarly agendas is underway in Russia, including a search for a new understanding of democracy itself. I would like to elaborate on this theme further.

The western idea of liberal insists on the importance of diversity of social phenomena. Yet in the course of my study several times I had reasons to question the link between democracy and diversity, specifically religious diversity. For instance, the Russian Empire is commonly considered to have been a more democratic state than the totalitarian Soviet Union. Yet in Tsarist Russia only during the brief period of 1905-17 was some relaxation in the religious sphere permitted, with Churches other than the main one receiving legal recognition. For the Old Believers, this allowed a short period of revival. Since many of the adherents of this oppressed community were the most successful entrepreneurs in Russia, the Old Believers managed, among other things, to build a large number of churches. Yet this revival was very short. The entrepreneurial basis of the Church was fatally affected by the 1917 Communist revolution. The schism splintered the Church community and weakened its political voice, allowing secular power to emerge as the sole arbiter in religious disputes. Because many of its most avid believers left the Church, it was left chiefly with those who were "lukewarm" and indifferent in religious matters. This led to a greater reliance on the state, police, and army to enforce the faith (Pankhurst 1996: 137).

Paradoxically, during the period of religious toleration in 1905-17 Tsar Nicholas II did not permit any reforms within the main Church, even preventing its Council from gathering. The All-Russian Church Council managed to meet only in 1917, in Moscow, in the country's largest Cathedral of Christ the Savior. It carried out a far-reaching program of reforms and restored the Patriarchate that Peter the Great had replaced with the Holy Synod. But, at some early sessions, members could hear the sound of Bolshevik artillery shelling the Kremlin, and two days after the election of the new Patriarch (Tikhon), Lenin and his associates gained full mastery over Moscow. The Church was allowed no time to consolidate the work of reform, providing a fruitful context for the Renovationist movement in the Church.

In contrast to Tsarist Russia, great religious diversity was characteristic of the early Bolshevik state of the first post-revolutionary decade. Not only were the state and religious matters separated, so that the privileging of one Church was stopped and other communities such as the Old Believers allowed to exist, but new Churches were also created (such as the Renovationist Church). This "creativity" in the field of religious diversity had little to do with democracy, but rather was a tool aimed at political goals.

However hostile to the Church, the Communists in a way plagiarized some essential Orthodox concepts, e.g., the veneration of rulers, the admiration of rituals, the dignity of suffering, and the commitment to collective, communal identity. The Orthodox prime concept of *sobornost'*, or "episcopal conciliarism," stems from *sobor* (meaning "cathedral" and "council"). Remarkably, the word *"soviet"* also means "council." It is only a limited paradox that the Bolsheviks found it useful to copy from the Church while at the same time igniting the Renovationist schism within the Church.

Post-Soviet development also questions the relationship between democracy and diversity in the religious sphere. Estonia, for example, is often considered one of the most liberal among the former Soviet republics, democratic enough to join many European institutions. Yet this seemingly democratic state has used the democratic rhetoric of fighting the Soviet heritage to decrease religious diversity by constraining the Russian Orthodox Church's branch in Estonia (Chapter 5).

Denationalization of church property is also seen as a part of the process because it supposedly increases pluralism of power in society. Close local analysis of this process in both Estonia and Moscow shows, however, that denationalization of churches often also serves hegemonic ends, e.g., it allows the state to privilege one Church at the expense of others.

The reversal of the anti-religious policies of the Communists in post-Soviet Russia is another example of a failed democratic ideal. The case of the restoration of the Cathedral of Christ the Savior is particu-

larly telling. Although the large-scale urban destruction and consequent restoration is not unique, there are few examples of a purposeful
demolition of a national monument and its eventual reconstruction.
Post-Soviet politicians and practitioners did have a rare chance to *re*-
construct such a landscape entirely, after reaching a unanimous con-
sensus about the unfairness of Communist manipulation of sacred
places and creation of a new social mythology. The way that the pit of
the Palace of the Soviets has been filled by post-Communist authorities
sheds light on the way in which they cope with the "historical gap" of
Communist rule (Chapter 7). The Pit would be a constant and painful
reminder of the recent Soviet past; therefore it had to be eliminated
from society's mental map by the "new" authorities. Filling the "pit"
bridges the "historical gap," and creates an association of post-Com-
munism with a different, "brighter," segment of the past. Although
the public could debate the speed, management, accuracy, and cost of
the reconstruction, it was unable to effectively discuss its location and
general purpose, perhaps the most burning issues.

Restoration could become an act of public repentance, a public
coming-to-terms with the Communist past. Unfortunately, the speed
of the reconstruction has prevented this. Not only was the public left
out of the reconstruction process, the country as a whole was in some
sense robbed. Areas of Russia other than "prosperous" Moscow are
struggling nowadays with problems of the kind the capital city solved
some time ago. They need time to recover from recent changes and to
participate in the restoration of a national monument. At the time of
its initial construction the Cathedral was the symbol of the Empire, not
just of Russia, and certainly not just of Moscow.

The result of this hectic filling in of the historical gap is that a
restoration of the recent past has become inevitable. Whereas an artist,
memorably named Christo, has wrapped Germany's Reichstag in fab-
ric to help denationalize the country, in Russia it works in the opposite
manner. The war memorial Cathedral of Christ the Savior has been
"unwrapped" to restore the "sense of national identity" and thus national tradition. The restoration will also certainly make the position
of the right wing in the Church stronger (Krotov 1994).

In the words of a Russian intellectual, with the Pit's erasure,
Moscow could become a *tabula rasa* ("Tsentr Novoi Utopii" 1995), nice
and fake, as shopping mall spaces are. The Cathedral is planned to be
linked by a new subway line to the Moscow-City business complex,
which is currently under construction. Only after that, perhaps, will
the project be fully completed. But the ideology of the reconstruction

will probably be recycled again and again, as already is seen with other "big" construction projects in the city (Chapter 6).

A fascination with new horizons opened by a new approach inevitably invites the skeptical question: so what? Perhaps the way to construct a public landscape in a less manipulative way is to allow a broader democratic participation in the construction process. Ironically, the Cathedral is publicized in exactly this light, as a whole nation's project, whereas in reality this is not and never was the case.

It would not be an exaggeration to say that the Russian Orthodox Church remains the most respected institution in post-Soviet Russia, despite (or because of) its continuing alliance with the state and lack of rapport with the contemporary social needs of the majority of the population. Perhaps the major finding of my study is that a quest for a new democracy is emerging, a democracy of the weak as opposed to a democracy of the powerful; a democracy of difference as opposed to a democracy of diversity, or a democracy demanded internally as opposed to a democracy supplied from outside. Russian Orthodoxy, with its tradition of communal justice has the potential to provide this new ideal. It remains to be seen if this potential will be realized.

SUPPLEMENT

Table A2.1. Religious profile of the Russian Empire by province, 1897. Percent of total population.

Map nos.	Province (guberniia)	Total population	Potential Orthodox (Actual Orthodox population)	Orth. & Edinoverie (Actual Orth.)	Actual Orth./ Potent.	Actual Orthodox/ Total Popul-n deficit	Old Belief	Old Belief/ Actual Orth. pop-n ratio	Roman Catholics	Protestants	Other Christians	Islam	Judaism	Other non-Christians
1	Arkhangel'sk	346536	85.18	97.33	12.15	-2.67	1.8	0.02	0.18	0.6	0	0.01	0.08	
2	Astrakhan'	1003542	54.13	52.74	-1.39	-47.26	1.54	0.03	0.15	0.52	0.42	30.6	0.31	3.72
3	Bessarabia	1936392	75.34	82.9	7.56	-17.1	1.46	0.02	0.95	2.88	0.13	0.03	11.7	0
4	Vilensk	1591207	61.05	26.1	-34.95	-73.9	1.61	0.06	58.8	0.29	0.01	0.28	12.9	0
5	Vitebsk	1489246	66.28	55.44	-10.84	-44.56	5.57	0.10	24	3.15	0.01	0.04	11.8	0
6	Vladimir	1515693	99.74	97.28	-2.46	-2.72	2.45	0.03	0.1	0.05	0	0.03	0.09	0
7	Vologda	1341785	91.32	99.31	7.99	-0.69	0.58	0.01	0.05	0.02	0	0.01	0.03	
8	Volyn'	2987970	73.77	70.52	-3.25	-29.48	0.26	0.00	9.93	5.8	0.01	0.16	13.3	0.01
9	Voronezh	2531253	99.65	99.11	-0.54	-0.89	0.58	0.01	0.09	0.09	0.01	0.01	0.11	
10	Vyatka	3032552	77.41	92.14	14.73	-7.86	3.17	0.03	0.02	0.01	0	4.27	0.03	0.36
11	Grodno	1602681	69.37	57.5	-11.87	-42.5	0.03	0.00	24	0.79	0.04	0.37	17.3	0
12	Don	2562754	95.28	90.37	-4.91	-9.63	5.07	0.06	0.38	1.14	1.06	0.12	0.6	1.26
13	Yekaterinoslav	2113384	86.85	90.29	3.44	-9.71	0.44	0.00	1.37	3.02	0.02	0.09	4.77	0.56
14	Kazan'	2176424	38.29	69.43	31.14	-30.57	1	0.01	0.09	0.06	0	28.8	0.11	0.56
15	Kaluga	1132843	99.58	95.88	-3.70	-4.12	3.71	0.04	0.19	0.07	0	0.02	0.13	0
16	Kiev	3559481	85.27	83.96	-1.31	-16.04	0.42	0.01	3.07	0.43	0	0.09	12	0
17	Kovno	1548410	7.26	2.98	-4.28	-97.02	2.08	0.70	76.6	4.47	0.03	0.11	13.7	0
18	Kostroma	1389812	99.42	96.98	-2.44	-3.02	2.81	0.03	0.06	0.04	0	0.05	0.06	0
19	Kurland	672308	5.69	3.79	-1.90	-96.21	1.23	0.32	11.1	76.4	0	0.09	7.33	0.05
20	Kursk	2371213	99.58	98.73	-0.85	-1.27	0.9	0.01	0.13	0.05	0	0.02	0.17	0
21	Lifland	1299523	5.36	14.33	8.97	-85.67	1.25	0.09	2.27	79.9	0	0.04	22.2	0
22	Minsk	2147911	80.41	72.8	-7.61	-27.2	0.74	0.01	10.2	0.26	0	0.21	15.8	0
23	Mogilev	1688573	85.96	83.18	-2.78	-16.82	1.35	0.02	3.04	0.4	0	0.1	11.9	0.01
24	Moscow	2427415	40.89	93.78	52.89	-6.22	4.01	0.04	0.61	0.94	0.07	0.23	0.36	0
25	Nizhnii Novgorod	1584774	93.24	91.58	-1.66	-8.42	5.54	0.06	0.08	0.06	0	2.62	0.12	0
26	Novgorod	1367022	96.90	96.11	-0.79	-3.89	2.24	0.02	0.33	0.94	0	0.03	0.35	
27	Olonets	364156	78.26	98.28	20.02	-1.72	0.81	0.01	0.11	0.67	0	0.02	0.11	
28	Orenburg	1600500	73.10	73.56	0.46	-26.44	3.08	0.04	0.24	0.33	0	22.7	0.13	0
29	Orel	2039808	99.09	99.18	0.09	-0.82	0.21	0.00	0.19	0.08	0.01	0.02	0.31	0
30	Penza	1470968	83.03	94.55	11.52	-5.45	1.29	0.01	0.08	0.06	0	3.98	0.04	0
31	Perm'	2993562	90.45	86.99	-3.46	-13.01	7.17	0.08	0.08	0.04	0	4.96	0.07	0.69
32	Podol'sk	3018551	85.12	78.17	-6.95	-21.83	0.62	0.01	8.7	0.13	0	0.23	12.2	0
33	Poltava	2780424	95.58	95.55	-0.03	-4.45	0.11	0.00	0.2	0.1	0	0.02	4.02	0
34	Pskov	1122152	94.94	93.53	-1.41	-6.47	3.17	0.03	0.49	2.23	0	0	0.58	
35	Ryazan'	1803617	99.39	98.54	-0.85	-1.46	0.95	0.01	0.09	0.06	0	0.27	0.09	0
36	Samara	2748876	68.96	77.51	8.55	-22.49	3.52	0.05	2.8	6.24	0	10.4	0.09	0.19
37	St.Petersburg	2109463	82.56	82.11	-0.45	-17.89	0.94	0.01	3.02	12.6	0.04	0.29	1.01	0
38	Saratov	2406919	82.98	84.14	1.16	-15.86	4.71	0.06	1.43	5.63	0.01	3.92	0.13	0.03
39	Simbirsk	1527481	68.17	89.03	20.86	-10.97	2.05	0.02	0.06	0.13	0	8.63	0.04	0.06
40	Smolensk	1525629	98.32	97.13	-1.19	-2.87	1.33	0.01	0.57	0.26	0	0.02	0.69	0
41	Tavrida	1448973	70.92	73.79	2.87	-26.21	0.89	0.01	2	4.81	0.8	13.1	4.57	0.01
42	Tambov	2683059	95.83	98.64	2.81	-1.36	0.57	0.01	0.07	0.05	0.01	0.58	0.08	0
43	Tver'	1769443	92.91	98.77	5.86	-1.23	0.87	0.01	0.1	0.16	0	0.02	0.08	0
44	Tula	1422291	99.43	99.55	0.12	-0.45	0.12	0.00	0.07	0.06	0	0.01	0.19	0
45	Ufa	2196642	38.22	43.65	5.43	-56.35	1.54	0.04	0.06	0.22	0.01	50	0.03	4.46
46	Khar'kov	2492367	98.73	98.43	-0.30	-1.57	0.29	0.00	0.33	0.32	0.02	0.06	0.55	0
47	Kherson	2738923	80.60	80.41	-0.19	-19.59	1.08	0.01	3.5	2.5	0.1	0.09	12.3	0
48	Chernigov	2298834	94.55	92.69	-1.86	-7.31	1.89	0.02	0.23	0.18	0	0.02	4.99	0
49	Estland	412817	5.06	9.17	4.11	-90.83	0.06	0.01	0.49	89.9	0.03	0.02	0.33	0.05
50	Yaroslavl'	1071579	99.49	98.7	-0.79	-1.3	0.85	0.01	0.15	0.12	0	0.03	0.15	0
	European Russia	93467738	79.69	81.81	2.12	-18.19	1.85	0.02	4.64	3.47	0.06	3.8	4.03	0.34

Table A2.1 (part 2).

Map nos.	Province (guberniia)	Total population	Potential Orthodox popu-lation	Orth. & Edinoverie (Actual Ortho-dox)	Actual Orth./ Potent. Orth. deficit	Actual Ortho-dox/ Total Popul-n deficit	Old Be-lief	Old Belief/ Actual Orth. pop-n ratio	Ro-man-Cath-olics	Pro-tes-tants	Other Chris-tians	Is-lam	Ju-da-ism	Other non-Chris-tians
51	Baku	826806	9.40	6.77	-2.63	-93.23	2.84	0.42	0.27	0.47	6.18	82.1	1.41	0.01
52	Dagestan	571381	2.82	2.82	0.00	-97.18	0.06	0.02	0.38	0.05	0.28	94.7	1.72	0
53	Yelisavetpol'	878185	2.05	1.14	-0.91	-98.86	1.16	1.02	0.08	0.38	34.05	63	0.23	0
54	Karsk	290654	9.60	16.96	7.36	-83.04	4.47	0.26	1.5	0.42	25.1	50.2	0.42	1.17
55	Kuban'	1919397	90.82	91.03	0.21	-8.97	1.21	0.01	0.38	0.97	0.76	5.38	0.25	0.02
56	Kutais	1057243	2.22	85.12	82.90	-14.88	0.02	0.00	0.39	0.16	2.34	11.1	0.84	0.01
57	Stavropol'	873805	91.93	91.27	-0.66	-8.73	1.22	0.01	0.24	0.95	0.61	4.39	0.15	1.17
58	Tersk	932341	33.76	39.55	5.79	-60.45	3.83	0.10	0.6	1.01	1.59	52.2	0.76	0.48
59	Tiflis	1054250	8.15	56.1	47.95	-43.9	1.52	0.03	1.01	0.72	21.83	18	0.81	0.03
60	Chernomor	57478	61.71	74.88	13.17	-25.12	0.14	0.00	4.21	2.65	10.85	5.41	1.83	0.03
61	Yerivan'	829550	1.92	2.15	0.23	-97.85	0.45	0.21	0.26	0.08	53	42.5	0.25	1.34
	Caucasus	9291090	34.03	49.48	15.45	-50.52	1.46	0.03	0.47	0.61	12.49	34.5	0.63	0.32
62	Amur	120306	86.33	76.16	-10.17	-23.84	11.9	0.16	0.35	0.6	0.01	0.54	0.33	10.12
63	Yenisey	570579	86.78	94.08	7.30	-5.92	1.96	0.02	1.08	0.66	0.01	0.86	1	0.35
64	Trans-Baikal	637777	69.76	75.24	5.48	-24.76	5.76	0.08	0.3	0.1	0.01	0.48	1.18	16.93
65	Irkutsk	514202	73.59	83.45	9.86	-16.55	0.17	0.00	0.78	0.15	0.03	1.48	1.6	12.34
66	Maritime	223336	50.97	62.82	11.85	-37.18	0.76	0.01	1.65	0.47	0.03	0.57	0.72	32.98
67	Sakhalin	28113	65.63	69.47	3.84	-30.53	0.76	0.01	6.56	1.74	0.45	6.52	0.45	14.05
68	Tobol'sk	1434482	91.49	89.08	-2.41	-10.92	5.04	0.06	0.5	0.43	0	4.47	0.17	0.31
69	Tomsk	1928257	91.38	90.48	-0.90	-9.52	5.14	0.06	0.44	0.1	0.01	2.12	0.4	1.31
70	Yakutsk	269667	11.42	98.06	86.64	-1.94	0.41	0.00	0.15	0.07	0	0.7	0.26	0.35
	Siberia	5726719	81.37	86.99	5.62	-13.01	4.15	0.05	0.6	0.28	0.01	2.2	0.6	5.13
71	Akmolinsk	682429	33.08	33.97	0.89	-66.03	0.34	0.01	0.25	0.77	0	64.4	0.24	
72	Trans-Caspian	380323	8.76	8.92	0.16	-91.08	0.11	0.01	1.23	0.28	1.13	88.1	0.24	0.02
73	Samarkand	859123	1.63	1.55	-0.08	-98.45	0.04	0.03	0.18	0.06	0.04	97.6	0.51	0
74	Semipalatinsk	686909	9.96	9.98	0.02	-90.02	0.22	0.02	0.03	0.02		89.7	0.04	0
75	Semirechensk	990211	9.64	9.74	0.10	-90.26	0.02	0.00	0.02	0.01		90.2	0.03	0
76	Syr-Dar'ya	1466249	3.06	2.92	-0.14	-97.08	0.2	0.07	0.19	0.13	0	96.4	0.19	0
77	Turgay	453691	7.72	8.92	1.20	-91.08	0.03	0.00	0.03	0.01	0	91	0.02	0
78	Ural'sk	645590	25.39	16.98	-8.41	-83.02	8.62	0.51	0.04	0.02	0	74.2	0.02	0.17
79	Fergana	1575869	0.62	0.63	0.01	-99.37	0	0.00	0.1	0.02	0.01	99.1	0.14	0.01
	Central Asia	7740394	8.92	8.36	-0.56	-91.64	0.82	0.10	0.17	0.12	0.06	90.3	0.16	0.02
80	Warsaw	1931168	5.56	5.46	-0.10	-94.54	0.05	0.01	71.6	4.7	0.01	0.08	18.1	0
81	Kalish	842398	1.06	1.09	0.03	-98.91	0.02	0.02	82.8	7.45	0	0.02	8.59	0.01
82	Kelets	761689	1.21	1.06	-0.15	-98.94	0	0.00	87.8	0.33	0	0.01	10.8	
83	Lomzhin	579300	5.54	5.42	-0.12	-94.58	0.1	0.02	77.5	1.24	0	0.08	15.7	0
84	Lyublin	1159273	21.17	21.81	0.64	-78.19	0.03	0.00	62.4	2.43	0	0.04	13.3	0.01
85	Petrokov	1404031	1.62	1.56	-0.06	-98.44	0.01	0.01	73.1	9.53	0	0.02	15.8	0
86	Plotsk	553094	3.18	3.1	-0.08	-96.9	0.11	0.04	81.1	6.55	0.01	0.04	9.13	0
87	Radom	815062	1.55	1.45	-0.10	-98.55	0.02	0.01	83.6	1.05	0	0	13.9	
88	Suvalk	582696	9.11	6.14	-2.97	-93.86	1.03	0.17	76.2	6.41	0	0.14	10.1	0.01
89	Sedlets	772386	16.54	22.05	5.51	-77.95	0.02	0.00	60.5	1.51	0	0.08	15.8	0
	Polish Provinces	9401097	6.77	7.06	0.29	-92.94	0.1	0.01	74.3	4.46	0	0.05	14	0
	Russian Empire	116225941	71.41	69.54	-1.87	-30.46	1.72	0.02	9.09	2.98	0.97	11.1	4.13	0.51
90	Russians in Finland	12907		73.7	73.70	-26.3	0.68	0.01	15.3	5.21	0.06	0.03	4.99	
91	Russians in Bukhara	11361		62.3	62.30	-37.7	1.26	0.02	10.3	2.46	3.17	14.1	6.4	0.02
92	Russians in Khiva	3917		1.43	1.43	-98.57	1.43	1.00	0.07	0.26	0.41	96.2	0.2	
	Navy abroad	12969		92.39	92.39	-7.61	0.62	0.01	2.34	3.66	0.01	0.77	0.02	0.19

Sources: Tsentral'nyi Statisticheskii (1901a: 2-3), *Pervaia Vseobschaia* (1903), author's calculations.

Table A2.2. Status of Old Belief property in the Russian Empire by province, 1912.

Map Nos.	Province (guberniia and oblast')	Chur-ches	Worship houses	Churches & Wor.H.	Cloi-sters	Scho-ols	Alms-houses	Total po-pulation 1.1.1914	Old Be-lief, % 1897	Estimated Old Belief popu-lation, 1.1.1914	Chur-ches	Worship houses	Churches & Wor.H.	Clois-ters	Schools	Alms-houses
			absolute numbers								number per 1 mln estim. 1914 Old Belief population					
1	Arkhangel'sk	4	6	10	2		1	483.5	1.8	8.7	459.6	689.4	1149.0	229.8	0.0	114.9
2	Astrakhan'	1	10	11		1		1315.9	1.54	20.3	49.3	493.5	542.8	0.0	49.3	49.3
3	Bessarabia	24	8	32	4	10	4	2657.3	1.46	38.8	618.6	206.2	824.8	103.1	257.8	103.1
4	Vil'na		29	29				2075.9	1.61	33.4	0.0	867.7	867.7	0.0	0.0	0.0
5	Vitebsk	5	80	85		2	3	1953.1	5.57	108.8	46.0	735.4	781.3	0.0	18.4	27.6
6	Vladimir	27	63	90	5		1	2027	2.45	49.7	543.7	1268.6	1812.3	100.7	0.0	20.1
7	Vologda	2	46	48	1		1	1751.6	0.58	10.2	196.9	4527.9	4724.7	98.4	0.0	98.4
8	Volynia		9	9				4189	0.26	10.9	0.0	826.3	826.3	0.0	0.0	0.0
9	Voronezh	2	27	29	1	1		3630.9	0.58	21.1	95.0	1282.1	1377.1	47.5	47.5	0.0
10	Vyatka	16	101	117				3996.7	3.17	126.7	126.3	797.2	923.5	0.0	0.0	7.9
11	Grodno			0				2048.2	0.03	0.6	0.0	0.0	0.0	0.0	0.0	0.0
12	Don Cossacks	17	72	89	2		1	3876	5.07	196.5	86.5	366.4	452.9	10.2	0.0	5.1
13	Yekaterinoslav	8	7	15	1	2		3455.5	0.44	15.2	526.2	460.4	986.6	65.8	131.5	0.0
14	Kazan'	7	55	62		1	3	2867	1	28.7	244.2	1918.4	2162.5	0.0	34.9	104.6
15	Kaluga	17	55	72	1	2		1476.6	3.71	54.8	310.3	1004.0	1314.3	18.3	36.5	0.0
16	Kiev	11	6	17	3			4792.5	0.42	20.1	546.5	298.1	844.6	149.0	0.0	0.0
17	Kovno	4	51	55				1857.1	2.08	38.6	103.6	1320.3	1423.8	0.0	0.0	0.0
18	Kostroma	26	102	128	3	2	4	1822.6	2.81	51.2	507.7	1991.6	2499.3	58.6	39.1	78.1
19	Kurlyandiya	3	10	13		13		798.3	1.23	9.8	305.5	1018.4	1324.0	0.0	1324.0	0.0
20	Kursk	3	46	49	2			3256.6	0.9	29.3	102.4	1569.5	1671.8	68.2	0.0	34.1
21	Liflyandiya	3	11	14		1	1	1744	1.25	21.8	137.6	504.6	642.2	0.0	45.9	45.9
22	Minsk	1	21	22				3035.8	0.74	22.5	44.5	934.8	979.3	0.0	0.0	0.0
23	Mogilev	8	33	41			1	2465.6	1.35	33.3	240.3	991.4	1231.8	0.0	0.0	0.0
24	Moscow	63	131	194	10	6	13	3591.3	4.01	144.0	437.5	909.7	1347.1	0.0	41.7	90.3
25	Nizhmiy Novgorod	38	205	243		5	3	2066.8	5.54	114.5	331.9	1790.4	2122.3	87.3	43.7	26.2
26	Novgorod	4	42	46			1	1671.5	2.24	37.4	106.8	1121.7	1228.6	0.0	0.0	26.7
27	Olonets		3	3				465.6	0.81	3.8	0.0	795.5	795.5	0.0	0.0	0.0
28	Orenburg	19	70	89	1	7	2	2170.8	3.08	66.9	284.2	1047.0	1331.1	15.0	104.7	29.9
29	Orel		18	18				2761.7	0.21	5.8	0.0	3103.7	3103.7	0.0	0.0	0.0
30	Penza	7	42	49				1911.6	1.29	24.7	283.9	1703.2	1987.1	0.0	0.0	0.0
31	Perm'	37	575	612	8	1		4007.5	7.17	287.3	128.8	2001.1	2129.9	27.8	3.5	0.0
32	Podol'sk	16	16	32				4057.3	0.62	25.2	636.0	636.0	1272.1	0.0	0.0	0.0
33	Poltava	1	1	2			2	3792.1	0.11	4.2	239.7	239.7	479.5	0.0	0.0	479.5
34	Pskov	8	19	27	1			1425.1	3.17	45.2	177.1	420.6	597.7	22.1	0.0	0.0

Table A2.2. (part 2)

Map Nos.	Province (guberniia and oblast')	Chur-ches	Worship houses	Churches & Wor.H.	Cloi-sters	Scho-ols	Alms-houses	Total po-pulation 1.1.1914	Old Be-lief % 1897	Estimated Old Belief popu-lation, 1.1.1914	Chur-ches	Worship houses	Churches & Wor.H. 1914 estim.	Clois-ters	Schools	Alms-houses
		absolute numbers									number per 1 mln Old Belief population					
35	Ryazan'	6	43	49	1	1		2773.9	0.95	26.4	227.7	1631.8	1859.4	37.9	37.9	0.0
36	Samara	10	179	189	1	1	1	3800.8	3.52	133.8	74.7	1337.9	1412.7	7.5	7.5	7.5
37	St.Petersburg	4	46	50	1		3	3136.5	0.94	29.5	135.7	1560.2	1695.9	0.0	33.9	101.8
38	Saratov	43	254	297	8	1	4	3269.3	4.71	154.0	279.2	1649.5	1928.8	52.0	6.5	26.0
39	Simbirsk	12	63	75				2067.8	2.05	42.4	283.1	1486.2	1769.3	0.0	0.0	0.0
40	Smolensk	9	12	21				2163.6	1.33	28.8	312.8	417.0	729.8	0.0	0.0	0.0
41	Tavrida	2	1	3		1		2059.3	0.89	18.3	109.1	54.6	163.7	0.0	54.6	0.0
42	Tambov		7	7				3530	0.57	20.1	0.0	347.9	347.9	0.0	0.0	0.0
43	Tver'	12	5	17	2	1	1	2394.1	0.87	20.8	576.1	240.1	816.2	96.0	48.0	48.0
44	Tula	2	4	6			2	1886.2	0.12	2.3	883.6	1767.2	2650.8	0.0	0.0	883.6
45	Ufa	5	47	52		6		3099.2	1.54	47.7	104.8	984.8	1089.5	0.0	125.7	0.0
46	Khar'kov		13	13		1		3416.8	0.29	9.9	0.0	1312.0	1312.0	0.0	100.9	0.0
47	Kherson	12	28	40	2	5	3	3744.6	1.08	40.4	296.7	692.4	989.1	49.5	123.6	74.2
48	Chernigov	7	64	71	4	3		3131.5	1.89	59.2	118.3	1081.3	1199.6	67.6	50.7	0.0
49	Estlyandiya [Estonia]		0	0				570.2	0.06	0.3	0.0	0.0	0.0	0.0	0.0	0.0
50	Yaroslavl'	9	45	54	1	2	7	1297.7	0.85	11.0	815.9	4079.6	4895.5	90.7	181.3	634.6
	European Russia	**515**	**2781**	**3296**	**64**	**77**	**64**	**128864**	**1.85**	**2384.0**	**216.0**	**1166.5**	**1382.6**	**26.8**	**32.3**	**26.8**
51	Baku		7	7				1100.4	2.84	31.3	0.0	224.0	224.0	0.0	0.0	0.0
52	Dagestan							724.2	0.06	0.4	0.0	0.0	0.0	0.0	0.0	0.0
53	Yelisavetpol'							1098	1.16	12.7	0.0	0.0	0.0	0.0	0.0	0.0
54	Kars							396.2	4.27	16.9	0.0	0.0	0.0	0.0	0.0	0.0
55	Kuban'	11	23	34				2984.5	1.21	36.1	304.6	636.9	941.5	0.0	0.0	0.0
56	Kutais+Sukhum+Batum							1397.2	0.02	0.3	0.0	0.0	0.0	0.0	0.0	0.0
57	Stavropol'	3	14	17				1329	1.22	16.2	185.0	863.5	1048.5	0.0	0.0	0.0
58	Terek (Tersk)	13	21	34	7	5		1261.2	3.83	48.3	269.1	434.7	703.9	144.9	103.5	0.0
59	Tiflis + Zakatal							1460	1.52	22.2	0.0	0.0	0.0	0.0	0.0	0.0
60	Black Sea		1	1				152.7	0.14	0.2	0.0	4677.7	4677.7	0.0	0.0	0.0
61	Yerivan'							1018.3	0.45	4.6	0.0	0.0	0.0	0.0	0.0	0.0
	Caucasus	**27**	**66**	**93**	**7**	**5**	**0**	**12921.7**	**1.46**	**188.7**	**143.1**	**349.8**	**493.0**	**37.1**	**26.5**	**0.0**
62	Amur	4	19	23				250.4	11.89	29.8	134.4	638.2	772.5	0.0	0.0	0.0
63	Yenisey	6	20	26		1		990.4	1.96	19.4	309.1	1030.3	1339.4	0.0	51.5	0.0
64	Trans-Baikal	5	44	49	1			945.7	5.76	54.5	91.8	807.7	899.5	0.0	0.0	0.0

Table A2.2. (part 3)

Map Nos.	Province (guberniia and oblast')	Churches	Worship houses	Churches & Wor.H.	Cloisters	Schools	Alms-houses	Total population 1.1.1914	Old Belief % 1897	Estimated Old Belief population, 1.1.1914	Churches	Worship houses	Churches & Wor.H.	Cloisters	Schools	Alms-houses
		absolute numbers									number per 1 mln estim. 1914 Old Belief population					
65	Irkutsk	3	3	6				750.2	0.17	1.3	2352.3	2352.3	4704.6	0.0	0.0	0.0
66	Primor'e+Kamchatka	3	7	10				647.1	0.76	4.9	610.0	1423.4	2033.4	0.0	0.0	0.0
67	Sakhalin			0				33.5	0.76	0.3	0.0	0.0	0.0	0.0	0.0	0.0
68	Tobol'sk	11	96	107	1			2054.4	5.04	103.5	106.2	927.2	1033.4	9.7	0.0	0.0
69	Tomsk	27	94	121	1	6		3999	5.14	205.5	131.4	457.3	588.7	4.9	29.2	0.0
70	Yakutsk	1	1	2		1		330	0.41	1.4	739.1	739.1	1478.2	0.0	739.1	0.0
	Siberia	**60**	**284**	**344**	**2**	**8**	**0**	**10000.7**	**4.15**	**415.0**	**144.6**	**684.3**	**828.9**	**4.8**	**19.3**	**0.0**
71	Akmolinsk		3	3				1523.7	0.34	5.2	0.0	579.1	579.1	0.0	0.0	0.0
72	Trans-Caspian							533.9	0.11	0.6	0.0	0.0	0.0	0.0	0.0	0.0
73	Samarkand							1198	0.04	0.5	0.0	0.0	0.0	0.0	0.0	0.0
74	Semipalatinsk		1	1				867.5	0.22	1.9	0.0	524.0	524.0	0.0	0.0	0.0
75	Semirechensk		1	1				1269.3	0.02	0.3	0.0	3939.2	3939.2	0.0	0.0	0.0
76	Syr-Dar'ya		5	5		1		2012.3	0.2	4.0	0.0	1242.4	1242.4	0.0	248.5	0.0
77	Turgay		3	3				697.7	0.03	0.2	0.0	14332.8	14332.8	0.0	0.0	0.0
78	Ural'sk	27	7	34		2		867.1	8.62	74.7	361.2	93.7	454.9	0.0	26.8	0.0
79	Fergana		1	1				2134		0.0						
	Central Asia	**27**	**21**	**48**	**0**	**3**	**0**	**11103.5**	**0.82**	**91.0**	**296.5**	**230.6**	**527.2**	**0.0**	**32.9**	**0.0**
80	Warsaw		2	2				2792.6	0.05	1.4	0.0	1432.4	1432.4	0.0	0.0	0.0
81	Kalish							1342.4	0.02	0.3	0.0	0.0	0.0	0.0	0.0	0.0
82	Kel'tsy							1029.8	0	0.0						
83	Lomzha							819.7	0.1	0.8	0.0	0.0	0.0	0.0	0.0	0.0
84	Lyublin							1481	0.03	0.4	0.0	0.0	0.0	0.0	0.0	0.0
85	Petrokov							2097.8	0.01	0.2	0.0	0.0	0.0	0.0	0.0	0.0
86	Plotsk							786	0.11	0.9	0.0	0.0	0.0	0.0	0.0	0.0
87	Radom							1180.2	0.02	0.2	0.0	0.0	0.0	0.0	0.0	0.0
88	Suvalki	1	7	8		6		718	1.03	7.4	135.2	946.5	1081.8	0.0	811.3	0.0
89	Sedlets								0.02	0.0						
	Polish provinces	**1**	**9**	**10**	**0**	**6**	**0**	**12247.5**	**0.1**	**12.2**	**81.6**	**734.8**	**816.5**	**0.0**	**489.9**	**0.0**
	Russian Empire	**630**	**3161**	**3791**	**73**	**99**	**64**	**175138**	**1.72**	**3012.4**	**209.1**	**1049.3**	**1258.5**	**24.2**	**32.9**	**21.2**

Sources: Departament Dukhovnykh Del (1913: 1-3), Tsentral'nyi Statisticheskii Komitet (1901b), Institute of Russian History (1995: 18-22).

Note: Precise location of Kholm province (population 1087.8) is unclear.

Table A2.3. Correlation between total, potentially Orthodox and actually Orthodox populations of the Russian Empire, 1897.

Map Province nos.	Total	Potentially Orthodox	% of Total	Actually Orthodox	Actual/ Potential Orth. Pop. Deficit	Total pop-n/ Orthodox Deficit	Old Belief/ Orthodox Ratio
1 Arkhangel'sk	346536	295174	85.18	337288	-12.5	2.7	1.8
2 Astrakhan'	1003542	543206	54.13	529170	2.7	89.6	2.9
3 Bessarabia	1936392	1458862	75.34	1605357	-9.1	20.6	1.8
4 Vilensk	1591207	971355	61.05	415291	133.9	283.2	6.2
5 Vitebsk	1489246	987020	66.28	825601	19.6	80.4	10.0
6 Vladimir	1515693	1511729	99.74	1474519	2.5	2.8	2.5
7 Vologda	1341785	1225350	91.32	1332477	-8.0	0.7	0.6
8 Volyn'	2987970	2204262	73.77	2106955	4.6	41.8	0.4
9 Voronezh	2531253	2522375	99.65	2508775	0.5	0.9	0.6
10 Vyatka	3032552	2347351	77.41	2794145	-16.0	8.5	3.4
11 Grodno	1602681	1111714	69.37	921557	20.6	73.9	0.1
12 Don	2562754	2441711	95.28	2315821	5.4	10.7	5.6
13 Yekaterinoslav	2113384	1835395	86.85	1908131	-3.8	10.8	0.5
14 Kazan'	2176424	833340	38.29	1510975	-44.8	44.0	1.4
15 Kaluga	1132843	1128044	99.58	1086188	3.9	4.3	3.9
16 Kiev	3559481	3035211	85.27	2988694	1.6	19.1	0.5
17 Kovno	1548410	112356	7.26	46161	143.4	3254.4	69.8
18 Kostroma	1389812	1381715	99.42	1347733	2.5	3.1	2.9
19 Kurland	672308	38278	5.69	25470	50.3	2539.6	32.5
20 Kursk	2371213	2361203	99.58	2341028	0.9	1.3	0.9
21 Lifland	1299523	69615	5.36	186274	-62.6	597.6	8.7
22 Minsk	2147911	1727169	80.41	1563791	10.4	37.4	1.0
23 Mogilev	1688573	1451510	85.96	1404572	3.3	20.2	1.6
24 Moscow	2427415	992578	40.89	2276244	-56.4	6.6	4.3
25 Nizhniy Novgorod	1584774	1477640	93.24	1451337	1.8	9.2	6.0
26 Novgorod	1367022	1324702	96.90	1313870	0.8	4.0	2.3
27 Olonets	364156	285006	78.26	357312	-20.2	1.9	0.8
28 Orenburg	1600500	1169979	73.10	1177240	-0.6	36.0	4.2
29 Orel	2039808	2021308	99.09	2023072	-0.1	0.8	0.2
30 Penza	1470968	1221353	83.03	1390796	-12.2	5.8	1.4
31 Perm'	2993562	2707634	90.45	2604227	4.0	15.0	8.2
32 Podol'sk	3018551	2569401	85.12	2359630	8.9	27.9	0.8
33 Poltava	2780424	2657434	95.58	2656933	0.0	4.6	0.1
34 Pskov	1122152	1065411	94.94	1049525	1.5	6.9	3.4
35 Ryazan'	1803617	1792683	99.39	1777244	0.9	1.5	1.0
36 Samara	2748876	1895713	68.96	2130724	-11.0	29.0	4.5
37 St. Petersburg	2109463	1741504	82.56	1732122	0.5	21.8	1.1
38 Saratov	2406919	1997201	82.98	2025323	-1.4	18.8	5.6
39 Simbirsk	1527481	1041308	68.17	1360005	-23.4	12.3	2.3
40 Smolensk	1525629	1500006	98.32	1481750	1.2	3.0	1.4
41 Tavrida	1448973	1027569	70.92	1069282	-3.9	35.5	1.2
42 Tambov	2683059	2571121	95.83	2646578	-2.9	1.4	0.6
43 Tver'	1769443	1644016	92.91	1747678	-5.9	1.2	0.9
44 Tula	1422291	1414131	99.43	1415850	-0.1	0.5	0.1
45 Ufa	2196642	839661	38.22	958756	-12.4	129.1	3.5
46 Khar'kov	2492367	2460631	98.73	2453349	0.3	1.6	0.3
47 Kherson	2738923	2207590	80.60	2202258	0.2	24.4	1.3
48 Chernigov	2298834	2173522	94.55	2130792	2.0	7.9	2.0
49 Estland	412817	20899	5.06	37842	-44.8	990.9	0.7
50 Yaroslavl'	1071579	1066064	99.49	1057663	0.8	1.3	0.9
European Russia	**93467738**	**74480010**	**79.69**	**76463375**	**-2.6**	**22.2**	**2.3**

51 Baku	826806	77729	9.40	56006	38.8	1376.3	41.9
52 Dagestan	571381	16110	2.82	16213	-0.6	3424.2	2.1
53 Yelisavetpol'	878185	17981	2.05	10016	79.5	8667.8	101.8
54 Karss	290654	27903	9.60	49295	-43.4	489.6	26.4
55 Kuban'	1919397	1743278	90.82	1747149	-0.2	9.9	1.3
56 Kutais	1057243	23499	2.22	899899	-97.4	17.5	0.0
57 Stavropol'	873805	803284	91.93	797545	0.7	9.6	1.3
58 Tersk	932341	314800	33.76	368776	-14.6	152.8	9.7
59 Tiflis	1054250	85970	8.15	591342	-85.5	78.3	2.7
60 Chernomor	57478	35469	61.71	43039	-17.6	33.5	0.2
61 Yerivan'	829550	15966	1.92	17848	-10.5	4547.9	20.9
Caucasus	**9291090**	**3161989**	**34.03**	**4597128**	**-31.2**	**102.1**	**3.0**
62 Amur	120306	103863	86.33	91621	13.4	31.3	15.6
63 Yenisey	570579	495148	86.78	536785	-7.8	6.3	2.1
64 Trans-Baikal	637777	444900	69.76	479861	-7.3	32.9	7.7
65 Irkutsk	514202	378424	73.59	429134	-11.8	19.8	0.2
66 Maritime	223336	113829	50.97	140310	-18.9	59.2	1.2
67 Sakhalin	28113	18451	65.63	19431	-5.0	44.7	1.1
68 Tobol'sk	1434482	1312412	91.49	1277781	2.7	12.3	5.7
69 Tomsk	1928257	1762052	91.38	1744766	1.0	10.5	5.7
70 Yakutsk	269667	30807	11.42	264443	-88.4	2.0	0.4
Siberia	**5726719**	**4659886**	**81.37**	**4984132**	**-6.5**	**14.9**	**4.8**
71 Akmolinsk	682429	225716	33.08	231812	-2.6	194.4	1.0
72 Trans-Caspian	380323	33320	8.76	33931	-1.8	1020.9	1.2
73 Samarkand	859123	14026	1.63	13307	5.4	6356.2	2.6
74 Semipalatinsk	686909	68433	9.96	68517	-0.1	902.5	2.2
75 Semirechensk	990211	95467	9.64	96463	-1.0	926.5	0.2
76 Syr-Dar'ya	1466249	44848	3.06	42819	4.7	3324.3	6.8
77 Turgay	453691	35028	7.72	40477	-13.5	1020.9	0.3
78 Ural'sk	645590	163926	25.39	109633	49.5	488.9	50.8
79 Fergana	1575869	9849	0.62	9791	0.6	15995.1	0.0
Central Asia	**7740394**	**690613**	**8.92**	**600750**	**15.0**	**1188.5**	**9.8**
80 Warsaw	1931168	107422	5.56	105444	1.9	1731.5	0.9
81 Kalish	842398	8932	1.06	9173	-2.6	9083.5	1.8
82 Kelets	761689	9181	1.21	8049	14.1	9363.2	0.0
83 Lomzhin	579300	32086	5.54	31399	2.2	1745.0	1.8
84 Lyublin	1159273	245407	21.17	252830	-2.9	358.5	0.1
85 Petrokov	1404031	22698	1.62	21900	3.6	6311.1	0.6
86 Plotsk	553094	17601	3.18	17140	2.7	3126.9	3.5
87 Radom	815062	12635	1.55	11755	7.5	6833.7	1.4
88 Suvalk	582696	53111	9.11	35775	48.5	1528.8	16.8
89 Sedlets	772386	127741	16.54	170319	-25.0	353.5	0.1
Vistula (Polish) Provinces	**9401097**	**636814**	**6.77**	**663784**	**-4.1**	**1316.3**	**1.4**
Russian Empire	**116225941**	**82992498**	**71.41**	**86645385**	**-4.2**	**34.1**	**2.5**
90 Russians in Finland	12907	12907	100.00	9513		35.7	0.9
91 Russians in Bukhara	11361	11361	100.00	7078		60.5	2.0
92 Russians in Khiva	3917	3917	100.00	56		6894 6	100.0
Navy abroad	12969		0.00	11982		8.2	0.7

Correlation	for the whole Russian Empire:			for the Russian provinces only:		
	Column 1	Column 2	Column 3	Column 1	Column 2	Column 3
Column 1	1			1		
Column 2	0.876175	1		0.90096	1	
Column 3	0.887064	0.9718858	1	0.9560404	0.95694	1

Sources: Tsentral'nyi Statisticheskii (1901a: 2-3), the author's calculations.

Table A2.4. The Orthodox Russian-State Church, dynamics of affiliational membership, 1913 (per 1 million 1913 Orthodox population).

Map Nos.	Diocese	Ortho-dox po-pulation 1913	Joined the ORSCh from					Left the ORSCh to					Balance				Total, net	Total, gross
			Old Be-lief	Sects	Other Chris-tian	Non-Chris-tian	Total	Old Be-lief	Sects	Other Chris-tian	Non-Chris-tian	Total	Old Be-lief	Sects	Other Chris-tian	Non-Chris-tian		
1	Arkhangel'sk	436924	68.66	0	13.73	9.15	91.55	105.28	6.87	18.31	2.29	132.75	83.81	15.71	10.48	-15.71	-41.20	224.30
2	Astrakhan'	542859	156.58	35.00	47.89	42.37	281.84	7.37	171.32	7.37	0.00	186.05	-274.86	251.11	-74.65	-78.05	95.79	467.89
3	Blagoveschensk	296050	33.78	67.56	30.40	3918.26	4049.99	6.76	256.71	43.91	0.00	307.38	-91.28	638.94	45.64	-13235.12	3742.61	4357.37
4	Chernigov	2461322	21.94	3.66	7.72	13.00	46.32	0.81	17.88	0.00	0.00	18.69	-8.58	5.78	-3.14	-5.28	27.63	65.01
5	Don	2215258	130.91	6.32	13.09	5.42	155.74	2.26	18.06	0.00	0.00	20.31	-58.08	5.30	-5.91	-2.45	135.42	176.05
6	Finland	62723	63.77	0.00	318.86	47.83	430.46	0.00	605.84	956.59	0.00	1562.43	-1016.73	9658.95	10167.32	-762.55	-1131.96	1992.89
7	Grodno	990373	4.04	0	261.52	6.06	271.61	0.00	8.08	418.02	2.02	428.12	-4.08	8.16	158.03	-4.08	-156.51	699.74
8	Irkutsk	412400	14.55	9.70	33.95	635.31	693.50	19.40	121.24	21.82	337.05	499.52	11.76	270.47	-29.40	-723.22	193.99	1193.02
9	Kaluga	1243642	127.85	4.02	4.02	4.02	139.91	28.14	25.73	0.00	1.61	55.48	-80.17	17.46	-3.23	-1.94	84.43	195.39
10	Kazan'	1643593	86.40	0.00	3.65	45.63	135.68	32.25	1.83	1.22	0.00	35.29	-32.95	1.11	-1.48	-27.76	100.39	170.97
11	Khar'kov	2872477	1.74	32.38	2.09	25.07	61.27	0.00	22.28	0.00	0.00	22.28	-0.61	-3.51	-0.73	-8.73	38.99	83.55
12	Kherson	2415112	29.40	121.73	23.60	33.54	208.27	0.00	96.48	5.80	0.00	102.27	-12.17	-10.46	-7.37	-13.89	106.00	310.54
13	Kholm	307481	0.00	6.50	614.67	9.76	630.93	0.00	0.00	97.57	0.00	97.57	0.00	-21.15	-1681.75	-31.73	533.37	728.50
14	Kiev	3320237	6.63	115.35	19.14	13.85	174.08	0.90	194.87	13.25	0.30	209.32	-1.72	23.95	-4.19	-4.08	-35.24	383.41
15	Kishinev	1619997	14.20	0.00	5.09	2.47	35.80	0.00	5.56	12.35	1.23	19.14	-8.76	3.43	-4.19	-0.76	16.67	54.94
16	Kostroma	1570181	266.85	0.00	5.09	4.46	276.40	71.33	5.73	3.82	0.00	80.88	-124.52	3.65	-0.81	-2.84	195.52	357.28
17	Kursk	2415795	6.21	11.18	3.73	1.66	22.77	7.04	160.20	0.83	0.41	168.47	0.34	61.69	-1.20	-0.51	-145.71	191.24
18	Lithuania	453811	46.27	0.00	489.19	55.09	590.55	6.61	26.44	713.95	6.61	753.62	-87.40	58.27	495.28	-106.82	-163.06	1344.17
19	Minsk	1856042	3.23	0	126.61	7.54	137.39	1.62	0.00	100.75	0.00	102.37	-0.87	0.00	-13.93	-4.06	35.02	239.76
20	Mogilev	1651365	16.35	8.48	18.17	10.90	53.89	0.61	27.86	33.91	2.42	64.79	-9.53	11.73	9.53	-5.13	-10.90	118.69
21	Moscow	1826691	116.06	0	35.58	66.79	218.43	77.19	78.28	83.76	3.28	242.52	-21.28	42.86	26.37	-34.76	-24.09	460.94
22	Nizh. Novgorod	1605094	85.35	0.00	0.62	6.85	92.83	419.91	0.00	3.12	1.25	424.27	208.44	0.00	1.55	-3.49	-331.44	517.10
23	Novgorod	1480357	49.31	0	14.86	2.03	66.20	57.42	5.40	6.76	0.00	69.58	5.48	3.65	-5.48	-1.37	-3.38	135.78
24	Olonets	430908	71.94	0	11.60	0.00	83.54	0.00	9.28	4.64	0.00	13.92	-166.95	21.54	-16.16	0.00	69.62	97.47
25	Omsk	1467963	106.95	29.29	17.71	12.26	166.22	27.93	147.82	9.54	0.00	185.29	-53.83	80.75	-5.57	-8.35	-19.07	351.51
26	Orel	1965703	3.56	0.51	4.07	12.72	20.86	0.51	9.67	2.03	0.00	11.70	-1.81	4.66	-1.04	-6.47	9.16	32.56
27	Orenburg	1628577	144.91	48.51	17.81	31.93	243.16	1.23	9.21	0.00	0.00	10.44	-88.23	-24.13	-10.93	-19.61	232.72	253.60
28	Penza	1606946	82.77	3.73	4.98	4.98	96.46	4.98	24.89	0.00	0.00	29.87	-48.41	13.17	-3.10	-3.10	66.59	126.33
29	Perm'	1550636	760.98	2.58	5.80	23.22	792.58	168.32	7.09	2.58	0.00	177.99	-382.20	2.91	-2.08	-14.97	614.59	970.57
30	Petrograd	1021840	131.14	0	313.16	113.52	557.82	15.66	67.53	68.50	1.96	153.64	-113.01	66.08	-239.43	-109.18	404.17	711.46
31	Podol'sk	2966413	1.69	3.03	35.06	1.69	41.46	1.69	61.02	40.12	0.00	101.13	-0.57	19.55	-0.57	-0.57	-59.67	142.60
32	Polotsk [Vitebski]	903394	38.74	0	92.98	22.14	153.86	30.99	13.28	121.76	0.00	166.04	-8.58	14.70	31.86	-24.51	-12.18	319.90
33	Poltava	2648679	0.38	0.00	1.13	12.08	13.59	0.76	83.44	6.80	0.00	90.99	0.14	31.50	2.14	-4.56	-77.40	104.58

Region	Pop	(2)	(3)	(4)	(5)	(6)	(7)	(8)	(9)	(10)	(11)	(12)	(13)	(14)	(15)	(16)	(17)
34 Pskov	1231918	60.07	0	21.11	4.87	86.04	21.11	14.61	6.49	0.00	42.21	-31.63	11.86	-11.86	-3.95	43.83	128.26
35 Riga	270574	140.44	25.87	2594.48	92.40	2853.19	66.53	192.18	3618.23	7.39	3884.33	-273.19	614.67	3783.62	-314.16	-1031.14	6737.53
36 Ryazan'	2059915	9.71	5.83	2.91	1.46	19.90	10.68	41.26	3.88	0.97	56.80	0.47	17.20	0.47	-0.24	-36.89	76.70
37 Samara	2671126	430.53	1.50	15.35	20.96	468.34	3.74	49.79	0.75	0.00	54.28	-159.78	18.08	-5.47	-7.85	414.06	522.63
38 Saratov	2422880	193.98	14.03	17.75	12.79	238.56	40.45	41.69	2.48	0.00	84.61	-63.37	11.41	-6.30	-5.28	153.95	323.17
39 Simbirsk	1683134	66.54	1.19	3.56	3.56	74.86	69.51	19.61	0.00	0.59	89.72	1.77	10.94	-2.12	-1.77	-14.85	164.58
40 Smolensk	1560805	12.81	0	10.25	3.20	26.27	1.92	33.32	8.33	0.00	43.57	-6.98	21.35	-1.23	-2.05	-17.30	69.84
41 Stavropol'	2669108	64.44	0.00	9.37	26.98	100.78	2.62	364.54	12.36	1.12	380.65	-23.16	136.58	1.12	-9.69	-279.87	481.43
42 Tambov	2998181	3.00	6.67	5.00	2.33	17.01	1.33	10.67	1.67	0.33	14.01	-0.56	1.33	-1.11	-0.67	3.00	31.02
43 Tavrida	1185847	7.59	17.71	58.19	62.40	145.89	1.69	238.65	30.36	0.00	270.69	-4.98	186.31	-23.47	-52.62	-124.81	416.58
44 Tobol'sk	1117055	206.79	1.79	8.06	238.13	454.77	50.13	36.70	0.90	0.00	87.73	-140.25	31.25	-6.41	-213.17	367.04	542.50
45 Tomsk	2902308	259.10	35.14	68.57	49.62	412.43	142.30	154.02	0.00	0.00	296.32	-40.25	40.96	-23.62	-17.10	116.11	708.75
46 Trans-Baikal	523987	5.73	0	19.08	250.01	274.82	0.00	1.91	7.63	5.73	15.27	-10.93	3.64	-21.85	-466.20	259.55	290.08
47 Tula	1636811	3.07	0.00	12.88	3.07	19.01	4.29	26.98	9.20	0.00	40.47	0.75	16.54	-2.26	-1.88	-21.46	59.48
48 Turkestan	366981	94.86	94.86	75.88	165.32	430.92	0.00	65.04	2.71	8.13	75.88	-257.08	-80.80	-198.32	-426.01	355.03	506.80
49 Tver'	1904672	7.35	0.00	4.20	1.05	12.60	0.53	3.15	1.05	0.00	4.73	-3.58	1.65	-1.65	-0.55	7.88	17.33
50 Ufa	1103404	94.73	0	15.34	19.85	129.92	16.24	8.12	11.73	1.80	37.89	-70.81	7.33	-3.26	-16.28	92.02	167.81
51 Vladikavkaz	433299	32.31	175.40	41.54	39.23	288.48	0.00	117.70	4.62	0.00	122.32	-74.57	-133.16	-85.22	-90.55	166.17	410.80
52 Vladimir	1589791	57.24	8.81	2.52	2.52	71.08	109.45	4.40	0.63	0.00	114.48	32.84	-2.77	-1.19	-1.58	-43.40	185.56
53 Vladivostok	334754	53.77	0.00	110.53	8011.85	8176.15	11.95	188.20	92.61	2.99	295.74	-124.93	562.20	-53.54	-2392.63	7880.41	8471.89
54 Vologda	1611412	5.59	0	3.72	3.72	13.03	17.38	4.34	1.86	0.00	23.58	7.32	2.70	-1.16	-2.31	-10.55	36.61
55 Volyn'	2175577	0.00	1.84	77.22	5.06	84.12	0.00	64.35	93.31	0.00	157.66	0.00	28.73	7.39	-2.32	-73.54	241.77
56 Voronezh	2934661	2.73	7.84	2.73	7.84	21.13	0.68	37.48	1.70	0.00	39.87	-0.70	10.10	-0.35	-2.67	-18.74	61.00
57 Vyatka	3243911	62.89	1.54	3.70	23.12	91.25	5.55	7.09	0.00	22.81	35.45	-17.68	1.71	-1.14	-0.10	55.80	126.70
58 Warsaw	91289	219.08	2508.52	251.95	251.95	2979.55	0.00	0.00	1347.37	0.00	1347.37	-2399.90	0.00	-12719.47	-2759.88	1632.18	4326.92
59 Yakutsk	264273	22.70	0.00	7.57	94.60	124.87	18.92	0.00	3.78	0.00	22.70	-14.32	0.00	-14.32	-357.96	102.17	147.57
60 Yaroslavl'	1150793	23.46	0.87	7.82	6.08	38.23	17.38	1.74	0.87	0.00	19.99	-5.29	0.76	-6.04	-5.29	18.25	58.22
61 Yekaterinburg	1504919	238.55	5.98	4.65	10.63	259.81	58.47	0.00	0.00	0.00	58.47	-119.66	-3.97	-3.09	-7.06	201.34	318.29
62 Yekaterinoslav	2247817	10.23	64.95	7.12	17.35	99.65	2.22	189.07	7.12	2.67	201.08	-3.56	55.22	0.00	-6.53	-101.43	300.74
63 Yenisey	765176	50.97	9.15	30.06	43.13	133.30	22.22	240.47	9.15	1.31	273.14	-37.58	302.31	-27.33	-54.65	-139.84	406.44
64 Georgia	1011344	0.99	14.83	9.89	7.91	33.62	0.00	35.60	25.71	1.98	63.28	-0.98	20.53	15.64	-5.87	-29.66	96.90
Moscow Synodal Court	16985	0.00	0.00	353.25	58.88	412.13	0.00	0.00	0.00	0.00	0.00	0.00	0.00	-20797.93	-3466.32	412.13	412.13
Army&Navy Abroad	958280	42.78	21.91	169.05	0.00	233.75	0.00	0.00	2.09	0.00	2.09	-44.65	-22.87	-174.23	0.00	231.67	235.84
TOTAL	98534800	79.29	16.10	40.08	62.82	198.29	27.55	62.07	32.97	2.70	125.30					72.99	323.58

Sources: *Vsepoddanneishii Otchet* (1916: 6-7), Institute of Russian History (1995: 18-22), Tsentral'nyi Statisticheskii (1901a). Density of churches is calculated by per capita of Orthodox population.

Note: Old Believers here are not considered as part of Orthodox population.

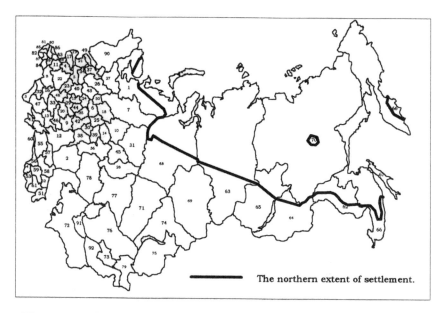

Figure A2.1. Civil division of the Russian Empire (gubernii), 1897. Source: the author's adaptation of Leasure and Lewis (1966).

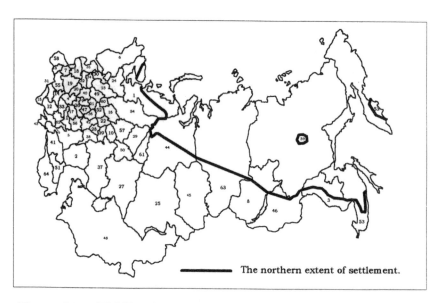

Figure A2.2. ORSCh's diocesan division of the Russian Empire, 1912. Source: the author's adaptation of Leasure and Lewis (1966). Note: see Chapter 2 for details.

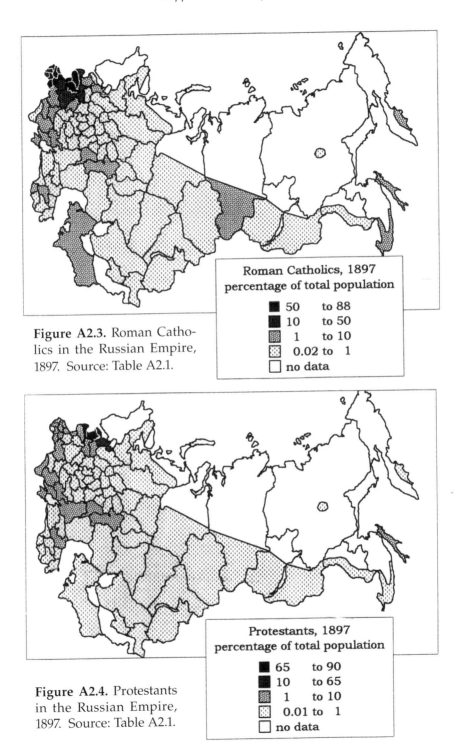

Figure A2.3. Roman Catholics in the Russian Empire, 1897. Source: Table A2.1.

Roman Catholics, 1897
percentage of total population

- 50 to 88
- 10 to 50
- 1 to 10
- 0.02 to 1
- no data

Figure A2.4. Protestants in the Russian Empire, 1897. Source: Table A2.1.

Protestants, 1897
percentage of total population

- 65 to 90
- 10 to 65
- 1 to 10
- 0.01 to 1
- no data

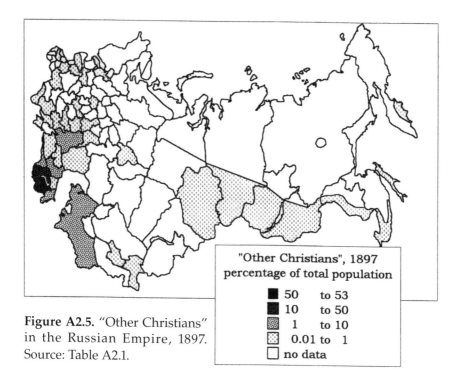

Figure A2.5. "Other Christians" in the Russian Empire, 1897. Source: Table A2.1.

"Other Christians", 1897 percentage of total population

- 50 to 53
- 10 to 50
- 1 to 10
- 0.01 to 1
- no data

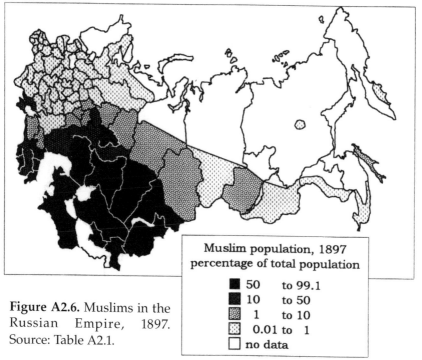

Figure A2.6. Muslims in the Russian Empire, 1897. Source: Table A2.1.

Muslim population, 1897 percentage of total population

- 50 to 99.1
- 10 to 50
- 1 to 10
- 0.01 to 1
- no data

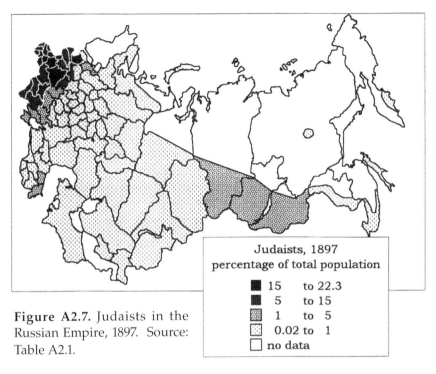

Figure A2.7. Judaists in the Russian Empire, 1897. Source: Table A2.1.

Judaists, 1897
percentage of total population

- 15 to 22.3
- 5 to 15
- 1 to 5
- 0.02 to 1
- no data

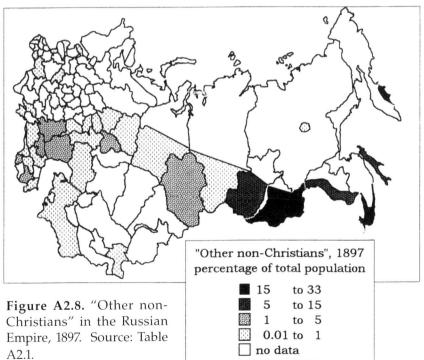

Figure A2.8. "Other non-Christians" in the Russian Empire, 1897. Source: Table A2.1.

"Other non-Christians", 1897
percentage of total population

- 15 to 33
- 5 to 15
- 1 to 5
- 0.01 to 1
- no data

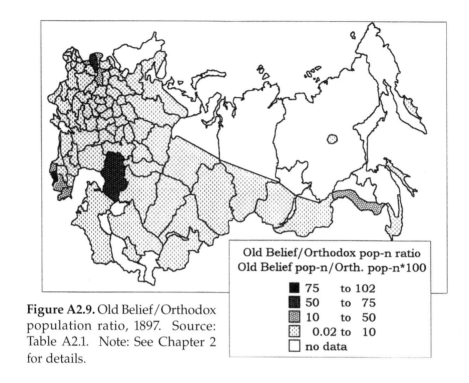

Old Belief/Orthodox pop-n ratio
Old Belief pop-n/Orth. pop-n*100

- ■ 75   to 102
- ■ 50   to 75
- ▨ 10   to 50
- ░ 0.02 to 10
- □ no data

Figure A2.9. Old Belief/Orthodox population ratio, 1897. Source: Table A2.1. Note: See Chapter 2 for details.

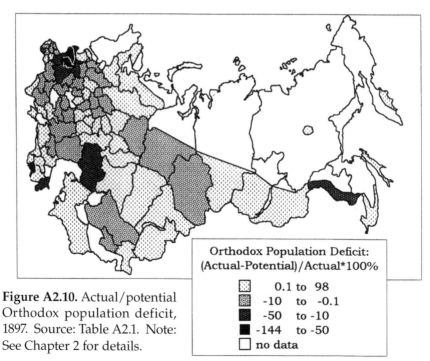

Orthodox Population Deficit:
(Actual-Potential)/Actual*100%

- ░   0.1 to 98
- ▨ -10   to -0.1
- ■ -50   to -10
- ■ -144 to -50
- □ no data

Figure A2.10. Actual/potential Orthodox population deficit, 1897. Source: Table A2.1. Note: See Chapter 2 for details.

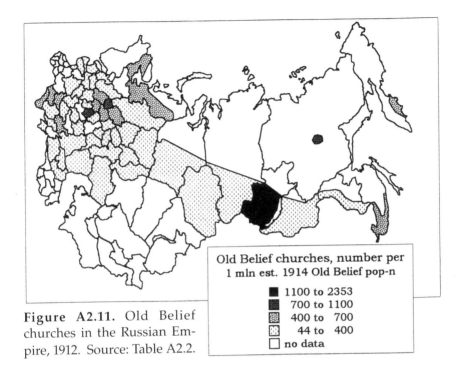

Figure A2.11. Old Belief churches in the Russian Empire, 1912. Source: Table A2.2.

Old Belief churches, number per 1 mln est. 1914 Old Belief pop-n

■ 1100 to 2353
▨ 700 to 1100
▨ 400 to 700
▨ 44 to 400
☐ no data

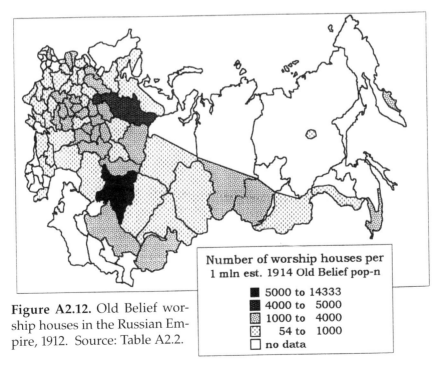

Figure A2.12. Old Belief worship houses in the Russian Empire, 1912. Source: Table A2.2.

Number of worship houses per 1 mln est. 1914 Old Belief pop-n

■ 5000 to 14333
■ 4000 to 5000
▨ 1000 to 4000
▨ 54 to 1000
☐ no data

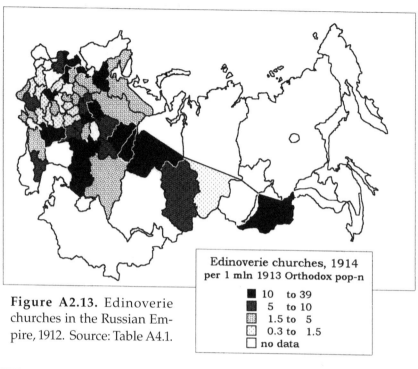

Figure A2.13. Edinoverie churches in the Russian Empire, 1912. Source: Table A4.1.

Edinoverie churches, 1914
per 1 mln 1913 Orthodox pop-n

- 10   to 39
- 5   to 10
- 1.5 to 5
- 0.3 to 1.5
- no data

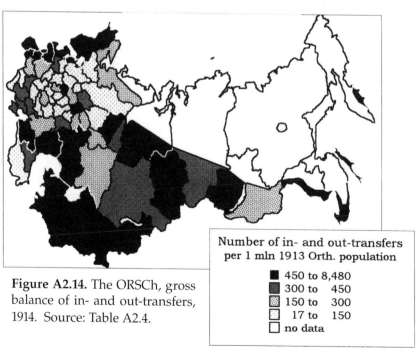

Figure A2.14. The ORSCh, gross balance of in- and out-transfers, 1914. Source: Table A2.4.

Number of in- and out-transfers
per 1 mln 1913 Orth. population

- 450 to 8,480
- 300 to   450
- 150 to   300
- 17 to   150
- no data

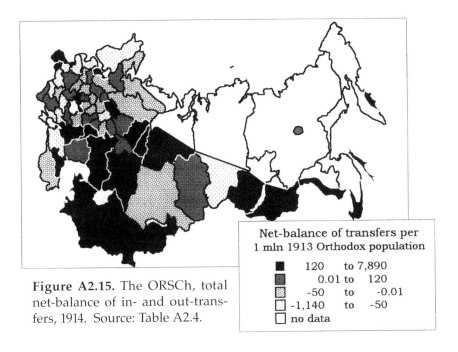

Figure A2.15. The ORSCh, total net-balance of in- and out-transfers, 1914. Source: Table A2.4.

Net-balance of transfers per 1 mln 1913 Orthodox population

- ■ 120 to 7,890
- ▨ 0.01 to 120
- ▨ -50 to -0.01
- □ -1,140 to -50
- □ no data

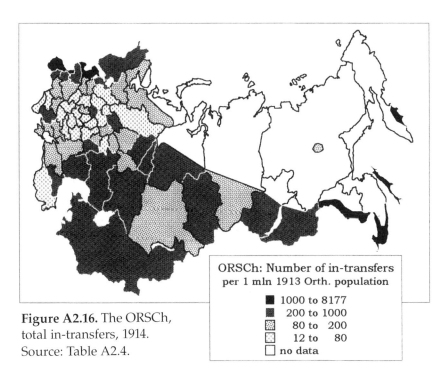

Figure A2.16. The ORSCh, total in-transfers, 1914. Source: Table A2.4.

ORSCh: Number of in-transfers per 1 mln 1913 Orth. population

- ■ 1000 to 8177
- ■ 200 to 1000
- ▨ 80 to 200
- ▨ 12 to 80
- □ no data

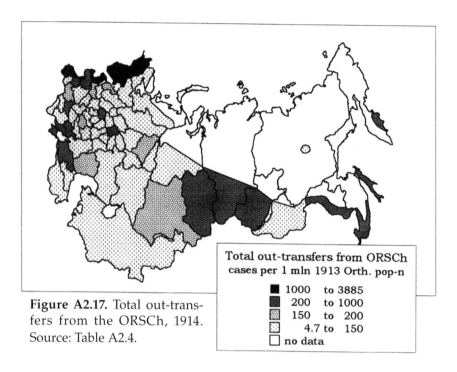

Figure A2.17. Total out-transfers from the ORSCh, 1914. Source: Table A2.4.

Total out-transfers from ORSCh cases per 1 mln 1913 Orth. pop-n

- 1000 to 3885
- 200 to 1000
- 150 to 200
- 4.7 to 150
- no data

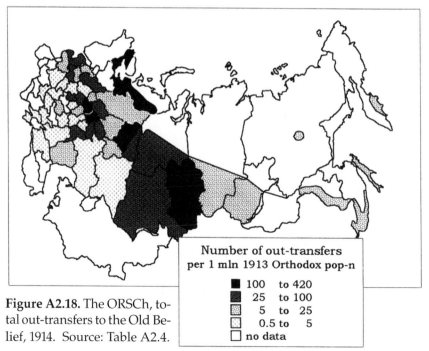

Figure A2.18. The ORSCh, total out-transfers to the Old Belief, 1914. Source: Table A2.4.

Number of out-transfers per 1 mln 1913 Orthodox pop-n

- 100 to 420
- 25 to 100
- 5 to 25
- 0.5 to 5
- no data

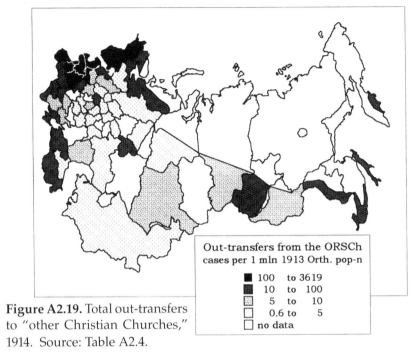

Figure A2.19. Total out-transfers to "other Christian Churches," 1914. Source: Table A2.4.

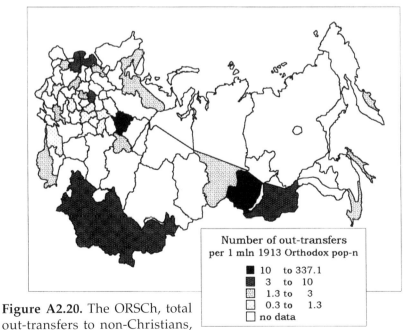

Figure A2.20. The ORSCh, total out-transfers to non-Christians, 1914. Source: Table A2.4.

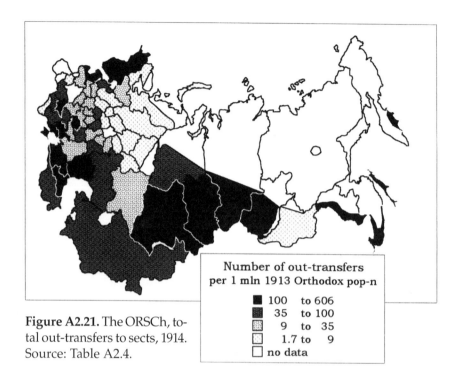

Figure A2.21. The ORSCh, total out-transfers to sects, 1914. Source: Table A2.4.

Number of out-transfers
per 1 mln 1913 Orthodox pop-n

■ 100 to 606
■ 35 to 100
▨ 9 to 35
▢ 1.7 to 9
□ no data

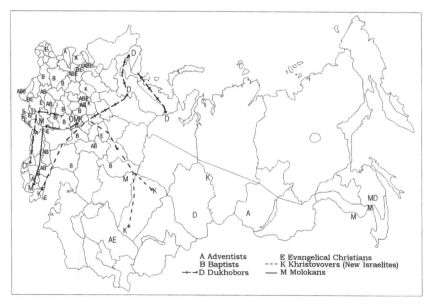

A Adventists   E Evangelical Christians
B Baptists   K Khristovovers (New Israelites)
D Dukhobors   M Molokans

Figure A2.22. Location and movement of sects in the late Russian Empire. Source: based on Klibanov (1982: 36, 67, 226).

Note on the Renovationist Statistics

Table A3.1. Status of Renovationist parishes, April 1924.
Sources: RTsKhIDNI f. 17, op. 87, d. 186, ll. 150-176; op. 60, d. 509, ll. 100-126; Roslof (1994: 211-12). Note: These data are based on the incomplete data compiled by Tuchkov in April 1924. Data for Astrakhan' and Kazan' provinces, marked by (*), refer to the province's center only. In some provinces data were not available, and the percentage of Renovationist parishes is only a conversion of Tuchkov's estimation: estimated "insignificant" Renovationist presence is treated here as 24.9 percent; "close to half" - as 49.9 percent; "above half" - as 50.1 percent, "significant" prevalence - as 75.1 percent. Neutral parishes in Ukrainian provinces were mostly of the Ukrainian autocephalous (independent) Church.

Table A3.2. Status of Renovationist parishes in 1925 and 1927 by diocese.
Sources: *Vestnik Sv. Sinoda* (1925), no. 1: 15-16; (1926) no. 7 (3): 2; (1927) no. 2 (15); (1928) no. 2 (25): 8; *Vsesoiuznaia Perepis'* (1928); Lemeshevskii (1979); the author's calculations and dioceses' adjustments.
Note: This set of dioceses is based on the latest report of the Renovationists [*Vestnik Sv. Sinoda* (1928), no. 2 (25): 8], because it contains the most complete listing of dioceses (101). Vol'sk diocese (in Saratov oblast'; 200 parishes on October 1, 1925), several other dioceses without data and some undeveloped areas have been excluded from this list. The order of metropolitanates has been changed and corresponds here to their proximity to the historical center of the country. Dioceses are ordered alphabetically with exception of some incorporated dioceses (for example, in 1925 Usol'e Upper Kama, Komi-Perm', Kungur and Sarapul dioceses were part of Perm' diocese and, therefore, are listed together). Average for the diocese's regional metropolitanate has been assigned if no specific figure is available. "Potentially Orthodox population" here includes Russians, Ukrainians, Belarusians and Moldovans.

Table A3.3. Status of Renovationist places of worship, early 1930s.
Source: GARF f. 5263, op. 1, d. 32, ll. 66-73; the author's calculations.
Note: A version of this table is published in Odintsov (1993: 64). Original data were compiled by the staff of the VTsIK Presidium's Permanent Commission for Cult Issues. These data were based on statistics from the provinces (the figures for Chechen AO and Ingush AO were only an estimation of the Commission) and, therefore, subject to permanent revisions. For instance, an earlier version of this table, March 1, 1932 (GARF f. 5263, op. 1, d. 90) gives significantly lower figures. "Places of worship" here mean church buildings and houses of worship. Their numbers roughly correspond to the number of parishes. The "1918-31" range is not accurate: strictly speaking, no Renovationist places of worship existed and could be closed prior to 1922.

Table A3.1. Status of Renovationist parishes, April 1924.

Nos.	Province (guberniia)	All Orthodox	of them, Neutral	Tikhonite	Renovationist	% of All
1	Altay	429	55	196	178	41.5
2	Arkhangel'sk					24.9
3	Astrakhan'*	23		8	15	65.2
4	Bashkir					50
5	Bryansk					24.9
6	Cherepovets					50
7	Chernigov	828	128	300	400	48.3
8	Chernomor	488		57	431	88.3
9	Chuvash	238		18	220	92.4
10	Crimea					50.1
11	Donetsk	450		260	190	42.2
12	Gomel'	800				50.1
13	Irkutsk	254		112	142	55.9
14	Ivanovo-Voznesensk	441		342	99	22.4
15	Kaluga					24.9
16	Kazan'*				102	50.0
17	Khar'kov	650	4	246	400	61.5
18	Kiev	1200	500	600	100	8.3
19	Komi (Zyryan)					49.9
20	Kostroma					5
21	Kuban'	488		57	431	88.3
22	Kursk					24.9
23	Leningrad	423		260	163	38.5
24	Minsk					24.9
25	Nikolaev					49.9
26	Nizhniy Novgorod	1322		1245	77	5.8
27	North Dvina					50.1
28	Novgorod				30	49.9
29	Novonikolaevsk	220		40	180	81.8
30	Odessa	1120	20	400	700	62.5
31	Omsk	399	25	82	292	73.2
32	Orel	598		173	425	71.1
33	Penza					50.0
34	Podol'sk	1098	298	550	250	22.8
35	Poltava	881	81	750	50	5.7
36	Pskov	393			57	14.5
37	Ryazan'					24.9
38	Smolensk					49.9
39	Stavropol'	225				24.9
40	Tambov	840		520	320	38.1
41	Tersk					24.9
42	Tomsk					75.1
43	Tsaritsyn	118			92	78.0
44	Tula	787	6	49	732	93.0
45	Tver'					24.9
46	Ural (Ishim)	102			82	80.4
47	Ural (Troitsk)	118		26	92	78.0
48	Vitebsk	426	239	44	143	33.6
49	Vladimir	606	206	207	193	31.8
50	Vologda	679	275	335	69	10.2
51	Volynia	798	18	700	80	10.0
52	Voronezh					49.9
53	Vyatka	555		251	304	54.8
54	Yaroslavl'					24.9
55	Yekaterinoslav	562	12	370	180	32.0
56	Yenisey	310	36	20	254	81.9
	TOTAL	18869	1903	8218	7473	39.6

Note: For explanations, see Note on the Renovationist Statistics.

Table A3.2. Status of Renovationist parishes in 1925 and 1927 by diocese.

Map nos.	Diocese	Potent. Orth. pop-n, 1926	Number of parishes			per 1 mln pot. Orth. pop-n			Change		% in ORSCh, 01.31.1927
			1.1.1925	10.1.1925	10.1.1927	1.1.1925	10.1.1925	10.1.1927	1.1.1925-27 1.1.1927	1.1.1925-10.1.10.1.25	
1	Astrakhan'	423,770	44	25		103.8	59.0			-44.8	16.6
2	Bryansk	1,959,157	103	103	112	52.6	52.6	57.2	4.6	0.0	16.6
3	Chuvash (incl. Mari&Krasnokokshaysk 1.1.25)	178,890	159	76	43	408.8	424.8	240.4	-168.5	16.0	16.6
4	Krasnokokshaysk	210,016		27	26	408.8	128.6	123.8	-285.0	-280.3	16.6
5	Ivanovo-Voznesensk	1,189,601	86	233	54	72.3	195.9	45.4	-26.9	123.6	6.6
6	Kaluga	1,144,907	83	83	65	72.5	72.5	56.8	-15.7	0.0	8.9
7	Kazan'	1,121,977	320	353	126	285.2	314.6	112.3	-172.9	29.4	16.6
8	Kostroma	807,615	15	19	15	18.6	23.5	18.6	0.0	5.0	3.2
9	Kursk	2,893,253	323	120	55	111.6	41.5	19.0	-92.6	-70.2	4.3
10	Kustanay (incl. Aktyubinsk)	383,848		38	55		99.0	143.3			59
11	Moscow	4,304,954	95	107		22.1	24.9			2.8	8.5
12	Nizhniy Novgorod	2,557,083	61	33	21	23.9	12.9	8.2	-15.6	-10.9	1.5
13	Orel	1,875,799	388	230	119	206.8	122.6	63.4	-143.4	-84.2	16.6
14	Orenburg	631,019	74	88	85	117.3	139.5	134.7	17.4	22.2	16.6
15	Penza	1,708,395	78	73	51	45.7	42.7	29.9	-15.8	-2.9	5.1
16	Petropavlovsk (Akmolinsk 1.1.25)	714,978	81	43	59	113.3	60.1	82.5	-30.8	-53.1	72
17	Ryazan'	2,415,054	49	15		20.3	6.2			-14.1	1.6
18	Samara	1,898,251	190	100		100.1	52.7			-47.4	7.6
19	Saratov	2,732,551	224	224		82.0	82.0			0.0	10.7
20	Semipalatinsk	548,636	142	103	81	258.8	187.7	147.6	-111.2	-71.1	62.3
21	Smolensk	2,236,751	386	352	245	172.6	157.4	109.5	-63.0	-15.2	40.2
22	Stalingrad	1,363,807	299	307	261	219.2	225.1	191.4	-27.9	5.9	69
23	Tambov	2,718,370	200	156	91	73.6	57.4	33.5	-40.1	-16.2	16.6
24	Tula	1,497,481	709	627	455	473.5	418.7	303.8	-169.6	-54.8	63.9
25	Tver'	2,087,792	16	6	22	7.7	2.9	10.5	2.9	-4.8	1.5
26	Ufa (incl. Zlatoust 1.1.25)	1,170,020	124	159	67	88.6	113.6	57.3	-31.4	25.0	16.6
27	Zlatoust	229,093			3	88.6	113.6	13.1	-75.5	25.0	16.6
28	Ul'yanovsk	1,114,411	309	170	37	277.3	152.5	33.2	-244.1	-124.7	8.6
29	Ural'sk	154,090	35	58		227.1	376.4			149.3	16.6
30	Vyatka	2,088,249	137	166	72	65.6	79.5	34.5	-31.1	13.9	16.6
31	Vladimir	1,315,912	390	224		296.4	170.2			-126.1	7.6
32	Voronezh	3,292,158	746	616	353	226.6	187.1	107.2	-119.4	-39.5	16.6
33	Yaroslavl'	1,332,271	7	9	26	5.3	6.8	19.5	14.3	1.5	2.6

Table A3.2 (part 2).

Map nos.	Diocese	Potent. Orth. pop-n, 1926	Number of parishes			per 1 mln pot. Orth. pop-n			Change		% in ORSCh, 01.31.1927
			1.1.1925	10.1.1925	10.1.1927	1.1.1925	10.1.1925	10.1.1927	1.1.1925-27 1.1.1.-10.1.27	1.1.1925-10.1.25	
	North-Western Metropolitanate										**18.2**
34	Arkhangel'sk	434,862	85	110	32	195.5	253.0	73.6	-121.9	57.5	18.2
35	Cherepovets	719,231	106	106	70	147.4	147.4	97.3	-50.1	0.0	18.2
36	Karelia	155,230	110	110	111	708.6	708.6	715.1	6.4	0.0	34.7
37	Leningrad	2,347,519	74	56	53	31.5	23.9	22.6	-8.9	-7.7	18.2
38	Novgorod	1,021,935	20	35	13	19.6	34.2	12.7	-6.8	14.7	2.4
39	Pskov	1,730,016	15	15	23	8.7	8.7	13.3	4.6	0.0	6.1
40	Velikiy Ustyug (Sysola-Vym')	687,321	139	139	50	202.2	202.2	72.7	-129.5	0.0	18.2
41	Vologda	1,049,591	167	141	128	159.1	134.3	122.0	-37.2	-24.8	18.2
42	**Crimean Metropolitanate**	382,645	55	55	13	143.7	143.7	34.0	-109.8	0.0	**30.1**
	Caucasian Metropolitanate										**57.9**
43	Baku	243,490	16	16	28	65.7	65.7	115.0	49.3	0.0	65.3
44	Don	1,355,134	312	312	83	172.3	172.3	45.8	-126.5	0.0	57.9
45	Kuban'-Chernomor	2,866,705	482	482	446	168.1	168.1	155.6	-12.6	0.0	81.3
46	Rostov	1,029,197	56	55	58	54.4	53.4	56.4	1.9	-1.0	57.9
47	Stavropol'	700,306	55	55	26	78.5	78.5	37.1	-41.4	0.0	13.6
48	Taganrog	252,702	36	36	15	142.5	142.5	59.4	-83.1	0.0	57.9
49	Tersk	573,480									15.1
50	Vladikavkaz	327,634	85	79	78	259.4	241.1	238.1	-21.4	-18.3	85
	Ural Metropolitanate										**34.2**
51	Irbit (Irbit-Turinsk)	274,039	115	115	66	419.6	419.6	240.8	-178.8	0.0	71.8
52	Chelyabinsk (incl. 53 and 54 in 1925)	437,392	212	212	42	153.5	153.5	96.0	68.9	0.0	34.2
53	Shadrinsk	670,453			16	153.5	153.5	23.9	68.9		34.2
54	Troitskoe	273,234			28	153.5	153.5	102.5	68.9		34.2
55	Ishim	430,640	77	77	48	178.8	178.8	111.5	-67.3	0.0	34.2
56	Kurgan	487,501	115	115	75	235.9	235.9	153.8	-82.1	0.0	34.2
57	Perm' (incl. 58, 59, 60, 61 in 1925)	687,138	200	200	58	67.4	67.4	84.4	-37.4	0.0	34.2
58	Usol'e Upper Kama	193,750			37	67.4	67.4	191.0	-37.4		34.2
59	Komi-Perm'	34,814			1	67.4	67.4	28.7	-37.4		34.2
60	Kungur	422,224			12	67.4	67.4	28.4	-37.4		34.2
61	Sarapul	815,583			18	67.4	67.4	22.1	-37.4		7.4
62	Tyumen'	465,502	17		12	36.5		25.8	-10.7	-36.5	34.2
63	Tobol'sk	130,199	10	10	6	76.8	76.8	46.1	-30.7	0.0	7.1

Table A3.2 (part 3).

Map nos.	Diocese	Potent. Orth. pop-n, 1926	Number of parishes			per 1 mln pot. Orth. pop-n			Change		% in ORSCh, 01.31.1927
			1.1.1925	10.1.1925	10.1.1927	1.1.1925	10.1.1925	10.1.1927	1.1.1925-27	1.1.-10.1.25	
64	Yekaterinburg (incl. Tag:l in 1925)	596,804	163	110	28	160.0	108.0	46.9	-113.1	-52.0	34.2
65	Tagil	421,762			47	160.0	108.0	111.4	-48.6	-52.0	34.2
	Siberian Metropolitanate										**35.1**
66	Altay	1,069,123	127	127		118.8	118.8		-118.8	0.0	35.1
67	Biysk-Oyrat	762,960	77	45	32	100.9	59.0	41.9	-59.0	-41.9	19.6
68	Irkutsk	640,323	101	103	63	157.7	160.9	98.4	-59.3	3.1	35.1
69	Kamensk	434,471	56	25	48	128.9	57.5	110.5	-18.4	-71.4	35.1
70	Krasnoyarsk (incl. Minusinsk&Kansk in 1925)	384,830	263	263	42	183.7	183.7	109.1	-74.5	0.0	35.1
71	Minusinsk	688,743			24	183.7	183.7	34.8	-148.8		75.5
72	Kansk	358,244			64	183.7	183.7	178.6	-5.0		35.1
73	Novonikolaevsk (incl. Kargat-Kainsk in 1927)	756,967	91	66	115	120.2	87.2	71.6	-48.7	-33.0	35.1
74	Kargat-Kainsk	850,172	68	67		80.0	78.8	71.6	-8.4	-1.2	35.1
75	Omsk	969,760	111	122	56	114.5	125.8	57.7	-56.7	11.3	35.1
76	Tomsk	991,567	227	176	66	228.9	177.5	66.6	-162.4	-51.4	46.8
	Far Eastern Metropolitanate	**1,761,328**	**400**			**227.1**					**58.8**
77	Amur (incl.Zeya in 1925)	373,262		86		227.1	206.0				58.8
78	Zeya	44,185				227.1					58.8
79	Khabarovsk	156,936		15		227.1	95.6				58.8
80	Trans-Baikal (Chita) (incl. Sretensk in 1925)	361,355		133	86	227.1	239.5	238.0			58.8
81	Sretensk	193,948				227.1					58.8
82	V.-Udinsk	260,778				227.1					58.8
83	Vladivostok	370,864		58	32	227.1	156.4	86.3			58.8
	Central Asian Metropolitanate										
84	Dzhetysuy	414,879	119	119	110	286.8	286.8	265.1	-21.7	0.0	86.6
85	Turkestan (Tashkent) (incl. Ashkhabad in 1925)	409,242	111	107	91	226.5	218.4	222.4	-4.2	-8.2	83.5
86	Ashkhabad	80,743				226.5	218.4			-8.2	83.5
87	Belarus (Veizh diocese only in 1927)	4,435,788	500	500	100	112.7	112.7	22.5	-90.2	0.0	
88	Ukraine (incl. Moldova)	26,003,808	3000	3000		115.4	115.4			0.0	50.1
89	Tiflis (1927 data refers to Sukhumi diocese)	125,532	40			318.6					50.1
90	Yerivan'	22,374									
	Total	113679046	13886	12304	5131	122.2	108.2	45.1	-77.0	-13.9	21.7

Note: For explanation, see Note on the Renovationist Statistics.

Table A3.3. Status of Orthodox places of worship, early 1930s.

Map nos.	Unit of the Russian Federation	Closed in 1918-31			Functioning Dec.1, 1933		
		Total	of them, Renovationist number	%	Total	of them, Renovationist number	%
1	Western Oblast'	527	51	9.7	1887	273	14.5
2	Ivanovo Industrial Obl.	530	28	5.3	2334	144	6.2
3	Leningrad Oblast'	686	55	8.0	2021	123	6.1
4	Moscow Oblast'	1331	107	8.0	3758	383	10.2
5	Ural Oblast'	996	247	24.8	1092	338	31.0
6	Central Black Soil Obl.	578	56	9.7	3121	385	12.3
7	East Siberian Kray	294	75	25.5	570	210	36.8
8	Northern Kray	346	51	14.7	971	97	10.0
9	North Caucasian Kray	187	51	27.3	1370	631	46.1
10	Middle Volga Kray	571	38	6.7	1858	64	3.4
11	Nizhniy Novgorod Kray	361	30	8.3	1477	130	8.8
12	Far Eastern Kray	584	192	32.9	289	39	13.5
13	Western Siberian Kray	288	45	15.6	1501	362	24.1
14	Low Volga Kray	459	58	12.6	1051	182	17.3
15	Adygey AO	3	3	100.0	14	12	85.7
16	Ingush AO				48		
17	Kalmyk AO	29	4	13.8	69	12	17.4
18	Karachaev AO				3		
19	Kara-Kalpak AO	102	25	24.5	27	9	33.3
20	Khakass AO				25	10	40.0
21	Oyrat AO	110			30		
22	Komi AO	52	13	25.0	195	49	25.1
23	Mari AO	12	7	58.3	85	41	48.2
24	Mordovian AO	168	15	8.9	679	81	11.9
25	Cherkess AO						
26	Chechen AO	22	6	27.3	173	79	45.7
27	Udmurt (Votyak) AO	31	7	22.6	152	12	7.9
28	Bashkir ASSR	184	22	12.0	290	33	11.4
29	Buryat-Mongol ASSR	61	6	9.8	82	16	19.5
30	Dagestan ASSR	24			20	15	75.0
31	Kabardino-Balkar ASSR	7			18	14	77.8
32	Kazakh ASSR	754	185	24.5	299	103	34.4
33	Karelian ASSR	179	35	19.6	338	143	42.3
34	Kyrgyz ASSR	84	21	25.0	126	43	34.1
35	Crimean ASSR	165	30	18.2	85	30	35.3
36	German Volga ASSR	25			92	3	3.3
37	Tatar ASSR	139	11	7.9	343	50	14.6
38	Chuvash ASSR	56	3	5.4	176	10	5.7
39	Yakutsk ASSR	111	11	9.9	164	31	18.9
	Total	10056	1488	14.8	26833	4157	15.5

Note: For explanation, see Note on the Renovationist statistics.

Table A3.4. Gross income of the Orthodox Russian-State Church by diocese, 1913 (in rubles).

Map nos.	Dioceses and provinces	Balance from 1912	Income in 1913	Sum	Expenditure in 1913	Net income	Number of churches	Per one church				
								balance 1912	income 1913	sum	expenditure	net income
1	Arkhangel'sk	667,035.95	243,854.67	910,890.61	198,480.13	45,374.54	325	2052.42	750.32	2802.74	610.71	139.61
2	Astrakhan'	490,505.65	339,927.66	830,433.31	312,556.26	27,371.40	224	2189.76	1517.53	3707.29	1395.34	122.19
3	Blagoveschensk	210,033.46	155,678.12	365,711.58	160,938.04	-5,259.92	150	1400.22	1037.85	2438.08	1072.92	-35.07
4	Chernigov	1,275,797.85	636,391.58	1,912,189.43			1,144	1115.21	556.29	1671.49		
5	Don	635,623.31	839,092.69	1,474,715.99	819,495.18	19,597.51	702	905.45	1195.29	2100.74	1167.37	27.92
6	Finland	108,033.45	30,293.07	138,326.52			47	2298.58	644.53	2943.12		
7	Grodno	304,052.15	191,291.52	495,343.66	188,292.00	2,999.52	365	833.02	524.09	1357.11	515.87	8.22
8	Irkutsk	935,296.32	225,463.80	1,160,760.11	235,399.16	-9,935.36	264	3542.79	854.03	4396.82	891.66	-37.63
9	Kaluga	1,324,452.38	865,497.94	2,189,950.32	795,640.44	69,857.50	661	2003.71	1309.38	3313.09	1203.69	105.68
10	Kazan'	696,435.15	344,225.46	1,040,660.61	313,063.57	31,161.89	676	1030.23	509.21	1539.44	463.11	46.10
11	Khar'kov	1,588,997.78	1,246,688.09	2,835,685.87			854	1860.65	1459.82	3320.48		
12	Kherson	1,290,423.58	846,705.60	2,137,129.18			670	1926.01	1263.74	3189.75		
13	Kholm	197,552.78	102,812.29	300,365.07			294	671.95	349.70	1021.65		
14	Kiev	2,132,697.43	1,339,087.38	3,471,784.81	1,367,151.78	-28,064.41	1,487	1434.23	900.53	2334.76	919.40	-18.87
15	Kishinev	961,828.67	784,412.66	1,746,241.33	741,015.22	43,397.44	1,119	859.54	700.99	1560.54	662.21	38.78
16	Kostroma	1,825,031.84	630,605.48	2,455,637.32	516,229.30	114,376.18	934	1954.00	675.17	2629.16	552.71	122.46
17	Kursk	1,576,475.18	870,042.83	2,446,518.01	856,671.72	13,371.11	1,050	1501.40	828.61	2330.02	815.88	12.73
18	Lithuania	202,071.32	123,435.56	325,506.88	118,007.85	5,427.71	215	939.87	574.12	1513.99	548.87	25.25
19	Minsk	430,727.59	283,660.68	714,388.27	276,716.66	6,944.02	561	767.79	505.63	1273.42	493.26	12.38
20	Mogilev	375,067.17	219,916.65	594,983.82	205,678.90	14,237.75	558	672.16	394.12	1066.28	368.60	25.52
21	Moscow	7,228,776.75	3,692,910.92	10,921,687.67	3,520,000.58	172,910.34	1,532	4718.52	2410.52	7129.04	2297.65	112.87
22	N. Novgorod	866,653.72	799,260.31	1,665,914.03	763,365.22	35,895.09	958	904.65	834.30	1738.95	796.83	37.47
23	Novgorod	1,067,647.61	499,401.83	1,567,049.43	496,419.80	2,982.03	765	1395.62	652.81	2048.43	648.91	3.90
24	Olonets	696,586.55	225,342.63	921,929.18	229,014.37	-3,671.74	363	1918.97	620.78	2539.75	630.89	-10.11
25	Omsk	438,256.99	313,354.09	751,611.08	293,704.76	19,649.33	475	922.65	659.69	1582.34	618.33	41.37
26	Orel	1,917,153.31	984,698.66	2,901,851.97			1,078	1778.44	913.45	2691.88		
27	Orenburg	537,177.24	514,557.19	1,051,734.43	494,132.97	20,424.22	677	793.47	760.05	1553.52	729.89	30.17
28	Penza	784,572.47	625,984.44	1,410,556.91			783	1002.01	799.47	1801.48		
29	Perm'	650,066.75	473,077.30	1,123,144.05			614	1058.74	770.48	1829.22		
30	Petrograd	2,258,824.23	2,580,657.20	4,839,481.42			350	6453.78	7373.31	13827.09		
31	Podol'sk	1,240,610.35	595,801.72	1,836,412.07			1,544	803.50	385.88	1189.39		
32	Polotsk [Vitebsk]	218,552.42	152,986.66	371,539.08			323	676.63	473.64	1150.28		
33	Poltava	1,817,519.16	1,212,375.52	3,029,894.68			1,177	1544.20	1030.06	2574.25		

34 Pskov	847,486.99	347,870.93	1,195,357.92			409	2072.10	850.54	2922.64		
35 Riga	293,656.94	169,003.08	462,660.02			212	1385.17	797.18	2182.36		
36 Ryazan'	1,571,604.59	906,980.39	2,478,584.97			967	1625.24	937.93	2563.17		
37 Samara	684,287.29	541,663.35	1,225,950.63			908	753.62	596.55	1350.17		
38 Saratov	1,000,005.14	616,289.93	1,616,295.07			829	1206.28	743.41	1949.69		
39 Simbirsk	560,695.24	396,130.86	956,826.10			745	752.61	531.72	1284.33		
40 Smolensk	1,962,696.21	858,229.50	2,820,925.71			658	2982.82	1304.30	4287.12		
41 Stavropol'	784,971.92	1,013,355.11	1,798,327.03			621	1264.04	1631.81	2895.86		
42 Tambov	1,052,307.24	1,469,573.61	2,521,880.85			1,170	899.41	1256.05	2155.45		
43 Tavrida	516,706.81	562,034.07	1,078,740.88			384	1345.59	1463.63	2809.22		
44 Tobol'sk	943,015.48	237,503.00	1,180,518.48			436	2162.88	544.73	2707.61		
45 Tomsk	580,867.50	483,586.94	1,064,454.44			977	594.54	494.97	1089.51		
46 Trans-Baikal	796,344.84	214,103.33	1,010,448.16	208,307.79	5,795.54	210	3792.12	1019.54	4811.66	991.94	27.60
47 Tula	1,797,514.50	792,310.33	2,589,824.83			885	2031.09	895.27	2926.36		
48 Turkestan	165,124.69	198,005.40	363,130.09			198	833.96	1000.03	1833.99		
49 Tver'	2,074,590.76	1,118,839.13	3,193,429.89			1,002	2070.45	1116.61	3187.06		
50 Ufa	243,997.70	195,811.45	439,809.15			460	530.43	425.68	956.11		
51 Vladikavkaz	61,458.12	151,350.10	212,808.22	152,025.02	-674.92	166	370.23	911.75	1281.98	915.81	-4.07
52 Vladimir	2,717,416.11	1,181,214.11	3,898,630.22	1,165,971.41	15,242.70	1,310	2074.36	901.69	2976.05	890.05	11.64
53 Vladivostok	269,256.14	186,268.77	455,524.91	189,237.06	-2,968.29	195	1380.80	955.22	2336.03	970.45	-15.22
54 Vologda	1,627,764.83	664,664.19	2,292,429.02	584,251.91	80,412.28	793	2052.67	838.16	2890.83	736.76	101.40
55 Volyn'	1,497,288.45	855,088.60	2,352,377.05	540,802.73	314,285.87	1,321	1133.45	647.30	1780.75	409.39	237.92
56 Voronezh	1,234,738.70	1,033,258.73	2,267,997.43	992,710.69	40,548.04	1,021	1209.34	1012.01	2221.35	972.29	39.71
57 Vyatka	840,055.86	729,266.20	1,569,322.06	711,919.66	17,346.54	777	1081.15	938.57	2019.72	916.24	22.33
58 Warsaw	117,153.96	102,586.94	219,740.89	105,929.33	-3,342.40	74	1583.16	1386.31	2969.47	1431.48	-45.17
59 Yakutsk	435,262.30	67,589.96	502,852.26			112	3886.27	603.48	4489.75		
60 Yaroslavl'	2,874,864.40	708,485.24	3,583,349.64			933	3081.31	759.36	3840.67		
61 Yekaterinburg	737,671.63	431,966.60	1,169,638.22	443,012.26	-11,045.67	480	1536.82	899.93	2436.15	922.94	-23.01
62 Yekaterinoslav	1,191,629.64	1,204,355.94	2,395,985.57	1,166,590.41	37,765.53	649	1836.10	1855.71	3691.81	1797.52	58.19
63 Yenisey	532,081.91	268,312.67	800,394.58	305,661.38	-37,348.71	304	1750.27	882.61	2632.88	1005.47	-122.86
64 Georgia	no data	no data									
Army&Navy	1,114,693.07	774,534.62	1,889,227.69			667	1671.20	1161.22	2832.43		
TOTAL	68,077,745.48	41,469,725.20	109,547,470.68			42,713	1593.84	970.89	2564.73		
sum	68,077,745.46	41,469,725.20	109,547,470.66			42,812.00	1590.16	968.65	2558.80		
difference	-0.02	0.00	-0.02			99.00					

Source: *Vsepoddanneishii Otchet* (1916: 42-5), the author's calculations. Note: The diocese of Finland, in addition to data in rubles and kopeks, had the following data in marks and pfennings: 1912 balance 110,987 m 79 p; 1913 income 102,323 m 82 p. "Total" figures are provided by the source; "sum" is the author's calculation.

Table A3.5. Categories of income of the Orthodox Russian-State Church by diocese, 1913.

Map nos.	Dioceses and provinces	Number of churches	Total income in 1913 rubles	Income per church rubles	Salver dues in churches rubles	Candle profit rubles	Quit-rent (obrok) items rubles	Donations to local churches rubles	Interest on capital of churches rubles	Misc. income rubles	Salver dues in churches	Candle profit	Quit-rent obrok items	Donations to local churches	Interest on capital	Misc income in 1913
											percentage of Total Income in 1913					
1	Arkhangel'sk	325	243,854.67	750.32	13,241.52	81,377.27	38,813.49	75,691.74	22,517.99	12,212.67	5.4	33.4	15.9	31.0	9.2	5.0
2	Astrakhan'	224	339,927.66	1517.53	16,991.63	216,952.62	46,813.98	33,513.40	13,135.91	12,520.12	5.0	63.8	13.8	9.9	3.9	3.7
3	Blagoveschensk	150	155,678.12	1037.85	12,462.25	84,123.54	12,062.22	17,132.69	7,192.20	22,705.22	8.0	54.0	7.7	11.0	4.6	14.6
4	Chernigov	1,144	636,391.58	556.29	61,097.26	239,241.67	101,435.99	136,635.56	38,694.97	59,286.13	9.6	37.6	15.9	21.5	6.1	9.3
5	Don	702	839,092.69	1195.29	54,828.32	566,331.65	19,231.83	89,903.77	18,629.03	90,168.09	6.5	67.5	2.3	10.7	2.2	10.7
6	Finland	47	30,293.07	644.53	5,390.89	13,857.80	1,596.48	2,902.82	3,836.70	2,708.38	17.8	45.7	5.3	9.6	12.7	8.9
7	Grodno	365	191,291.52	524.09	30,157.29	89,234.84	4,020.90	24,292.79	8,254.20	35,331.50	15.8	46.6	2.1	12.7	4.3	18.5
8	Irkutsk	264	225,463.80	854.03	9,857.38	119,589.31	7,081.72	21,037.67	31,059.56	36,838.16	4.4	53.0	3.1	9.3	13.8	16.3
9	Kaluga	661	865,497.94	1309.38	256,579.66	272,799.04	21,138.91	92,331.94	42,474.00	180,174.39	29.6	31.5	2.4	10.7	4.9	20.8
10	Kazan'	676	344,225.46	509.21	42,993.50	94,292.78	19,362.20	129,352.94	19,188.07	39,035.97	12.5	27.4	5.6	37.6	5.6	11.3
11	Khar'kov	854	1,246,688.09	1459.82	138,425.30	550,202.26	95,789.68	263,602.43	47,994.66	150,673.77	11.1	44.1	7.7	21.1	3.8	12.1
12	Kherson	670	846,705.60	1263.74	66,336.71	414,404.28	117,436.14	136,553.49	47,142.44	64,832.54	7.8	48.9	13.9	16.1	5.6	7.7
13	Kholm	294	102,812.29	349.70	30,081.51	33,872.61	4,256.52	10,522.02	6,214.03	17,865.60	29.3	32.9	4.1	10.2	6.0	17.4
14	Kiev	1,487	1,339,087.38	900.53	158,411.54	467,040.25	100,655.79	327,123.66	60,602.13	225,254.01	11.8	34.9	7.5	24.4	4.5	16.8
15	Kishinev	1,119	784,412.66	700.99	26,374.02	538,216.93	29,527.07	72,328.46	23,472.29	94,493.90	3.4	68.6	3.8	9.2	3.0	12.0
16	Kostroma	934	630,605.48	675.17	145,623.76	114,103.57	38,809.94	213,904.08	59,532.36	58,631.77	23.1	18.1	6.2	33.9	9.4	9.3
17	Kursk	1,050	870,042.83	828.61	93,583.11	382,721.02	58,961.78	158,904.55	37,827.01	138,045.36	10.8	44.0	6.8	18.3	4.3	15.9
18	Lithuania	215	123,435.56	574.12	18,665.04	45,206.89	11,535.38	12,472.13	8,311.40	27,244.72	15.1	36.6	9.3	10.1	6.7	22.1
19	Minsk	561	283,660.68	505.63	65,771.08	113,973.29	8,145.77	30,637.37	15,371.51	49,761.66	23.2	40.2	2.9	10.8	5.4	17.5
20	Mogilev	558	219,916.65	394.12	52,415.56	84,403.77	11,393.06	36,502.48	9,351.12	25,850.66	23.8	38.4	5.2	16.6	4.3	11.8
21	Moscow	1,532	3,692,910.92	2410.52	542,643.94	776,926.76	929,040.00	654,774.51	240,522.67	549,003.04	14.7	21.0	25.2	17.7	6.5	14.9
22	N. Novgorod	958	799,260.31	834.30	135,148.35	171,699.65	31,071.62	317,485.83	28,205.06	115,649.80	16.9	21.5	3.9	39.7	3.5	14.5
23	Novgorod	765	499,401.83	652.81	106,863.38	168,996.66	27,376.70	84,521.28	34,119.70	77,524.11	21.4	33.8	5.5	16.9	6.8	15.5
24	Olonets	363	225,342.63	620.78	24,404.14	56,110.92	20,218.82	29,814.04	24,269.01	70,525.70	10.8	24.9	9.0	13.2	10.8	31.3
25	Omsk	475	313,354.09	659.69	25,106.70	184,265.86	6,559.67	52,573.87	14,375.21	30,472.78	8.0	58.8	2.1	16.8	4.6	9.7
26	Orel	1,078	984,698.66	913.45	134,722.30	319,240.49	166,595.65	204,500.42	49,455.94	110,183.86	13.7	32.4	16.9	20.8	5.0	11.2
27	Orenburg	677	514,557.19	760.05	51,756.24	268,409.97	12,306.00	117,343.55	19,442.42	45,299.01	10.1	52.2	2.4	22.8	3.8	8.8
28	Penza	783	625,984.44	799.47	118,940.53	214,613.50	17,842.40	168,105.36	22,214.85	84,267.80	19.0	34.3	2.9	26.9	3.5	13.5
29	Perm'	614	473,077.30	770.48	64,762.69	175,286.72	27,677.83	151,195.09	20,296.36	33,858.61	13.7	37.1	5.9	32.0	4.3	7.2
30	Petrograd	350	2,580,657.20	7373.31	107,009.33	873,264.34	1,089,610.01	136,317.82	103,360.20	271,095.50	4.1	33.8	42.2	5.3	4.0	10.5

31 Podol'sk	1,544	595,801.72	385.88	101,950.39	311,185.62	25,493.64	67,751.14	28,593.15	60,827.78	17.1	52.2	4.3	11.4	4.8	10.2
32 Polotsk [Vitebsk]	323	152,986.66	473.64	20,905.86	82,298.53	3,981.79	20,253.05	6,323.27	19,224.16	13.7	53.8	2.6	13.2	4.1	12.6
33 Poltava	1,177	1,212,375.52	1030.06	108,040.95	499,083.68	146,664.47	292,440.21	60,386.36	105,759.85	8.9	41.2	12.1	24.1	5.0	8.7
34 Pskov	409	347,870.93	850.54	28,017.88	184,275.89	14,583.81	58,247.92	25,456.14	37,289.29	8.1	53.0	4.2	16.7	7.3	10.7
35 Riga	212	169,003.08	797.18	27,865.03	48,058.21	66,537.18	10,573.02	10,069.60	5,900.04	16.5	28.4	39.4	6.3	6.0	3.5
36 Ryazan'	967	906,980.39	937.93	254,734.38	188,239.86	38,017.87	267,090.08	44,930.79	113,967.41	28.1	20.8	4.2	29.4	5.0	12.6
37 Samara	908	541,663.35	596.55	57,273.49	261,545.70	25,437.84	115,521.98	16,510.51	65,373.83	10.6	48.3	4.7	21.3	3.0	12.1
38 Saratov	829	616,289.93	743.41	41,239.80	280,228.89	42,335.14	91,849.85	29,129.06	131,507.19	6.7	45.5	6.9	14.9	4.7	21.3
39 Simbirsk	745	396,130.86	531.72	51,873.93	180,745.26	10,766.51	96,795.85	14,251.42	41,697.89	13.1	45.6	2.7	24.4	3.6	10.5
40 Smolensk	658	858,229.50	1304.30	123,569.01	289,966.02	66,878.50	157,236.85	65,785.55	154,793.57	14.4	33.8	7.8	18.3	7.7	18.0
41 Stavropol'	621	1,013,355.11	1631.81	34,904.25	749,375.21	24,668.57	95,330.11	22,877.63	86,199.34	3.4	73.9	2.4	9.4	2.3	8.5
42 Tambov	1,170	1,469,573.61	1256.05	263,575.05	537,039.59	46,489.49	228,466.39	34,330.16	359,672.93	17.9	36.5	3.2	15.5	2.3	24.5
43 Tavrida	384	562,034.07	1463.63	25,494.17	357,266.01	35,136.12	76,848.74	13,969.18	53,319.85	4.5	63.6	6.3	13.7	2.5	9.5
44 Tobol'sk	436	237,503.00	544.73	20,025	100,514	4,439	39,712	30,241	42,572	8.4	42.3	1.9	16.7	12.7	17.9
45 Tomsk	977	483,586.94	494.97	43,691.35	267,287.28	17,497.20	99,547.97	17,659.18	37,903.96	9.0	55.3	3.6	20.6	3.7	7.8
46 Trans-Baikal	210	214,103.33	1019.54	10,701.29	121,664.74	5,252.92	22,950.41	29,179.40	24,354.57	5.0	56.8	2.5	10.7	13.6	11.4
47 Tula	885	792,310.33	895.27	197,723.28	239,552.21	25,434.07	158,782.37	56,128.67	114,689.73	25.0	30.2	3.2	20.0	7.1	14.5
48 Turkestan	198	198,005.40	1000.03	21,430.18	107,122.32	3,438.72	22,725.57	6,230.17	37,058.44	10.8	54.1	1.7	11.5	3.1	18.7
49 Tver'	1,002	1,118,839.13	1116.61	407,312.86	245,425.71	39,034.02	242,278.53	66,721.49	118,066.52	36.4	21.9	3.5	21.7	6.0	10.6
50 Ufa	460	195,811.45	425.68	21,811.89	25,125.52	2,022.19	123,152.74	6,800.59	16,898.53	11.1	12.8	1.0	62.9	3.5	8.6
51 Vladikavkaz	166	151,350.10	911.75	5,670.36	106,265.31	5,910.33	22,310.16	1,531.29	9,662.65	3.7	70.2	3.9	14.7	1.0	6.4
52 Vladimir	1,310	1,181,214.11	901.69	340,295.13	237,045.89	36,601.64	376,900.69	87,573.43	102,797.33	28.8	20.1	3.1	31.9	7.4	8.7
53 Vladivostok	195	186,268.77	955.22	14,285.76	82,844.45	16,872.46	15,206.87	8,482.39	48,576.84	7.7	44.5	9.1	8.2	4.6	26.1
54 Vologda	793	664,664.19	838.16	142,332.27	107,091.99	55,234.30	223,698.80	50,625.11	85,681.72	21.4	16.1	8.3	33.7	7.6	12.9
55 Volyn'	1,321	855,088.60	647.30	157,651.12	221,647.10	29,574.57	304,954.49	32,305.45	108,955.87	18.4	25.9	3.5	35.7	3.8	12.7
56 Voronezh	1,021	1,033,258.73	1012.01	165,440.45	452,238.39	41,233.18	265,608.02	29,531.32	79,207.37	16.0	43.8	4.0	25.7	2.9	7.7
57 Vyatka	777	729,266.20	938.57	120,464.40	325,129.18	80,878.92	111,304.16	29,084.78	62,404.76	16.5	44.6	11.1	15.3	6.0	8.6
58 Warsaw	74	102,586.94	1386.31	23,398.69	34,088.67	22,381.61	7,842.59	4,827.30	10,048.08	22.8	33.2	21.8	7.6	4.7	9.8
59 Yakutsk	112	67,589.96	603.48	5,074.54	14,836.67	3,753.72	22,282.36	13,717.86	7,924.81	7.5	22.0	5.6	33.0	20.3	11.7
60 Yaroslavl'	933	708,485.24	759.36	214,128.17	106,515.66	46,408.53	173,516.79	99,239.09	68,677.00	30.2	15.0	6.6	24.5	14.0	9.7
61 Yekaterinburg	480	431,966.60	899.93	50,744.04	232,105.38	27,385.10	66,194.20	24,003.30	31,534.58	11.7	53.7	6.3	15.3	5.6	7.3
62 Yekaterinoslav	649	1,204,355.94	1855.71	110,385.03	674,893.70	35,911.72	144,725.64	33,277.14	205,162.71	9.2	56.0	3.0	12.0	2.8	17.0
63 Yenisey	304	268,312.67	882.61	17,457.65	89,840.65	10,146.26	52,851.72	16,394.41	81,621.98	6.5	33.5	3.8	19.7	6.1	30.4
64 Georgia				no data											
Army & Navy	667	774,534.62	1161.22	145,593.19	397,115.50	76,745.46	61,722.50	37,174.78	56,183.19	18.8	51.3	9.9	8.0	4.8	7.3
TOTAL	42,812.0	41,469,725.2	968.65	5,985,705.84	15,888,419.27	4,209,514.16	7,938,651.84	2,130,403.97	5,317,030.12	14.4	38.3	10.2	19.1	5.1	12.8

Source: *Vsepoddanneishii Otchet* (1916: 42-5), the author's calculations. Note: The diocese of Finland, in addition had the following data in marks and pfennings: 1912 balance 110,987 m 79 p; 1913 income 102,323 m 82 p. Underlined figures differ from original ones, which most likely were erroneous.

Table A3.6. Renovationist churches in the USSR, 04.01.1936.

Unit (Oblast)	Number	Unit (Oblast)	Number
Moscow Metropolitanate	225	Central Asia	42
of them, in Moscow	11	Kazakhstan	28
Leningrad Metropolitanate	143	Kazan'	90
Kalinin	91	Sverdlovsk	105
Kursk	94	Chelyabinsk	54
Voronezh	232	Western Siberia	80
Ivanov	185	Omsk	64
Yaroslavl'	170	Belarus	16
Western	195	Ukrainian Exarchate	365
Kirov and Gor'kiy	100	Ufa	24
Arkhangel'sk	98	Irkutsk	15
Kuybyshev	13	Krasnoyarsk	34
Stalingrad	68	under direct rule by the Patriarch:	
Orenburg	6	Vladivostok city	1
Azovo-Chernomorsk	210	Baku	1
North Caucasian	110	Yakutsk	1
Crimea	17	Total in the USSR	2875

Source: GARF 5263, op. 2, d. 12, ll.192-192ob.

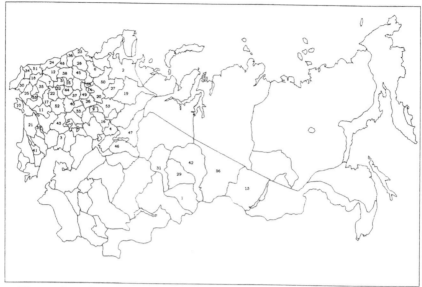

Figure A3.1. Provinces of the Soviet Union considered in Tuchkov's Report, 1924. Source: Rossiiskaia Sotsialisticheskaia (1921). Note: Units' numbers correspond to Table A3.1.

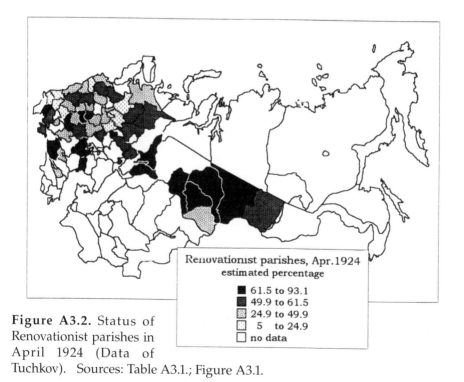

Figure A3.2. Status of Renovationist parishes in April 1924 (Data of Tuchkov). Sources: Table A3.1.; Figure A3.1.

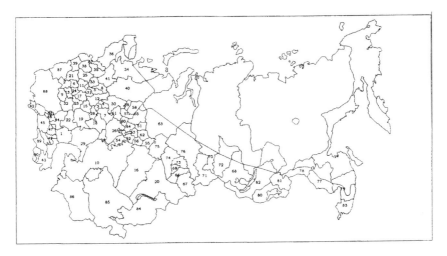

Figure A3.3. Renovationist diocesan division of the Soviet Union in 1927. Source: the author's reconstruction based on the Renovationist statistics (Table A3.2) and December 1926 map of the USSR from Leasure and Lewis (1966: vii). Note: Units' numbers correspond to Table A3.2.

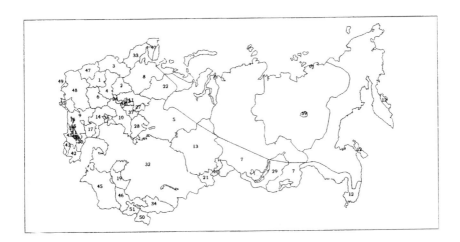

Figure A3.4. Statistical-administrative division of the USSR in 1931. Source: Administrativno-Territorial'noe Delenie (1931). Note: Units' numbers correspond to Table A3.3.

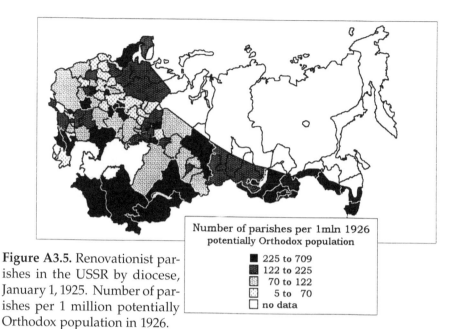

Figure A3.5. Renovationist parishes in the USSR by diocese, January 1, 1925. Number of parishes per 1 million potentially Orthodox population in 1926.

Sources: Table A3.2; base map: the author's reconstruction based on based on Renovationist statistics (Table A3.2) and the December 1926 map of the USSR from Leasure and Lewis (1966: vii).

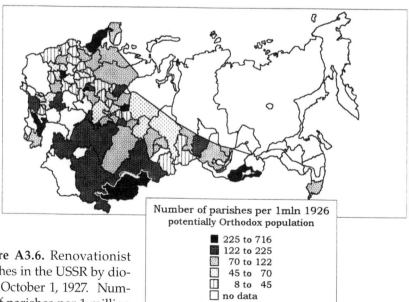

Figure A3.6. Renovationist parishes in the USSR by diocese, October 1, 1927. Number of parishes per 1 million potentially Orthodox population in 1926.

Sources: Table A3.2.; base map: Leasure and Lewis (1966: vii); the author's adjustment.

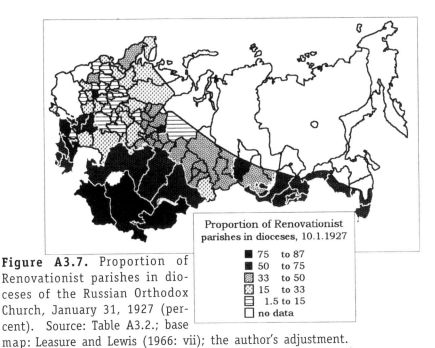

Figure A3.7. Proportion of Renovationist parishes in dioceses of the Russian Orthodox Church, January 31, 1927 (percent). Source: Table A3.2.; base map: Leasure and Lewis (1966: vii); the author's adjustment.

Proportion of Renovationist parishes in dioceses, 10.1.1927

- 75 to 87
- 50 to 75
- 33 to 50
- 15 to 33
- 1.5 to 15
- no data

Figure A3.8. Change in the number of Renovationist parishes, January 1, 1925 — October 1, 1927. Number of parishes per 1 million potentially Orthodox population in 1926.

Change per 1 mln 1926 potentially Orthodox population

- 10 to 69
- -35 to -10
- -100 to -35
- -286 to -100
- no data or no change

Sources: Table A3.2.; base map: Leasure and Lewis (1966: vii); the author's adjustment.

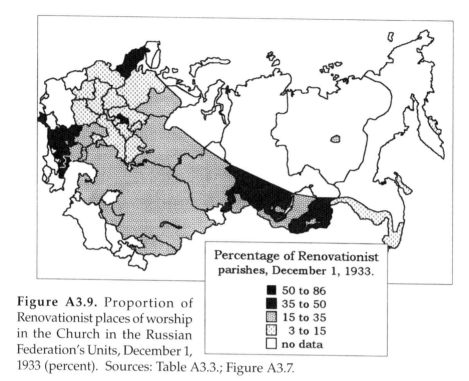

Percentage of Renovationist
parishes, December 1, 1933.

■ 50 to 86
■ 35 to 50
▨ 15 to 35
▦ 3 to 15
□ no data

Figure A3.9. Proportion of Renovationist places of worship in the Church in the Russian Federation's Units, December 1, 1933 (percent). Sources: Table A3.3.; Figure A3.7.

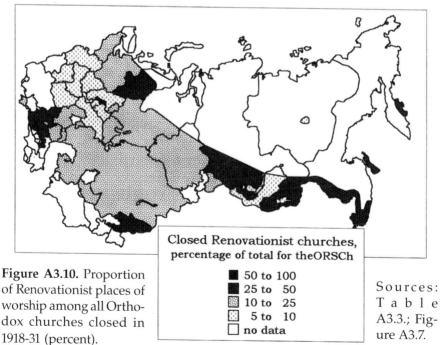

Closed Renovationist churches,
percentage of total for theORSCh

■ 50 to 100
■ 25 to 50
▨ 10 to 25
▦ 5 to 10
□ no data

Figure A3.10. Proportion of Renovationist places of worship among all Orthodox churches closed in 1918-31 (percent).

Sources: Table A3.3.; Figure A3.7.

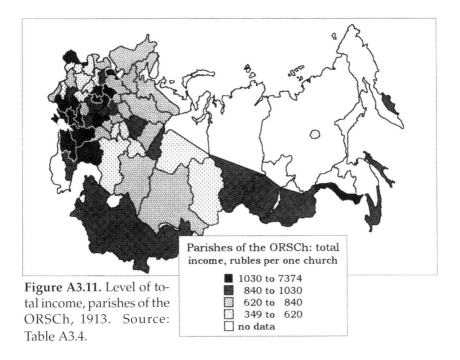

Figure A3.11. Level of total income, parishes of the ORSCh, 1913. Source: Table A3.4.

Parishes of the ORSCh: total income, rubles per one church

■ 1030 to 7374
■ 840 to 1030
▨ 620 to 840
▨ 349 to 620
□ no data

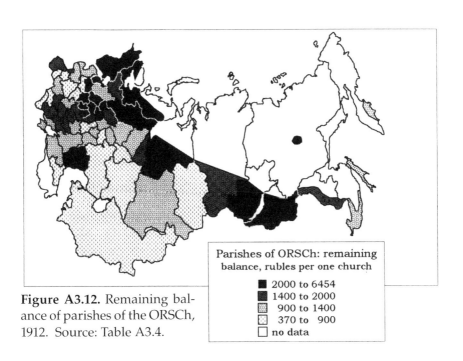

Figure A3.12. Remaining balance of parishes of the ORSCh, 1912. Source: Table A3.4.

Parishes of ORSCh: remaining balance, rubles per one church

■ 2000 to 6454
■ 1400 to 2000
▨ 900 to 1400
▨ 370 to 900
□ no data

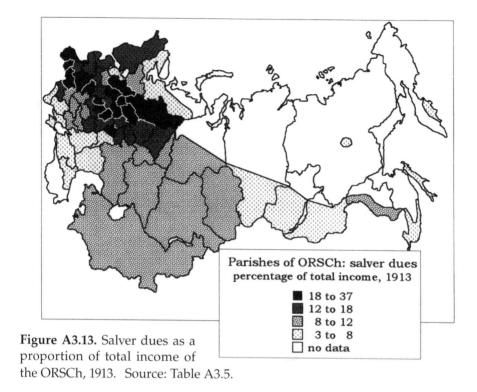

Figure A3.13. Salver dues as a proportion of total income of the ORSCh, 1913. Source: Table A3.5.

Parishes of ORSCh: salver dues
percentage of total income, 1913

■ 18 to 37
▨ 12 to 18
▧ 8 to 12
▨ 3 to 8
□ no data

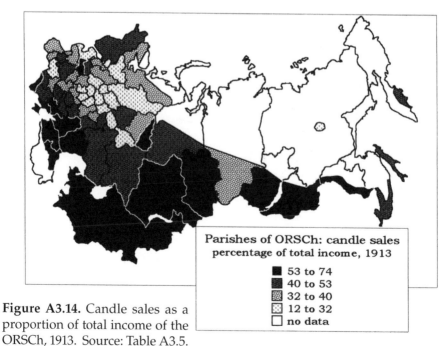

Figure A3.14. Candle sales as a proportion of total income of the ORSCh, 1913. Source: Table A3.5.

Parishes of ORSCh: candle sales
percentage of total income, 1913

■ 53 to 74
▨ 40 to 53
▨ 32 to 40
▨ 12 to 32
□ no data

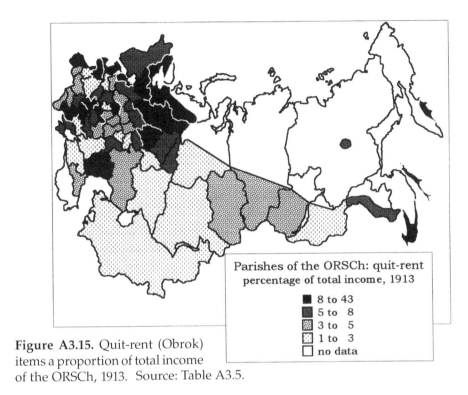

Figure A3.15. Quit-rent (Obrok) items a proportion of total income of the ORSCh, 1913. Source: Table A3.5.

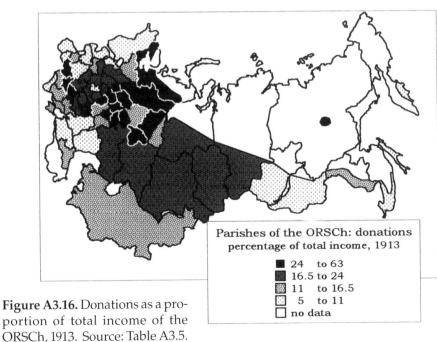

Figure A3.16. Donations as a proportion of total income of the ORSCh, 1913. Source: Table A3.5.

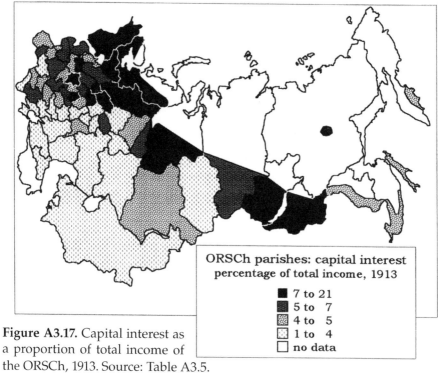

Figure A3.17. Capital interest as a proportion of total income of the ORSCh, 1913. Source: Table A3.5.

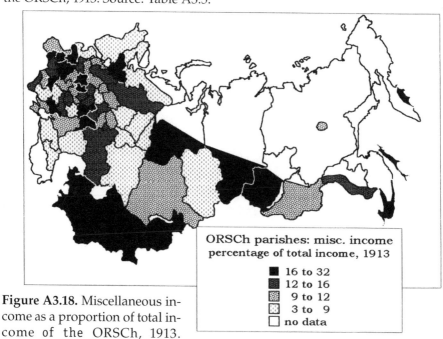

Figure A3.18. Miscellaneous income as a proportion of total income of the ORSCh, 1913. Source: Table A3.5.

Table A4.1. Property of the Orthodox Russian-State Church by type, 1914

Map nos.	Dioceses/ provinces	Orthodox population 1913	Number of churches, by type											Density per 1 million 1913 Orthodox population										
			cathrals	monastery	parish	home/ state	Edinoverie	branch	cetery	field	missionary	Total	Chapels	cathedrals	monastery	parish	home/ state	Edinoverie	branch	cemetery	field	missionary	Total	Chapels
1	Arkhangel'sk	436924	15	51	454	9	2	146	35			712	452	34.3	116.7	1039.1	20.6	4.6	334.2	80.1	0.0	0.0	1629.6	1034.5
2	Astrakhan'	542859	6	9	197	12		44	6	1	4	279	35	11.1	16.6	362.9	22.1	0.0	81.1	11.1	1.8	7.4	513.9	64.5
3	Blagoveschensk	296050	3	2	130	7			2			144	154	10.1	6.8	439.1	23.6	0.0	0.0	6.8	0.0	0.0	486.4	520.2
4	Chernigov	2461322	15	46	1029	138	27	90				1345	105	6.1	18.7	418.1	56.1	11.0	36.6	0.0	0.0	0.0	546.5	42.7
5	Don	2215258	6	8	673	25	34	62	11			819	35	2.7	3.6	303.8	11.3	15.3	28.0	5.0	0.0	0.0	369.7	15.8
6	Finland	62723	3	29	31	7		22	3	3		98	98	47.8	462.4	494.2	111.6	0.0	350.7	47.8	47.8	0.0	1562.4	1562.4
7	Grodno	990373	8	5	351	7		108	135			614	42	8.1	5.0	354.4	7.1	0.0	109.0	136.3	0.0	0.0	620.0	42.4
8	Irkutsk	412400	6	13	231	18		68	1			337	207	14.5	31.5	560.1	43.6	0.0	164.9	2.4	0.0	0.0	817.2	501.9
9	Kaluga	1243642	15	30	615	22	2	59	9			752	147	12.1	24.1	494.5	17.7	1.6	47.4	7.2	0.0	0.0	604.7	118.2
10	Kazan'	1643593	18	27	658	38		19	9			769	343	11.0	16.4	400.3	23.1	0.0	11.6	5.5	0.0	0.0	467.9	208.7
11	Khar'kov	2872477	12	43	824	47	4	25	23			978	77	4.2	15.0	286.9	16.4	1.4	8.7	8.0	0.0	0.0	340.5	26.8
12	Kherson	2415112	12	10	616	60	15	34	8			755	31	5.0	4.1	255.1	24.8	6.2	14.1	3.3	0.0	0.0	312.6	12.8
13	Kholm	307481	8	40	275	17		92	29			461	53	26.0	130.1	894.4	55.3	0.0	299.2	94.3	0.0	0.0	1499.3	172.4
14	Kiev	3320237	14	52	1378	43	1	139	11			1638	119	4.2	15.7	415.0	13.0	0.3	41.9	3.3	0.0	0.0	493.3	35.8
15	Kishinev	1619997	13	46	909	22	3	116	8			1117	7	8.0	28.4	561.1	13.6	1.9	71.6	4.9	0.0	0.0	689.5	4.3
16	Kostroma	1570181	28	66	1033	18	22	10	30			1207	1735	17.8	42.0	657.9	11.5	14.0	6.4	19.1	0.0	0.0	768.7	1105.0
17	Kursk	2415795	17	46	1053	35	6	12	17			1186	18	7.0	19.0	435.9	14.5	2.5	5.0	7.0	0.0	0.0	490.9	7.5
18	Lithuania	453811	5	9	204	27	3	67	103			418	56	11.0	19.8	449.5	59.5	6.6	147.6	227.0	0.0	0.0	921.1	123.4
19	Minsk	1856042	10	8	548	26		396	242			1230	319	5.4	4.3	295.3	14.0	0.0	213.4	130.4	0.0	0.0	662.7	171.9
20	Mogilev	1651365	8	26	561	15	2	139	94			845	47	4.8	15.7	339.7	9.1	1.2	84.2	56.9	0.0	0.0	511.7	28.5
21	Moscow	1826661	15	114	1228	132	9	114	40			1652	513	8.2	62.4	672.3	72.3	4.9	62.4	21.9	0.0	0.0	904.4	280.8
22	N.Novgorod	1605094	18	72	893	39	24	24	65			1135	211	11.2	44.9	556.4	24.3	15.0	15.0	40.5	0.0	0.0	707.1	131.5
23	Novgorod	1480357	15	15	753	31	7	119	39			979	3264	10.1	10.1	508.7	20.9	4.7	80.4	26.3	0.0	0.0	661.3	2204.9
24	Olonets	430908	10	37	292	17	5	208	20		3	592	1715	23.2	85.9	677.6	39.5	11.6	482.7	46.4	0.0	7.0	1373.8	3980.0
25	Omsk	1467963	7	6	429	15		57	5			519	302	4.8	4.1	292.2	10.2	0.0	38.8	3.4	0.0	0.0	353.6	205.7
26	Orel	1965703	12	48	882	40		59	37			1078	58	6.1	24.4	448.7	20.3	0.0	30.0	18.8	0.0	0.0	548.4	29.5
27	Orenburg	1628577	7	17	660	23	5	137	11		1	861	84	4.3	10.4	405.3	14.1	3.1	84.1	6.8	0.0	0.6	528.7	51.6
28	Penza	1606946	10	52	753	40	11	14	50			930	65	6.2	32.4	468.6	24.9	6.8	8.7	31.1	0.0	0.0	578.7	40.4
29	Perm'	1550635	11	24	428	21	41	72	23			620	1169	7.1	15.5	276.0	13.5	26.4	46.4	14.8	0.0	0.0	399.8	753.9
30	Petrograd	1021840	19	57	301	190	13	166	38			784	1638	18.6	55.8	294.6	185.9	12.7	162.5	37.2	0.0	0.3	767.2	1603.0
31	Podol'sk	2966413	12	34	1429	26	1	174	59			1735	94	4.0	11.5	481.7	8.8	0.3	58.7	19.9	0.0	0.0	584.9	31.7
32	Polotsk [Vitebsk]	903394	13	20	301	23	11	93	100			561	216	14.4	22.1	333.2	25.5	12.2	102.9	110.7	0.0	0.0	621.0	239.1

	Pop.																							
33 Poltava	2648679	17	13	1146	45	3	43	44			7	1311	33	6.4	4.9	432.7	17.0	1.1	16.2	16.6	0.0	0.0	495.0	12.5
34 Pskov	1231918	10	32	377	40	5	67	27				558	997	8.1	26.0	306.0	32.5	4.1	54.4	21.9	0.0	0.0	453.0	809.3
35 Riga	270574	3	9	195	32	3	18	7				267	71	11.1	33.3	720.7	118.3	11.1	66.5	25.9	0.0	0.0	986.8	262.4
36 Ryazan'	2059915	12	14	926	19	2	3	9	7			985	56	5.8	6.8	449.5	9.2	1.0	1.5	4.4	3.4	0.0	478.2	27.2
37 Samara	2671126	15	45	935	53	103	93	11	10			1235	131	5.6	16.8	350.0	8.6	38.6	34.8	4.1	3.7	0.0	462.4	49.0
38 Saratov	2422880	11	33	733	21	14	64	23				971	93	4.5	13.6	302.5	21.9	5.8	26.4	9.5	0.0	0.0	400.8	38.4
39 Simbirsk	1683104	9	23	703	21	6	136	16				914	133	5.3	13.7	417.7	12.5	3.6	80.8	9.5	0.0	0.0	543.0	79.0
40 Smolensk	1560805	19	40	654	22		21	7				816	102	12.2	25.6	419.0	14.1	0.0	13.5	38.4	0.0	0.0	522.8	65.4
41 Stavropol'	2669108	8	12	582	25	7		60				641	50	3.0	4.5	218.1	9.4	2.6	2.6	0.0	0.0	0.0	240.2	18.7
42 Tambov	2998181	13	60	1155	68	3	30	7				1379	29	4.3	20.0	385.2	22.7	1.0	10.0	16.7	0.0	0.0	459.9	9.7
43 Tavrida	1185847	15	43	348	35	3	24	5	50			473	65	12.6	36.3	293.5	29.5	2.5	20.2	4.2	0.0	0.0	398.9	54.8
44 Tobol'sk	1117055	7	7	384	18	15	80	9				520	435	6.3	6.3	343.8	16.1	13.4	71.6	8.1	0.0	0.0	465.5	389.4
45 Tomsk	2902308	9	16	793	31	20	229	9	7	3	30	1138	363	3.1	5.5	273.2	10.7	6.9	78.9	2.4	1.0	10.3	392.1	125.1
46 Trans-Baikal	523987	9	13	196	17	7	147	10				399	403	17.2	24.8	374.1	32.4	13.4	280.5	19.1	0.0	0.0	761.5	769.1
47 Tula	1630811	14	32	836	42	2	61	23				1010	257	8.6	19.6	512.6	25.8	1.2	37.4	14.1	0.0	0.0	619.3	157.6
48 Turkestan	368981	11	4	125	22		17	5	12	1		197	69	29.8	10.8	338.8	59.6	0.0	46.1	13.6	32.5	2.7	533.9	187.0
49 Tver'	1904672	15	77	926	36	5	123	73				1255	1031	7.9	40.4	486.2	18.9	2.6	64.6	38.3	0.0	0.0	658.9	541.3
50 Ufa	1108404	6	28	474	26	11	17	6				568	266	5.4	25.3	427.6	23.5	9.9	15.3	5.4	0.0	0.0	512.4	240.0
51 Vladikavkaz	433299	8	6	162	17	4	21	11				229	19	18.5	13.8	373.9	39.2	9.2	48.5	25.4	0.0	0.0	528.5	43.8
52 Vladimir	1589791	18	35	1124	34	12	67	25				1315	18	11.3	22.0	707.0	21.4	7.5	42.1	15.7	0.0	0.0	827.2	11.3
53 Vladivostok	334754	4	5	180	8		29	2				228	75	11.9	14.9	537.7	23.9	0.0	86.6	6.0	0.0	0.0	681.1	224.0
54 Vologda	1611412	14	67	748	23	3	89	33	4			981	1607	8.7	41.6	464.2	14.3	1.9	55.2	20.5	2.5	0.0	608.8	997.3
55 Volyn'	2175577	13	40	1274	25	1	479	173				2005	207	6.0	18.4	585.6	11.5	0.5	220.2	79.5	0.0	0.0	921.6	95.1
56 Voronezh	2934661	13	54	984	26	2	28	13				1120	58	4.4	18.4	335.3	8.9	0.7	9.5	4.4	0.0	0.0	381.6	19.8
57 Vyatka	3243911	20	27	677	44	17	80	47				912	750	6.2	21.9	646.3	13.6	5.2	24.7	14.5	0.0	0.0	281.1	231.2
58 Warsaw	91289	10	2	59	6		21	6			1	130	16	109.5	3.8	208.7	350.5	0.0	230.0	65.7	0.0	0.0	1424.0	175.3
59 Yakutsk	264273	5	1	106	32		10					131	146	18.9	21.9	401.1	22.7	0.0	37.8	0.0	3.8	7.6	495.7	552.5
60 Yaroslavl'	1150793	12	26	861	43	7	18		1		2	967	790	10.4	22.6	748.2	37.4	6.1	0.0	15.6	0.0	0.0	840.3	686.5
61 Yekaterinburg	1504919	14	33	414	21	35	64	23		1		605	746	9.3	21.9	275.1	14.0	23.3	42.5	15.3	0.7	0.0	402.0	495.7
62 Yekaterinoslav	2247817	11	15	607	45	2	53	9				742	73	4.9	6.7	270.0	20.0	0.9	23.6	4.0	0.0	0.0	330.1	32.5
63 Yenisey	765176	7	9	257	9	1	36	6	1		11	337	317	9.1	11.8	335.9	11.8	1.3	47.0	7.8	1.3	14.4	440.4	414.3
64 Georgia	1011344	18	90	1589	40		788	39				2564	130	17.8	89.0	1571.2	39.6	0.0	779.2	38.6	0.0	0.0	2535.2	128.5
TOTAL	98534800	741	1973	40649	2138	541	5823	2058	48		49	54053	22945	7.5	20.0	412.5	21.7	5.5	59.1	20.9	0.5	0.5	548.6	232.9
Moscow Synodal Court	16985	7	47	1			7					56	42	412.1	0.0	3297.0	0.0	0.0	0.0	0.0	0.0	0.0		353.3
Army&Navy	958280	23		56				2		37	304	65	6	24.0	0.0	0.0	434.1	0.0	0.0	117.8	0.0	0.0		83.5
Abroad	55			416			29	37				809	80						30.3	38.6	317.2			

Sources: *Vsepoddanneishii Otchet* (1916: 6-7), Institute of Russian History (1995: 18-22), Tsentral'nyi Statisticheskii (1901a).

Note: Old Believers here are not considered as part of Orthodox population.

Table A4.2. Orthodox church closures by units of the Russian Federation, 1918-33.

Map nos.	Unit of the Russian Federation	Total Population (TP), 1.1.31	Closures, 1918-1931 churches	per 1 mln TP	Places of worship, 1931 number	per 1 mln TP	Closures, 1931-33 places	per 1 mln TP	Places of worship, 12.1.1933 number	per 1 mln TP
1	Western Oblast'	6,731,200	527	78.3	1915	284.5	28	4.2	1887	280.3
2	Ivanovo Industrial Oblast'	4,404,700	530	120.3	2377	539.7	43	9.8	2334	529.9
3	Leningrad Oblast'	6,174,900	686	111.1	2071	335.4	50	8.1	2021	327.3
4	Moscow Oblast'	11,359,300	1,331	117.2	3887	342.2	129	11.4	3758	330.8
5	Ural Oblast'	7,785,500	996	127.9	1147	147.3	55	7.1	1092	140.3
6	Central Black Soil Oblast'	11,878,100	578	48.7	3150	265.2	29	2.4	3121	262.8
7	East Siberian Kray	2,402,800	294	122.4	580	241.4	10	4.2	570	237.2
8	Northern Kray	2,429,100	346	142.4	984	405.1	13	5.4	971	399.7
9	North Caucasian Kray	8,296,700	187	22.5	1382	166.6	12	1.4	1370	165.1
10	Middle Volga Kray	6,285,500	571	90.8	1888	300.4	30	4.8	1858	295.6
11	Nizhniy Novgorod Kray	5,444,800	361	66.3	1533	281.6	56	10.3	1477	271.3
12	Far Eastern Kray	1,559,900	584	374.4	294	188.5	5	3.2	289	185.3
13	Western Siberian Kray	8,057,200	288	35.7	1514	187.9	13	1.6	1501	186.3
14	Low Volga Kray	5,049,000	459	90.9	1075	212.9	24	4.8	1051	208.2
15	Adygey AO	126,500	3	23.7	15	118.6	1	7.9	14	110.7
16	Ingush AO	81,900			48	586.1			48	586.1
17	Kalmyk AO	176,300	29	164.5	69	391.4			69	391.4
18	Karachaev AO	72,100			3	41.6			3	41.6
19	Kara-Kalpak AO	338,100	102	301.7	27	79.9			27	79.9
20	Khakass AO	135,600			25	184.4			25	184.4
21	Oyrat AO	114,500	110	960.7	30	262.0			30	262.0
22	Komi AO	251,200	52	207.0	196	780.3	1	4.0	195	776.3
23	Mari AO	519,300	12	23.1	90	173.3	5	9.6	85	163.7
24	Mordovian AO	1,389,600	168	120.9	682	490.8	3	2.2	679	488.6
25	Cherkess AO	41,100								
26	Chechen AO	525,800	22	41.8	173	329.0			173	329.0
27	Udmurt (Votyak) AO	880,700	31	35.2	153	173.7	1	1.1	152	172.6
28	Bashkir ASSR	2,955,700	184	62.3	298	100.8	8	2.7	290	98.1
29	Buryat-Mongol ASSR	571,900	61	106.7	84	146.9	2	3.5	82	143.4
30	Dagestan ASSR	871,100	24	27.6	20	23.0			20	23.0
31	Kabardino-Balkar ASSR	224,400	7	31.2	18	80.2			18	80.2
32	Kazakh SSR	7,058,500	754	106.8	305	43.2	6	0.9	299	42.4
33	Karelian ASSR	284,100	179	630.1	341	1200.3	3	10.6	338	1189.7
34	Kyrgyz ASSR	1,108,200	84	75.8	126	113.7			126	113.7
35	Crimean ASSR	800,900	165	206.0	89	111.1	4	5.0	85	106.1
36	German Volga ASSR	623,500	25	40.1	92	147.6			92	147.6
37	Tatar ASSR	2,726,100	139	51.0	346	126.9	3	1.1	343	125.8
38	Chuvash ASSR	909,100	56	61.6	181	199.1	5	5.5	176	193.6
39	Yakutsk ASSR	308,900	111	359.3	164	530.9			164	530.9
	TOTAL	110,953,800	10,056	90.6	27372	246.7	539	4.9	26833	241.8

Sources: GARF f. 5263, op. 1, d. 32, ll. 66-73, *Administrativno-Territorial'noe Delenie* (1931: vi-xiii), the author's calculation.

Table A4.3. Dynamics of places of worship of the Russian Orthodox Church, 1946-48.

Map nos.	Division (oblast', kray, ASSR)	1959 potential Orth.population	IV.1. 1946	I.1. 1948	Change		
					absolute	relative	%
1	Karelia	508,242	10	9	-1	-2.0	90
2	Komi	492,466	1	1	0	0.0	100
3	Arkhangel'sk	1,233,676	19	32	13	10.5	168.4
5	Vologda	1,290,365	10	17	7	5.4	170
6	Murmansk	536,579	1	4	3	5.6	400
7	Leningrad	4,250,191	71	58	-13	-3.1	81.7
8	Novgorod	722,680	55	41	-14	-19.4	74.5
9	Pskov+Velikie Luki	932,132	94	117	23	24.7	124.5
10	Bryansk	1,523,420	98	88	-10	-6.6	89.8
11	Vladimir	1,377,936	60	75	15	10.9	125
12	Ivanovo	1,297,973	43	56	13	10.0	130.2
19	Kalinin	1,720,036	89	97	8	4.7	109.0
13	Kaluga	921,704	33	37	4	4.3	112.1
14	Kostroma	905,317	94	99	5	5.5	105.3
15	Moscow	10,340,210	198	211	13	1.3	106.6
17	Ryazan'	1,428,273	57	85	28	19.6	149.1
18	Smolensk	1,130,337	54	60	6	5.3	111.1
20	Tula	1,876,269	16	38	22	11.7	238
21	Yaroslavl'	1,374,023	148	149	1	0.7	100.7
22	Mari	312,252	10	16	6	19.2	160
23	Mordovia	597,111	9	27	18	30.1	300
24	Chuvashia	267,529	33	39	6	22.4	118.2
25	Kirov	1,776,563	50	84	34	19.1	168
26	Gor'kiy+Arzamas	3,411,305	30	46	16	4.7	153.3
28	Voronezh	2,349,324	114	131	17	7.2	114.9
29	Kursk	1,471,994	326	323	-3	-2.0	99.1
27	Belgorod	1,219,747			0	0.0	
30	Lipetsk	1,134,171			0	0.0	
16	Orel	922,724	25	27	2	2.2	108
31	Tambov	1,538,305	31	50	19	12.4	161.3
33	Tatarstan	1,268,512	13	15	2	1.6	115.4
34	Astrakhan'	550,665	11	15	4	7.3	136.4
35	Stalingrad [Volgograd]	1,691,215	34	39	5	3.0	114.7
36	Penza	1,322,541	22	33	11	8.3	150
37	Kuybyshev [Samara]	1,917,561	9	19	10	5.2	211.1
38	Saratov+Balashov	2,011,893	5	13	8	4.0	260
39	Ul'yanovsk	877,483	11	19	8	9.1	172.7
41	Dagestan	224,010	3	3	0	0.0	100
43	Kabardino-Balkar	170,986	11	10	-1	-5.8	90.9
45	North Ossetian	188,016	8	9	1	5.3	113
42	Checheno-Ingushetia	362,053	4	5	1	2.8	125
47	Kradnodar	3,530,783	259	239	-20	-5.7	92.3

Table A4.3 (part 2).

Map nos.	Division (oblast', kray, ASSR)	1959 potential Orth.population	IV.1 1946	I.1. 1948	Change absolute	relative	%
48	Stavropol'	1,650,274	147	140	-7	-4.2	95.2
49	Rostov+Kamensk	3,182,075	214	243	29	9.1	113.6
100	Crimea	-	60	58	-2		96.7
50	Bashkiria [Bashkortostan]	1,522,533	24	39	15	9.9	163
51	Udmurt	766,291	22	28	6	7.8	127.3
52	Kurgan	938,885	2	12	10	10.7	600
53	Chkalov [Orenburg]	1,424,999	9	16	7	4.9	177.8
54	Molotov [Perm']	2,525,015	59	73	14	5.5	123.7
56	Sverdlovsk [Yekaterinburg]	3,688,204	29	33	4	1.1	113.8
57	Chelyabinsk	2,537,775	26	37	11	4.3	142.3
59	Altay Kray	2,425,073	4	11	7	2.9	275
60	Kemerovo	2,520,490	6	15	9	3.6	250
61	Novosibirsk	2,130,890	4	7	3	1.4	175
62	Omsk	1,411,381	6	7	1	0.7	116.7
63	Tomsk	673,865	4	4	0	0.0	100
64	Tyumen'	911,651	12	17	5	5.5	141.7
67	Buryatia	512,751	1	2	1	2.0	200
68	Tuva	70,029	1	2	1	14.3	200
70	Krasnoyarsk	2,315,354	12	19	7	3.0	158.3
73	Irkutsk	1,782,292	10	16	6	3.4	160
74	Chita	963,281	2	3	1	1.0	150
75	Yakutia	230,058		2	2	8.7	
76	Maritime	1,315,433	3	5	2	1.5	166.7
77	Khabarovsk	1,043,581	1	3	2	1.9	300
	Russia (total)	**102,067,000**	**2827**	**3228**	**401**	**3.9**	**114.2**
86	Ukraine	39,540,000	6077	8903	2826	71.5	146.5
87	Moldova	714,000	582	612	30	42.0	105.2
88	Belarus	7,324,000	621	993	372	50.8	159.9
89	Estonia	267,000	132	137	5	18.7	103.8
90	Latvia	647,000	147	130	-17	-26.3	88.4
91	Lithuania	279,000	64	68	4	14.3	106
92	Armenia	56,000	1	1	0	0.0	100
93	Azerbaijan	501,000	2	3	1	2.0	150
94	Georgia	460,000	40	53	13	28.3	133
95	Kazakhstan	4,843,000	17	52	35	7.2	305.9
96	Kyrgyzstan	761,000	14	31	17	22.3	221.4
97	Tajikistan	290,000	3	4	1	3.4	133.3
98	Turkmenistan	284,000	2	5	3	10.6	250
99	Uzbekistan	1,179,000	15	24	9	7.6	160
	Total for the USSR	**159,280,000**	**10544**	**14244**	**3700**	**23229.5**	**135.1**

Source: GARF f. 6991s, op. 2, d. 180, ll.22-25; f. 6991s, op. 2, d. 263, l.2.
Note: Units with no data available are excluded from this table.

Figure A4.4. Dynamics of communities of the Russian Orthodox Church in the USSR, 1949-57.

Map Division (oblast', nos. kray, ASSR)	X.1. 1949	I.1. 1957	Change absolute	Change relative	1959 potentially Orth. population
1 Karelia	9	6	-3	-5.9	508,242
2 Komi	1	1	0	0.0	492,466
3 Arkhangel'sk	32	25	-7	-5.7	1,233,676
5 Vologda	17	17	0	0.0	1,290,365
6 Murmansk	4	4	0	0.0	536,579
7 Leningrad	57	57	0	0.0	4,250,191
8 Novgorod	42	41	-1	-1.4	722,680
9 Pskov+Velikie Luki	95	92	-3	-3.2	932,132
10 Bryansk	80	74	-6	-3.9	1,523,420
11 Vladimir	74	69	-5	-3.6	1,377,936
12 Ivanovo	57	56	-1	-0.8	1,297,973
19 Kalinin [Tver']	94	87	-7	-4.1	1,720,036
13 Kaluga	38	38	0	0.0	921,704
14 Kostroma	92	80	-12	-13.3	905,317
15 Moscow	215	213	-2	-0.2	10,340,210
17 Ryazan'	85	76	-9	-6.3	1,428,273
18 Smolensk	59	54	-5	-4.4	1,130,337
20 Tula	39	39	0	0.0	1,876,269
21 Yaroslavl'	147	143	-4	-2.9	1,374,023
22 Mari	16	16	0	0.0	312,252
23 Mordvinia	27	27	0	0.0	597,111
24 Chuvashia	41	41	0	0.0	267,529
25 Kirov	86	80	-6	-3.4	1,776,563
26 Gor'kiy+Arzamas	47	48	1	0.3	3,411,305
28 Voronezh	133	58	-75		2,349,324
29 Kursk	318	155	-163		1,471,994
27 Belgorod		133	133		1,219,747
30 Lipetsk		31	31		1,134,171
16 Orel	26	23	-3	-3.3	922,724
31 Tambov	49	47	-2	-1.3	1,538,305
33 Tatarstan	15	15	0	0.0	1,268,512
34 Astrakhan'	17	16	-1	-1.8	550,665
35 Stalingrad	34	23	-11	-6.5	1,691,215
36 Penza	32	33	1	0.8	1,322,541
37 Kuybyshev	19	19	0	0.0	1,917,561
38 Saratov+Balashov	15	11	-4	-2.0	2,011,893
39 Ul'yanovsk	19	19	0	0.0	877,483
41 Dagestan	3	3	0	0.0	224,010
43 Kabardino-Balkaria	9	8	-1	-5.8	170,986
45 North Ossetia	9	9	0	0.0	188,016
42 Checheno-Ingushetia	5	5	0	0.0	362,053
47 Kradnodar	230	208	-22	-6.2	3,530,783
48 Stavropol'	140	129	-11	-6.7	1,650,274
49 Rostov+Kamensk	238	121	-117	-36.8	3,182,075

Figure A4.4 (part 2).

Map nos.	Division (oblast', kray, ASSR)	X.1. 1949	I.1. 1957	Change absolute	Change relative	1959 potentially Orth. population
100	Crimea	51	49	-2	-1.7	1,147,604
50	Bashkiria [Bashkortostan]	39	41	2	1.3	1,522,533
51	Udmurt	29	29	0	0.0	766,291
52	Kurgan	13	13	0	0.0	938,885
53	Chkalov [Orenburg]	24	23	-1	-0.7	1,424,999
54	Molotov [Perm']	67	63	-4	-1.6	2,525,015
56	Sverdlovsk [Yekaterinburg]	33	33	0	0.0	3,688,204
57	Chelyabinsk	35	29	-6	-2.4	2,537,775
59	Altay	11	11	0	0.0	2,425,073
60	Kemerovo	14	14	0	0.0	2,520,490
61	Novosibirsk	7	7	0	0.0	2,130,890
62	Omsk	6	5	-1	-0.7	1,411,381
63	Tomsk	4	4	0	0.0	673,865
64	Tyumen'	15	15	0	0.0	911,651
67	Buryatia	2	2	0	0.0	512,751
68	Tuva	2	2	0	0.0	70,029
70	Krasnoyarsk	18	18	0	0.0	2,315,354
73	Irkutsk	15	14	-1	-0.6	1,782,292
74	Chita	3	2	-1	-1.0	963,281
75	Yakutia	2	2	0	0.0	230,058
76	Maritime	5	5	0	0.0	1,315,433
77	Khabarovsk	2	2	0	0.0	1,043,581
79	Amur	3	4	1	1.4	695,727
86	Ukraine	9176	8548	-628	-15.9	39,540,000
87	Moldova	565	546	-19	-26.6	714,000
88	Belarus	1040	968	-72	-9.8	7,324,000
89	Estonia	137	125	-12	-44.9	267,000
90	Latvia	131	123	-8	-12.4	647,000
91	Lithuania	60	55	-5	-17.9	279,000
92	Armenia	1	1	0	0.0	56,000
93	Azerbaijan	4	4	0	0.0	501,000
94	Georgia	56	46	-10	-21.7	460,000
95	Kazakhstan	55	60	5	1.0	4,843,000
96	Kyrgyzstan	33	32	-1	-1.3	761,000
97	Tajikistan	6	6	0	0.0	290,000
98	Turkmenistan	5	5	0	0.0	284,000
99	Uzbekistan	23	25	2	1.7	1,179,000
	Total	**14457**	**13381**	**-1076**	**-282.2**	**158,509,083**

Source: GARF f. 6991s, op. 2, d. 180, ll. 22-25; f. 6991s, op. 2, d. 263, l. 2.
Note: Units with no data available are excluded from this table.

Table A4.5. Density of registered communities of the Russian Orthodox Church by diocese, 1958-1994.

Map nos.	Diocese	Potent. Orth. pop-n 1959	Potent. Orth. pop-n 1989	Communities per 1 mln POP* 1.1.1958	Communities per 1 mln POP* 1.1.1966	Communities per 1 mln POP* 1.1.1986	Communities per 1 mln POP* 1.1.1991	Communities per 1 mln POP* 1.1.1994	Change per 1 mln POP* 1966/1958	Change per 1 mln POP* 1986/1966	Change per 1 mln POP* 1991/1986	Change per 1 mln POP* 1994/1991
1	Alma Ata	4843000	7306390	12.4	9.5	7.8	10.9	14.0	-2.9	2.3	3.1	3.0
2	Arkhangel'sk	2596607	3522135	12.7	8.9	6.0	14.2	17.9	-3.9	-0.8	8.2	3.7
3	Astrakhan'	550665	732272	29.1	30.9	23.2	41.0	49.2	1.8	0.0	17.8	8.2
4	Cheboksary	267529	357120	153.3	138.3	103.6	210.0	210.0	-15.0	0.0	106.4	0.0
5	Chelyabinsk	2537775	3039122	11.4	5.9	4.9	8.2	18.4	-5.5	0.0	3.3	10.2
6	Chernigov	1535899	1388668	234.4	104.2	79.2	141.9	201.6	-130.2	-32.6	62.6	59.8
7	Chernovtsy	569457	729161	635.7	463.6	353.8	493.7	507.4	-172.1	-10.5	139.9	13.7
8	Dnepropetrovsk	3992439	6391053	71.6	8.8	5.2	16.0	22.7	-62.9	-0.5	10.8	6.7
9	Gor'kiy [N. Novgorod]	3411305	3555492	14.1	13.5	12.7	33.8	25.3	-0.6	-0.3	21.1	-8.4
10	Irkutsk	4327393	6573327	4.2	3.7	2.6	4.6	7.6	-0.5	0.2	2.0	3.0
11	Ivano-Frankovsk	1075685	1399893	600.5	347.7	238.6	21.4	10.0	-252.9	-37.2	-217.2	-11.4
12	Ivanovo	1297973	1273361	43.1	33.9	34.6	62.8	104.4	-9.2	0.0	28.3	41.6
13	Izhevsk	766291	959383	37.8	23.5	18.8	36.5	37.5	-14.4	0.0	17.7	1.0
14	Kalinin [Tver]	1720036	1594911	52.9	31.4	30.7	62.7	97.2	-21.5	-2.9	32.0	34.5
15	Kaluga	921704	1037208	41.2	30.4	23.1	49.2	46.3	-10.8	-4.3	26.0	-2.9
16	Kazan'	1580764	1964156	19.6	15.2	13.2	25.5	42.8	-4.4	1.3	12.2	17.3
17	Khabarovsk	2359014	5588120	5.5	5.1	2.9	6.4	14.9	-0.4	1.7	3.6	8.4
18	Khar'kov	2411442	3070081	65.5	31.9	19.9	28.3	42.3	-33.6	-6.6	8.5	14.0
19	Khmel'nitskiy	1514448	1462767	259.5	92.4	94.3	272.1	341.8	-167.1	-1.3	177.7	69.7
20	Kiev (Kyiv)	4095705	5839000	142.1	52.7	31.2	62.0	36.0	-89.4	-8.3	30.8	-26.0
21	Kirov	1776563	1550564	45.0	19.1	20.6	80.6	78.7	-25.9	-1.1	60.0	-1.9
22	Kirovograd	2166164	1573830	117.7	51.2	50.8	88.3	133.4	-66.5	-14.3	37.5	45.1
23	Kishinev [Chisinau]	714000	1182043	764.7	312.3	167.5	549.9	549.9	-452.4	-35.0	382.4	0.0
24	Kostroma	905317	787234	88.4	78.4	81.3	123.2	123.2	-9.9	-7.7	41.9	0.0
25	Krasnodar	3530783	4841118	58.9	21.8	15.7	30.0	41.1	-37.1	-0.3	14.3	11.2
26	Kuybyshev [Samara]	1917561	2801891	9.9	9.4	6.4	17.1	12.1	-0.5	0.0	10.7	-5.0
27	Kursk	2691741	2680472	107.0	73.2	64.2	74.6	90.3	-33.8	-9.3	10.4	15.7
28	Leningrad [St. Petersburg]	4250191	6279217	13.4	10.6	7.0	13.7	31.7	-2.8	-0.2	6.7	18.0
29	L'vov	3065444	3812860	675.6	391.8	282.2	184.6	68.7	-283.8	-40.8	-97.6	-115.9
30	Minsk	7324000	9537730	132.0	57.8	38.8	64.0	89.1	-74.3	-7.2	25.2	25.2
31	Moscow	10340210	14743249	20.5	16.6	11.9	17.0	50.6	-3.9	0.3	5.1	33.6
32	Mukachevo Transcarpathia	716063	1026207	715.0	597.7	411.2	435.6	497.0	-117.3	-8.4	24.4	61.4
33	Novgorod	722680	732929	56.7	34.6	34.1	58.7	69.6	-22.1	0.0	24.6	10.9
34	Novosibirsk	10135701	1650215	5.5	3.3	23.0	44.2	106.7	-2.3	0.5	21.2	62.4

35 Odessa	2377961	164.8	60.6	35.9	73.8	97.9	-104.3	-9.7	38.0	24.0
36 Olonets	508242	11.8	7.9	7.5	16.5	40.6	-3.9	2.0	9.0	24.0
37 Omsk	2323032	8.6	5.2	5.9	19.4	29.3	-3.4	0.4	13.5	9.9
38 Orel	2446144	39.7	26.6	23.7	43.1	64.1	-13.1	-4.1	19.4	21.1
39 Orenburg	1424999	16.1	9.1	7.2	20.4	13.2	-7.0	-0.7	13.2	-7.2
40 Penza	1919652	31.3	24.0	24.2	47.4	92.2	-7.3	0.0	23.2	44.8
41 Perm'	2525015	25.0	16.2	15.2	29.3	29.3	-8.7	0.0	14.1	0.0
42 Poltava	1607897	162.9	38.6	30.1	50.4	75.4	-124.4	-6.2	20.3	24.9
43 Pskov	932132	114.8	97.6	104.2	127.2	218.1	-17.2	-5.4	23.0	90.9
44 Riga	647000	190.1	146.8	77.9	80.6	77.9	-43.3	-12.4	2.7	-2.7
45 Rostov-on-Don	3182075	66.9	22.9	15.8	27.6	49.2	-44.0	-2.8	11.8	21.7
46 Ryazan'	1428273	53.2	41.3	40.4	81.6	57.2	-11.9	-4.2	41.2	-24.4
47 Saratov	3703108	12.2	8.6	6.4	13.5	38.8	-3.5	-0.3	7.0	25.3
48 Simferopol	1147604	41.8	12.2	6.1	17.3	21.7	-29.6	0.0	11.3	4.3
49 Smolensk	1130337	47.8	33.6	32.8	54.9	100.9	-14.2	-0.9	22.1	46.0
50 Stavropol	3201277	49.4	32.5	25.8	63.7	63.7	-16.9	-0.9	38.0	0.0
51 Sumy	1498356	146.2	94.8	65.2	91.5	120.5	-51.4	-33.4	26.2	29.1
52 Sverdlovsk [Yekaterinburg]	4627089	9.9	6.5	6.0	18.6	20.9	-3.5	0.4	12.6	2.3
53 Tallin	267000	460.7	337.1	148.9	150.7	114.4	-123.6	-30.0	1.8	-36.3
54 Tambov	1538305	31.2	26.7	29.2	38.4	60.6	-4.6	-2.0	9.2	22.3
55 Tashkent	2514000	27.0	20.3	13.7	18.1	27.4	-6.8	-0.4	4.4	9.3
56 Tula	1876269	21.3	17.1	17.7	31.5	27.6	-4.3	0.0	13.8	-3.9
57 Ufa	1522533	26.9	12.5	10.5	24.6	59.1	-14.4	-1.3	14.2	34.5
58 Ulyanovsk	877483	21.7	13.7	8.7	30.0	67.7	-8.0	-3.4	21.3	37.7
59 Vilnyus	279000	197.1	154.1	90.6	110.5	181.3	-43.0	-7.2	19.9	70.7
60 Vinnitsa	2059929	290.3	169.9	142.2	228.3	326.1	-120.4	-40.8	86.1	97.8
61 Vladimir	1377936	47.2	39.2	31.7	61.6	46.6	-8.0	-2.2	29.9	-14.9
62 Vologda	1290365	13.2	13.2	12.8	18.8	44.4	0.0	0.0	6.0	25.6
63 Volyn'	1783037	444.2	274.3	206.5	363.0	508.2	-169.9	-19.1	156.6	145.2
64 Voronezh	3483495	31.9	23.0	20.5	39.5	41.1	-8.9	-1.4	18.9	1.6
65 Voroshilovgrad [Donetsk]	6424874	47.6	24.9	18.0	28.5	40.6	-22.7	-2.8	10.5	12.1
66 Yaroslavl'	1374023	104.1	62.6	54.4	73.9	139.4	-41.5	-5.8	19.5	65.5
67 Zhitomir	1448173	203.7	119.5	108.6	173.7	238.2	-84.2	-12.4	65.1	64.4
Total	157378164 185559191	85.2	47.4	36.3	54.5	69.1	-37.8	-4.6	18.2	14.6

Sources: Davis (1995: 33, 44, 54, 88, 111), *Tsentral'noe Statisticheskoe* (1975), Gosudarstvennyi Komitet (1991), the author's calculations.

Notes: Potentially OrthoĊox population (POP) here includes Russians, Ukrainians, and Belarusians.

*Density of communities in 1958 and 1966 is based on POP in 1959; density in 1986, 1991, and 1994 -- on POP in 1989.

Table A4.6. The ROCh' communities among all religious organizations in the Russian Federation, 1.1.1995.

M Region/ a civil division p	Relig. org., total	ROCh	% of Total	Popu-lation 1.1.1994	Total per 1 mln population	ROCh per 1 mln population
North	**315**	**185**	**58.73**	**6021.9**	**52.3**	**30.7**
1 Karelian republic	84	37	44.05	794.2	105.8	46.6
2 Komi republic	49	17	34.69	1228.1	39.9	13.8
3 Arkhangel'sk obl.	51	36	70.59	1497.1	34.1	24.0
4 Nenets AO	1	1	100	50.9	19.6	19.6
5 Vologda oblast'	89	75	84.27	1360.1	65.4	55.1
6 Murmansk oblast'	41	19	46.34	1091.5	37.6	17.4
Northwest	**659**	**427**	**64.8**	**8135.5**	**81.0**	**52.5**
7 Leningrad oblast'	168	100	59.52	1668.9	100.7	59.9
7a St.Petersburg city	247	119	48.18	4882.6	50.6	24.4
8 Novgorod oblast'	91	73	80.22	747.4	121.8	97.7
9 Pskov oblast'	153	135	88.24	836.6	182.9	161.4
Central	**3191**	**1848**	**57.91**	**30118**	**105.9**	**61.4**
10 Bryansk oblast'	145	118	81.38	1471.6	98.5	80.2
11 Vladimir oblast'	188	155	82.45	1648.3	114.1	94.0
12 Ivanovo oblast'	168	150	89.29	1300.4	129.2	115.3
13 Kaluga oblast'	60	41	68.33	1087.6	55.2	37.7
14 Kostroma oblast'	126	113	89.68	810.2	155.5	139.5
15 Moscow oblast'	680	560	82.35	6644	102.3	84.3
15a Moscow city	437	233	53.32	8792.9	49.7	26.5
16 Orel oblast'	71	51	71.83	913.2	77.7	55.8
17 Ryazan' oblast'	178	169	94.94	1336.9	133.1	126.4
18 Smolensk oblast'	97	76	78.35	1166.5	83.2	65.2
19 Tver' [Kalinin] ob.	189	162	85.71	1654.5	114.2	97.9
20 Tula oblast'	99	81	81.82	1832.3	54.0	44.2
21 Yaroslavl' oblast'	172	156	90.7	1459.8	117.8	106.9
Volga-Vyatka	**829**	**665**	**80.22**	**8463.5**	**98.0**	**78.6**
22 Mari-El (republic)	61	40	65.57	764.7	79.8	52.3
23 Mordvinian rep.	147	136	92.52	962.7	152.7	141.3
24 Chuvashia (rep.)	132	115	87.12	1359	97.1	84.6
25 Kirov oblast'	167	132	79.04	1694.4	98.6	77.9
26 N.Novgorod ob. [Gor'kiy]	322	242	75.16	3682.7	87.4	65.7
Central Chernozem	**710**	**589**	**82.96**	**7840.1**	**90.6**	**75.1**
27 Belgorod oblast'	161	127	78.88	1437.6	112.0	88.3
28 Voronezh oblast'	163	139	85.28	2498.5	65.2	55.6
29 Kursk oblast'	196	154	78.57	1343.8	145.9	114.6
30 Lipetsk oblast'	89	80	89.89	1245.5	71.5	64.2
31 Tambov oblast'	101	89	88.12	1314.7	76.8	67.7
Volga	**1542**	**666**	**43.19**	**16808**	**91.7**	**39.6**
32 Kalmyk republic	30	11	36.67	320.6	93.6	34.3
33 Tatarstan [rep.]	665	126	18.95	3743.6	177.6	33.7
34 Astrakhan' oblast'	61	33	54.1	1015.4	60.1	32.5
35 Volgograd oblast'	179	113	63.13	2674.3	66.9	42.3
36 Penza oblast'	153	110	71.9	1523.3	100.4	72.2
37 Samara ob. [Kuybyshev]	170	94	55.29	3322.4	51.2	28.3
38 Saratov oblast'	147	101	68.71	2728.4	53.9	37.0
39 Ul'yanovsk oblast'	137	78	56.93	1479.6	92.6	52.7
North Caucasus	**957**	**437**	**45.66**	**17518**	**54.6**	**24.9**

40 Adygey republic	34	13	38.24	449	75.7	29.0
41 Dagestan (republic)	818	7	0.86	1953	418.8	3.6
42 Chechnya						
43 Kabardino-Balkar rep.	97	12	12.37	785.8	123.4	15.3
44 Karachay-Cherkess r.	96	16	16.67	434.1	221.1	36.9
45 North Ossetian rep.	37	10	27.03	650.4	56.9	15.4
46 Ingushetia (republic)	6		0.00	1290	4.7	0.0
47 Krasnodar Kray	397	239	60.20	4939.5	80.4	48.4
48 Stavropol' Kray	162	76	46.91	2615.1	61.9	29.1
49 Rostov oblast'	162	84	51.85	4401.3	36.8	19.1
Ural	**1356**	**630**	**46.46**	**20421**	**66.4**	**30.9**
50 Bashkortostan (rep.)	460	96	20.87	4055.3	113.4	23.7
51 Udmurt republic	101	72	71.29	1640.7	61.6	43.9
52 Kurgan oblast'	70	41	58.57	1114.8	62.8	36.8
53 Orenburg oblast'	179	85	47.49	2234.7	80.1	38.0
54 Perm' oblast'	196	130	66.33	2931.2	66.9	44.4
55 Komi-Permyak AO				160.3	0.0	0.0
56 Sverdlovsk oblast'	234	144	61.54	4666.7	50.1	30.9
57 Chelyabinsk oblast'	116	62	53.45	3616.9	32.1	17.1
West Siberia	**400**	**235**	**58.75**	**15138**	**26.4**	**15.5**
58 [Gorno-] Altay rep.	17	13	76.47	198.3	85.7	65.6
59 Altay Kray	95	61	64.21	2686.4	35.4	22.7
60 Kemerovo oblast'	107	69	64.49	3157.9	33.9	21.8
61 Novosibirsk oblast'	78	48	61.54	2792.1	27.9	17.2
62 Omsk oblast'	103	44	42.72	2172.6	47.4	20.3
63 Tomsk oblast'	39	22	56.41	1000.6	39.0	22.0
64 Tyumen' oblast'	63	22	34.92	1348.8	46.7	16.3
65 Khanty-Mansi AO	27	19	70.37	1312.6	20.6	14.5
66 Yamal-Nenets AO	22	8	36.36	468.8	46.9	17.1
East Siberia	**321**	**122**	**38.01**	**9200.7**	**34.9**	**13.3**
67 Buryatia (republic)	56	17	30.36	1052.8	53.2	16.1
68 Tuva (republic)	16	3	18.75	306.3	52.2	9.8
69 Khakassia (republic)	16	3	18.75	584	27.4	5.1
70 Krasnoyarsk Kray	113	56	49.56	2956.7	38.2	18.9
71 Taymyr AO				49.2	0.0	0.0
72 Evenki AO				22.6	0.0	0.0
73 Irkutsk oblast'	89	34	38.20	2860.9	31.1	11.9
74 Chita oblast'	31	9	29.03	1368.2	22.7	6.6
Far East	**402**	**144**	**35.82**	**7788.3**	**51.6**	**18.5**
75 Sakha rep. [Yakutia]	41	9	21.95	1060.7	38.7	8.5
76 Maritime Kray	88	30	34.09	2286.9	38.5	13.1
77 Khabarovsk Kray	73	24	32.88	1608.2	45.4	14.9
78 Jewish AO	16	6	37.50	217.8	73.5	27.5
79 Amur oblast'	42	15	35.71	1056.7	39.7	14.2
80 Kamchatka oblast'	24	12	50.00	404	59.4	29.7
81 Koryak AO				35.4	0.0	0.0
82 Magadan oblast'	35	19	54.29	306.9	114.0	61.9
83 Chukchi AO	10	3	30.00	113.1	88.4	26.5
84 Sakhalin oblast'	73	26	35.62	698.6	104.5	37.2
85 Kaliningrad oblast'	**126**	**44**	**34.92**	**913.1**	**138.0**	**48.2**
TOTAL	*10808*	*5992*	**55.44**	*148366*	**72.8**	**40.4**

Note: Population is Total Present on Jan. 1, 1994.

Source: *Gosudarstvenno-Tserkovnye* (1996: 246-48), *Chislennost' Naseleniia* (1994: 3-5).

Table A4.7. Parishes of principal churches in Ukraine by oblast', 1.1.1993.

Map nos.	Oblast' / city	Population	UOCh-Moscow Patriar. number	per 1 mln	UOCh-Kievan Patriar. number	per 1 mln	Greek-Catholics number	per 1 mln
1	Cherkasy	1,531,800	194	126.65	7	4.57		
2	Chernihiv	1,398,000	232	165.95	17	12.16	1	0.72
3	Chernivtsi	940,000	335	356.38	68	72.34	9	9.57
4	Dnipropetrovs'k	3,918,600	124	31.64	5	1.28		
5	Donets'k	5,352,600	163	30.45	1	0.19	4	0.75
6	Ivano-Frankivs'k	1,451,500	18	12.40	377	259.73	608	418.88
7	Kharkiv	3,188,600	110	34.50	4	1.25		
8	Kherson	1,270,000	101	79.53	12	9.45	1	0.79
9	Khmel'nyts'kyi	1,521,500	521	342.43	33	21.69	3	1.97
10	Kyiv (Kiev)	1,948,000	226	116.02	67	34.39	1	0.51
26	*Kyiv (Kiev) city*	2,624,000	37	14.10	20	7.62	2	0.76
11	Kirovohrad	1,247,500	116	92.99	1	0.80		
12	Krym (Crimea)	2,235,000	73	32.66			2	0.89
27	*Sevastopol*	361,000	10	27.70	1	2.77	1	2.77
13	Luhans'k	2,877,400	120	41.70	1	0.35	1	0.35
14	L'viv	2,771,300	138	49.80	618	223.00	1288	464.76
15	Mykolaiv	1,350,800	89	65.89	22	16.29		
16	Odessa	2,634,500	252	95.65	3	1.14	1	0.38
17	Poltava	1,762,800	122	69.21	5	2.84		
18	Rivne	1,181,600	360	304.67	65	55.01	1	0.85
19	Sumy	1,430,700	166	116.03	2	1.40	1	0.70
20	Ternopil'	1,177,100	153	129.98	356	302.44	670	569.20
21	Transcarpathia	1,271,600	459	360.96			209	164.36
22	Vinnytsia	1,908,400	531	278.24	16	8.38	2	1.05
23	Volhynia	1,072,700	439	409.25	55	51.27	2	1.86
24	Zaporizhia	2,108,500	81	38.42	3	1.42		
25	Zhytomyr	1,503,700	320	212.81	4	2.66		
	Total	**52,039,200**	**5,490**	**105.50**	**1763**	**33.88**	**2807**	**53.94**

Source: Markus (1995: 175).
Notes: Sevastopol, Kyiv (Kiev) oblast', and Kyiv city population as of January 1, 1990.
UOCh-Moscow Patriar. stands for the Ukrainian Orthodox Church-Moscow Patriarchate;
UOCh-Kievan Patriar. -- the Ukrainian Orthodox Church-Kievan Patriarchate.

Table A4.8. Status of the ROCh's registered societies in republics of the USSR, 1944-89 (number and % of total).

Republic	1944	%	1948	%	1954	%	1958	%	1964	%	1969	%	1974	%	1979	%	1984	%	1989	%
RSFSR	2,785	22.5	3,205	22.3	2,922	21.8	2,920	21.9	1,995	26.3	1,906	26.1	1,874	26.5	1,865	26.9	1,866	27.4	2,519	24.9
Ukraine	7,040	56.9	9,061	62.9	8,517	63.7	8,468	63.5	4,587	60.5	4,468	61.3	4,291	60.8	4,175	60.3	4,049	59.5	6,110	60.4
Belarus	1,238	10.0	1,065	7.4	967	7.2	966	7.2	426	5.6	382	5.2	376	5.3	370	5.3	370	5.4	477	4.7
Moldova	924	7.5	617	4.3	544	4.1	544	4.1	223	2.9	219	3.0	204	2.9	199	2.9	199	2.9	675	6.7
Azerbaijan			4	0.0	4	0.0	4	0.0	4	0.1	4	0.1	4	0.1	4	0.1	4	0.1	4	0.0
Kazakhstan	17	0.1	55	0.4	54	0.4	60	0.5	46	0.6	46	0.6	45	0.6	49	0.7	57	0.8	71	0.7
Kyrgyzstan	11	0.1	33	0.2	32	0.2	32	0.2	22	0.3	21	0.3	21	0.3	21	0.3	21	0.3	23	0.2
Latvia	138	1.1	131	0.9	123	0.9	123	0.9	106	1.4	92	1.3	90	1.3	89	1.3	87	1.3	86	0.9
Lithuania	65	0.5	60	0.4	54	0.4	55	0.4	45	0.6	42	0.6	42	0.6	41	0.6	41	0.6	43	0.4
Tadjikistan	5	0.0	6	0.0	6	0.0	6	0.0	5	0.1	3	0.0	3	0.0	3	0.0	3	0.0	3	0.0
Turkmenistan	2	0.0	5	0.0	5	0.0	5	0.0	4	0.1	4	0.1	4	0.1	4	0.1	4	0.1	5	0.0
Uzbekistan	13	0.1	24	0.2	23	0.2	25	0.2	20	0.3	20	0.3	20	0.3	21	0.3	22	0.3	23	0.2
Estonia	125	1.0	137	1.0	125	0.9	125	0.9	94	1.2	87	1.2	88	1.2	84	1.2	83	1.2	77	0.8
USSR	12,363	100.0	14,403	100.0	13,376	100.0	13,333	100.0	7,577	100.0	7,294	100.0	7,062	100.0	6,925	100.0	6,806	100.0	10,116	100.0

Source: *Gosudarstvenno-Tserkovnye* (1996: 244), the author's calculations.

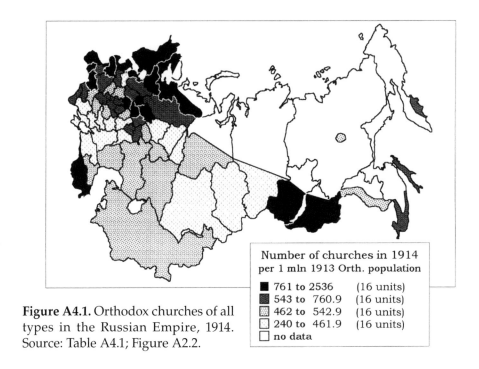

Figure A4.1. Orthodox churches of all types in the Russian Empire, 1914. Source: Table A4.1; Figure A2.2.

Number of churches in 1914 per 1 mln 1913 Orth. population

■ 761 to 2536   (16 units)
■ 543 to 760.9   (16 units)
▨ 462 to 542.9   (16 units)
□ 240 to 461.9   (16 units)
□ no data

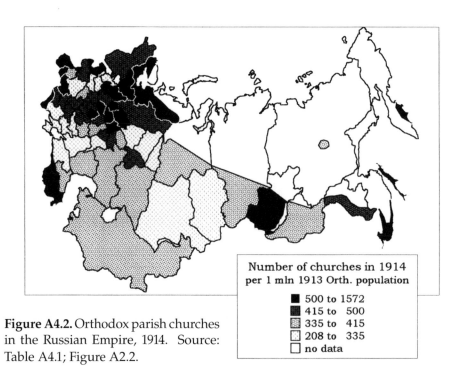

Number of churches in 1914 per 1 mln 1913 Orth. population

■ 500 to 1572
■ 415 to 500
▨ 335 to 415
□ 208 to 335
□ no data

Figure A4.2. Orthodox parish churches in the Russian Empire, 1914. Source: Table A4.1; Figure A2.2.

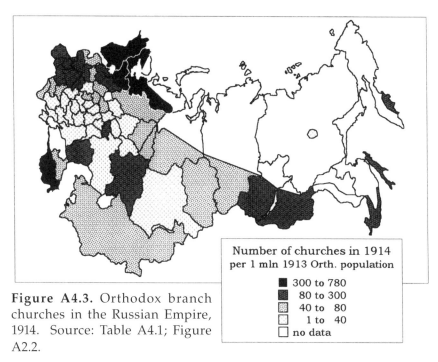

**Number of churches in 1914
per 1 mln 1913 Orth. population**

- 300 to 780
- 80 to 300
- 40 to 80
- 1 to 40
- no data

Figure A4.3. Orthodox branch churches in the Russian Empire, 1914. Source: Table A4.1; Figure A2.2.

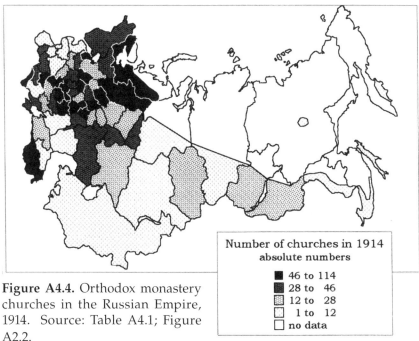

**Number of churches in 1914
absolute numbers**

- 46 to 114
- 28 to 46
- 12 to 28
- 1 to 12
- no data

Figure A4.4. Orthodox monastery churches in the Russian Empire, 1914. Source: Table A4.1; Figure A2.2.

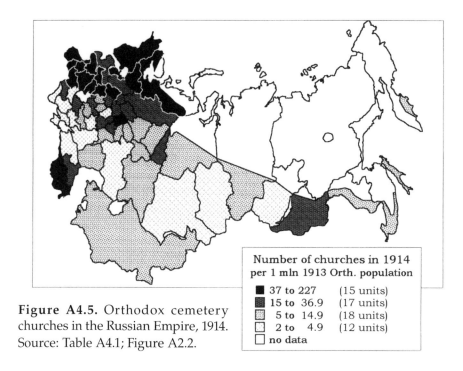

Figure A4.5. Orthodox cemetery churches in the Russian Empire, 1914. Source: Table A4.1; Figure A2.2.

Number of churches in 1914 per 1 mln 1913 Orth. population

- 37 to 227   (15 units)
- 15 to 36.9   (17 units)
- 5 to 14.9   (18 units)
- 2 to 4.9   (12 units)
- no data

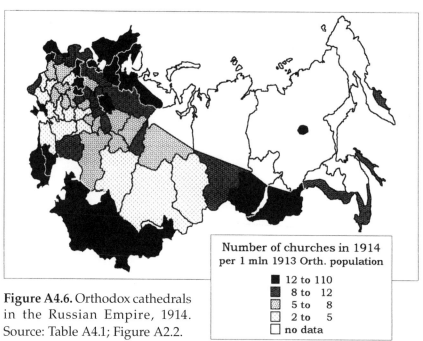

Figure A4.6. Orthodox cathedrals in the Russian Empire, 1914. Source: Table A4.1; Figure A2.2.

Number of churches in 1914 per 1 mln 1913 Orth. population

- 12 to 110
- 8 to 12
- 5 to   8
- 2 to   5
- no data

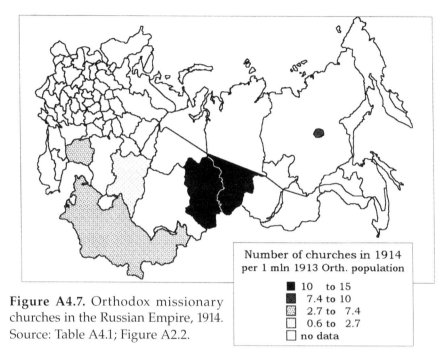

Figure A4.7. Orthodox missionary churches in the Russian Empire, 1914. Source: Table A4.1; Figure A2.2.

Number of churches in 1914
per 1 mln 1913 Orth. population

- ■ 10   to 15
- ■ 7.4 to 10
- ▨ 2.7 to 7.4
- ☐ 0.6 to 2.7
- ☐ no data

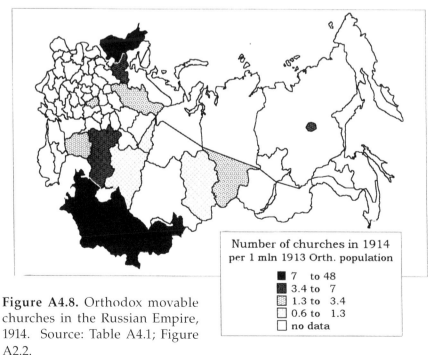

Figure A4.8. Orthodox movable churches in the Russian Empire, 1914. Source: Table A4.1; Figure A2.2.

Number of churches in 1914
per 1 mln 1913 Orth. population

- ■ 7   to 48
- ■ 3.4 to 7
- ▨ 1.3 to 3.4
- ☐ 0.6 to 1.3
- ☐ no data

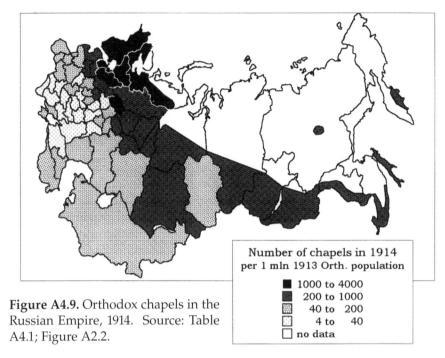

Figure A4.9. Orthodox chapels in the Russian Empire, 1914. Source: Table A4.1; Figure A2.2.

Number of chapels in 1914
per 1 mln 1913 Orth. population

- 1000 to 4000
- 200 to 1000
- 40 to 200
- 4 to 40
- no data

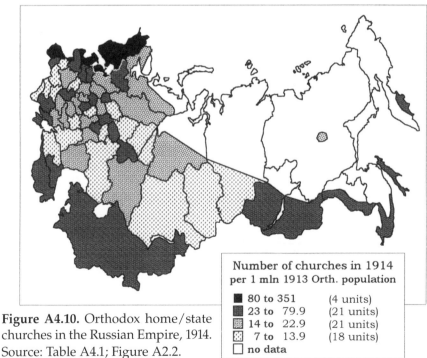

Figure A4.10. Orthodox home/state churches in the Russian Empire, 1914. Source: Table A4.1; Figure A2.2.

Number of churches in 1914
per 1 mln 1913 Orth. population

- 80 to 351 (4 units)
- 23 to 79.9 (21 units)
- 14 to 22.9 (21 units)
- 7 to 13.9 (18 units)
- no data

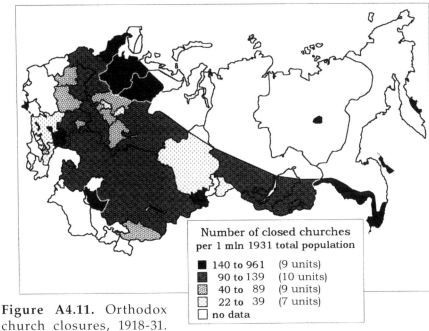

Number of closed churches
per 1 mln 1931 total population

■	140 to 961	(9 units)
▨	90 to 139	(10 units)
▨	40 to 89	(9 units)
▨	22 to 39	(7 units)
□	no data	

Figure A4.11. Orthodox church closures, 1918-31. Source: Table A4.2.

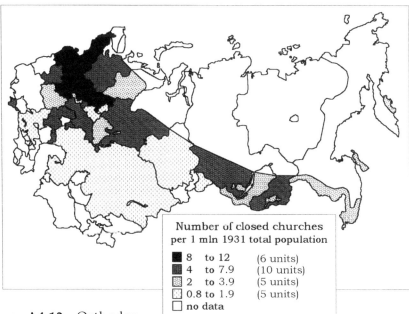

Number of closed churches
per 1 mln 1931 total population

■	8 to 12	(6 units)
▨	4 to 7.9	(10 units)
▨	2 to 3.9	(5 units)
▨	0.8 to 1.9	(5 units)
□	no data	

Figure A4.12. Orthodox church closures in the USSR, 1931-33. Source: Table A4.2.

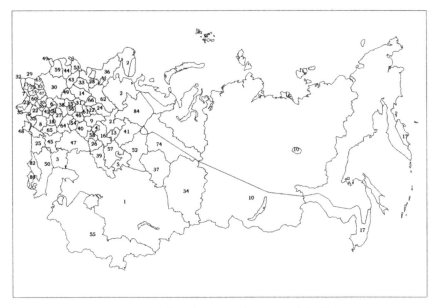

Figure A4.13. Orthodox diocesan division of the Russian Orthodox Church, 1950-80s. Source: Ellis (1986).

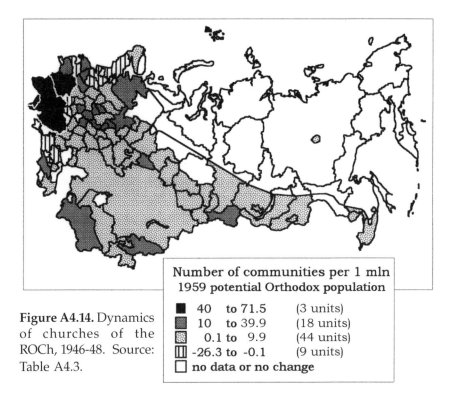

Figure A4.14. Dynamics of churches of the ROCh, 1946-48. Source: Table A4.3.

Number of communities per 1 mln
1959 potential Orthodox population

■	40 to 71.5	(3 units)
▨	10 to 39.9	(18 units)
▦	0.1 to 9.9	(44 units)
⦀	-26.3 to -0.1	(9 units)
☐	no data or no change	

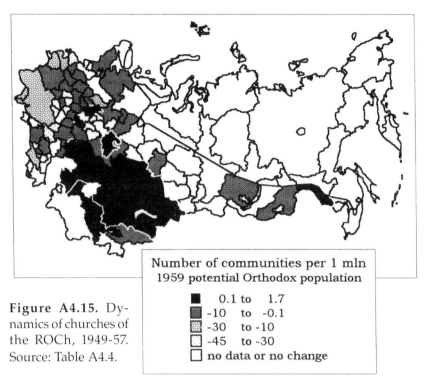

Figure A4.15. Dynamics of churches of the ROCh, 1949-57. Source: Table A4.4.

Number of communities per 1 mln 1959 potential Orthodox population

- 0.1 to 1.7
- -10 to -0.1
- -30 to -10
- -45 to -30
- no data or no change

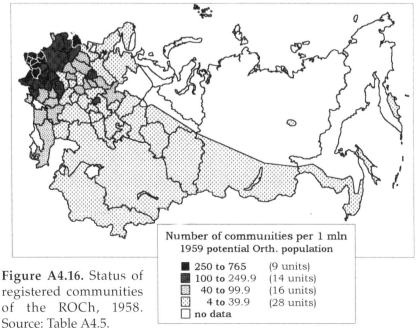

Figure A4.16. Status of registered communities of the ROCh, 1958. Source: Table A4.5.

Number of communities per 1 mln 1959 potential Orth. population

- 250 to 765 (9 units)
- 100 to 249.9 (14 units)
- 40 to 99.9 (16 units)
- 4 to 39.9 (28 units)
- no data

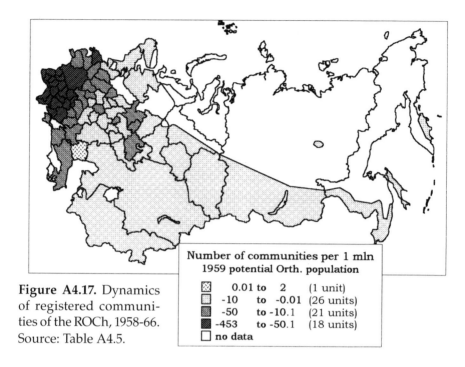

Figure A4.17. Dynamics of registered communities of the ROCh, 1958-66. Source: Table A4.5.

Number of communities per 1 mln 1959 potential Orth. population

0.01 to	2	(1 unit)
-10 to	-0.01	(26 units)
-50 to	-10.1	(21 units)
-453 to	-50.1	(18 units)
no data		

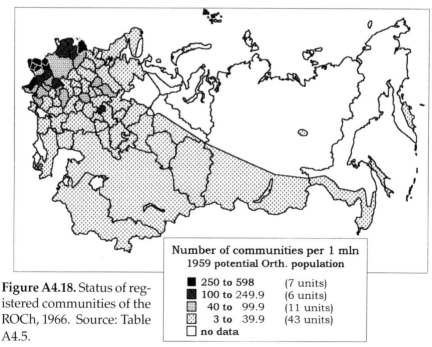

Figure A4.18. Status of registered communities of the ROCh, 1966. Source: Table A4.5.

Number of communities per 1 mln 1959 potential Orth. population

250 to 598	(7 units)
100 to 249.9	(6 units)
40 to 99.9	(11 units)
3 to 39.9	(43 units)
no data	

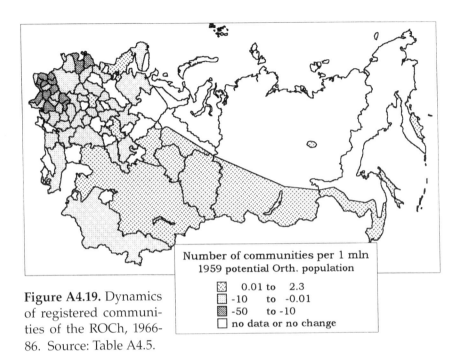

Number of communities per 1 mln 1959 potential Orth. population

▨	0.01 to 2.3
☐	-10 to -0.01
▧	-50 to -10
☐	no data or no change

Figure A4.19. Dynamics of registered communities of the ROCh, 1966-86. Source: Table A4.5.

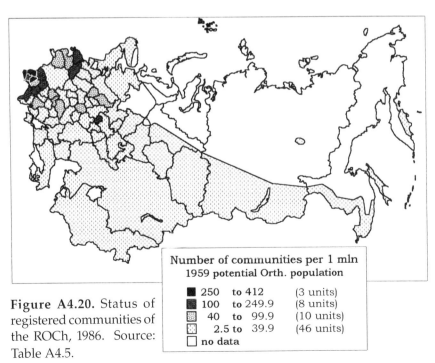

Number of communities per 1 mln 1959 potential Orth. population

■	250	to 412	(3 units)
■	100	to 249.9	(8 units)
▨	40	to 99.9	(10 units)
▧	2.5 to	39.9	(46 units)
☐	no data		

Figure A4.20. Status of registered communities of the ROCh, 1986. Source: Table A4.5.

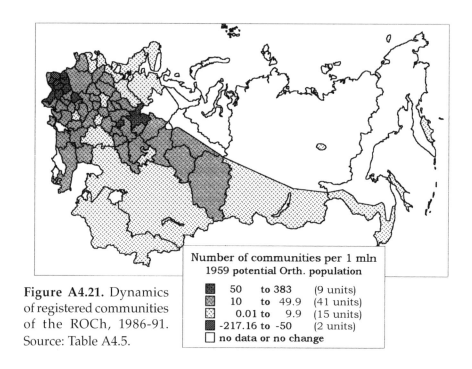

Figure A4.21. Dynamics
of registered communities
of the ROCh, 1986-91.
Source: Table A4.5.

**Number of communities per 1 mln
1959 potential Orth. population**

50 to 383	(9 units)
10 to 49.9	(41 units)
0.01 to 9.9	(15 units)
-217.16 to -50	(2 units)
no data or no change	

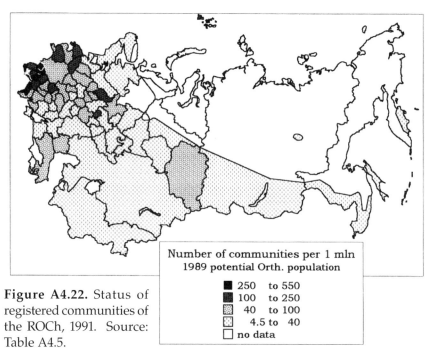

Figure A4.22. Status of
registered communities of
the ROCh, 1991. Source:
Table A4.5.

**Number of communities per 1 mln
1989 potential Orth. population**

250 to 550
100 to 250
40 to 100
4.5 to 40
no data

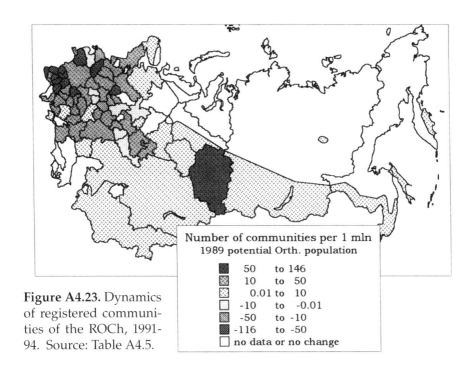

Figure A4.23. Dynamics of registered communities of the ROCh, 1991-94. Source: Table A4.5.

Number of communities per 1 mln
1989 potential Orth. population

	50	to 146
	10	to 50
	0.01 to 10
	-10	to -0.01
	-50	to -10
	-116	to -50
	no data or no change

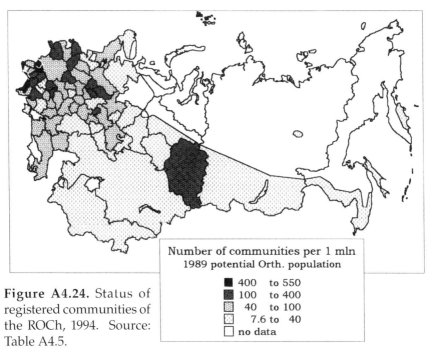

Figure A4.24. Status of registered communities of the ROCh, 1994. Source: Table A4.5.

Number of communities per 1 mln
1989 potential Orth. population

	400	to 550
	100	to 400
	40	to 100
	7.6 to 40
	no data

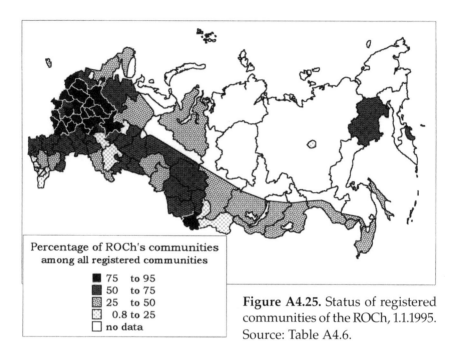

Percentage of ROCh's communities
among all registered communities

- 75 to 95
- 50 to 75
- 25 to 50
- 0.8 to 25
- no data

Figure A4.25. Status of registered communities of the ROCh, 1.1.1995. Source: Table A4.6.

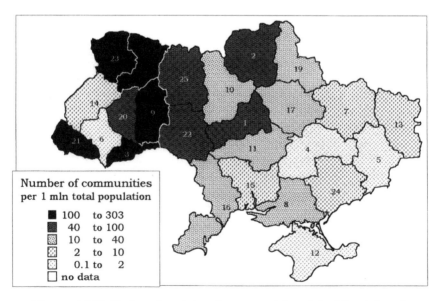

Number of communities
per 1 mln total population

- 100 to 303
- 40 to 100
- 10 to 40
- 2 to 10
- 0.1 to 2
- no data

Figure A4.26. Status of registered communities of the Ukrainian Orthodox Church-Moscow Patriarchate, 1.1.1993. Source: Table A4.7.

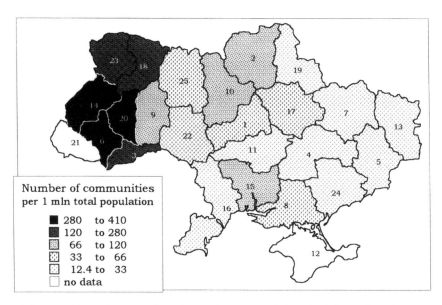

Figure A4.27. Status of registered communities the Ukrainian Orthodox Church-Kievan Patriarchate, 1.1.1993. Source: Table A4.7.

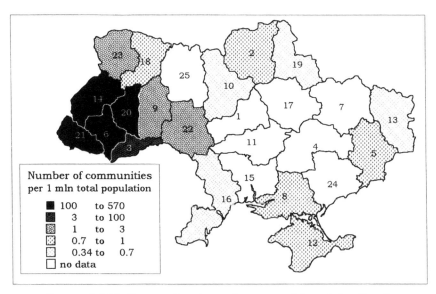

Figure A4.28. Status of registered communities of the Greek-
Catholic Church, 1.1.1993. Source: Table A4.7.

Table A5.1. The Catacomb Orthodox Church's adherents in the USSR, 1.1.1962.

Map nos.	File (delo) nos.	Division	Number of comm-unities	members	Potentially Orthodox po-pulation, 1959	Per 1 mln 1959 potentially Orthodox population communities	members
1	279	Alma-Ata	1	12	790,409	1.3	164.5
2	321	Altay	1	15	2,425,073	2.1	42.9
3	331	Belgorod	2	55	1,219,747	8.2	125.4
4	423	Cherkassy	1	15	1,479,978	4.1	35.1
5	424	Chernigov	1	130	1,535,899	4.6	85.9
6	373	Chita	3	65	963,281	2.1	11.4
7	320	Chuvash	2	68	267,529	18.7	119.6
8	409	Crimea	2	476	1,147,604	0.9	26.1
9	398	Donetsk	3	80	4,032,664	0.2	1.7
10	279	Eastern Kazakh	7	75	543,084	5.5	119.7
11	276	Georgia	5	101	460,000	2.2	32.6
12	270	Gomel'	8	83	1,304,133	0.8	11.5
13	337	Gor'kiy	3	28	3,411,305	0.9	24.6
14	326	Karachaevo-Cherkess	5	32	92,480	0.0	800.2
15	280	Karaganda	5	104	599,701	3.3	113.4
16	420	Khar'kov	2	18	2,411,442	0.8	7.5
17	422	Khmel'nitskiy	15	420	1,514,448	0.7	9.2
18	408	Kirovograd		74	1,191,531	1.7	36.9
19	307	Komi	10	153	492,466	14.2	152.3
20	322	Krasnodar	3	50	3,530,783	0.6	5.1
21	348	Kurgan	14	277	938,885	9.6	136.3
22	347	Kuybyshev	3	84	1,917,561	2.1	23.5
23	350	Leningrad	4	45	4,250,191	0.7	11.8
24	351	Lipetsk	9	128	1,134,171	2.6	35.3
25	308	Mari	3	50	312,252	16.0	323.5
26	274	Minsk	3	40	459,522	4.4	119.7
27	355	Novosibirsk	2	25	2,130,890	0.9	11.7
28	414	Odessa	2	77	1,699,788	4.1	35.3
29	358	Orel	3	53	922,724	3.3	57.4
30	357	Orenburg	7	116	1,424,999	1.4	54.0
31	359	Penza	7	127	1,322,541	5.3	87.7
32	360	Perm'	4	45	2,525,015	2.8	50.3
33	362	Rostov	8	308	3,182,075	1.3	14.1
34	363	Ryazan'	2	18	1,428,273	5.6	215.6
35	364	Saratov	1	10	2,011,893	1.0	8.9
36	280	Southern Kazakh	16	406	517,391	3.9	920.0
37	325	Stavropol'	12	385	1,650,274	9.1	254.5
38	365	Sverdlovsk	8	112	3,688,204	0.3	2.7
39	367	Tambov	2	11	1,538,305	10.4	263.9
40	316	Tatar	1	50	1,268,512	6.3	65.4
41	368	Tomsk	1	7	673,865	17.8	571.3
42	282	Tselinograd	1	16	348,731	8.6	229.4
43	370	Tyumen'	2	44	911,651	8.8	122.9
44	318	Udmurt	1	30	766,291	3.9	36.5
45	395	Vinnitsa	7	60	2,059,929	0.5	24.3
46	269	Vitebsk	2	18	1,167,002	0.9	10.3
47	334	Volgograd	1	14	1,691,215	1.8	29.6
48	336	Voronezh	6	52	2,349,324	6.0	117.9
49	399	Zhitomir	7	132	1,448,173	0.7	11.0
		TOTAL	**218**	**4794**	**75,943,613**	**2.9**	**63.1**

Sources: GARF f. 6991 op. 4, file numbers are in the table; Tsentral'noe Statisticheskoe (1975).

Table A5.2. Parishes of the True and Free/Foreign Orthodox Churches in the Russian Federation, 1.1.1996.

Map Unit nos.	True Orthodox Church	Free/Foreign Church	Present population (PP), thousand	per 1 mln PP True Orthodox Church	per 1 mln PP Free/Foreign Church
North	**1**	**2**	**5,889.10**	**0.017**	**0.34**
1 Karelia	1	1	785	1.27	1.27
6 Murmansk		1	1,048		0.95
Northwest		**3**	**8,052.30**		**0.037**
7a St. Petersburg city		1	4,801.50		0.21
7 Leningrad Oblast'		1	1,675.90		0.60
9 Pskov Oblas'		1	832.3		1.20
Central	**12**	**34**	**29,883**	**0.4**	**1.14**
10 Bryansk Oblast'			1,479.70		0.68
11 Vladimir Oblast'		12	1,644.70		7.3
13 Kaluga Oblast'		1	1,097.30		0.91
14 Kostroma Oblast'	1		805.7	1.24	
15a Moscow city	3	14	8,664.40	0.35	1.62
15 Moscow Oblast'	7	2	6,596.60	1.06	0.3
17 Ryazan' Oblast'			1,325.30		0.75
19 Tver' Oblast'			1,650.60		0.61
20 Tula Oblast'	1	1	1,814.50	0.55	0.55
21 Yaroslavl' Oblast'		1	1,451.40		0.69
Volga-Vyatka	**1**	**3**	**8,443.80**	**0.13**	**0.36**
25 Kirov Oblast'	1	1	1,634.50	0.68	0.61
26 N. Novgorod Obl.		2	3,726.40		0.54
Central Chernozem	**1**	**9**	**7,880.60**	**0.13**	**1.14**
27 Belgorod Oblast'	1	5	1,469.10	0.68	3.4
29 Kursk Oblast'		3	1,346.90		2.23
31 Tambov Oblast'		1	1,250.20		0.8
Volga		**14**	**16,920.10**		**0.83**
33 Tatarstan (republic)		3	3,760.50		0.8
34 Astrakhan' Oblast'		1	1,028.90		0.97
35 Volgograd Oblast'		7	2,703.70		2.59
36 Penza Oblast'		2	1,562.30		1.28
38 Saratov Oblast'		1	2,739.50		0.37
North Caucasus	**2**	**13**	**17,737.90**	**0.11**	**0.73**
47 Krasnodar Kray		4	5,043.90		0.79
48 Stavropol' Kray	1	3	2,667	0.37	1.12
49 Rostov Oblast'	1	6	4,425.40	0.23	1.36
Ural	**6**	**9**	**20,460.90**	**0.29**	**0.44**
52 Kurgan Oblast'	4	3	1,112.20	3.6	2.7
53 Orenburg Oblast'		1	2,228.60		0.45
54 Perm' Oblast'		4	3,009.40		1.33
56 Sverdlovsk Oblast'	1		4,686.30	0.21	
57 Chelyabinsk Oblast'	1	1	3,688.70	0.27	0.27
West Siberia	**2**	**5**	**15,127.70**	**0.13**	**0.33**
59 Altay Kray	1		2,690.10	0.37	
60 Kemerovo Oblast'	1		3,063.50	0.33	
62 Omsk Oblast'		1	2,176.40		0.46
63 Tomsk Oblast'		2	1,077.60		1.86
64 Tyumen' Oblast'		2	3,169.90		0.63
East Siberia			**9,144.10**		
Far East	**1**	**1**	**7,504.70**	**0.13**	**0.13**
76 Maritime Kray	1	1	2,255.40	0.44	0.44
82 Magadan Oblast'	1		258.2	3.87	
85 Kaliningrad Oblast'		4	932.2		4.29
TOTAL	**13**	**59.5**	**147,976.4**	**0.17**	**0.66**
Diocesan centers	1	3			

Source: The Russiar Federation's Ministry of Justice, unpub. data; Goskomstat Rossii (1996).

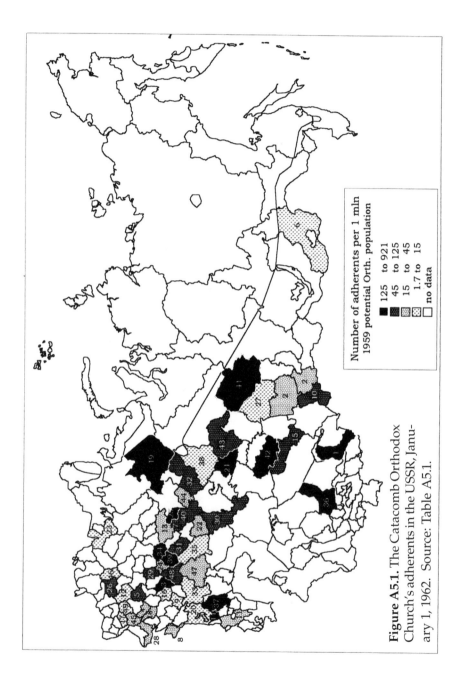

Figure A5.1. The Catacomb Orthodox Church's adherents in the USSR, January 1, 1962. Source: Table A5.1.

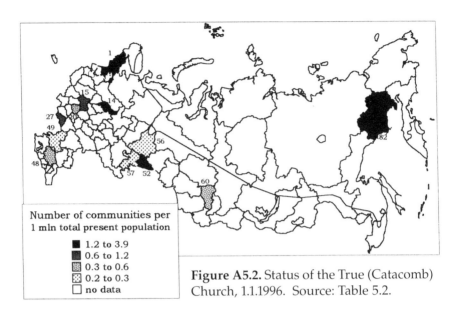

Figure A5.2. Status of the True (Catacomb) Church, 1.1.1996. Source: Table 5.2.

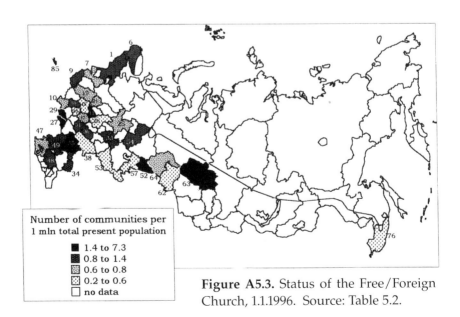

Figure A5.3. Status of the Free/Foreign Church, 1.1.1996. Source: Table 5.2.

Table A6.1. Registration of communities of religious organizations in Moscow, 1991-94.

Nos.	Religious Organization	Communities' Registrations				
		1991	1992	1993	1994	Total
1	Russian Orthodox Church	138	97	43	30	308
	Old Believers Churches [Nos.2-4]	3	6	2	1	12
2	Russian Orthodox Old Belief Church	3	2		1	6
3	Ancient Orthodox Church		2		1	3
4	Ancient Orthodox Pomor Church		1			1
5	Edinoverie Church	1				1
	Free Orth. Russ.-State Church (foreign) [6-7]	3	5	1	3	12
6	Free Orthodox Russian-State Church		3	2	1	6
7	Orthodox Russian-State Church Abroad	2	1		1	4
8	True Russian Orthodox (Catacomb) Church		4			4
9	Ukrainian Orthodox Church–Kievan Patriarchate			1	1	2
10	Catholic Orthodoxy		2			2
11	Independent Orthodox communities		1		1	2
12	Valaam Society of America, branch		1			1
13	Bulgarian Orthodox Church, podvor'e		1			1
14	Armenian Apostolic Church	1	2			3
15	Apostolic Catholic Assirian Church "Orient"		1			1
16	God's Mother's Brotherhood		1			1
17	God's Mother's Society		1			1
18	Roman-Catholics	8	2	1		11
19	Muslims	2	3	6	5	16
	Buddhists [20-21]	4	1	4	3	12
20	Lamaism	3	2	2		7
21	Other Buddhists	1		2		3
	Judaism [22-23]	5	3	3		11
22	Reform Judaism (Hasidim)	1				1
23	Orthodox Judaism (Siphardim)		1			1
24	Methodist Church	2	2	5	2	11
	Lutheran Churches [25-28]	2	4	1		7
25	Evangelic-Lutheran Church		1			1
26	United Evangelic-Lutheran Churches of Russia	1				2
27	Finnish parish	1				1
28	Latvian parish	1				1
29	Evangelical Christians-Baptists	13	5	10	6	34
30	Seventh-Day Adventists	1	3	6	2	12
31	Pentecostals	2	7	5	7	21
32	Charismatic Churches		4	3	1	8
33	Church of Christ		2	1		3
34	New Apostolic Church	3			1	4
35	Full Evangelics			3	3	6
36	Evangelical Christians in Spirit of Apostles		1			2
37	Evangelical Christians	5	7	8	11	31
	Evangelical Christians-abstainers	1				1
38	Evangelical Church		2	1	2	5
39	Evangelical Free Church		1			1
40	Jehovah's Witnesses		1	1		2
41	Presbyterian Church	7	10	26	11	54
42	Disciples of Bahai Faith	1	1			2
43	Krishnaits	1	5	2		8
44	Pagan Beliefs (ethno-confessional)				1	1
45	Mormons (Christ's St. Latter Days Church.)			1		1
46	Mennonites		1			1
47	Church of England		1			1
48	Church of Unification			1		1
49	Salvation Army		1			1
50	Spiritual Christians-Molokans	2				2
51	Tantrism		1			1
52	Daocism		1		2	3
53	Scientological Church				1	1
54	Tolstoians	1				1
55	Church of God		1			1
56	Knowledge of Truth AUM [Sinriko]				1	1
57	Church Khaydakandi Samage (Santana Dharma)				1	1
	Non-confessional societies					
58	Interconfessional missions	1	21	15	2	39
59	Church of the Moscow Christian Center		1			1
60	Moscow Christian Church		1			1
61	God's Grace Church [Korean protestant]			1		1
62	Local Church of Love "Agape"				1	1
	Total (sum)	184	136	90	54	464

Source: Moscow Mayor's Committee on Relationships with Religious Organizations, unpub. data.

Table A6.2. Types of registered religious organizations in Moscow in 1991-1994

Religious Organization	Societies/ communities					Centers/ unions				Brother/ sisterhoods			
	91	92	93	94	Sum	92	93	94	Sum	92	93	94	Sum
Russian Orthodox Church	116	69	14	9	208	3			10	10	12	9	44
Old Believers Churches	**2**	**3**		**1**	**6**	**2**			**3**		**1**		**1**
Russian Orthodox Old Belief Church	2	2		1	5				1				
Ancient Orthodox Church		1			1	1			1		1		1
Ancient Orthodox Pomor Church						1			1				
Edinoverie Church	1				1								
Free Orth.Russian-State Ch. (foreign)	**3**	**4**		**3**	**10**					**1**	**1**		**2**
Free Orth. Russian Church	1	3		2	6								
Orthodox Russian-State Church Abroad	2	1		1	4					1	1		2
True Russ. Orth. (Catacomb) Church		3			3	1			1				
Ukrainian Orth.Church-Kievan Patriarchate													
Catholic Orthodoxy			2		2								
Independent Orthodox communities			1	1	2								
Valaam Society of America, branch													
Bulgarian Orthodox Church, podvor'e													
Armenian Apostolic Church			2		2				1				
Apostolic Catholic Assirian Church "Orient"			1		1								
God's Mother's Brotherhood										1			1
God's Mother's Society		1			1								
Roman-Catholics	6	1			7				1				
Muslims	1	1	4	3	9	1		1	3				
Buddhists	**4**		**4**	**2**	**10**	**1**		**1**	**2**				
Lamaism													
Other Buddhists													
Judaism	**4**		**1**		**5**		**1**		**1**				
Reform Judaism (Hasidim)	1				1								
Orthodox Judaism (Siphardim)			1		1								
Methodist Church	2	2	5	1	10			1	1				
Lutheran Churches	**1**	**3**			**4**		**1**		**1**				
Evangelic-Lutheran Church							1		1				
United Ev.-Lutheran Churches of Russia	1	1			2								
Finnish parish		1			1								
Latvian parish		1			1								
Evangelical Christians-Baptists	7	3	4	4	18		1	1	6		1		1
Seventh-Day' Adventists	1	3	5	2	11								
Pentecostals		3	4	3	10			2	3				
Charismatic Churches		4	1	1	6		2		2				
Church of Christ		1	1		2								
New Apostolic Church	1		1		2				2				
Full Evangelics			1	3	4		1		1				
Ev.Christ-s in Spirit of Apostles	1	1			2								
Evangelical Christians	3	3	5	6	17	1		2	4				
Ev. Christians-abstainers									1				
Evangelical Church		1	1	2	4								
Evangelical Free Church		1			1								
Jehovah's Witnesses			1		1				1				
Presbyterian Church	6	10	23	11	50		1		1				
Disciples of Bahai Faith	1				1	1			1				
Krishnaits	1	4	1		6	1			1				
Pagan Beliefs (ethno-confessional)				1	1								
Mormons (Christ's St. Latter Days Church.)													
Mennonites													
Church of England			1		1								
Church of Unification													
Salvation Army													
Spiritual Christians-Molokans	1				1				1				
Tantrism		1			1								
Daocism		1			1								
Scientological Church				1	1								
Tolstoians													
Church of God													
Knowledge of Truth AUM [Sinriko]				1	1								
Church Khaydakandi Samage (Santana Dharma)				1	1								
Non-denominational societies													
Interdenominational missions													
Church of the Moscow Christian Center													
Moscow Christian Church													
God's Grace Church [Korean protestant]													
Local Church of Love "Agape"													
Total (sum)	162	123	83	56	424	11	7	8	49	12	14	10	49

Religious Organization	Missions					Seminaries/ schools					Podvor'ia (townhouses)					Monasteries/ nunneries				
	91	92	93	94	Sum	91	92	93	94	Sum	91	92	93	94	Sum	91	92	93	94	Sum
Russian Orthodox Church	1				1	1				1	12	15	11		38	2	1	2	1	6
Old Believers Churches						1	1			2										
Russian Orthodox Old Belief Church																				
Ancient Orthodox Church																				
Ancient Orthodox Pomor Church																				
Edinoverie Church																				
Free Orth. Russian-State Ch. (foreign)																				
Free Orthodox Russian-State Church																				
Orthodox Russian-State Church Abroad																				
True Russ. Orth. (Catacomb) Church																				
Ukrainian Orth.Church-Kievan Patriarchate		1	1		2															
Catholic Orthodoxy																				
Independent Orthodox communities																				
Valaam Society of America, branch		1			1															
Bulgarian Orthodox Church, podvor'e												1		1						
Armenian Apostolic Church																				
Apostolic Catholic Assirian Church "Orient"																				
God's Mother's Brotherhood																				
God's Mother's Society																				
Roman-Catholics						1		1		2						1				1
Muslims		1	2		3				1	1										
Buddhists																				
Lamaism																				
Other Buddhists																				
Judaism		1	1		2	1	2			3										
Reform Judaism (Hasidim)																				
Orthodox Judaism (Siphardim)																				
Methodist Church																				
Lutheran Churches																				
Evangelic-Lutheran Church																				
United Ev.-Lutheran Churches of Russia																				
Finnish parish																				
Latvian parish																				
Evangelical Christians-Baptists	2	2	4		8		1			1										
Seventh-Day' Adventists			1		1															
Pentecostals	1	3	1	2	7	1				1										
Charismatic Churches																				
Church of Christ		1			1															
New Apostolic Church																				
Full Evangelics			1		1															
Ev.Christ-s in Spirit of Apostles																				
Evangelical Christians	1	3	3	3	10															
Ev. Christians-abstainers																				
Evangelical Church		1			1															
Evangelical Free Church																				
Jehovah's Witnesses																				
Presbyterian Church	1		2		3															
Disciples of Bahai Faith																				
Krishnaits							1			1										
Pagan Beliefs (ethno-confessional)																				
Mormons (Christ's St. Latter Days Church.)																				
Mennonites			1		1															
Church of England																				
Church of Unification																				
Salvation Army																				
Spiritual Christians-Molokans																				
Tantrism																				
Daocism			2		2															
Scientological Church																				
Tolstoians																				
Church of God																				
Knowledge of Truth AUM [Sinriko]																				
Church Khaydakandi Samage (Santana Dharma)																				
Non-denominational societies																				
Interdenominational missions	1	21	15	2	39															
Church of the Moscow Christian Center																				
Moscow Christian Church																				
God's Grace Church [Korean protestant]																				
Local Church of Love "Agafe"																				
Total (sum)	6	34	33	10	83	2	5	4	1	12	0	12	16	11	39	2	2	2	1	7

Source: Moscow Mayor's Committee on Relationships with Religious Organizations, unpublished data.

Table A6.3. Registered religious organizations in Moscow oblast', May 15, 1994 (number per 1 million total population)

Map nos.	Rayons and cities	Present popul-n, 1.1.1994 mln	ROCh all	Old Believers all	Catacomb Chur.	Rus. Orth. Independ	Judaism	Islam	Buddhists	Protestants all	Evang. Christ. Baptist	Evan. Faith Christians	Evan. Christians ntists	7th Day Adventists	Charism L	Methodism	"Emmanuil" Faith ists	Chur. of Christians	Presbyterians	Total
1	Balashikha	0.1676	41.77				5.97	5.97		23.87	11.93						5.97			77.57
44	Zheleznodorozhnyy city	0.1045	9.57							9.57	9.57									19.14
45	Reutov city	0.0696	14.37																	14.37
2	Volokolamsk	0.0548	109.49		18.25															145.99
3	Voskresensk	0.1577	88.78							6.34	6.34									95.12
4	Dmitrov	0.1545	135.92							12.94	12.94									155.34
5	Domodedovsk	0.1237	194.02							16.17	8.08	8.08								210.19
6	Egor'evsk	0.1063	103.48	18.81			9.41	9.41												141.11
7	Zaraysk	0.0449	89.09																	89.09
8	Istra	0.1245	128.51							32.13	32.13									176.71
9	Kashira	0.0785	140.13		25.48															165.61
10	Klin	0.1405	163.70							14.23	14.23									177.94
11	Kolomna	0.0434	207.37																	253.46
46	Kolomna city	0.1621	18.51	6.17						6.17	6.17									30.85
12	Krasnogorsk	0.1139	79.02							17.56	17.56									96.58
47	Krasnoarmeysk city	0.0272	36.76							36.76	36.76									73.53
13	Leninsk	0.1297	107.94							7.71	7.71									131.07
14	Lotoshino	0.0186	107.53																	107.53
15	Lukhovitsk	0.065	200.00							15.38	15.38									215.38
16	Lubertsy	0.3032	23.09	3.30	3.30	3.30		3.30		16.49	9.89			3.30					3.30	52.77
48	Lytkarino city	0.0511	19.57																	19.57
17	Mozhaysk	0.0721	97.09							13.87	13.87									138.70
18	Mytischi	0.1882	69.08		5.31					26.57	10.63			5.31		5.31	5.31			100.96
49	Dolgoprudnyy city	0.0761	39.42																	39.42
50	Lobnya city	0.0605	16.53																	16.53
19	Naro-Fominsk	0.1727	57.90	5.79						5.79	5.79									69.48
20	Noginsk	0.2392	87.79	4.18						12.54	8.36							4.18		104.52
21	Odintsovo	0.258	81.40							11.63	11.63									93.02
51	Zvenigorod city	0.0187	106.95							53.48	53.48									160.43

No.	Name	Weight	1	2	3	4	5	6	7	8	9	10	11	12	13	14	15	16	Total
22	Ozery	0.04	25.00	25.00															100.00
23	Orekhovo-Zuevo	0.1292	75.00	77.40	23.22														100.62
52	*Orekhovo-Zuevo city*	0.1336	7.49	7.49	14.97	14.97													29.94
24	Pavlov Posad	0.109	82.57	18.35	9.17	9.17													119.27
25	Podol'sk	0.0751	253.00	26.63															279.63
53	*Podol'sk city*	0.2041	4.90	4.90	19.60	4.90	4.90	4.90											34.30
54	*Klimovsk city*	0.0566	0.00																0.00
55	*Troitsk city*	0.0306	32.68	32.68															65.36
56	*Scherbinka city*	0.0291	34.36																34.36
26	Pushkinsk	0.1923	67.60	5.20	15.60	10.40	5.20												88.40
57	*Ivanteevka city*	0.0518	38.61																38.61
27	Ramenki	0.2224	112.41	4.50	8.99	4.50	4.50												125.90
58	*Bronnitsy city*	0.0166	60.24																60.24
28	Ruza	0.0689	116.11	14.51	14.51														130.62
29	Sergiev Posad	0.2375	130.53	4.21	4.21														143.16
30	Serebryanye Prudy	0.025	80.00																80.00
31	Serpukhov	0.035	200.00	57.14	28.57	28.57													285.71
59	*Serpukhov city*	0.1391	7.19	7.19	28.76	14.38	7.19												43.13
60	*Puschino city*	0.0206	48.54																48.54
61	*Protvino city*	0.0365	27.40																27.40
32	Solnechnogorsk	0.1282	85.80	7.80	7.80														93.60
33	Stupino	0.122	409.84	8.20	24.59	8.20	8.20	8.20											450.82
34	Taldom	0.0518	154.44	57.92	19.31	38.61													212.36
35	Khimki	0.1727	17.37	11.58	11.58														28.95
36	Chekhov	0.0981	132.52	20.39	10.19	10.19													152.91
37	Shatura	0.0983	61.04	20.35	10.17	10.17													81.38
38	Shakhovskoy	0.024	125.00																125.00
39	Schelkovo	0.2078	91.43																91.43
62	*Fryazino city*	0.0536	0.00																0.00
40	*Dubna city*	0.0674	44.51	29.67	14.84	14.84													74.18
41	*Zhukovskiy city*	0.1	10.00	10.00	10.00	10.00													30.00
42	*Kaliningrad city*	0.1891	10.58																10.58
43	*Elektrostal' city*	0.151	6.62	6.62	6.62														13.25
	Total	**6.6438**	80.23	2.11	1.81	0.15	0.30	0.45	0.15	11.89	7.68	1.51	0.30	1.20	0.60	0.15	0.15	0.15	99.34

Sources: the Committee on Relationship with Religious Organizations of Moscow Oblast; unpub. data; *Sotsial'no-Ekonomicheskoe* (1994: 27-37).

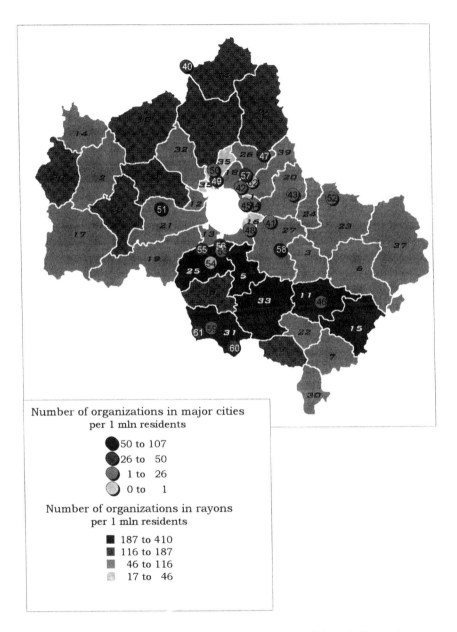

Number of organizations in major cities
per 1 mln residents

- 50 to 107
- 26 to 50
- 1 to 26
- 0 to 1

Number of organizations in rayons
per 1 mln residents

- 187 to 410
- 116 to 187
- 46 to 116
- 17 to 46

Figure A6.1. Status of registered organizations of the ROCh in Moscow oblast, Jan. 1, 1995. Source: Table A7.3, Sidorov (1998: 161).

REFERENCES

The following is a list of cited works only. Unless specified, all works with translated titles are in Russian. All Russian-language periodicals, unless specified, are published in Moscow.

Adams, P. 1996. Protest and the Scale Politics of Telecommunications. *Political Geography* 15:419-41.

Administrativno-Territorial'noe Delenie Soiuza SSR (raiony i goroda SSSR) [Administrative-Territorial Division of the Union of the SSRs (districts and cities of the USSR)]. 1931. Moscow: PrezidiumVTsIK.

Agnew, J. 1987. *Place and Politics: The Geographical Mediation of State and Society.* Boston: Allen and Unwin.

___. 1993. Representing Space - Space, Scale and Culture in Social Science. In *Place/Culture/Representation*, ed. J. Duncan and D. Ley, pp. 251-71. London and New York: Routledge.

Agnew, J., and S. Corbridge. 1995. *Mastering Space: Hegemony, Territory and International Political Economy.* London and New York: Routledge.

Aksenov, S. 1994. Chuzhoi Monastyr' so Svoim Zaborom [Alien Monastery with Its Own Wall]. *Glagol*, 26.

Al-Faruqi, I. 1974. *Historical Atlas of the Religions of the World.* New York: Macmillan.

Alexeev, W. 1954-55. *Materials for the History of the Russian Orthodox Church in the U.S.S.R.* New York: Research Program on the USSR.

Alexeev, W., and Th. Stavrou. 1976. *The Great Revival: The Russian Church under German Occupation.* Minneapolis: Burgess Publishing Co.

Alexeeva, G. et al. 1993. Net Pokoia Poklonnoy Gore… [No Rest for Poklonnaya Gora] *Sovetskaia Rossiia*, December 31.

Alexii II, Patriarch of Moscow and All Russia. 1996. Interview, *Ta Nea*, February 28. [Trans. from Greek. Published in "Podborka po Presse".]

Anderson, B. 1983. *Imagined Communities: Reflections on the Origin and Spread of Nationalism.* London and New York: Verso.

Anderson, J. 1994. *Religion, the State and Politics in the Soviet Union and Successor States.* Cambridge: Cambridge University Press.

Anderson, P. B. 1944. *People, Church and State in Modern Russia.* London: Student Christian Movement Press, Ltd.

Angapov, S. B. 1979. Etnograficheskii Muzey Kul'tury i Byta Narodov Zabaykal'ia [Ethnographic Museum of Culture and Everyday Life of Trans-Baikal Peoples]. In *Pamiatniki Otechestva* [Monuments of Fatherland], vol. 4. Moscow: Sovremennik.

Anisimov, V. 1995. Ne Filaretstvuia Lukavo? [Tricky Filaret?]. *Nezavisimost'*, August 2.

Antonov, V. and Kobak, A.. 1994. *Sviatyni Sankt-Peterburga*. [The Treasures of St.Petersburg], vol.1. St.-Petersburg: Izdatel'stvo Chernysheva.

Appadurai, A.. 1996. *Modernity at Large: Cultural Dimensions of Globalization*. Minneapolis: University of Minnesota Press.

Ardov, M. 1994. Interview. Moscow, December.

___. 1996a. Kto i Kak Boretsia s "Raskolom" v Sovremennoi Rossii [Who and How Is Fighting "Schism" in Contemporary Russia]. In *Religiia i Prava Cheloveka. Na Puti k Svobode Sovesti*, vol. 3, ed. S. Filatov. Moscow: Nauka.

___. 1996b. Interview with A. V. Mikhal'chenkov. Manuscript.

Armeev, R. 1993. Krasnoi Ploschadi Vernuli Otniatoe — Kazanskii Sobor [Red Square Has Got Back the Stolen – Kazanskii Church]. *Izvestiia*, November 3.

___. 1994. Kazanskii Sobor Vozrozhden [Kazanskii Church Is Restored]. *Moskovskii Zhurnal* 1:2-3.

Arpishkin, Yu. 2000. Peredav Tserkov' v Filiakh Obschine, Gosudarstvo Obreklo Ee na Medlennoe Razrushenie [Having Transferred Church in Fili to Parish, State Made Its Slow Deconstruction Inevitable]. VremiaMN, April 7.

Atkinson, D. and D. Cosgrove. 1998. Urban Rhetoric and Embodied Identities: City, Nation, and Empire at the Vittorio Emanuele II Monument in Rome, 1870-1945. *Annals of the Association of American Geographers* 88:28-49.

Babaeva, S. 2000. Rossiyskomu Narodu Predpisano Stat' Dukhovnym [Russian People Are Prescribed to Become Spiritual]. *Izvestia*, June 2.

Babasian, N. 1992. Zarubezhnaia Tserkov' Proiavliaet Aktivnost' v Rossii: Vladyka Varnava Druzhit s "Pamiat'iu" [The Foreign Church Shows Interest in Russia: Bishop Varnava Is Friendly with Pamiat']. *Nezavisimaia Gazeta*, June 9.

___. 1996. Pravoslavnye Raspri: Spor Moskvy i Konstantinopolia ob Estonskoi Pravoslavnoi Tserkvi Imeet Imuschestvennuiu Podopleku [Orthodox Quarrel: Property Is the Underlying Reason for the Dispute between Moscow and Constantinople Over the Estonian Orthodox Church]. *Novoe Vremia* 10.

Babris, P. J. 1978. *Silent Churches: Persecution of Religions in the Soviet-Dominated Areas.* Arlington Heights, Illinois: Research Publishers.

Balabanov, V. 1995. Khram Oprokinutyy -- Khram Voskresshii [Cathedral Reversed -- Cathedral Resurrected]. *Nauka i Religiia* 12: 6, 66.

Barnes, T. 1994. Probable Writing: Derrida, Deconstruction, and the Quantitative Revolution in Human Geography. *Environment and Planning A* 26: 1021-40.

Barron, J. B., and H. M. Waddams. 1950. *Communism and the Churches, a Documentation.* London: SCM Press, Ltd.

Barry, E. 1995. Critic Queries Church Funding. *The Moscow Times*, July 8.

Bartholomew I. 1996. Letter of Ecumenical Patriarch Bartholomew I to Patriarch Alexy II of Moscow Concerning the Orthodox Church in Estonia, February 24. Protocol no. 206. The Official Website of the Patriarchate of Constantinople.

Baskov, V. 1994. Bol'shomu Basseinu — Bol'shoe Plavanie [Long Life to Big Swimming Pool]. *Novoe Vremia* 3:54-56.

Bassin, M. 1992. Geographical Determinism in Fin-de-siecle Marxism: Georgii Plekhanov and the Environmental Basis of Russian History. *Annals of the Association of American Geographers* 82:3-22.

Batalden, S. K., ed. 1993. *Seeking God: The Recovery of Religious Identity in Orthodox Russia, Ukraine, and Georgia.* DeKalb, Ill.: Northern Illinois University Press.

Beeson, T. 1982. *Discretion and Valour: Religious Conditions in Russia and Eastern Europe.* London: Collins, Fount Paperback.

Beglov, A. 1994. Sviaschennik Maksim Kozlov Mechtaet o Soiuze Religii i Nauki [Priest Maksim Kozlov Dreams about the Union of Religion and Science]. *Segodnia*, March 12.

Beliaev, L. A., and G. A. Pavlovich. 1993. *Kazanskii Sobor na Krasnoi Ploschadi* [Kazanskii Church on Red Square]. Moscow: Biznes MN.

Belliustin, I. S. 1985. *Description of the Clergy in Rural Russia: The Memoir of a Nineteenth-Century Parish Priest.* Trans. with an interpretive essay by Gregory L. Freeze. Ithaca and London: Cornell University Press.

Billington, J. H. 1970. *The Icon and the Axe: An Interpretive History of Russian Culture.* New York: Random House, Vintage Books.

Bilokhin, S. 1995. The Kiev Patriarchate and the State. In *The Politics of Religion in Russia and the New States of Eurasia*, ed. M. Bourdeaux, pp. 183-201. Armonk, NY; London, England: M. E. Sharpe.

BNS. 1996. Konflikt v Pravoslavnom Mire Grozit Rasshireniem Masshtabov [Conflict in Orthodox World Threatens to Enlarge]. *Vechernie Vesti*, March 9.

Bociurkiw, B. R. 1969. Church-State Relations in the USSR. In *Religion and the Soviet State: A Dilemma of Power*, ed. M. Hayward, and W. C. Fletcher, pp. 71-104. London: Pall Mall Press.

___. 1984. *Ukrainian Churches under Soviet Rule: Two Case Studies*. Cambridge, MA: Harvard University Ukrainian Studies Fund.

Bociurkiw, B. R., and J. W. Strong. 1975. *Religion and Atheism in the USSR and Eastern Europe*. London: The Macmillan Co.

Boiter, A. 1980. *Religion in the Soviet Union*. Beverly Hills: Sage Publications.

Bolshakoff, S. 1942. *The Christian Church and the Soviet State*. London: Society for Promoting Christian Knowledge.

Bossart, A. 1995. Teatr Vremen Luzhkova i Sinoda [Theater of the Time of Luzhkov and Synod]. *Stolitsa* 2:10-13.

Bourdeaux, M. 1975. *Patriarch and Prophets: Persecution of the Russian Orthodox Church*. London: Mowbrays.

___. 1983. *Risen Indeed: Lessons in Faith from the USSR*. London: Darton, Longman and Todd.

___. 1990. *Gorbachev, Glasnost and the Gospel*. London: Hodder and Stoughton.

___. ed. 1995. *The Politics of Religion in Russia and the New States of Eurasia*. Armonk, NY, and London, England: M.E. Sharpe.

Bourdeaux, M., and M. Rowe, eds. 1980. *May One Believe in Russia? Violations of Religious Liberty in the Soviet Union*. London: Darton, Longman and Todd.

Burakov, Yu. 1991. *Pod Sen'iu Monastyrei Moskovskikh* [In the Shadow of Moscow Monasteries]. Moscow: Moskovskii Rabochii.

Buss, G. 1987. *The Bear's Hug: Christian Belief and the Soviet State, 1917-86*. Grand Rapids, MI.: Wm. B. Eerdmans Publishing Co.

Butorov, A. 1992. *Khram Khrista Spasitelia: Istoriia Stroitel'stva i Razrusheniia* [Cathedral of Christ the Savior: History of Construction and Demolition]. Moscow: Yunyi Khudozhnik.

Buttner, M. 1974. Religion and Geography: Impulses for a New Dialogue between Religionswissenschaftlern and Geography. *Numen* 21: 165-96.

___. 1980. Survey Article on the History and Philosophy of the Geography of Religion in Germany. *Religion*, 86-119.

Central Statistical Board of the USSR. 1927. *Ten Years of Soviet Power in Figures, 1917-1927*. Moscow: Central Statistical Board of the USSR.

Charondin, V. 1994. Srazhenie za Novyy Ierusalim [Battle for New Jerusalem]. *Vek* 14: April 15-21.

Cherkasov-Georgievskii. B. 1992. *Moskva: Religioznye Tsentry i Obschiny* [Moscow: Religious Centers and Communities]. Moscow: Profizdat.

Chislennost' Naseleniia Rossiiskoi Federatsii: po gorodam, rabochim poselkam i raionam na 1 ianvaria 1994 g. [Population of the Russian Federation: by cities, workers' settlements and districts on January 1, 1994]. Moscow: Respublikanskii informatsionno-izdatel'skii tsentr.

Chrysostomus, J. 1965-68. *Kirchengeschichte Russlands der Neusten Zeit.* Munich-Salzburg, 3 vols.

Chulaki, M. 1994. Doroga k Khramu? [Road to Church?]. *Kul'tura* 4, February 5.

Chumachenko, T. 1999. *Gosudarstvo, Pravoslavnaia Tserkov', Veruiuschie. 1941-1961* [State, Orthodox Church, Believers. 1941- 1961]. Moscow: AIRO-XX.

Cleman, O. 1996. Raskolotaia Tserkov'? [Split Church?]. *Russkaia Mysl'*, April 11-17. [Trans. from French. Originally published in *Avvenire.* Milan, March 24.]

Colton, T. 1995. *Moscow: Governing the Socialist Metropolis.* Cambridge, MA: Belknap Press of the Harvard University Press.

Cooper, S. 1992. New Directions in the Geography of Religion. *Area* 24:123-129.

Cox, K. 1991. Comment: Redefining 'Territory'. *Political Geography Quarterly* 10:5-7.

___. 1996. Editorial: The Difference that Scale Makes. *Political Geography* 15:667-669.

___. 1997. Introduction: Globalization and Its Politics in Question. In *Spaces of Globalization: Reasserting the Power of the Local*, ed. K. Cox, pp. 1-18. New York: Guilford Press.

Cross, S. 1949. *Medieval Russian Churches.* Cambridge, MA: The Mediaeval Academy of America.

Cunningham, J. W. 1981. *A Vanquished Hope: The Movement for Church Renewal in Russia, 1905-1906.* Crestwood, New York: St. Vladimir's Seminary Press.

Curtis, J. R. 1980. Miami's Little Havana: Yard Shrines, Cult Religion and Landscape. *Journal of Cultural Geography* 1:1-15.

Curtiss, J. S. 1953. *The Russian Church and the Soviet State, 1917-1950.* Boston: Little, Brown and Co.

Dalby, S. 1990. American Security Discourse: The Persistence of Geopolitics. *Political Geography Quarterly* 9:171-188.

___. 1993. The 'Kiwi Disease': Geopolitical Discourse in Aotearon/ New Zealand and the South Pacific. *Political Geography* 12:437-456.

Davis, M. 1990. *City of Quartz: Excavating the Future in Los Angeles.* New York: Verso.

Davis, N. 1995. *A Long Walk to Church: A Contemporary History of Russian Orthodoxy.* Boulder, CO: Westview Press.

De Custine, A., marquise. 1989 (1839). *Empire of the Czar: A Journey Through Eternal Russia.* Foreword by D. J. Boorstin. Intr. by G. F. Kennan. New York: Doubleday.

Deffontaines, P. 1953. The Place of Believing. *Landscape* 3:22-28.

Deich, M. 1995. Prokliatie Igumen'i [Damnation of Mother Superior]. *Novoe Vremia* 52:40-44.

Degtiarev, Yu. M. 1995. Otkryval li Stalin Tserkvi? [Did Stalin Open Churches?]. In *Religioznye Organizatsii Sovetskogo Soiuza v Gody Velikoy Otechestvennoy Voyny 1941-1945 gg.: Materialy "Kruglogo Stola", Posviaschennye 50-letiiu Pobedy 13 aprelia 1995 g.* [Religious Organizations during the Great Patriotic War 1941-1945: Materials of the Round Table Devoted to the 50th Anniversary of the Victory, April 13, 1995], pp. 130-43. Moscow: Rossiiskaia Akademiia Gosudarstvennoy Sluzhby pri Prezidente Rossiiskoy Federatsii.

Deich, M. 1994. Prokliatie Igumen'i [Damnation of Mother Superior]. *Novoe Vremia* 52:40-44.

Delaney, D., and Leitner, H. 1997. The Political Construction of Scale. *Political Geography* 16:93-98.

Departament Dukhovnykh Del Ministerstva Vnutrennikh Del. 1913. *Statisticheskie Svedeniia o Staroobriadtsakh (k 1 ianvaria 1912 g.)* [Statistical Data on Old Believers (January 1, 1912)]. St. Petersburg.

Divakov, V. 1996. Interview. Moscow, September 13.

Dmitriev, G. 1994. Vozvraschenie Tret'iakovki: Sviatoi Nikola Vsekh Pomirit [Return of Tret'iakov Gallery: Holy Nikola Will Befriend Everyone]. *Moskovskaia Pravda*, April 5.

Dmitriev, P. 1994. Ne Nam, no Imeni Tvoemu [Not for Us, but in the Sake of Your Name]. *Moskovskaia Pravda*, December 20.

Dodgshon, R. A. 1987. *The European Past: Social Evolution and Spatial Order.* London: Macmillan Education Ltd.

Doel, M. A. 1992. In Stalling Deconstruction: Striking Out the Postmodern. *Environment and Planning D: Society and Space* 10:163-179.

Dorovskikh, I. 2000. Militsiia Vosstanovila Khram [Police Restored Church]. *Literaturnaia Rossia,* August 11.

Doughty, R. W. 1994. Environmetal Theology: Trends in Christian Thought. In *Re-Reading Cultural Geography*, ed. Foote, K. E. et al., pp. 313-322. Austin: University of Texas Press.

Driver, F. 1985. Power, Space and the Body: a Critical Reassessment of Foucault's 'Discipline and Punish'. *Environment and Planning D: Society and Space* 3:425-46.

Dunaev, M. 1994. Nasazhdaemaia Raspria [Propagated Quarrel]. *Nezavisimaia Gazeta*, March 26.

Duncan, J. 1990. *The City as Text: The Politics of Landscape Interpretation in the Kandian Kingdom.* Cambridge, UK: Cambridge University Press.

Duncan, P. J. S. 1991. Orthodoxy and Russian Nationalism in the USSR, 1917-88. In *Church, Nation and State in Russia and Ukraine*, ed. G. Hosking, pp. 312-332. New York: St. Martin's Press.

Duncan, S., and M. Savage. 1989. Space, Scale and Locality. *Antipode* 21:179-206.

Dunlop, J. B. 1995. The Russian Orthodox Church as an "Empire-Saving" Institution. In *The Politics of Religion in Russia and the New States of Eurasia*, ed. M. Bourdeaux, pp. 14-40. Armonk, NY, and London, England: M. E. Sharpe.

Dunn, D. J., ed. 1987. *Religion and Nationalism in Eastern Europe and the Soviet Union.* Boulder, Co.: Lynne Rienner.

Dvorkin, A. 1994. Chto Takoe Russkaia Pravoslavnaia Tserkov' za Granitsei? [What Is the Russian Orthodox Church Abroad?]. *Vestnik Russkogo Khristianskogo Dvizheniia* (Paris) 170:217-38.

Eesti Ringvaade. 1996. A Weekly Review of Estonian News. Internet Edition 5:50, Dec.10-16.

Ellis, J. 1986. *The Russian Orthodox Church: A Contemporary History.* Bloomington: Indiana University Press.

___. 1996. *The Russian Orthodox Church, 1985-94: Triumphalism and Defensiveness.* New York: St. Martin's Press, Inc. in association with St. Antony's College, Oxford, UK.

Estonia Today. 1993. Infoleht/Info Sheet, Internet Edition.

___. 1996. Infoleht/Info Sheet, Internet Edition.

Estonian Review. 1996. 6 (34), August 19-25.

Fickeler, P. 1962. Fundamental Questions in the Geography of Religions. In *Readings in Cultural Geography*, ed. P. L. Wagner, and M. W. Mikesell, pp. 94-117. Chicago: University of Chicago Press.

Filonova, S. 1994. Molitva + Pikety = ? [Pray + Pickets = ?]. *Rossiia* 10, March 16-22.

Fireside, H. 1971. *Icon and Swastika: The Russian Orthodox Church under Nazi and Soviet Control.* Cambridge, MA: Harvard University Press.

First Victims of Communism – White Book on the Religious Persecutions in Ukraine. 1953. Rome: Analecta O.S.B.M.

Fischer, L. 1990. The Geography of Protestant Monasticism. Ph.D. diss. Minneapolis, MN: University of Minnesota.

Fletcher, W. C. 1965. *A Study in Survival: The Church in Russia, 1927-1943.* New York: Macmillan Publishing Co.

___. 1971. *The Russian Orthodox Church Underground, 1917-1970.* London: Oxford University Press.

___. 1981. *Soviet Believers: The Religious Sector of the Population.* Lawrence: The Regents Press of Kansas.

Fletcher, W., and A. Strover. 1967. *Religion and the Search for New Ideals in the USSR.* New York: Frederick A. Praeger.

Fogarty, M. P. 1957. *Christian Democracy in Western Europe.* London: Routledge & Kegan Paul.

Forest, J. 1990. *Religion in the New Russia.* New York: Crossroad.

Foucault, M. 1972. *The Archaeology of Knowledge and the Discourse on Language.* Trans. from French by A. M. Sheridan Smith. New York: Pantheon Books.

___. 1977. *Discipline and Punish: The Birth of the Prison.* Trans. by A.M. Sheridan Smith. Andover, UK: Tavistock.

___. 1980. Questions on Geography. In *Power/Knowledge: Selected Interviews and Other Writings by Michel Foucault 1972-1977*, ed. by C. Gordon, pp. 63-77. New York: Pantheon Books.

___. 1984. Space, Knowledge, and Power. In *The Foucault Reader*, ed. P. Rabinow, pp. 239-257. New York: Pantheon Books.

Freeze, G. L. 1977. *The Russian Levites: Parish Clergy in the Eighteenth Century.* Cambridge, MA, and London, England: Harvard University Press.

___. 1983. *The Parish Clergy in Nineteenth-Century Russia: Crisis, Reform, Counter-Reform.* Princeton, NJ: Princeton University Press.

___. 1995. Counter-Reformation in Russian Orthodoxy: Popular Response to Religious Innovation, 1922-1925. *Slavic Review* 54:305-339.

Freitag, A. 1963. *The Twentieth Century Atlas of the Christian World: The Expansion of Christianity Through the Centuries.* New York: Hawthorn Books, Inc.

Friland, K. 1995. Khram Khrista Spasitelia Stanovitsia Simvolom Rossiiskogo Kapitalizma [Cathedral of Christ the Savior Is Becoming a Symbol of Russian Capitalism]. *Izvestiia*, August 29.

GARF (Gosudarstvennyi Arkhiv Rossiiskoi Federatsii) f. 5263, op. 1, d. 6, ll. 22, 25-26ob.

___. f. 5263, op. 1, d. 23.

___. f. 5263, op. 1, d. 32, ll. 66-73.

___. f. 5263, op. 1, d. 90

___. f. 5263, op. 2, d. 2, ll. 60-60ob., 77-77ob.

___. f. 5263, op. 2, d. 10.

___. f. 5263, op. 2, d. 12, ll.192-192ob.

___. f. 5263, op. 2, d. 13.

___. f. 6991, op. 1, d. 3, ll. 7-8.

___. f. 6991, op. 2, d. 82.

___. f. 6991s, op. 2, d. 180, ll. 22-25.

___. f. 6991s, op. 2, d. 263, l. 2.

___. f. 6991, op. 6, d. 2971, l. 40.

Gay, J. D. 1971. *The Geography of Religion in England*. London: Gerald Duckworth.

Gidulianov, P. V. 1926. *Otdelenie Tserkvi ot Gosudarstva. Polnyi Sbornik Dekretov, Vedomstvennykh Rasporiazhenii i Opredelenii Verkhovnogo Suda RSFSR i Drugikh Sovetskikh Sotsialisticheskikh Respublik* [Separation of the Church and the State. Complete Collection of Decrees, Administrative Decisions and Statements of the Supreme Court of the RSFSR]. Moscow.

Gilbert, M. 1972. *Russian History Atlas*. New York: The Macmillan Company.

Glacken, C. 1967. *Traces on the Rhodian Shore*. Berkeley: University of California Press.

Godienko, N., et al., eds. 1988. *Pravoslavie: Slovar' Ateista* [Orthodoxy: Atheist's Dictionary]. Moscow: Politizdat.

Goriacheva, Yu. 1994. Protiv ili Vmeste: Otets Viktor Potapov ne Vozlagaet Nadezhd na Razvitie Zarubezhnoi Tserkvi v Rossii [Against or Together: Father Viktor Potapov Has no Hopes for the Foreign Church's Advancement in Russia]. *Nezavisimaia Gazeta*, January 27.

Goskomstat Rossii. 1996. *Chislennost' Naseleniia Rossiiskoi Federatsii: po gorodam, rabochim poselkam i raionam na 1 ianvaria 1996 g.* [Population of the Russian Federation: by cities, workers' settlements and districts on January 1, 1996]. Moscow: Goskomstat Rossii.

Gosudarstvenno-Tserkovnye Otnosheniia v Rossii (Opyt Proshlogo i Sovremennoe Sostoianie) [State-Church Relations in Russia (Past Experience and Current State)]. 1996. Moscow: Rossiiskaia Akademiia Gosudarstvennoi Sluzhby pri Prezidente RF.

Gosudarstvennyi Komitet SSSR po Statistike. 1991. *Natsional'nyi Sostav Naseleniia SSSR: po Dannym Vsesoiuznoi Perepisi Naseleniia 1989 g.* [Ethnic Composition of Population of the USSR: Data of the 1989 All-Union Population Census]. Moscow: Finansy i Statistika.

Gramsci, A. 1992. *Prison Notebooks.* Ed. with intro. by J. Buttigieg. Trans. by J. Buttigieg and A. Callari. New York: Columbia University Press.

Gregory, D. 1994. *Geographical Imaginations.* Cambridge, MA: Blackwell.

Grigor'eva, Y. 1994. V Stolitse Budet Gde Zamolit' Grekhi [There Will Be in Moscow a Place to Atone for One's Sins by Prayer]. *Izvestiia,* August 2.

Grollenberg, L. H. 1956. *Atlas of the Bible.* London and Edinburgh: Nelson.

Gronskii, D. 1994. My Pamiatnik Sebe Vozdvig... Vosstanovlenie Kazanskogo Sobora Tozhe Mozhno Oposhlit' [We Have Erected Monument to Ourselves... Restoration of Kazanskii Church Could Be Cheapened Too]. *Nezavisimaia Gazeta,* January 4.

Gsovski, V., ed. 1955. *Church and State Behind the Iron Curtain.* New York: Frederick A. Praeger.

Gubonin, M. E. 1994. *Akty Sviateishego Tikhona, Patriarkha Moskovskogo i Vseia Rossii, Pozdneishie Dokumenty i Perepiska o Kanonicheskom Preemstve Vysshei Tserkovnoi Vlasti 1917-1943.* [Acts of Holy Tikhon, Patriarch of Moscow and All Russia, Later Documents and Letters on the Canonical Succession of the Highest Church Authority 1917-1943]. Moscow: Pravoslavnyi Sviato-Tikhonovskii Bogoslovskii Institut; Bratstvo vo Imia Vsemilostivogo Spasa.

The Harriman Institute Newsletter. 1996.

Harvey, D. 1979. Monument and Myth. *Annals of the Association of American Geographers* 69:362-81.

___. 1989. *The Condition of Postmodernity: An Enquiry into the Origins of Cultural Change.* Oxford: Blackwell.

___. 1992. Social Justice, Postmodernism and the City. *International Journal of Urban and Regional Research* 16:588-601.

Herbert, S. 1996. The Normative Ordering of Police Territoriality: Making and Marking Space with the Los Angeles Police Department. *Annals of the Association of American Geographers* 86:567-82.

Herod, A. 1991. The Production of Scale in US Labour Relations. *Area* 23:82-88.

_____. 1997. Labor's Spatial Praxis and the Geography of Contract Bargaining in the U.S. East Coast Longshore Industry, 1953-1989. *Political Geography* 16:145-69.

Hewryk, T. D. 1982. *The Lost Architecture of Kiev.* New York: The Ukrainian Museum.

Hill, K. 1989. *The Puzzle of the Soviet Church: An Inside Look at Christianity and Glasnost.* Portland, Oregon: Multnomah Press.

___. 1991. *The Soviet Union on the Brink: An Inside Look at Christianity and Glasnost'.* Portland, Oregon: Multnomah in cooperation with the Institute on Religion and Democracy.

Hobsbawm, E. and Ranger, T., ed. 1983. *The Invention of Tradition.* Cambridge: Cambridge University Press.

Hotchkiss, W. A. 1950. *Areal Pattern of Religious Institutions in Cincinnati.* Chicago: The University of Chicago.

House, F. 1988. *The Russian Phoenix.* London: SPCK.

Howitt, R. 1993. "A World in a Grain of Sand": Towards a Reconceptualisation of Geographical Scale. *Australian Geographer* 24:33-44.

Hultkrantz, A. 1966. An Ecological Approach to Religion. *Ethnos* 31:131-150.

Huntington, E. 1926. *The Pulse of Progress.* New York and London: Charles Scribner's Sons.

Hughes, R., and N. Paperno, eds. 1994. *Russian Culture in Modern Times.* Berkeley: University of California Press.

Iashunskii, I. 1992. Nashi Katakomby [Our Catacombs]. *Vestnik Russkogo Khristianskogo Dvizheniia* 166:243-260.

Institut Russkogo Iazyka AN SSSR. 1984. *Slovar' Russkogo Iazyka* [Dictionary of Russian Language], vol. 4. Moscow: Russkii Iazyk.

Institute of Russian History of the Russian Academy of Sciences. 1995. *Rossiia 1913 god: Statisticheskо-Dokumental'nyy Spravochnik* [Russia in 1913: Statistics and Documentary Guide]. St.Petersburg: Blits.

Interesnoe Nabliudenie, Mezhdu Prochim [Interesting Observation, by the Way]. 1996. *Estonia.* February 27.

Ioasaf. 1993. Vchera Il'inskii Skit, Segodnia Oboyan' — Kto Zavtra...?

[Yesterday Il'inskii Skit, Today Oboyan' — Who Will Be Tomorrow?]. *Pravoslavnaia Rus'* 17.

Isaak, E. 1959-60. Religion, Landscape and Space. *Landscape* 9: 14-18.

___. 1965. Religious Geography and the Geography of Religion. *Man and the Earth, University of Colorado Studies, Series in Earth Sciences* 3:1-14. Boulder, CO: University of Colorado Press.

Istoriia Moskvy v Gody Velikoy Otechestvennoy Voyny i v Poslevoennyy Period [History of Moscow during and after WWII]. 1967. Moscow: Nauka.

Izvlechenie iz Otcheta po Vedomstvu Dukhovnykh Del Pravoslavnogo Ispovedaniia za 1835 God [Summary of the Report of the Orthodox Faith Department in 1835]. 1837. Saint-Petersburg: Tipografiia Sviateyschego Pravitel'stvuiuschego Sinoda.

Jackson, P. 1989. *Maps of Meaning: An Introduction to Cultural Geography*. London: Unwin Hyman.

Johnston, R., D. Gregory, and D. Smith, eds. 1994. *The Dictionary of Human Geography*. Cambridge, MA: Blackwell.

Jonas, A. 1994. The Scale of Politics of Spatiality. *Environment and Planning D: Society and Space* 12:257-264.

K., O. 1997. Zakladka Novoy Chasovni v Moskve [Foundation Ceremony for a New Chapel in Moscow]. *Zhurnal Moskovskoi Patriarkhii* [Journal of the Moscow Patriarchate] 6.

Kaganskii, V. 1995. Sovetskoe Prostranstvo: Konstruktsiia i Destruktsiia [Soviet Space: Construction and Destruction]. In *Inoe: Kherstomatiia Novogo Rossiiskogo Samosoznaniia. Rossiia kak Predmet* [Other: Readings in New Russian Self-Identification. Russia as Object], compiled by S. B. Chernyshev, pp. 89-130. Moscow: Argus.

Kak Byla Kreschena Rus' [How Rus' Had Been Baptized]. 1998. Moscow: Politizdat.

Katys, M. 1995. Lechit' Zuby ... k Nastoiatel'nitse: Skandal Vokrug Rozhdestvenskogo Monastyria Prodolzhetsia [To Seek Dental Treatment ... from Prioress: Scandal Over Rozhdestvenskii Monastery Ccontinues]. *Golos*, 3.

Khmilevskii, N. 1993. Vybor [Choice]. *Khristianskii Vestnik* 10 (24), March: 15-20.

Khozhdenie vo Vlast' [Walking to the Powerful]. 1994. *Komsomol'skaia Pravda*. February 22.

Khram Khrista Spasitelia [Cathedral of Christ the Savior]. 1993 (1891,1918). Moscow: "Otechestvo"-Kraytur.

Khram Khrista Spasitelia Budet Vossozdan [Cathedral of Christ the

Savior Will Be Restored]. 1994. *Rossiiskaia Gazeta.* March 31.

Khram, Pariaschii nad Moskvoi? [Cathedral Flying Over Moscow?]. 1994. *Vecherniaia Moskva,* August 22.

King, L. 1964. *Missionary Atlas: A Manual of the Foreign Work of the Christian and Missionary Alliance.* Nurrisburg, PA: Christian Publications, Inc.

Kirichenko, E. I. 1992. *Khram Khrista Spasitelia v Moskve: Istoriia Proektirovaniia i Sozdaniia Sobora; Stranitsy Zhizni i Gibel'* [Cathedral of Christ the Savior: History of Design and Construction; Pages of Life and Death]. Moscow: Planeta & Kuznetskii Most.

Kirillov, I. A. 1913. *Statistika Staroobriadchestva* [Statistics of the Old Belief]. Moscow: Tipo-litografiia I. M. Mashistova. Edition of journal "Staroobriadcheskaia Mysl'."

Kirpichnikov, A. 1994. S Dumoi o Tserkvi [Thinking about the Church]. *Segodnia,* July 23.

Klenskii, D. 1996. Ugroza Miru vo Imia Unichtozheniia "Shestoi Chasti Sveta" [Threat to Peace in the Name of Destruction of One-Sixth of the World]. *Vechernie Vesti,* March 9.

Klibanov, A. 1982. *History of Religious Sectarianism in Russia, 1860s-1917.* Trans. By E. Dunn. Oxford and New York: Pergamon Press.

Klin, B. 2000. "Kommersant" i Khram Khrista Spasitelia [*Kommersant* and the Cathedral of Christ the Savior]. *Kommersant* August 9.

Kliuev, B. 1993. Zakatilos' Iabloko Razdora azh na Poklonnuiu Goru… [Apple of Discord Rolled Up Poklonnaia Gora]. *Rabochaia Tribuna,* December 28.

Kolarz, W. 1961. *Religion in the Soviet Union.* New York: St. Martin's Press.

Kolomayets, M. 1995. Two Orthodox Churches in Ukraine Discuss Unification. *The Ukrainian Weekly* 47, November 19.

Kolomeytsev, P. 1993. Est' li Buduschee u Staroobryadtsev? [Do the Old Believers Have the Future?]. In *Religiia i Demokratiia: Na Puti k Svobode Sovesti,* ed. S. B. Filatov, and D. E. Furman, pp. 517-532. Moscow: Progress.

Kolpakov, A. 1993. Vosstal Brat na Brata [Brother-Against-Brother Rebellion]. *Moskovskii Komsomolets,* September 9.

___. 1994a. Sny Velikana v Tsifrakh i Giperbolakh [Giant's Dreams in Figures and Hyperboles]. *Moskovskii Komsomolets,* March 16.

___. 1994b. Khram, Kotoryi Postroit Mer [Cathedral, Which Will Be Built by Major]. *Moskovskii Komsomolets,* September 23.

Komarov, E. 1999. Merskie Podarki: Pravitel'stvo Moskvy Razdaet Gorodskuiu Nedvizhimost' Kommersantam cherez Tserkov'

[Mayor's Gifts: The Government of Moscow Transfers City Property to Merchants via the Church]. *Novye Izvestiia*, December 16.

Komlev, G. 1996. Ne Dopustite Religioznogo Konflikta! [Prevent Religious Conflict!]. *Estoniia*, March 1.

Kondrat'ev, A. 1995. Alexandr Nikiforovich Kondrat'ev: o Vremeni i o Sebe [Alexandr Nikiforovich Kondrat'ev about His Time and about Himself]. *Arkhitektura i Stroitel'stvo Moskvy* 4:11-21.

Kong, L. 1990. Geography and Religion: Trends and Prospects. *Progress in Human Geography* 14:355-71.

___. 1993. Ideological Hegemony and the Political Symbolism of Religious Buildings in Singapore. *Environment and Planning D: Society and Space* 11:23-45.

Konovalov, V. 1999. Sokhranenie Istoriko-Kul'turnogo Naslediia Moskvy [Preservation of Moscow's Historico-Cultural Heritage]. *Arkhitektura. Stroitel'stvo. Dezayn* 4: 56-61.

Konstantinov, D. 1984. *Stations of the Cross: The Russian Orthodox Church, 1970-1980*. London: Zarya.

Korneev, A. 1993. Ostanovit' Koschunstvo na Poklonnoi Gore [Stop Blasphemy on Poklonnaia Hill]. *Domostroi* 51.

Korneeva, K. 1999. Khram Khrista Spasitelia i Politicheskaia Bor'ba [The Cathedral of Christ the Savior and Political Struggle]. *Russkaya Mysl'* (Paris) 4293, November 18.

Korolev, A. 1993a. Kolokola Pamiati [Bells of Memory]. *Trud*, November 5.

___. 1993b. Kolokol'naia "Nakladka" [Bell "Error"]. *Trud*, November 25.

___. 1996a. Verolomstvo [Betrayal]. *Trud*, March 2.

___. 1996b. Voznikla Opasnost' Raskola [Threat of Schism Emerged]. *Trud*, February 27.

Kosukha, P., and P. Iarotskii. 1993. Ukrainskii Ekumenizm ili Ideia Natsional'noi Tserkvi? [Ukrainian Ecumenism or the Idea of National Church]. *Khristianskii Vestnik* 37(51-52):28-31.

Kozarzhevskii, A. Ch. 1989. A. I. Vvedenskii i Obnovlencheskii Raskol v Moskve [A. I. Vvedenskii and Renovationist Schism in Moscow]. *Vestnik Moskovskogo Universiteta, seriia 8*, 1:54-66.

Kozlov, M. 1994. Bozhii Khram v Khrame Nauki [God's Temple in the Temple of Science]. *Literaturnaia Rossiia* 11, March 18.

Kozlov, V. 1991a. Gibel' Khrama [Death of a Cathedral]. *Moskovskii Zhurnal* 9:8-18.

___. 1991b. Delo ob Ograblenii Tserkvi: 1920-1930-e Gody [Case of Church's Robbery: 1920-1930s]. *Moskovskii Zhurnal* 7.

___. 1991c. Pod Flagom Nigilizma: God 1930-i [Under the Banner of Nigilism: the Year of 1930]. *Moskovskii Zhurnal* 6.

___. 1991d. Chernye Gody Moskovskikh Obitelei [Black Years of Moscow Cloisters]. *Moskovskii Zhurnal* 4.

___. 1997. Khram Sv. Borisa i Gleba na Arbatskoi Ploschadi: Istoriia i Sud'by [SS Boris and Gleb Church on Arbat Square: History and Destiny]. In *Arbatskii Arkhiv: Istoriko-Kraevedcheskii Al'manakh* [Arbat Archive: Local History Literary Miscellany]. 1997. Moscow: Tverskaia 13.

Krasnov-Levitin, A. 1977. *Likhie Gody, 1925-1941: Vospominaniia* [Dramatic Years, 1925-1941: Memoirs]. Paris: YMCA-Press.

Krestnikov, A. 1993. Igumen Schet Liubit [Father Superior Likes Counting]. *Komsomol'skaia Pravda*, November 16.

Krindatch, A. 1992. Geografiia Religii kak Nauchnoe Napravlenie. *Izvestiia Akademii Nauk. Ser. Geograficheskaia*, 3:63-69.

___. 1996. *Geography of Religions in Russia*. Decatur, GA: Glenmary Research Center.

Krolenko, I. 1994. Budet Vechnyi Glukhoi Zabor... [There Will Be an Eternal Monotonous Wall]. *Moskovskie Novosti* 48, October.

Krotov, Ya. 1994. Vechno Vzryvat' i Rekonstruirovat' [To Ruin and Reconstruct Endlessly]. *Moskovskie Novosti* 15, April.

___. 1995. Alexandr Men': Ateizm — Dar Bozhii [Alexander Men': Atheism Is God's Providence]. *Kuranty*, January 21.

___. 1996. Khristos Prishel ko Vsem? [Did Christ Come to Everyone?]. *Kuranty*, March 12.

Kulakova, V. 1994. Patriarkh i "Dukh Vremeni" [Patriarch and the Spirit of Time]. *Segodnia*, June 25.

Kuprach, A. 1993. Muzey Pozhral Khram [Museum Has Eaten Church]. *Den'*, September 23.

Kuraev, A. 1995. *Razmyshleniia Pravoslavnogo Pragmatika o Tom, Nado li Stroit' Khram Khrista Spasitelia* [Thoughts of an Orthodox Pragmatist About Whether It Is Worth Restoring the Cathedral of Christ the Savior]. Moscow: Otdel Religioznogo Obrazovaniia i Katekhizatsii Moskovskogo Patriarkhata.

Kuranty. 1994. April 5.

Kusov, V. 1995. Gora Poklonnaia [Poklonnaia Hill]. *Moskovskii Zhurnal* 5:15-6.

Kuznetsov, A. I. 1956-9. *Obnovlencheskii Raskol v Russkoi Tserkvi*. 3 vols. Typescript.

Laatsch, W., and C. Calkins. 1986. The Belgian Roadside Chapels of Wisconsin's Door Peninsula. *Journal of Cultural Geography* 7:117-28.

Lagopoulos, A. P. 1993. Postmodernism, Geography, and the Social Semiotics of Space. *Environment and Planning D: Society and Space* 11:255-278.

Lane, C. 1978. *Christian Religion in the Soviet Union: A Sociological Study.* Albany, New York: State University of New York Press.

Lang, D. M. 1969. Religion and Nationalism: a Case Study: the Caucasus. In *Religion and the Soviet State: A Dilemma of Power*, ed. M. Hayward, and W. C. Fletcher, 169-186. London: Pall Mall Press.

(Larin), Sergii. 1953-9. *Obnovlencheskii Raskol* [Renovationist Schism]. Typescript.

Leasure, J. W., and R. Lewis. 1966. *Population Changes in Russia and the USSR: a Set of Comparable Territorial Units.* Social Science Monograph Series 1(2). San Diego: San Diego State College Press.

Lebedeva, E. 1996. Raskol Neizbezhen? [Is the Split Unavoidable?]. *Den' za dnem*, February 22.

Lefebvre, H. 1991. *The Production of Space.* Oxford, UK; Cambridge, MA: Blackwell. Trans. by D. Nickolson-Smith.

Leitner, H. 1997. Reconfiguring the Spatiality of Power: the Construction of a Supranational Migration Framework for the European Union. *Political Geography* 16:123-144.

(Lemeshevskii), Manuil, Metropolitan. 1979-89. *Die Russischen Orthodoxen Bischofe von 1893 bis 1965.* 6 vols. Erlangen: OIKONOMIA.

Lenin, V. 1933. The Attitude of the Workers' Party Towards Religion. In V. Lenin *Religion*, pp. 11-20. New York: International Publishers.

Leningrad: Vidy Goroda [Leningrad: Town's Views]. 1960. Moscow-Leningrad: Gosudarstvennoe Izdatel'stvo Izobrazitel'nogo Iskusstva.

Levine, G. J. 1986. On the Geography of Religion. *Transactions of the IBG, N.S.* 11:428-40.

Levitin, A. and V. Shavrov. 1977. *Ocherki po Istorii Russkoi Tserkovnoi Smuty.* 3 vols. Switzerland, Kusnacht: Institut Glaube in der 2 Welt.

Lewandowski, S. J. 1984. The Built Environment and Cultural Symbolism in Post-Colonial Madras. In *The City in Cultural Context*, ed. J. A.. Agnew et al., pp. 237-54. Boston: Allen and Unwin.

Livanov, V. 1926. Antireligioznaia Propaganda na Ukraine [Anti-Religious Propaganda in Ukraine]. *Antireligioznik* 5:39-47.

Lobacheva, I. 1994. Peizazh Posle Bitvy — Zrelische ne iz Priatnykh

[Landscape after Battle Is Nnot a Pleasant View]. *Kuranty*, August 14.

Loriia, Y. 1995. Ob Obiazatel'nykh Pozhertvovaniiakh Khrista Radi [On Obligatory Donations for the Sake of Christ]. *Komsomol'skaia Pravda*, February 21.

Lorimer, F. 1946. *The Population of the Soviet Union: History and Prospects*. Geneva: League of Nations.

Loukaki, A. 1997. Whose Genius Loci?: Contrasting Interpretations of the "Sacred Rock of the Athenian Acropolis." *Annals of the Association of American Geographers* 87:306-329.

Lutskii, I. 1995. Skazhite, Etot Mostik Vedet k Khramu? [Tell Me, Is This Bridge Leading to the Cathedral?]. *Argumenty i Fakty* 30.

Luzhnyts'kyi, H. 1960. *Persecution and Destruction of the Ukrainian Church by the Russian Bolsheviks*. New York, NY: The Ukrainian Congress Committee of America.

Lypkivsky, Vasyl, Metropolitan. 1959. *Vidrodzhennia Tserky v Ukraini* [Revival of Church in Ukraine] (in Ukrainian). Toronto: Dobra Knyzhka.

M., K. 1995. City Scape Changing in a Hurry. *Moscow News* 1: January 6.

Makeev, M. 1994. Interview. Moscow, November.

Malinin, N. 1994. Dorogi k Khramu, Kotorye My Vybiraem [Roads to Church Which We Choose]. *Argumenty i Fakty* 11: March.

___. 1995. Konstantin Ton kak Bon i kak Mauvrais Ton [Konstantin Ton as Bon Ton and Mauvrais Ton]. *Stolitsa* 2: 93-96.

Markus, V. 1985. *Religion and Nationalism in Soviet Ukraine After 1945*. Cambridge, MA: Ukrainian Studies Fund, Harvard University.

___. 1995. Politics and Religion in Ukraine: In Search of a New Pluralistic Dimension. In *The Politics of Religion in Russia and the New States of Eurasia*, ed. by M. Bourdeaux, pp. 163-81. Armonk, NY, and London, England: M.E. Sharpe.

Marshall, R., T. Bird, and A. Blane, eds. 1971. *Aspects of Religion in the Soviet Union, 1917-1967*. Chicago: University of Chicago Press.

Marston, Sallie A. 2000. The Social Construction of Scale. *Progress in Human Geography* 24: 219-42.

Matless, D. 1992. An Occasion for Geography: Landscape, Representation, and Foucault's Corpus. *Environment and Planning D: Society and Space* 10:41-56.

May, H. G., et al., ed. 1962. *Oxford Bible Atlas*. London: Oxford University Press.

Melikiants, G. 1994. Stenka na Stenku u Monastyrskikh Vorot [Wall-to-Wall Fight Near Monastery Gates]. *Izvestiia*, July 8.

Meyer, W., et al. 1992. The Local-Global Continuum. In *Geography's Inner Worlds: Pervasive Themes in Contemporary American Geography*, ed. R. Abler, M. Marcus, and J. Olson, pp. 255-79. New Brunswick, NJ: Rutgers University Press.

Mezentseva, G. and Mezentsev, I. 1981. *Kiev* [Kiev]. Kiev: Budivel'nik.

Mikhailov, A. 1994. Imuschestvo Kul'tury: Zdaniia Tserkvei kak Ochagi Misticheskogo Ppragmatizma [Property of Culture: Church Buildings as Centers of Mystical Pragmatism]. *Nezavisimaia Gazeta*, April 7.

Miller, B. 1994. Political Empowerment, Local-Central State Relations, and Geographical Shifting Political Opportunity Structures: Strategies of the Cambridge, Massachusetts Peace Movement. *Political Geography* 13:393-406.

_____. 1995. The Power of Place, the Significance of Scale: The Geographic Structuring of Collective Action in the Boston Area Peace Movement. Ph.D. diss. Minneapolis, MN: University of Minnesota.

The Minnesota Geography Reading Group. 1992. Collective Response: Social Justice, Difference, and the City. *Environment and Planning D: Society and Space* 10:589-595.

Mitrofanov, G. 1995. *Russkaia Pravoslavnaia Tserkov' v Rossii i v Emigratsii v 1920-e Gody: k Voprosu o Vzaimootnosheniiakh Moskovskoi Patriarkhii i Russkoi Tserkovnoi Emigratsii v Period 1920-1927 gg.* [The Russian Orthodox Church in Russian and in Emigration in the 1920s: On the Question of Relationship between the Moscow Patriarchate and Russian Church Emigration in 1920-1927]. St. Petersburg: Noakh.

Mitrokhin, N. and S. Timofeeva. 1997. *Episkopy i Eparkhii Russkoy Pravoslavnoy Tserkvi: po sostoianiiu na 1 oktiabria 1997 g.* [Bishops and Dioceses of the Russian Orthodox Church: on October 1, 1997]. Moscow: Panorama.

Mol, H. J. J., ed. 1972. *U.S.S.R., Western Religion: A Country by Country Sociological Inquiry*. The Hague, Paris: Mouton.

Moscow Patriarchate. 1942. *Pravda o Religii v Rossii* [Truth about Religion in Russia]. Moscow: Moskovskaia Patriarkhiia.

Moscow Patriarchate's "Arkhkhram". 1995. Predlozheniia po Vosstanovleniiu Khrama Khrista Spasitelia [Suggestions on the Restoration of the Cathedral of Christ the Savior]. *K Svetu* 17:116-39.

Moscow Times. 1996. February.

Moskovskie Novosti. 1996. no. 8.

Moskovskii Komsomolets. 1993a. November 5.

___. 1993b. December 7.

Moskva: Fotoetiudy [Moscow: Photostudy]. 1957. Photo by Il'ia Goland.

Moskva i Konstantinopol': Istoriia Razryva [Moscow and Constantinople: the History of Split]. 1996. *Russkaia Mysl'* (Paris), February 29 - March 6.

Muir, E., and F. Weissman. 1989. Social and Symbolic Places in Renaissance Venice and Florence. In *The Power of Place: Bringing Together Geographical and Sociological Imaginations*, ed. J. Agnew, and J. Duncan, pp. 81-104. Winchester, MA: Unwin Hyman.

Mydlowsky, L. 1962. *Bolshevist Persecution of Religion and Church in Ukraine, 1917-1957: Informative Outline*. London: Ukrainian Publishers Ltd.

Mykorskiy, B. 1951. *Razrusheniye Kulturno-Istoricheskikh Pamiatnikov v Kieve v 1934-1936 Godakh* [Destruction of Cultural-Historical Monuments in Kiev in 1934-1936]. Munich.

Nadeemsia, Chto Nash Golos Budet Uslyshan [We Hope That Our Voice Will Be Heard]. 1993. *Podol'skii Rabochii* (Podol'sk, Moscow oblast'). September 3.

Nauka i Religiia. 1993. no. 6, 14-15.

Nekrasov, I. 1994. Radi Vysshego Smysla: Khram Khrista Spasitelia Sobiraiutsia Vossozdat' uzhe bez Gosudarstvennogo Uchastiia [Cathedral of Christ the Savior Is to Be Restored without State Participation]. *Nezavisimaia Gazeta*, December 1.

Nevidimye [Invisible]. 1996. *Eleftherotypia.* February 29. [Trans. from Greek. Published in *Podborka po Presse*.]

Nezavisimaia Gazeta. 1994. February 25.

___. 1996. January 5.

Nezhnyi, A. 1993a. Ukradennyi Kolokol [Stolen Bell]. *Rossiiskaia Gazeta*, December 30.

___. 1993b. Kolokola Oboyani [Bells of Oboyan']. *Rossiiskaia Gazeta*, December 7.

___. 1993c. Raspiatie v Oboyani [Crucifix in Oboyan']. *Rossiiskaia Gazeta*, November 4.

___. 1993d. *Komissar D'iavola* [Evil's Commissar]. Moscow: Protestant.

___. 1994. Raspiatie v Oboyani [Crucifix in Oboyan']. *Russkaia Mysl'*, 4011, January 6.

___. 1995. Krest na Sobstvennosti: Zametki o Dvizhimom i Nedvizhimom Imuschestve Russkoi Pravoslavnoi Tserkvi [Cross on Property: Notes on Movable and Real Property of the Russian Orthodox Church]. *Russkaia Mysl'*, January 26 - February 1.

NIIiPI Genplana Moskvy. 1991. (Nauchno-Issledovatel'skii i Proektnyi Institut General'nogo Plana Moskvy, Glavnoe Upravlenie Arkhitektury i Gradostroitel'stva Moskvy. Otdel GIiIG). Gradostroitel'naia Kontseptsiia Razvitiia i Razmescheniia Religioznykh Organizatsii, Obschin i Kul'tovykh Ob'ektov v g. Moskve [Town-Planning Concept of Development and Location of Religious Organizations, Communities, and Churches in the City of Moscow]. Poiasnitelniaia zapiska." Kniga 1, chast' 1., no. 17-91/29. Unpub. report.

___. 1992. (Nauchno-Issledovatel'skii i Proektnyi Institut General'nogo Plana Moskvy, Glavnoe Upravlenie Arkhitektury i Gradostroitel'stva Moskvy. Otdel GIiIG), Issledovanie Sotsial'no-Gradostroitel'nykh Problem Razvitiia Religioznykh Organizatsii i Obschin v g. Moskve i Razmeschenie Neobkhodimykh dlia Ikh Deiatel'nosti Ob'ektov [Research of the Social and Urban Planning Problems of Development of Religious Organizations and Communities in the City of Moscow and Allocation of Objects Necessary for Their Functioning], I and II stages (December), no. 17-92/11. Unpub. report.

___. 1997. Podgotovka Materialov dlia Rassmotreniia Pravitel'stvom Moskvy. Skhemy Razmescheniia Kul'tovykh Zdanii Razlichnykh Konfessii na Territorii Moskvy. Poiasnitel'naia Zapiska [Preliminary Materials for Consideration by Moscow City Government. Design of Location of Cult Buildings of Various Denominations in Moscow. Explanation Notes], unpub. report.

Nikol'skaia, O. 1993. Kolokola Kazanskogo Sobora Zapoiut Blagovest [Bells of Kazan' Church Will Sing Good News]. *Vecherniaia Moskva*, November 2.

___. 1994a. Tserkov' Tat'iany: Konflikt Ischerpan? [Church of Tat'iana: the Conflict is Over?]. *Vecherniaia Moskva*, March 21.

___. 1994b. Zlatoglavaia Simphoniia [Golden Cupols' Symphony]. *Vecherniaia Moskva*, January 21.

___. 1999. Vsevidiashchee Oko Elektroniki: Chto Skryto v Nishakh Khrama? [Omnipresent Electronic Gaze: What Is Hidden in the Cathdral's Niches?]. *Vecherniaia Moskva*, May 27.

Nikonov, A. 2000. Netzenzurnaia Dermocratia [Dermocracy of Harsh Words: Interview with Sergey Yushinkov]. *Ogonyek* 47(4674).

Nochuykina, A. 2000. Moskva-City, na Uglu Sprosite: Moskovskii Mankhetten, Novoe Litso Rossii, Gorod v Oblakakh [Ask Someone Else Where Is Moscow-City: Moscow Manhattan, New Face of Russia, the City in the Clouds]. *Moscow News* 13(1031), April 4-10.

Nolan, M. L. 1986. Pilgrimage Traditions and the Nature Mystique in Western European Culture. *Journal of Cultural Geography* 7:5-20.

Novikov, P. 1996a. K Tserkovnoi Situatsii v Estonii: Deistvitel'nost' i Perspektivy [On the Church Situation in Estonia: Status Quo and Perspectives]. *Russkaia Mysl'*, June 13-19.

___. 1996b. Spor mezhdu Moskvoi i Konstantinopolem: Zastarelaia Bolezn' i Neobkhodimost' Ee Uvrachevaniia [Dispute between Moscow and Constantinople: Old Disease Which Needs to Be Cured]. *Russkaia Mysl'*, March 14-27, March 28-April 3.

Odintsov, M. I. 1993. Purgatory. *Russian Studies in History*, 32(2): 53-81.

___. 1994. *Gosudarstvo i Tserkov' v Rossii: XX Vek.* [State and Church in Russia: The XX Century]. Moscow: Rossiiskaia Akademiia Upravleniia.

Odintsov, M. I., Pinkevich, V.K., and O. Y. Red'kina. 1995. Gosudarstvenno-tserkovnye Otnosheniia v Politicheskoi Istorii Rossii. In *Gosudarstvenno-tserkovnye Otnosheniia v Rossii: kurs lektsii* [State-Church Relations in Russia: Lecture Course]. Moscow: Rossiiskaia Akademiia Gosudarstvennoi Sluzhby pri Prezidente RF.

Olsson, G. 1993. Chiasm of Thought-and-Action. *Environment and Planning D: Society and Space* 11:279-294.

Opolznev, M. 1994. Sviato Mesto Pusto Ne Budet [Holy Place Will Not Be Empty]. *Moskovskaia Pravda*, October 7.

Orthodox Churches Avoid Schism over Estonia Row. 1996. *Reuters News Service. Internet edition.*

(Osetrov), Andrei, press-secretary of the Russian Free Church. 1994. Interview. Suzdal', September.

Ostrowski, D. 1993. Why Did the Metropolitan Move from Kiev to Vladimir in the Thirteenth Century? In *Slavic Cultures in the Middle Ages.* Vol. 1 of Christianity and the Eastern Slavs, ed. B. Gasparov, and O. Raevsky-Hughes, pp. 83-101. Berkeley: University of California Press.

Ovrutskii, L. 2000. Dogovor Dorozhe Deneg? [Agreement Is Less Important than Money?]. *Vremia I Den'gi: Gazeta Delovykh Krugov Tatarstana* (Kazan'), 21 èþíÿ 2000 ã.

Palamarchuk, P. 1989. *Sorok Sorokov* [Forty by Forty]. Vol 1: Kreml' i Monastyri. Paris: YMCA-Press.

___. 1992. *Sorok Sorokov: Kratkaia Illiustrirovannaia Istoriia Vsekh Moskovskikh Khramov* [Forty by Forty: A Brief Illustrated History of All Moscow Churches]. Vol. 1. Kreml' i Monastyri. Moscow: Kniga i biznes.

___. 1994. *Sorok Sorokov: Kratkaia Illiustrirovannaia Istoriia Vsekh Moskovskikh Khramov* [Forty by Forty: A Brief Illustrated History of All Moscow Churches]. Vol. 2. Moscow: Kniga i biznes.

Palishin, V. 1994. Grekh Tscheslaviia [Sin of Vanity]. *Sovetskaia Rossiia,* February 3.

Pankhurst, J. 1996. Religious Culture. In *Russian Culture at the Crossroads: Paradoxes of Postcommunist Consciousness,* ed. D. Shalin, pp. 127-156. Boulder, CO: Westview Press.

Park, C. 1994. *Sacred Worlds: an Introduction to Geography and Religion.* London and New York: Routledge.

Parsons, H. L. 1972. *Christianity in the Soviet Union.* New York: The American Institute for Marxist Studies.

Paskhal'nyi Podarok Patriarkhu [Easter Present to Patriarch]. 1994. *Moskovskii Komsomolets.* April 22.

Patriarchate of Constantinople. 1996. Patriarchal and Synodical Act Concerning the Re-Activation of the Patriarchal and Synodical Tomos of 1923 Regarding the Orthodox Metropolitanate of Estonia, February 20. Protocol No. 201. The Official Website of the Patriarchate of Constantinople.

Patriarkh Alexii and Prezident Yel'tsin Obsudili Konflikt Vokrug Estonskoi Pravoslavnoy Tserkvi [Patriarch Alexii and President Yel'tsin Discussed the Conflict Over the Estonian Orthodox Church]. 1996. *Estonia.* February 29.

Pavlov, I. 1993. Ukrainskaia Pravoslabnaia Tserkov' v Proshlom i Nastoiaschem [Ukrainian Orthodox Church in the Past and Present]. *Nezavisimaia Gazeta,* April 8.

___. 1994a. Vox Populi. *Segodnia,* October 1.

___. 1994b. Stalinu i Ne Snilos': Kommentarii k Postanovleniiu Pravitel'stva Rossiiskoi Federatsii ot 6 maia 1994 goda no. 466 [Stalin Did Not Even Dream about That: Commentary on the Russian Federal Government's Resolution no. 466, May 6, 1994]. *Segodnia,* July 9.

___. 1996. Restitutsiia and Sviaschennoe Pravo Sobstvennosti: Nyneshnii Moskovskii Patriarkhat Ne Mozhet byt' Priznan Pravopreemnikom Rossiiskoi Tserkvi [Restitution and the Holy Right of Property: the Current Moscow Patriarchate Cannot Be Recognized as Legal Successor of the State-Russian Church], *Russkaia Mysl',* no. 4153, December 12-18. "Tserkovno-Obschestvennyi Vestnik", no. 5, 8.

Pavlovskii, A. I. 1991. Iama: o Khudozhestvenno-Filosofskoi Kontseptsii Povesti Andreia Platonova "Kotlovan" [Pit: On the Esthetical-Philosophical Conception of Andrei Platonov's Novel "Foundation Pit"]. *Russkaia Literatura* 1:22-41.

Peet, R. 1996. A Sign Taken for History: Daniel Shay's Memorial in Petersham, Massachusetts. *Annals of the Association of American Geographers* 86:21-43.

Pervaia Vseobschaia Perepis' Naseleniia Rossiiskoi Imperii 1897 Goda [The First General Population Census of the Russian Empire 1897]. 1903. St.Petersburg.

Petro, N. N., ed. 1990. *Christianity and Russian Culture in Soviet Society. Part One: Christianity and the Soviet State.* Boulder, CO: Westview Press.

Petrov, M. 1996. Komissiia Gotovit Vstrechu [Commission Is Preparing Meeting]. *Estonia*, July 25.

Philo, C. 1992. Foucault's Geography. *Environment and Planning D: Society and Space* 10:137-161.

Platonov, A. 1973. *Foundation Pit/Kotlovan.* Ann Arbor, Mich.: Ardis. Bi-lingual edition. English tr. by Thomas P. Whitney. Preface by Joseph Brodsky.

___. 1987. Kotlovan. *Novyi Mir* 6: 50-123.

Pokrovskii, I. 1994. Nas Spaset Khram Khrista Spasitelia [Cathedral of Christ the Savior Will Save Us]. *Izvestiia*, September 2.

Pokrovskii, I. M. 1897-1913. *Russkiia Eparkhii v XVI-XIX vv., Ikh Otkrytie, Sostav, i Predely. Opyt Tserkovno-Istoricheskogo i Geograficheskogo Issledovaniia* [Russian Dioceses in the 16-19 Cen., Their Creation, Structure, and Extent. A Church-Historical and Geographic Study]. Kazan': Tipo-lit. Imp. Un-ta.

Poloznev, G. 1994. Untitled. *Novoe Vremia* 48.

Popov, D. 1994. Den'gi dlia Khrama [Money for Cathedral]. *Moskovskaia Pravda*, December 6.

Posokhin, M. M. 1995. Vossozdaetsia v Istoricheskom Oblike [Restoration in Historical Image]. *Arkhitektura i Stroilel'stvo Moskvy* 4: 23-28.

Pospielovsky, D. V. 1984. *The Russian Church under the Soviet Regime, 1917-1982.* Crestwood, New York: St. Vladimir's Seminary Press. 2 vols.

___. 1988. *A History of Soviet Atheism in Theory and Practice, and the Believer,* 3 vols. New York: St. Martin's Press.

___. 1989. *Some Observations on Russian Self-Awareness and the Orthodox Church in the Era of Gorbachev.* Koln: Bunderinstitut fur Ostwissenschaftliche und Internationale Studien.

___. 1995a. *Russkaia Pravoslavnaia Tserkov' v XX Veke* [Russian Ortho-
   dox Church in the 20th Century]. Moscow: Respublika.

___. 1995b. Nekotorye Problemy Sovremennoi Russkoi Pravoslavnoi
   Tserkvi – Ee Vnutrennei Zhizni, Kul'tury, Obrazovaniia [Some
   Problems in Contemporary Russian Orthodox Church]. *Vestnik
   Russkogo Khristianskogo Dvizheniia* 172:198-231.

Pozdniaev, M. 1994. Khram Khrista Spasitelia ... Imeni Dvortsa Sovetov?
   [Cathedral of Christ the Savior ... Named after the Palace of the
   Soviets?]. *Novoe Vremia* 36:36-39.

___. n.d. Lazar' Smerdiaschii [Lazar' the Fetid]. *Stolitsa* 46.

Pravoslavnaia Moskva. 1995. Moscow: Izdatel'stvo bratstva Sviatitelia
   Tikhona.

Pushkarev, S. G. 1970. *Dictionary of Russian Historical Terms from the
   Eleventh Century to 1917.* New Haven and London: Yale University Press.

Ramet, P. 1987. *Cross and Commissar: the Politics of Religion in Eastern
   Europe and the USSR.* Bloomington: Indiana University Press.

___. ed. 1989. *Soviet and East European Politics.* Durham: Duke Univer-
   sity Press.

Ramet, S., ed. 1993. *Religious Policy in the Soviet Union.* New York:
   Cambridge University Press.

Raskol Pravoslavnoi Tserkvi v Moldove i Ego Politicheskaia Podopleka
   [The Orthodox Church Schism in Moldova and Its Political Con-
   text]. 1993. *Khristianskii Vestnik* no. 35-36 (49-50).

Reader's Digest Atlas of the Bible: an Illustrated Guide to the Holy Land.
   1981. Pleasantville, N.Y. and Montreal: the Reader's Digest Association, Inc.

Regel'son, L. 1977. *Tragediia Russkoi Tserkvi 1917-1945* [Tragedy of the
   Russian Church 1917-1945]. Paris: YMCA-Press.

Religioznye Ob'edineniia Rossiiskoi Federatsii: Spravochnik [Religious Organizations of the Russian Federation]. 1996. Moscow:
   Respublika.

Revzin, G. 1999. Bronza Pretknoveniia: Esche Odin Skandal Vokrug
   Khrama Khrista Spasitelia [Bronze of Tension: One More Scandal over the Cathedral of Christ the Savior]. *Kommersant*, May 1.

___. 2000a. Vladimir Putin Peredal Pravoslavnoy Tserkvi Unikal'nyy
   Pamiatnik Rossiyskogo Zodchestva [[Vladimir Putin Transferred
   to Orthodox Church a Uniqie Monument of Russian Architec-
   ture]. *Kommersant*, April 5.

___. 2000b. Khrista Spasitelia Sdali v Khram [Cathedral Has Utilized
   Christ the Savior]. *Kommersant* August 8.

Rinschede, G. 1986. The Pilgrimage Town of Lourdes. *Journal of Cultural Geography* 7:21-34.

Robson, R. R. 1995. *Old Believers in Modern Russia*. DeKalb, Illinois: Northern Illinois University Press.

Rodin, I. 1994. Duma Otkazalas' Sozdat' Precedent: Ideologicheski Raznye Deputaty Presledovali Odni i Te Zhe Teni Proshlogo [The Duma Has Refused to Create a Precedent: Ideologically Different Deputies Chased the Same Shadows of the Past]. *Nezavisimaia Gazeta*, July 30.

Rodina. 1995. Winter, 1:16.

Rogerson, J. 1985. *Atlas of the Bible*. New York: Facts on File Publications.

Rokhlin, A. 1995. Georgiia Pobedonostsa Zakovali v Bronyu: Khram na Poklonnoy Gore Raspisan Vopreki Kanonam Pravoslavnoy Tserkvi [St. George the Victorious Put into Bronze: Church on Poklonnaya Hill Is Decorated Not in Accordance with Orthodox Church's Canons]. *Moskovskii Komsomolets*, April 26.

Romanov, V. 1996. Otvety Bez Otveta [Answers without Answers]. *Russkii Telegraph*, February 26.

Rosbizneskonsalting News Agency. 2000. News report, 06.01.

Roslof, E. 1994. The Renovationist Movement in the Russian Orthodox Church, 1922-1946. Unpub. Ph.D. diss. Chapel Hill, NC: University of North Carolina at Chapel Hill.

Rossiiskaia Gazeta. 1994. July 28.

Rossiiskaia Sotsialisticheskaia Federativnaia Sovetskaia Respublika. 1921. Moscow: Vysshee Geodezicheskoe Upravlenie. [Map of the RSFSR].

RTsKhIDNI (Rossiiskii Tsentr Khraneniia i Izucheniia Dokumentov Noveishei Istorii, now RGASPI) f. 17, op. 60, d. 509, ll. 100-26.

———. f. 17, op. 84, d. 309, ll. 124-140.

———. f. 17, op.87, d.186, ll. 150-176.

———. f. 17, op.112, d. 443a, l.3ob.

———. f. 17, op. 113, d. 871, l. 33. Notes of Meeting on May 18, 1929.

———. f. 17, op. 113, d. 871, l. 36. Notes of Meeting on May 29, 1929.

———. f. 89, op 4, d. 162, ll. 66-67, 141-142.

———. f. 89, op. 4, d. 171, ll. 1-4.

Rusantsov, Valentin, archbishop of Suzdal' and Vladimir. 1994. Interview. Suzdal', September.

Russkaia Pravoslavnaia Tserkov' i Kommunistiveskoe Gosudartsvo 1917-1941. Dokumenty i Fotomaterialy [Russian Orthodox Church and Communist State 1917-1941. Documents and Photomaterials]. 1996. Moscow: Bibleisko-Bogoslovskii Institut Sv. apostola Andreia.

Russkoe Zarubezh'e v God Tysiacheletiia Krescheniia Rusi: Sbornik [Russian Diaspora in the Year of Rus' Baptizing's Millenium: Collection of Essays]. 1991. Comp. by M. Nazarov. Moscow: Stolitsa.

Rutter, E. 1929. The Muslim Pilgrimage. *Geographical Journal* 74:271-73.

Rybakov, B. 1993. Russkaia Kul'tura Novogo Peredela Ne Pereneset [Russian Culture Would Not Survive another Redistribution]. *Pravda*, December 15.

Sack, R. D. 1986. *Human Territoriality: Its Theory and History.* Cambridge: Cambridge University Press.

Safronov, S. 1998. Geograficheskie Aspekty Izucheniia Religioznoi Sfery Rossii [Geographic Aspects of the Study of Religious Sphere in Russia]. Ph.D. diss. Moscow: Moscow State University.

Santalov, A. A. and L. Segal, eds. 1930. *Soviet Union Year-Book 1930.* London: George Allen and Unwin Ltd.

Savel'ev, O. 1996. Zhizn' v Moskve Otlichaetsia ot Zhizni v Rossii [Life in Moscow Differs from Life in Russia]. *Segodnia*, January 31.

Savostiuk, O. et al. 1994. I Tserkov' Ne Izbezhala Konfrontatsii [The Church Has Failed to avoid Confrontation]. *Izvestiia*, June 25.

Scherbina, N. 1993. Izgnannye [Expelled]. *Rossiiskie Vesti*, December 11.

Schipanova. 1994. Smuta v Derevne Liubytino [Unrest in the Village of Liubytino]. *Segodnia*, August 5.

Scientific Publishing Institute of Pictorial Statistics. 1938. *USSR: An Album Illustrating the State of Organization and National Economy of the U.S.S.R.* Moscow.

Scott, J., and P. Simpson-Housley, eds. 1991. *Sacred Places and Profane Spaces: Essays in the Geographics of Judaism, Christianity, and Islam.* New York: Greenwood Press.

Segodnia. 1993. August 3.

___. 1994. Vo Cho by to Ni Stalo [At Any Cost]. November 18.

Semenov, N. 1994. Dorogu k Khramu Vymostiat Torgovtsy? [Road to Church Will Be Paved by Sellers?]. *Reklamnyi Vestnik* 11: March 18.

Semple, E. 1911. *Influences of Geographic Environment: on the Basis of Ratzel's System of Anthropo-Geography.* New York: Henry Holt and Co.; London: Constable and Co.

Separatizm Ne Po-Khristianski [Separatism Not According to Christ]. 1996. *Rossiiskaia Gazeta.* February 28.

Sh., M. 1996. Yakunin Podderzhal Patriarkha Varfolomeia [Yakunin Supports Patriarch Bartholomew]. *Nezavisimaia Gazeta*, March 12.

Shakhov, M. 1994. Komu Prinadlezhat Relikvii? Drevlepravoslavie and Patriarkhiia [To Whom Do the Relics Belong? Ancient Orthodoxy and the Patriarchate]. *Nezavisimaia Gazeta*, July 9-15.

Shalaev, G. 1993. Proval Imeni Khrama Khrista Spasitelia [Pit Named after the Cathedral of Christ the Savior]. *Utro Rossii*, November 4.

Shalin, D., ed. 1996. *Russian Culture at the Crossroads: Paradoxes of Postcommunist Consciousness.* Boulder, CO: Westview Press.

Shebanov, I. 1995. Khram Khrista Spasitelia — na Plyvunakh [The Cathedral of Christ the Savior Is on Quicksand]. *Pravda*, January 11.

Shevchenko, M. 1996. Sinod RPTs Rvet Otnosheniia s Konstantinopolem: Tserkovnyi Raskol v Estonii Nosit Ne Tol'ko Religioznyi Kharakter [The Synod of the ROCh Breaks Relations with Constantinople: the Church Split in Estonia Does Not Have Exclusive Religious Character]. *Nezavisimaia Gazeta*, n. d.

Shilhav, Y. 1983. Principles for the Location of Synagogues: Symbolism and Functionalism in a Spatial Context. *Professional Geographer* 35:324-29.

Shimanskii, D. 1994b. My Nash, My Novyi Khram Postroim... Pokaianie Tozhe Mozhet Byt' Vygodnym [We Will Build Our New Church... Repentance Could Be Profitable Too]. *Nezavisimaia Gazeta*, April 7.

___. 1994a. Agressiia Surrogata: Khram Khrista Spasitelia — Ne Roskosh', a Sredstvo Peredvizheniia [Aggression of Substitute: Cathedral of Christ the Savior [Is] Not a Luxury, but a Vehicle]. *Nezavisimaia Gazeta*, December 31.

___. 1996. Tretii Rim Epokhi Raspada: Chto Ob'ediniaet Moskovskie "Stroiki Veka"? [The Third Rome of Decay Epoch: What Units Moscow's "Constructions of the Century"?]. *Nezavisimaia Gazeta*, January 24.

Shinkin, A. 1996. Krestovyi Khod Protiv Krestovogo Pokhoda [March Against Crusade]. *Rossiiskaia Gazeta*, March 3.

Shishkin, A. A. 1970. *Suschnost' i Kriticheskaia Otsenka "Obnovlencheskogo" Raskola Russkoi Pravoslavnoi Tserkvi.* Kazan': Izdatel'stvo Kazanskogo Universiteta.

Shkarovsky, M. 1999. Russkaia Pravoslavnaia Tserkov' pri Staline i Khrushcheve: Gosudarstvenno-Tserkovnye Otnoshenia v SSSR v 1939-1964 Godakh [The Russian Orthodox Church under Stalin and Khrushchev: State-Church Relationship in the USSR in 1939-1964]. Moscow: Krutitskoe Patriarshee Podvor'e.

Shugaikina, A. 1994. Glavnoe, Nachat' Ryt'? [To Start Digging Is Most Important?]. *Vecherniaia Moskva*, August 22.

Shusharin, D. 1992. My Prosto Vozvraschaemsia v Rossiiu: Interv'iu s Episkopom Kannskim Varnava [We Have Just Returned Back to Russia: Interview with Varnava, Bishop of Cannes]. *Nezavisimaia Gazeta*, February 21.

___. 1994. Vokrug Khrama [Around the Cathedral]. *Segodnia*, October 1.

Sidorov, D. 1992. Variations in Perceived Level of Prestige of Residential Areas in the Former USSR. *Urban Geography* 13:355-373.

___. 1994-5. Review of John Anderson's "Religion, State and Politics in the Soviet Union and Successor States" and M.I. Odintsov's "Gosudarstvo i Tserkov' v Rossii: XX Vek." *Modern Greek Studies* 10/11:968-970.

___. 1996. Review of I. Prosvirnin, ed. "Istoriia Russkoi Pravoslavnoi Tserkvi v Dokumentakh Regional'nykh Arkhivov Rossii" and M. Odintsov, ed. "Arkhiv Soveta po Delam Religioznykh Kul'tov pri SM SSSR (1944-1965). Katalog dokumentov." *Modern Greek Studies Yearbook* 12/13:679-681.

___. 1997a. Sovremennye Zapadnye Issledovaniia Gosudarstvenno-Tserkovnykh Otnoshenii v SSSR i Rossii [Contemporary Western Studies of State-church Relations in the USSR and Russia]. In *Religiia, Tserkov' v Rossii i za Rubezhom: Informatsionno-Analiticheskii Biuleten'* 9-10:117-126.

___. 1997b. Review of J. Ellis, "The Russian Orthodox Church: Triumphalism and Defensiveness" (London: MacMillan Press Ltd. in ass. with St. Antony's College, Oxford, 1996). *Modern Greek Studies Yearbook* 12/13: 683-85.

___. 1998. Orthodoxy, Difference, and Scale: The Evolving Geopolitics of Russian Orthodox Church(es) in the 20th Century. Ph.D. diss. Minneapolis: University of Minnesota.

___. 2000a. Playing Chess with Churches: Russian Orthodoxy as Re(li)gion. *Historical Geography* 28:208-233.

___. 2000b. National Monumentalization and the Politics of Scale: The Resurrections of the Cathedral of Christ the Savior in Moscow. *Annals of the Association of American Geographers* 90:548-572.

___. 2000c. Review of D. Harvey, "Justice, Nature and the Geography of Difference." *Ethics, Place and Environment* 3:105-9 (with the Minnesota Geography Reading Group).

Sigida, A. 2000. Putin and Yel'tsin Priniali Uchastie v Osviaschenii Khrama [Putin and Yel'tsin Attended Consecration of Church]. *Nezavisimaia Gazeta*, June 2.

Simon, G. 1970. *Church, State and Opposition in the U.S.S.R.* Transl. K. Matchett. Berkeley, Calif.: University of California Press.

Sirotkin, V. 1995. Pervyi Khram Khrista Spasitelia [First Cathedral of Christ the Savior]. *Russkaia Mysl'* 4088-9, July 27.

Sivers, Amvrosii, Bishop von. 1994. "Katakombnye" Khristiane — Grazhdane Nebesnogo Ierusalima [Catacomb Christians Are the Citizens of the Heavenly Jerusalem]. *Smena* (St. Petersburg), Jine 25.

___. 1996. Gosudarstvo i "Katakomby" [The State and the Catacombs]. In *Na Puti k Svobode Sovesti: Religiia i Prava Cheloveka*, ed. S. Filatov, pp. 99-101. Vol. 3. Moscow: Nauka.

Slovar' Russkago Iazyka, Sostavlennyi vtorym Otdeleniem Imperatorskoi akademii Nauk. 1895. Vol. 3. St. Petersburg: Tipografiia Imperatorskoi Akademii Nauk.

Sluzhenie Tserkvi Nikogda Ne Bylo Legkim: Zametki s Eparkhial'nogo Sobraniia Goroda Moskvy [Serving the Church Never Was Easy: Notes from Diocesan Meeting of the City of Moscow]. 1994. *Pravoslavnaia Moskva* 2, February.

Small, J. and M. Witherick. 1989. A Modern Dictionary of Geography. London : E. Arnold.

Smith, K. 1997. An Old Cathedral for a New Russia: The Symbolic Politics of the Reconstituted Church of Christ the Saviour. *Religion, State & Society* 25: 163-75.

Smith, N. 1992. Geography, Difference and the Politics of Scale. In *Postmodernism and the Social Sciences,* ed. J. Doherty, E. Graham, and M. Malek, pp. 57-79. London: McMillan.

_____. 1993. Homeless/Global: Scaling Places. In *Mapping the Futures: Local Cultures, Global Change,* ed. J. Bird, pp. 87-119. London and New York: Routledge.

_____. 1994. Contours of a Spatialized Politics: Homeless Vehicles and the Production of Geographical Scale. *Social Text* 33:54-81.

_____. and Dennis, W. 1987. The Restructuring of Geographical Scale: Coalescence and Fragmentation of the Northern Core Region. *Economic Geography* 63:160-82.

Smolitsch, I. 1964-1991. *Gerchichte der Russischen Kirche, 1700- 1917.* Leiden: E.J. Brill.

Smolkin, S. 1994. Zhalko Khram, No Byl li On Shedevrom? [Pity for Cathedral, But Was It a Masterpiece?]. *Rossiiskaia Gazeta*, October 15.

___. 1996. Khram, Kotoryi My Zasluzhili: Pochemu Yurii Luzhkov Liubit Konstantina Tona [Cathedral, Which We Have Deserved:

Why Yurii Luzhkov Likes Konstantin Ton]. *Nezavisimaia Gazeta*, February 8.

(Snychev), Ioann. 1993. *Tserkovnye Raskoly Russkoi Tserkvi 20-kh i 30-kh Godov XX Stoletiia — Grigorianskii, Yaroslavskii, Iosiflianskii, Viktorianskii i Drugie, Ikh Osobennosti i Istoriia* [Church Schisms in the Russian Church in the 1920-30s of the XX Century — Grigogian, Yaroslavian', Iosifian, Victorian and Others, Their Particulars and History]. Sortavala, Karelia.

Soja, E. 1989. *Postmodern Geographies: The Reassertion of Space in Critical Social Theory*. London: Verso.

Sokolov, Y. 1994. Pervaia Zhertva Vozrozhdeniia Khrama [First Victim of the Cathedral's Reconstruction]. *Izvestiia*, December 7.

Soldatov, A. 1996. Vozderzhanie ot Obscheniia [Abstinence from Communication]. *Moskovskie Novosti* 13.

Sopher, D. 1967. *Geography of Religions*. Englewood Cliffs, NJ: Prentice-Hall, Inc.

___. 1981. Geography and Religions. *Progress in Human Geography* 5:510-524.

Sorokin, S. 1993. Tserkovnaia Ekspansiia [Church Expansion]. *Moskovskii Komsomolets*, October 9.

Sotsial'no-Ekonomicheskoe Razvitie Gorodov i Rayonov Moskovskoi Oblasti za 1993 God: Statisticheskii Sbornik [Social-Economic Development of Moscow Oblast' Cities and Districts in 1993: Statistics]. 1994. Moscow: Moskovskii Oblastnoi Komitet Gosudarstvennoi Statistiki.

Spasitel' i Deputaty [Savior and Deputies]. 1994. *Segodnia*. December 8.

Spinka, M. 1956. *The Church in Soviet Russia*. New York: Oxford University Press.

Staeheli, L. 1994. Empowering Political Struggle: Spaces and Scales of Resistance. *Political Geography* 13:387-391.

Statisticheskii Ezhegodnik Rossii. 1914 g. [Statistical Annual of Russia. 1914]. 1915. Petrograd.

Statistika Religioznykh Ob'edinenii [Statistics of Religious Organizations]. 1926. *Antireligioznik* 6:61-62.

Stepanova, I. 1995. Strannyi Spisok [Strange Listing]. *Russkaia Mysl'*, 4052, November 10-16.

Stewart, L. 1995. Bodies, Visions, and Spatial Politics: A Review Essay on Lefebvre's 'The Production of Space'. *Environment and Planning D: Society and Space* 13:609-618.

Strannoe Mesto [Strange Place]. 1994. *Nezavisimaia Gazeta*. August 8.

Stratonov, I. 1932. *Russkaia Tserkovnaia Smuta, 1921-1931* [Russian Church Unrest, 1921-1931]. Berlin.

Strel'chik, E. 1993. Khram Isskustva Gotovitsia v Vozvrascheniiu ... Gospoda [Temple of arts Prepares to Restoration of ... God]. *Vecherniaia Moskva*, November 28.

Stroyen, W. B. 1967. *Communist Russia and the Russian Orthodox Church, 1943-1962.* Washington: The Catholic University of America Press.

Struve, N. 1967. *Christians in Contemporary Russia.* Trans. by Lancelot Sheppard, and A. Manson. New York: Charles Scribner's Sons.

Sushchii, S. Ia., and A. G. Druzhinin. 1994. *Ocherki Geografii Russkoi Kul'tury* [Essays on Geography of Russian Culture]. Rostov-on-Don: Izdatel'stvo SKNTS VSh.

Suzdal'skii Palomnik. 1994. (Suzdal'), no. 18-20, special issue.

Sventsytskii, A. B. 1994. Vospominaniia Moskovskogo Prikhozhanina [Memories of a Moscow Parishioner]. *Zhurnal Moskovskoi Patriarkhii* 4:110-127.

Sviatyni Drevnei Moskvy/Sacred Places of Ancient Moscow. 1993. Moscow: Nikos-Kontakt, bi-lingual edition.

Swyngedouw, E. 1992. The Mammon Quest. 'Glocalisation', Interspatial Competition and the Monetary Order: the Construction of New Scales. In *Cities and Regions in the New Europe: the Global-Local Interplay and Spatial Development Strategies*, ed. M. Dunford, and G. Kafkalas, pp. 39-67. London: Belhaven Press.

Sysyn, F. E. 1993. The Third Rebirth of the Ukrainian Autocephalous Orthodox Church and the Religious Situation in Ukraine, 1989-1991. In *Seeking God: The Recovery of Religious Identity in Orthodox Russia, Ukraine, and Georgia*, ed. S. Batalden, pp. 191-219. DeKalb: Northern Illinois University Press.

Szczesniak, B., ed. 1959. *The Russian Revolution and Religion: A Collection of Documents Concerning the Suppression of Religion by the Communists, 1917-1925.* Notre Dame, Ind.: University of Notre Dame Press.

Tanaka, H. 1981. The Evolution of Pilgrimage as a Spatial- Symbolic System. *The Canadian Geographer* 25:240-51.

Tarkhanov, A. and S. Kavtaradze. 1992. *Architecture of the Stalin Era.* New York; Rizzoli.

Taylor, P. 1982. A Materialist Framework for Political Geography. *Transactions of the Institute of British Geographers* 7:15-34.

___. 1989. Oneworldism. *Political Geography* 8:211-213.

Tikhomirov, I. 1900. *Raskol v Predelakh Kaluzhskoi Eparkhii: Proshloe i Nastoiaschee Mestnogo Raskola* [Schism in Kaluga Diocese: the Past and Present of the Local Schism]. Kaluga: Tipo-litografiia gubernskogo pravleniia.

Tolstikhina, A. and I. Mel'nikova. 2001. Tvorets Dovolen: Zavershilos' Stroitel'stvo Khrama Khrista Spasitelia [Creator Is Satisfied: Construction of the Cathedral of Christ the Savior Is Completed]. *Segodnya*, January 6.

Trebuiutsia Milliardery-Romantiki: Arkhitektor Boris Tkhor Melochey Ne Liubit [Seeking Milliarders-Romantics: Architect Boris Tkhor Does Not Like Small Problems]. *Moscow News* 13 (1031), April 4-10.

Trofimov, A. 1993. Dvazhdy Rozhdennyi [Born Twice]. *Rossiiskie Vesti*, November 3.

Tsarevskii, A. A. 1991 (1898). *Znachenie Pravoslaviia v Zhizni i Istoricheskoi Sud'be Rossii.* [The Meaning of the Orthodoxy in Life and Historical Destiny of Russia]. Leningrad: Al'fa. (Reprint of 1898 edition, Kazan'.)

Tsentr Novoi Utopii? [Center of New Utopia?]. 1995. *Segodnia*, February 18.

Tsentral'noe Statisticheskoe Upravlenie pri Sovete Ministrov SSSR. 1975. *Itogi Vsesoiuznoi Perepisi Naseleniia 1959 Goda* [Results of the 1959 All-Union Population Census]. Nendeln: Kraus Reprint.

Tsentral'nyi Statisticheskii Komitet Ministerstva Vnutrennikh Del. 1901a. *Raspredelenie Naseleniia Imperii po Glavnym Veroispovedaniiam* [Distribution of Empire's Population among Main Religions]. St. Petersburg.

Tsentral'nyi Statisticheskii Komitet Ministerstva Vnutrennikh Del. 1901b. *Raspredelenie Staroobriadtsev i Sektantov po Tolkam i Sektam* [Distribution of Old Believers and Sectarians among Subgroups and Sects]. St. Petersburg.

Tsypin, V. 1994. *Istoriia Russkoi Pravoslavnoi Tserkvi 1917-1990* [History of the Russian Orthodox Church 1917-1990]. Moscow: Moskovskaia Patriarkhiia.

Tuan, Y. F. 1977. Sacred Space: Exploration of an Idea. In *Dimensions of Human Geography: Essays on Some Familiar and Neglected Themes*, ed. K. W. Butzer. Research Paper 186, pp. 84-99. Chicago: the University of Chicago, the Department of Geography.

Tumarkin, M. 1995. Nevynosimaia Legkost' Ofitsioza [Unbearable Lightness of the Official]. *Segodnia*, July 1.

Turner, V. 1978. *Image and Pilgrimage in Christian Culture: Anthropological Perspectives.* New York: Columbia University Press.

Tysiacheletie Kreshceniia Rusi [Millennium of Rus' Baptizm]. 1988. International Theological-Historical Conference, Kiev, 21-28 July, 1986, Proceedings. Moscow: Moskovskaia Patriarkhiia.

Tyssovskaia, T. 1994. I Vnov' Prodolzhetsia Boy... [Fight Continues Again]. *Rossiia* 29, August 3-9.

USSR Academy of Sciences. 1986. *Religion in the USSR: The Truth and Falsehood*. Moscow: Social Sciences Today.

Uzzell, L. 1996a. The Church Mouse That Roared: Estonian Orthodoxy's Road to Independence. Oxford, UK: Keston News Service.

___. 1996b. Orthodox in Estonia Choose Sides. Oxford, UK: Keston News Service.

V MGU Budet Domovaia Tserkov' [Home Church Will Be in MSU]. 1993. *Segodnia*. December 24.

Vandenko, I. 1996. Vyshe — Tol'ko Krest [Only Cross Is Higher]. *Izvestiia*, February 2.

Vaneeva, N. 1992. Budet li v Rossii Muzey Pravoslavnoi Kul'tury? [Is There to Be the Museum of Orthodox Culture in Russia in the Future?]. *Nezavisimaia Gazeta*, April 30.

Vasil'ev, A. 1994. I Vernetsia Khram Tserkvi [Temple Will Be Returned to the Church]. *Moskovskaia Pravda*, March 15.

Tserkovnyy Konflikt v Estonii [Church Conflict in Estonia]. 1996. *Vecherniaia Moskva*, March 2.

Vershillo, R. 1993. Zarubezhnaia Tserkov' Podelilas' na Chistykh i Nechistykh [The Foreign Church Has Divided into the Pure and Impure]. *Segodnia*, July 6.

Vestnik Merii Moskvy. 1994a. O Vossozdanii Khrama Khrista Spasitelia v g.Moskve po ul. Volkhonke, Vladeniia 15-17 (Tsentral'nyi Administrativnyi Okrug). Postanovlenie Pravitel'stva Moskvy ot 31.05.94 g. no.463 [On Restoration of the Cathedral of Christ the Savior in the City of Moscow on Volkhonka St., #15-17 (Central Administrative Okrug). Decree of the Government of Moscow, 05.31.94. no.463]. no. 14 (1268), July.

___. 1994b. Ob Obrazovanii Nabliudatel'nogo Soveta po Kontroliu za Vosstanovleniem Khrama Khrista Spasitelia. Rasporiazhenie mera Moskvy ot 21.07.94 no. 346-PM. [On Creation of an Observation Council for Control of Restoration of the Cathedral of Christ the Savior. Order of the Mayor of Moscow, 07.21.94 no..346-RM]. no. 18 (1272), September.

___. 1994c. O Poriadke Peredachi Kul'tovykh Zdanii i Sooruzhenii Religioznym Organizatsiiam v g. Moskve. Rasporiazhenie mera Moskvy ot 12.08.94 no. 394-PM [On the Order of Transfer of Cult Buildings and Constructions to Religious Organizations in Moscow. Decree of the mayor of Moscow, August 12, 1994, no. 394-PM], no. 20 (1274), October.

___. 1995. Ob Inzhenernom Obespechenii Khrama Khrista Spasitelia. Rasporiazhenie Prem'era Pravitel'stva Moskvy ot 01.02.95g. no. 89-RP [On Infrastructural Support of the Cathedral of Christ the Savior. Order of the Premier of Moscow Government, 02.01.95g. no. 89-RP]. no. 5 (1283), March.

Vestnik Sviaschennogo Sinoda Pravoslavnoi Rossiiskoi Tserkvii. 1925-27.

Vestnik Sviaschennogo Sinoda Pravoslavnykh Tserkvei v SSSR. 1928.

Volin, B. M., and D. N. Ushakov, eds. 1940. *Tolkovyi Slovar' Russkogo Iazyka* [Explanatory Dictionary of Russian Language], v. 4. Moscow: Gosudarstvennoe izdatel'stvo inostrannykh i natsional'nykh slovarei.

Vpervye za Tysiacheletie [For the First Time in 1000 Years]. 1996. *Sovetskaia Rossiia.* February 27.

Vsepoddanneishii Otchet Ober-Prokurora Sviateishego Sinoda po Vedomstvu Pravoslavnogo Ispovedaniia za 1913 God. [Report of the Holy Synod's Over-Procurator on Orthodox Faith Department in 1913]. 1914. Petrograd.

Vsepoddanneishii Otchet Ober-Prokurora Sviateishego Sinoda po Vedomstvu Pravoslavnogo Ispovedaniia za 1914 God. [Report of the Holy Synod's Over-Procurator on Orthodox Faith Department in 1914]. 1916. Petrograd.

Vsesoiuznaia Perepis' Naseleniia 17 Dekabria 1926 g. Kratkie Svodki [All-Union Population Census December 17, 1926. Brief Summary]. 1928. Vols. 4, 7, 8. Moscow: Izdanie TsSU SSSR.

Vsevoiuznaia Perepis' Naseleniia 1937 Goda. Kratkie Itogi [All-Union Population Census 1937]. 1991. Moscow: Institut Istorii SSSR, Akademiia Nauk SSSR.

Vsesoiuznaia Perepis' Naseleniia 1939 Goda. Osnovnye Itogi [All-Union Population Census 1939. Main Results]. 1991. Moscow: Nauka.

Vvedenskii, A. 1925. Apologeticheskoe Obosnovanie Obnovlenchestva. Doklad na Plenume Sv. Sinoda 27 ianvaria 1925 Goda [Apologetic Foundation of the Renovationism: Report on Session of the Holy Synod, January 27, 1925]. *Vestnik Sviaschennogo Sinoda Pravoslavnoi Rossiiskoi Tserkvi* 1:21.

Vystorobest, A. 1994. Interesy Ne Sovpali: Novoierusalimskii Monastyr' Dolzhen Byt' Peredan Russkoi Pravoslavnoi Tserkvi [Discord in Interests: New Jerusalem Monastery Must Be Transferred to the Russian Orthodox Church]. *Rossiiskaia Gazeta*, July 20.

Wallerstein, I. 1991. *Geopolitics and Geoculture: Essays on the Changing World-System.* Cambridge: Cambridge University Press.

Ware, T. 1963. *The Orthodox Way.* Baltimore, Maryland: Penguin Books.

Warhola, J. W. 1993. *Russian Orthodoxy and Political Culture Transformation*. The Carl Beck Papers. Pittsburg: Center for Russian and East European Studies.

Weber, M. 1976. *The Protestant Ethic and the Spirit of Capitalism*. Trans. by Talcott Parsons. London: Allen and Unwin.

Wheatley, P. 1971. *The Pivot of the Four Quarters: A Preliminary Enquiry into the Origins and Character of the Ancient Chinese City*. Chicago: Aldine Publishing Co.

White, L. 1967. The Historical Roots of Our Ecological Crisis. *Science* 155:203-207.

Young, I. 1990. *Justice and the Politics of Difference*. Princeton: Princeton University Press.

Zabavskikh, E. 1993. Stroit' Vmeste [To Build Together]. *Moskovskie Novosti*, November 7.

Zavrazhin, K. 1993. Sobor Otkrut i Osviaschen. Pri Otsutstvii Pressy [Cathedral Is Opened and Blessed. In the Absence of Press]. *Megapolis-Express*, November 10.

Zelinsky, W. 1961. An Approach to the Religious Geography of the United States. *Annals of the Association of American Geographers* LI:139-93.

Zenkovsky, S. A. 1955. Raskol i Sud'by Imperii [Schism and the Empire's Fate]. *Vozrozhdenie/La Renaissance* 39:112-125.

—. 1957. The Russian Church Schism: Its Background and Repercussions. *The Russian Review* 16:37-58.

—. 1970. *Russkoe Staroobriadchestvo: Dukhovnye Dvizheniia Semnadtsatogo Veka* [Russian Old Belief: Spiritual Movement of the 17th Century]. Munchen: Wilhelm Fink Verlag.

Zinov'ev, A. 1979. *The Yawning Heights*. New York: Random House.

Zybkovets, V. 1975. *Natsionalizatsiia Monastyrskikh Imuschestv v Sovetskoii Rossii (1917-1921 gg.)* [Nationalization of Monastery Property in Soviet Russia (1917-1921)]. Moscow: Nauka.

Zubtsova, Ia., and I. Lutskii. 1995. Nika Nikuda Ne Uletit [Nika Will Not Fly Away]. *Argumenty i Fakty* 33.

INDEX